THE

WAR

YEARS

1939 — 1945

EYEWITNESS ACCOUNTS

THE WAR YEARS
1939 – 1945
EYEWITNESS ACCOUNTS

MARSHALL CAVENDISH

Published by Marshall Cavendish Books
(a division of Marshall Cavendish Partworks Ltd),
119 Wardour Street, London W1V 3TD

Copyright © Marshall Cavendish 1994

ISBN 1 85435 720 4

Printed and bound in Malaysia

Some of this material has previously appeared in the Marshall Cavendish partwork
IMAGES OF WAR

CONTENTS

Jubilant scenes in Brussels after the city was liberated by British, Canadian and Polish forces on September, 1944. The German Army was now in headlong retreat in Belgium. Picture by Sergeant Hardy of the British Army's Photographic Unit.

INTRODUCTION

Between the end of World War I on November 11, 1918, and the declaration of war against Germany on September 3, 1939, a generation had grown up which had never known war. It was these 20-year-olds who were to bear the burden of the first years of World War II.

With the exception of Nazi Germany, the nations that went to war in 1939 went armed with weapons and equipment that were in effect improved versions of those with which they ended World War I – The Great War – The War to End all Wars. They went to war on horseback as cavalry, with horse-drawn artillery and waggons, or as infantry who marched or bicycled into action supported by comparatively slow-moving aircraft, some of which were biplanes. However, the German armoured attack on Poland in 1939, supported by dive bombers and fighters, gave the startled world the first indication that land warfare was going to be very different from the mud and squalor of the trenches. On May 14, 1940, German air attacks on Rotterdam made 78,000 people homeless and killed 1,000; the world condemned the attack as an act of airborne terror. In the subsequent five years attitudes to such air attacks hardened.

Clothes and Weapons

Even the clothing at the beginning of the war was similar in many ways to that worn 20 years earlier. For the men and women in the Navy, Army and Air Force uniforms were made from wool serge with button closures, and many soldiers, like their comrades in World War I, wore the spiral puttees wrapped around their calves and ankles and boots with metal-studs.

Personal weapons had changed little. In the late 1930s the British War Office evaluated the American Thompson sub-machine gun, described it as "a gangster's weapon" and in 1939 sent its soldiers to fight the Germans armed with bolt action rifles, the new Bren light machine gun and the Vickers medium machine gun – a weapon developed in World War I.

After six years of conflict the world had changed beyond recognition. The war lasted long enough to include fathers and sons – one 14-year-old whose father died at Dunkirk in 1940 was a platoon commander at Arnhem in 1944. At Arnhem, paratroopers fought Waffen-SS soldiers with each side armed with self-loading rifles, submachine guns and flame throwers and kitted out with close-weave, camouflaged smocks over their uniforms. During the course of the war, there were other small but significant changes to uniforms including press studs, zip fasteners and rubber-soled boots.

A New Age

In 1945 the world entered a new and frightening age. The United States employed the first nuclear weapons at Hiroshima and Nagasaki. In the first attack five square miles of the city was destroyed and 70,000 people killed. At the second, at Nagasaki, the city was protected by the surrounding hills, but although the damage was less severe 35,000 people still died. The death tolls seem enormous viewed from the perspective of the mid-1990s, but in earlier conventional missions by USAAF B-29s against Tokyo in March

1945, incendiary and high explosive bombing killed 100,000 people; RAF incendiary attacks on Hamburg in July 1943, in the grimly named operation Gomorrah, killed 45,000.

By 1945 the world political map had changed – in Eastern Europe the Soviet Union moved its influence into Germany and formerly democratic countries or even monarchies became Communist satellites. In Africa and the Far East, countries that had been colonies of the former European combatants fought for their freedom. In the Far East, Dutch, French and British colonies had been over-run by the Japanese, and the native population had seen their European colonial masters humbled by Orientals. This gave a profound spur to native independence movements. In 1945 the United States emerged from war in Europe and the Pacific the richest and most powerful nation in the world. In 1939 it had looked at the European war from an isolationist perspective, reluctant to be drawn into the conflict.

Unexpected Challenges

For many of those who lived then and survive today, recalling these events is recalling their teens and early twenties, a time when young people normally leave home, begin to grow up, experiment with life and romance and start their first job. However, this was a generation that took on responsibilities and faced challenges which seem awesome from the perspective of peace in the mid-1990s. As a 40-year-old on a recent visit to the Royal Air Force Museum in Hendon, London, remarked to a member of the museum staff,
"I have just looked at the Lancaster bomber and realised that at 19 my father was flying one of those to Germany on bombing missions – my son is 19 and I don't even trust him with the family car."

Men and women were trusted with the lives of, or trusted their lives to, people who weeks, days and even hours before had been strangers. It was a time when ordinary

USAAF ground crew in Normandy, draped with ammunition belts, line up to rearm a squadron of Mustang during the French campaign.

people were asked to do extraordinary things – men and women found that some of them were capable of being heroes, others of being quietly brave for months and years, and some were broken by fatigue and fear.

About This Book

The War Years gives a unique insight into the lives of these ordinary men and women caught up, willingly or reluctantly, in the greatest adventure of their lives. In eight chapters it gives an eyewitness account of the pre-war to postwar years.

The first chapter, *1939 The Day War Broke Out*, covers Hitler's pre-war expansion into Czechoslovakia and the attack on Poland which triggered the war. The mood and period is well represented by personal accounts. An Austrian who was working on a farm near the Czech border describes the treatment of the Jews in that village and his own experience at Dachau. A freedom fighter in the Czech airforce also describes the entry of Hitler; later he made his way to Britain to fly Hurricanes against the Germans. An American remembers rescuing women and children from a sinking ship in the Atlantic. Descriptions of ordinary life in London, like the young woman trying to get to work once war had been declared, are also very telling.

In Chapter Two, *1940 Britain Alone,* Britain was faced, for the first time since the Napoleonic wars, with the possibility of a seaborne invasion; and in the skies above Britain German bombers battled with the RAF. Europe was already occupied. Read what it was like in France – for both German and English soldiers – and glimpse life in Jersey for the inhabitants with the Germans there. In Norway eye-witness accounts give a feel of the cold, the danger and the difficulty of fighting without knowing enemy plans and movements.

In 1941 the War became truly worldwide, and Chapter Three, *The World on Fire*, describes how war exploded from Africa and Europe into the Far East and Russia. Read the *Afrika Korps* soldier's account of war in the desert and the Royal Tank regiment meeting the retreating Italians on the Tripoli road. Experience the terror of the last moments of a sinking German U-boat or British submarine. A Russian describes life on the Russian border, and both a Japanese and American give insights into the situation at Pearl Harbor.

Chapter Four, *1942 Total War*, covers the lowest ebb of the war for the Allies. Germany and her Axis partners were deep inside the USSR and most of western Europe was under occupation, represented here by the report from a major who led a raid in occupied France and a woman civilian digging in the ruins after RAF and USAAF air attacks in Cologne. In the Pacific the Japanese Imperial Army and Navy plunged south seizing the Philippines and the British colony of Malaya and base of Singapore. A captain describes being present at the conference at which Allied leaders discussed the surrender to the Japanese, whilst a Japanese petty officer in East New Guinea recounts a raid on an Australian air force base. It was not all bad news for the Allies – as an American at the Battle of Midway reports.

Chapter Five, *1943 In the Balance*, quite aptly describes the point when the strategic balance shifted in favour of the Allies. In Europe the German 6th Army had

In June 1944 Anglo-American bombers were hitting German targets night and day and Allied victory was closer than at any time, but it was also the first time VI flying bombs were being used, against Britain. The picture here shows the effect of one of these bombs in Clapham, London.

surrendered to the Red Army at Stalingrad during the winter. In the summer the Germans attempted to retaliate at Kursk. The eyewitnesses in Russia, from both sides, tell the same terrible story of inhumanity.

As in the other chapters, accounts of the Far East, Europe, the Mediterranean, Atlantic and the Eastern Front give real meaning to the war, with fierce action, the deaths of friends, tricks of battle and contrasts in approach to the job among the various army groups.

Chapter Six is called *1944 The Tide Turns*. In January the Red Army lifted the siege of Leningrad. In June Rome was liberated and the Allies landed in Normandy – read the account by an SS Officer captured in Normandy. Also in June, the first B-29 raids hit Japan and the British 14th Army won the battle of Kohima/Imphal in Burma. Susumu Nishida recounts the offensive against the Allies from his viewpoint. Most of the chapter, although it covers accounts from the Far East and the Eastern Front, is concerned with Europe: Both Russian and German eyewitnesses give accounts from Russian soil; there are stories from resistance workers, German

1944 in the Far East. Japan was at last being outfought despite its strong beginnings. Here, US soldiers watch for Japanese snipers in jungle territory.

and British bomber pilots, from wireless operators and a ship's stoker.

Chapter Seven, *1945 V For Victory*, marks the climax of World War II. Soviet troops stormed into Budapest in February and captured Vienna on April 13. Three days later the final assault on Berlin began. On May 7 German forces formally surrendered to the Allies. Several British witnesses recall Germany after its surrender and the haunting effects of seeing the concentration camps. In the Far East, however, the war continued. Troops who had fought in Europe were warned to prepare for service in the Pacific. On July 16, in the Alamagordo desert in New Mexico, the first atomic bomb was successfully tested. A Japanese schoolboy remembers the effects of the US air raids and a POW recalls seeing the bomb being dropped in Nagasaki. On September 2, 1945, the Japanese government formally surrendered aboard the USS *Missouri* in Tokyo Bay. We read that it was not easy for either the winners or the losers.

Chapter Eight vividly reveals the enormous problems left by the war. Initially Europe was still chaotic as displaced persons (DPs) roamed east and west searching for homes and families. A 13-year-old girl in Germany whose parents had died describes what it was like in 1946 for her. An interpreter gives his impressions of Berlin, which he had known before the war; and a Czech pilot who had served in the RAF returns to Czechoslovakia now under the Soviets.

Reconstruction began, but across the world wars did not cease, as accounts from Palestine, Burma and Corfu show. It took nearly 50 years before Eastern Europe and East Germany ceased to be satellites of the Soviet Empire and when the Iron Curtain came down and the Cold War ended the last vestiges of World War II disappeared.

Of all the accounts in the book, those in the final section, *Remembrance*, are a powerful summation of the war. These personal stories by ordinary people bring alive the reality of war for those who did not share the experience and enable them to begin to understand the good and bad implications and effects of the War Years.

1939
THE DAY WAR BROKE OUT

Eyewitnesses chronicle the days that led to World War II

By 1939, war in Europe was virtually inevitable. The Munich Crisis of late 1938, in which Britain and France had allowed Hitler to dismember Czechoslovakia, had acted as an ominous warning, while the growth of the German armed forces, coupled to the beginnings of overt anti-semitism, had shown the true nature of Hitler's regime. As the new year dawned, the Allies began to prepare for the worst.

It was to take nine months for the storm to break – on 3 September – with only one early scare in March when German troops invaded what remained of Czechoslovakia. This triggered increased war preparations in the democracies: in Britain, for example, it occasioned the introduction of conscription for the first time during peace.

This was in response to Hitler's invasion of Poland, a country protected by agreements with Britain and France. There was little they could do to offer practical help, watching the destruction of their ally by both German and Soviet troops.

Action took place only at sea, where German U-boats began their campaign to destroy Allied merchant shipping from the very first day of the war. At the same time, German capital ships moved out to threaten Britain's lifeline in the Atlantic, only to discover that the Royal Navy was still an effective instrument of war.

Thus, by the end of 1939, there was a feeling of anti-climax. The Germans and Soviets had taken Poland, and the Soviets had invaded Finland, but elsewhere, all was quiet.

ESCAPE TO THE WEST

Their armies beaten, Czechs and Poles make their way west to fight on in Allied forces. Their story, told in their own words, is one of unflinching courage.

T hroughout the 1930s a variety of people fled from the countries of Europe directly affected by the spread of fascism, seeking asylum in the free democracies. Many were Jews, alerted by the introduction of anti-semitic laws by the Nazis in Germany; others were political refugees. Not all were welcomed in their new homes – indeed, when war broke out in 1939, many were interned as 'enemy aliens' – but quite often their skills proved of inestimable value to the Allied cause. By 1939, a different class of refugees had begun to appear – servicemen who escaped from their homelands as the Germans closed in. Of necessity, given the difficulties of escape by other means, these were primarily airmen, all fired with a determination to continue to fight. Some flew from Czechoslovakia or Poland into the Balkans; many made it to France and, eventually, some reached Britain. Their flying expertise and ruthless determination to win were welcome assets.

Robert Bruckner (25) was a farm worker in Baden in Austria (about 17 miles from Vienna) in 1938 when the Germans took the country over. A socialist, he was arrested in November 1938 for sabotage and taken off to Dachau for six months. When he was released, he fled to England, where he still lives.

❝ When Hitler marched in in 1938, I was working on a farm in a little village near the Czech border. Every farmer had a swastika flag in his house, and when Hitler took over they all hung them out of the window. As soon as I saw this I left the village and returned to Baden. I have always been a socialist

▲ Prague citizens, restrained by police, shout abuse at German troops entering the city, 15 March 1939.

▲ ▶ Robert Bruckner, Austrian socialist and Dachau survivor, whose youthful sabotage acts enraged the Nazis.

▶ ▲ In a posed picture, German troops are welcomed by ethnic Germans as they annex the Sudetenland in 1938.

and so was all my family. When I got back to Baden I joined an organisation called the Freedom Fighters of Baden, which was affiliated to the Austrian Socialist Party – the same party which still exists today. Austria had a Christian Socialist government, which supported the Nazis.

The Nazis came into Baden in trucks and they were picking up Jews all over the place, taking them away. We thought, 'That can't be right, they're our friends,' but we couldn't do a thing.

The Jews were dragged out of their houses. They had found their names and addresses from a register in the Jewish community centre. Another thing, the Nazis flattened the Jewish cemetery. I remember that somebody had written a slogan on the wall of the cemetery. Wherever the Nazis went they would daub 'Juden 'raus' (Jews out) on the walls, and they'd daubed it on the cemetery wall, but next to it somebody had written 'Nazis in', meaning 'throw the Nazis into the graves'.

There was no escape for the Jews. As soon as the Nazis moved in, the borders were sealed off. We discussed the matter at the Freedom Fighters' meeting, but there was no channel of escape. They were all picked up in the end.

The only thing we did do was to

going. I remember we were put on a train at Vienna Westbahnhof – there were about ten coaches divided into compartments. In my compartment there were four prisoners on one side, four on the other and four on the floor, and on top of each man another prisoner was sat on his lap. There were about six Jews in that compartment and the rest were from the Freedom Fighters. It was about 8 o'clock in the evening when we were put into the train and the two SS men (Blackshirts) who were guarding us told us we had to sit with our eyes on the light in the ceiling the whole time. Now there was one old man there, he couldn't keep his head up to look at the light – I mean, I couldn't either – if you let your head fall they would hit you on both sides of the head with the side of their

on each side, each hut divided into four compartments. Beside the huts was a grass strip, and next to that was an electric fence, and then next to that a river, and then an SS camp with a moat around it. So if you wanted to escape you had to go through the SS camp. Now there were watchtowers outside the SS camp, and there was a little path beneath the watchtowers. The SS men in the watchtowers would play this little game. They threw a handkerchief down on to the grass, and you weren't allowed to go on the grass. They told this man to fetch the handkerchief. If you said you couldn't fetch it they would shoot you, and if you went on the grass to fetch it the other man would shoot you from the other watchtower. This actually happened. I saw it.

As soon as we got to Dachau we had to strip naked and take an ice-cold shower. Some of the prisoners had to be deloused. Now that was something, I can tell you! They had to run naked from one hut to another through the snow. That would kill all the lice!

Now, up there in the winter it's a morass, and the ground is a swamp. Our work was to put the mud on one side into wheelbarrows, take it to the other side and make a heap, and when you'd done that, you carried it back to the other side. Useless work, purposeless. The wheelbarrows were big heavy things with wooden planks for handles. There were some old Jews there, 60 or 70 years old. We helped them. We tied some pieces of string together, slipping them through their jackets, let the string run through the sleeves with a loop around the handles of the wheelbarrow. So they could bear the weight of the barrow not only with their

remove the man-hole covers during the blackouts. The Germans organised practice blackouts, and the only people allowed on the streets were the German soldiers, in trucks or on foot. This caused a lot of accidents, I can tell you. They wanted to have three blackouts, but they abandoned it after the second one, because of the man-holes. During the second blackout I was caught red-handed. I was put in a police cell, and on 12 November I was taken to Dachau.

We weren't told where we were

bayonets. Anyway, the elderly man, they shot him, and the bullet went through him and into the man sitting behind him, killing them both.

When the train pulled in at Munich we were taken off and loaded into cattle wagons to make the rest of the journey to Dachau (about 16 km). You couldn't stand or sit, crammed in like sardines. It was a very foggy morning when we arrived. One man tried to run away and he was shot.

In Dachau, there were 24 huts, 12

▼ Come 1939, Austrian Nazis take up their positions – albeit in somewhat makeshift uniforms.

hands but with their shoulders. It was a great help.

Anyway, an SS man saved one of these old Jews – I mustn't forget that. The old man must have gone mad. He ran away, knowing they would shoot him. He ran towards one of the SS men, but instead of shooting him, he threw down his rifle and grabbed the Jew by the hand. He talked to him for about half an hour and then let him go. This was the only good thing I saw.

I was in barrack No 24. It had four compartments, and in each room there were over 100 men. We had no beds. We all had to sleep crammed together on benches covered with straw. We had a little blanket. The man sleeping next to me was the Lord Mayor of Vienna.

On 22nd of January 1939 the sirens went at 6.40 in the evening. Everybody was ordered out on to the parade ground. We heard that a man had escaped. How he did it I'll never know. So we had to stand on the parade ground – we had caps and gloves – and at around midnight the weather got bitterly cold, a snow-storm. The order was issued: Caps

off, gloves off. We had to stand there until 6.40 in the morning in the bitter cold. Some of the men dropped down, frozen to death. At 6.40 the sirens went and we were herded back into the barracks for a cup of coffee and a piece of bread. At 7.00 am – back to the parade ground, standing there until 6.40 in the evening. It was snowing the whole time – you are in the Alps in Dachau, that's what Dachau means – 'roof'. About 50 people dropped down dead. At 6.40 again in the evening, we were allowed to go back into the barracks. All this meticulous time-keeping!

About ten days later the sirens went again – on to the parade ground again. We saw a lone figure with a drum hanging from string round his neck, walking towards the stage on the parade ground, drumming, drumming. It was the man who had escaped. When he got up on the stage, still drumming, one SS man at each shoulder, he was shot. Both of them shot him with their rifles. I didn't know him – I mean, there were 34,000 prisoners there. My number was 24,346 – it will always be in my mind, that number.

I remember once we had a visit from Himmler. He inspected us. We had a very good meal that day. He told us: 'You are all *Verbrecher* (criminals)!' In my barracks we were all political prisoners.

One thing – if you had money – the SS ran a shop. You could buy food from the shop. You could buy lovely bread there, jam, any foodstuffs, whatever you needed. It was of course peacetime. So I could write home to my family and they would send me money – so I bought jam from there. Apart from what was in the shop the prison food was just about adequate.

At the time my sisters found a job in England as domestic servants. Anyway, the man they worked for,

▲▲ Massed ranks of SA (Storm Troopers) with swastika banners. Many SA men had served in World War I and joined the Nazi Party partly for its beery social gatherings.

▲ Miroslav Mansfeld, Sergeant Pilot with the RAF (left) with fellow Czech pilot. Mansfeld is wearing a life jacket for operations over the Channel.

he swore an affidavit and sent a letter to Dachau applying for my release. And as there was no war on, I could be released.

When I returned to Baden the whole place was covered in swastikas. I set off for England in May 1939 and in June 1940, a policeman called to say that they were rounding up every Austrian and German refugee. I was transferred to a camp on the Isle of Man and then to Canada. **"**

Miroslav Mansfeld was a 26-year-old pilot in the Czech Air Force in 1939 when the Germans invaded. He would not surrender, and, driven by an inner fury to fight for his country, he made his way through Europe, eventually arriving in England after the fall of France.

" I started flying at school in 1930, so by 1938 I was an experienced pilot, a sergeant in the air force. That year I was given the task of going to Russia to fly back six Russian light bombers for my squadron. This was the sort of strange job I was often given – outside normal flying duties.

Another time I was assigned as the personal pilot to the Czech chief-of-staff, who was, in time, to become the president. But when we got to Prague he disembarked and went to meet the MPOs – but he never came back. I was told that I could fly out.

That evening I heard awful broadcasts on the radio – announcers in tears crying out, 'We cannot defend ourselves, we have to give in' – it must have been October or November. Politically we were not sure who was going to be president, although we were still flying and I was transferred to a special test-pilot unit.

Then came the Germans. Their General, Udet, came to our airfield and flew one of our planes. I must say he was very good, but it meant the end of flying for me. I and all the other Czech pilots were sent on leave for an unspecified time.

I went home, to my village just outside Prague, where my family ran a restaurant. After a few days, I cannot remember exactly, the Germans appeared in tanks and armoured cars. One small armoured car stopped at our restaurant, where I was serving, and a young German got out of the car and came to sit at one of the tables. I had to serve him so I asked what he would like. He replied by asking me what we had. I told him eggs . . . would he like scrambled eggs, or steak or chocolate? His eyes opened wide in surprise and his mouth fell open: 'Real eggs, real chocolate?' he asked. 'Yes,' I said, and he replied, 'Then I want scrambled eggs and chocolate.'

So I brought him these two things and watched him eat – he was eating egg, and with it chocolate.

My step-sister, who spoke a little more German than me – and, in any case, as a pilot I didn't like to speak

KRISTALLNACHT

Hitler's anti-semitism was summed up in his book *Mein Kampf*, for all to see as early as the 1920s. However, despite the Nuremberg Laws of 1935, prohibiting mixed Jewish-Aryan marriages and restricting the rights of Jews to work in certain professions, it was not until November 1938 that more vicious persecutions began. On 9 November Ernst vom Rath, a German embassy official shot by a 17-year-old Jew in Paris, died of his wounds. Nazi propaganda chief Josef Goebbels sent SA and SS squads throughout Germany on an orgy of anti-semitic destruction. In 24 hours over 7,000 Jewish businesses had been destroyed, along with nearly 200 synagogues; over 100 Jews were killed.

Kristallnacht ('Night of [Broken] Glass') was a sign of the horrors to come.

◄ A German girl sniggers at the photographer the morning after *Kristallnacht* as she passes the shattered shop-front of a Jewish business. Attacks on Jews and their shops proved crudely popular.

to the Germans – spoke to him and found out that he had only eaten egg powder before, never fresh eggs, and the only chocolate he had eaten was *ersatz* chocolate. So much for the German superiority – they couldn't even feed their people properly.

Soon I was bored and troubled by staying at home. I had to escape. I went to Prague to meet a few friends to talk about escape. One day in the city, where I was staying in a hotel, I found myself summoned to the phone and told to report immedi-ately to the airfield.

So I went back to the airfield and was told to test aircraft for the Ger-mans – mostly Russian planes. There were many incidents of misunder-standing with the Germans and sometimes they would arrest a pilot if they thought he was trying to sabo-tage the aircraft. It was usually a stu-pid mistake.

After a while I was back at home listening to stories of how our people were fighting in Russia, France and even Italy. I had to get out. So off I went to Prague again where my old commanding officer helped make ar-rangements.

There was a group of six of us and we were put on a train to Silesia and from there we went to Poland, where we were met by other Czechs who arranged for us to go to France, but first we had to join the French Foreign Legion; so I signed on.

We left Prague on 2 June, and by the end of the month we were on a Polish ship bound for Dover. Of course, the British wouldn't let us off the ship because we were military, only the political refugees were let in. So we went to Boulogne where we were met by the Czech air at-taché. He arranged for us to be taken to Paris by train and made to sign on again, have another medical examination and afterwards sent to North Africa via Marseilles.

Now I felt proud again. I was a trained soldier ready to fight. We were sent to Algeria and then back to France to train in some ancient aircraft – there were no fighting planes. When France declared war on Germany, we were moved to an airfield just outside Paris to a fighter school, but there was no progress, just routine flying, nothing that would prepare you for fighting on the front. At last, the Germans in-vaded France – by now it was 1940 – and there was fighting, but not for me. I was sent back to Africa!

France was then defeated, we were told it was finished, that we were leaving the French Air Force and being sent to England. We were moved to Casablanca, from where we were shipped to Gibraltar to transfer to a British ship which took us through the straits out into the Atlantic in convoy with French naval vessels that were heading towards Africa. We had to go more or less to America, because there were too many submarines near the coast of France. About 80 of us arrived in Liverpool. I had left home in May 1939 and arrived here in July 1940, over a year of travelling through Europe. But it was worth it, because by 25 September I was flying Hur-ricanes and five days later I joined 111 Squadron, and was ready to fight. In France it had taken five months to become a pilot, in Eng-land one flight! That was the dif-ference, I had one flight with an in-structor and the next time up I was the instructing pilot! Soon I was to shoot down my first German plane.

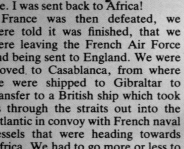

▲ A completed PzKw III tank on a production line in Germany at the beginning of the war.

▶ A flag-bedecked Vienna in 1938, after the German takeover, awaits the arrival of the Führer.

would not be here now, and if I'd known what 'pilot training' actually meant, I'd have stayed in the cavalry!

Our introduction to flying involved what I can only describe as being thrown off a mountain in a balsa-wood glider, tied together with bits of string. If you survived, you became a pilot. Many didn't.

Becoming a pilot was wonderful. I loved flying and there was considerable glamour in being in the air force. We found time to go skiing in the mountains at Zakopane, which was wonderful, as I came from a very flat part of eastern Poland, now Russia. Sadly, it became clear that there was going to be a war and the peacetime exercises became much more serious. For me, the outbreak of war in September 1939 was a double blow, as it coincided with the death of my father and I was unable to

▼ Hitler, surrounded by Nazi Party staff, talks to Dr Seyss-Inquart, the last Chancellor of Austria, in March 1938.

Michal Leszkiewicz began his military career as a cavalryman in the Polish Army, then became a pilot in the country's air force. As the Germans invaded and defeated his homeland in September 1939 he, like many others, determined to fight on.

" I started my military service in the army and, coming from a farm where we bred horses, I suppose it was only natural that I should become a cavalryman. Because I could ride well, I was trained to lay field-telephone cables – a job which might sound easy, but I can assure you wasn't. You had to ride sidesaddle in order to carry the cable-drum and pay out the line at the gallop – not easy on exercises, let alone under fire!

I can't say I enjoyed the cavalry, which was subject to very harsh discipline, and I was very homesick. I hated having to groom the horses constantly, and being told to clean the latrines! Under these circumstances, you'll understand why, when a recruiting drive for the air force was announced, I jumped at the chance of becoming a pilot.

Looking back on it, I think this was the point in my life where I began to realise that I had a lucky streak. If I'd stayed in the cavalry, I

▼ Michal Leszkiewicz, in flying kit marked with the Polish insignia, at the beginning of the war.

attend his funeral because of the military situation.

When war broke out, I was based at Torun, flying an aeroplane called the Karas, which was designed for army co-operation missions. Our air force was, for the most part, attached to Poland's field armies and my unit was attached to the Army Pomorze.

When the German attack began, we had been moved to wartime airfields so that the enemy could not destroy our aircraft on the ground. Although the fighting was bitter, I had a feeling that there was a lack of direction in our high command, because our missions often seemed to have little point to them.

Despite everything, we fought on for as long as we could, but it was hopeless, especially after the Rus-

MARCH

1 After a decision by the League of Nations, the Saar area is officially returned to Germany after 16 years

11 The new German Luftwaffe comes into being

16 Hitler reinstates compulsory military service in Germany

MAY

19 Elections in Czechoslovakia reveal overwhelming support by the German population for the Sudeten Party

JUNE

28 Germany commissions its first U-boat since World War I

SEPTEMBER

15 The German parliament adopts the Nuremberg Laws, depriving Jews of their citizenship

1936

MARCH

7 German troops march into the Rhineland, demilitarised since the Treaty of Versailles

AUGUST

1 Hitler opens the Berlin Olympic Games amid much Aryan celebration

30 Britain announces launch of its biggest naval expansion programme, calling for the building of 38 new warships

OCTOBER

25 The 'Axis' Berlin-Rome is created

sians invaded eastern Poland. It was like being a nut in a nutcracker. At the end, we were ordered to evacuate all flyable aircraft to Romania, and I took off for the last time from my homeland – and have not seen it since.

Luck came to my rescue again during the evacuation flight. Near the border, we were fired on by anti-aircraft artillery – whether it was Polish or Romanian, I don't know. Whoever it was, their aim was good, because they shot off my propeller. The aircraft became uncontrollable, at first rearing up, then stalling, and it was only with a semblance of control that we hit the ground. In the crash, my bomb-aimer was killed – his position in a gondola underneath the fuselage was destroyed in the impact. My gunner and myself were badly shaken – but alive – and got out of the wreck as quickly as possible. As far as I could judge, we were somewhere in the Carpathians and there was only one way to go – south.

We set off walking across the mountains along with many other refugees, trying to escape both the Germans and the Russian secret police (NKVD). Some were captured and sent to the Kamchatka Peninsula to die in horrible conditions. How many ended up in Katyn?

The two of us had not gone far when we had an incredible stroke of good fortune – we saw a Polish military convoy! What was even more extraordinary was the fact that the troops were the ground echelon from our own squadron! We joined them and made it over the border into Romania. Although relations between Poland and Romania were good before the war, it was soon clear that there were going to be problems, and we were eventually interned in a makeshift camp in southern Romania, near the Danube.

Conditions were grim – we had our heads shaved, and for beds we had the hard, bare earth. Being young and hot-headed, we decided to escape. We bribed the guards, who were local peasants, and they brought us civilian clothes and food.

We knew that it could not be long before the Germans turned their attention towards Romania, and a group of us determined to travel east along the Danube to the Black Sea and try to find a ship that would carry us to freedom. At first we made reasonable progress, travelling only at night, but we started fighting amongst ourselves. No-one was in charge and the arguments were about travelling in daylight, which would be much easier. In the end we started creeping along the riverbank in daylight, trying to keep as much under cover as possible.

Eventually someone did break cover. We were in a clearing in the woods, having some food. Someone went down to the water to wash a tin can and all hell broke loose. Firing came from all sides without any warning! We had been surrounded and had no option but to surrender. When our captors emerged from the bushes, we saw they were no more than a bunch of terrified locals with pitchforks and anything else they

▲ Anti-tank ditches and a sacrificed tramcar block a main road in Warsaw.

ALLIED WAR PLANS

Soon after war was declared on 3 September 1939 the British Expeditionary Force (BEF) – nearly 150,000 men and over 24,000 vehicles under General Lord Gort – crossed the Channel, joining French armies to prevent a German attack on the West. The French had constructed an elaborate series of defences – the Maginot Line – along the border with Germany. This did not cover the borders with Luxemburg and Belgium, so the BEF, along with French troops, was deployed to cover the gap. The Allies planned to fight off any invasion from the north, although by the end of 1939 this had been amended to include an advance to the River Dyle as soon as Belgium was attacked. No preparations could be made and, of course, no account was taken of the possibility of an armoured thrust through the 'impassable' Ardennes.

▶ British troops embark for France, October 1939.

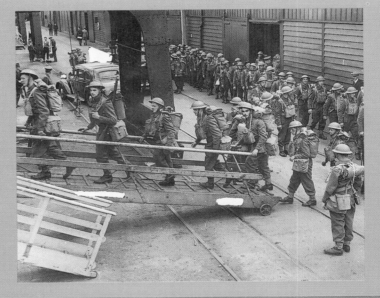

could lay their hands on.

After this, we were escorted to Bucharest where, to our surprise, we found a fully operational Polish military staff who were organising our papers for evacuation to France.

From Bucharest we travelled by train to the seaside resort of Balchik on the Black Sea, where we were billeted in local *pensions* prior to taking ship for, we supposed, France.

When we did leave Balchik, which is now in Bulgaria, we sailed into the Mediterranean. Our destination turned out to be Beirut in the Lebanon, which was then under French control. Here we were to

change ships. Beirut in the autumn of 1939 was marvellous – wonderful, light, beautiful houses and a sophisticated atmosphere. We were fascinated by the Arab way of life. We eventually set sail for France.

Our arrival in France was far less welcoming – the French didn't seem to want us and the weather was so cold that you would wake up in the morning with your blankets frozen solid! One good thing I do remember was drinking Champagne, which was cheaper to buy than table wine!

As I've said, the French didn't appear to know what to do with us, and we just waited and waited for something to happen. Eventually, we

were transferred to Lyons where, as part of the *Armée de l'Air Polonaise*, we were to receive training on French machines. With my background, I was to go to a reconnaissance unit, which was to be equipped with an aeroplane called the Potez 63. Before I could get to grips with it, the Germans invaded France and our airfield was bombed, which put paid to any thoughts of operations.

As the military situation got worse, chaos developed. Our officers, seeing the way things were going, determined to get us to the coast where we could be picked up by the British. Doing this was easier said than done, and we had to commandeer a train to make the journey. Our escape was successful, and when we reached the Atlantic coast there was a British destroyer waiting to take us off. We boarded but did not set sail for some time. I will never forget that three-day voyage: hundreds of us crammed into this tiny, heaving ship. The weather was rough and when we did set sail, the situation was made worse by the kindness of the British sailors who gave us their own rum rations to cheer us up. To this day, just the smell of rum makes me feel sick.

Our first sight of England was Liverpool, and I was soon on my way to RAF Innsworth in Gloucestershire to begin my career in the RAF – but that's another story. **"**

▼ **German Me1-09 fighters take off from a grass strip at the beginning of the war with Poland, September 1939.**

1937

JANUARY

30 Hitler formally renounces the Treaty of Versailles which had stood since 1919

MAY

28 Neville Chamberlain becomes Prime Minister of Britain

NOVEMBER

5 Hitler reveals his war plans in a secret speech

1938

MARCH

12 German troops march into Austria 'to quell public disorder'

13 Official annexation of Austria by Germany

SEPTEMBER

23 Hitler demands that Czechs evacuate the Sudetenland

30 Hitler, Chamberlain, Mussolini and Daladier sign Munich Agreement which divides up the territory of Czechoslovakia

OCTOBER

1 German troops march into Sudetenland

NOVEMBER

9 10 During *Kristallnacht*, Jewish property is destroyed all over Germany

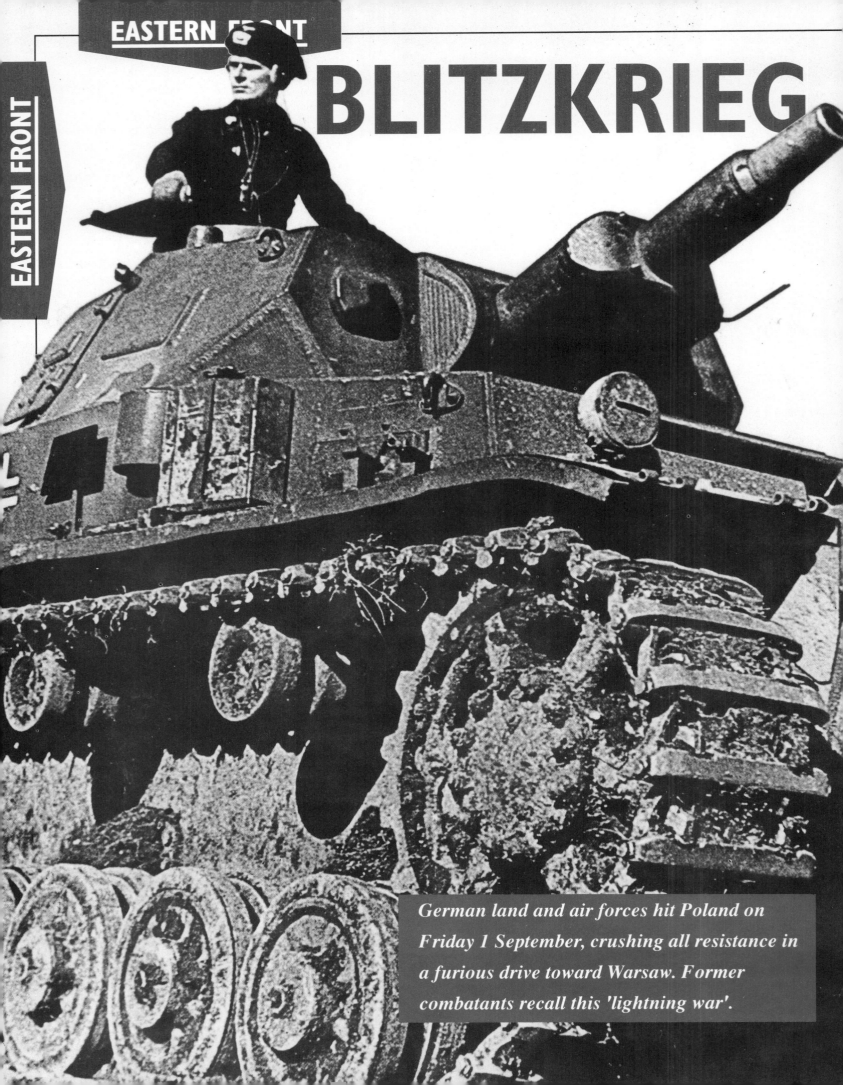

BLITZKRIEG

German land and air forces hit Poland on Friday 1 September, crushing all resistance in a furious drive toward Warsaw. Former combatants recall this 'lightning war'.

World War II began as a territorial war – an attempt by the Germans to recover land which they believed had been taken away from them by the Treaty of Versailles in 1919 and given to the reborn state of Poland, and to create *Lebensraum* (living space) in the east. It was clearly in Hitler's interests to make the campaign as short, sharp and decisive as possible, to present the Anglo-French allies with a *fait accompli* before they could intervene.

But even though the campaign lasted barely a month, the human suffering was appalling. Ethnic Germans, caught on the wrong side of an imposed border in 1919, may have welcomed the Wehrmacht as 'liberators', but to the Poles themselves it was a catastrophe. As their country began to collapse, torn apart by the force of Hitler's panzers and betrayed by the sudden Soviet attack from the east, ordinary people struggled to make sense of the chaos. For them it was only the beginning of what was to be a nightmare of foreign occupation.

Arno Pommerenke was a young ethnic German from the border territory of Wollstein, in Posen, who had been living in Eastern Germany since 1935. He was anxious to join the German Army in 1939, but for him the enemy would mean his brother and many of his schoolmates.

❝ In 1939 when the tensions were growing between Germany and Poland, someone suggested to me that I should apply for full German citizenship. I was born in Wollstein in Posen (Poznan), part of the disputed border territory, and had come to Germany four years ago.

I got all the official papers in June 1939, and was now able to join the army. I was posted to the 8th Infantry Regiment in Frankfurt an der Oder in the Hindenburg barracks. We didn't know then how close to war we were, but we sensed there was something in the air.

On 30 August I was ordered to report to the Regimental commander. The first thing he asked was whether it was true that I had a good command of both spoken and written Polish. I said that I did. 'Right,' he said, 'you are going to be a military interpreter at Army High Command.'

My superior there was a young major and we were both assigned to the 122nd Infantry Regiment in Meseritz. That same evening we found ourselves on the Polish border. The place was called Wirzebau. In the night of 30 August/1 September the whole of the German invasion force assembled at the border, camouflaged with bits of trees and bushes.

It was a very cool night. In the grey dawn light I could make out the

red and white border post and the empty Polish border hut. At 4 o'clock in the morning we got some food and hot coffee. The major and I wrapped ourselves in tarpaulin and waited for something to happen.

My home town, Wollstein, lay about 250 yards away from where we

were dug in. I had to tell him about my worst fears. 'It's like this', I said, 'about seven of my schoolmates are fighting on our side, the rest of my class are in Polish uniform. You know, my older brother, Kurt, graduated from the German Grammar School in Lissa and is now a lieutenant and platoon commander in a Polish regiment. Can you imagine – not only old schoolfriends, but your own brother!'

The major became pensive and then shook his head. 'That's your misfortune', he said, 'to come from a border territory. But the issue has to be settled.'

It was 5.30 in the morning – the calm before the storm. A Polish military aircraft flew over us about 100 metres off the ground. We could make out clearly the red and white insignia and the faces of the two men in the plane. No shots were fired. But now we knew we were entering the last few minutes of peace. The aircraft turned round and came back, then flew away towards Posen.

5.45 am. A young lieutenant from the staff brought over the order to attack. The advance units started moving eastwards. At 6.00 am we crossed the border. No sign of the enemy anywhere. Still no sound of gunfire. At about 6.10 we heard the first shot. It came from inside a windmill, of all places. The major ordered us to bombard it with incendiaries. The windmill went up like a flaming torch. Right next to me a corporal fell to the ground. He'd got one in the head. We pressed slowly on, but the major and myself soon had to come back. The first prisoners had been taken and we had to interrogate them. I was praying I didn't recognise any of them. ❞

JANUARY

4 President Roosevelt calls for increase in US defence budget

5 Hitler calls for the return of Danzig to Germany

9 Hitler reopens the *Reichstag* building, which was destroyed in the 1933 fire

10 Chamberlain meets Mussolini in Rome

17 A law is passed in Germany forbidding Jews to drive cars

19 The former president of the *Reichsbank* is dismissed by Hitler, after issuing a warning that Germany's rearmament programme threatens the economy

24 *Gestapo* officer Heydrich is asked to speed up evacuation of Jews from Germany

28 A report is published in Sweden on the principle of nuclear fission – the splitting of the atom

30 Hitler threatens the annihilation of the Jewish race in Europe in case of war

▲ Arno Pommerenke, a German living on the border with Poland, joined the Luftwaffe after a spell in the army.

◄ A German panzer heads for the Polish border. Along with the Luftwaffe, German tanks were in the forefront of the assault on Poland in 1939.

► A Polish border outpost gives way under attack from a German anti-tank gun and an armoured vehicle.

SS *Herbert Brunnegger was 16 and a fresh recruit in the SS Totenkopf (Death's Head) Regiment. His first taste of action was during the annexation of the Sudetenland in 1938 – his account of the invasion of Poland shows how Blitzkrieg really was.*

" The end of summer 1939, and with it the end of my holiday. A storm was brewing on the political horizon. Suddenly our unit was provided with a great number of transport trucks. The whole of the SS camp was jolted into a state of alarm. We gathered up all our ammunition, Teller-mines and explosives were also loaded. The mood in the camp was one of tense anticipation. In contrast to the Sudetenland crisis, it was very clear to us that something entirely different was in the offing – something which was not going to be resolved 'diplomatically'. The issue, and for us it was a clear one, was to protect German people from the brutal actions of another nation. Every day we read of the mistreatment and murder of Germans in Poland. The new *Reich* could not sit idly by while our own countrymen were being harmed, and the Poles were behaving provocatively towards us at the border. We had to come to the aid of the Germans in the Polish territories, if they were not to be driven out of their home towns.

I was very young at the time, and if I was not the most committed National Socialist, I was certainly a committed nationalist. I wanted above all, to be a soldier and to fight for my Fatherland. Everyone has to take his place in the field which attracts him. I wanted to be a soldier.

On 1 September 1939, I was walking over the wide parade ground and drew closer to our provisional accommodation, the green canteen building, when suddenly the loudspeaker attached to the wooden

▶ Herbert Brunnegger after he joined up with the SS *Totenkopf* Regiment, which took him to fight in Czechoslovakia and Poland.

▲ Early reconnaissance flights enabled the Germans to spot and destroy almost the entire Polish Air Force within the first hours of their attack.

▼ The bomb aimer/nose gunner of a German Heinkel He-111 bomber overlooks a Warsaw suburb as the crew prepares to attack enemy positions.

building began to crackle. The Führer addressed the German people. The time had arrived when the Poles had to be taken on: 'From 5.45 this morning we have returned fire!' All the young soldiers around me danced with joy. The war had begun.

The next day we were on our way in trucks heading for Breslau. Day and night the regiment rumbled on towards the south east. Together with a large battalion of the Wehrmacht we crossed the Polish border in the area of the Bartsch bridge and advanced north-east

through Ostrowo, Kalisz and Turek towards Lodz. Day after day encircling, cordoning off whole areas, breaking through enemy resistance.

The mighty iron construction of the Vistula bridge had collapsed into the river. Here our advance was stopped again, as it had been before in Lodz. Our lightning advance through swamp tracks, forest paths and sandy fields, through colonies of refugees and Polish units giving themselves up had stopped.

It was a hard campaign, but it was over in no time for us. At the beginning of October we were heading back south-west. We thought we were going back to Berlin, but as soon as we reached German soil again, we were put on a train in the direction of Munich. Before we reached the city where I'd sworn my oath of allegiance to the Führer two years beforehand, we were taken off the train and the sentry on the Autobahn directed us to Dachau. We got an awful feeling in the pit of our stomachs, as we had after the march into the Sudetenland. **"**

FEBRUARY

10 Poland declares it will not permit German road or rail traffic across the Danzig Corridor

14 The German battleship *Bismarck* is launched

19 A trade agreement is signed between the governments of Poland and the Soviet Union

23 Jews are ordered to hand in all precious stones and metals

MARCH

13 Berlin demands the dismissal of anti-Nazi ministers from the government

15 Hitler marches into Prague. Czechoslovakia effectively ceases to exist

20 The United States recall their ambassador from Berlin in protest at the invasion of Czechoslovakia

21 Annexation of the German-speaking Memel area into the German *Reich*

28 Civil war ends in Spain. Franco is in control of Madrid

31 Britain and France jointly declare their intention of defending Poland against any aggressor

◄A formation of Junkers JU-87 Stukas provides support from the air.

▼Brought up to full strength during the past few months, an armoured division of the German Army rolls into Poland.

▲ **The German Army ploughs into Poland.** Though Polish units demolished many bridges to stem the advance, the overwhelming German superiority soon crushed any resistance. Within a day of the invasion, Westerplatte's fort is blown up (background).

▼ **A German 15 cm howitzer pounds a Polish defensive position.** The Germans had modern and efficient artillery.

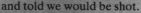

Alfred Fritz was an ethnic German living in a village called Mühltal, close to Bromberg (Bydgoszez), near the Polish border with Germany. He describes in particular what he witnessed of the events of 3 September 1939, which ethnic Germans in the area refer to as 'Bloody Sunday'.

❝ I have to say that relations between the Poles and the German minority living in this area had been very good up until 1939. I myself went to a Polish school and later on I was a member of the Evangelical Church Youth Group in a neighbouring village. On Sundays we would have a barrel-organ and folk dances – no politics, just a good time.

But, of course, we Germans were overjoyed when we heard on the radio on 1 September that the war with Poland had begun, and now, at last, these territories would be German again. This was German land, which had been robbed from the Fatherland by the Treaty of Versailles.

On 2 September the *soltys* (mayor) came to the village and declared that we were to be evacuated: all civilians should make their way to the freight station in Mühltal, from where we would be taken as far away from the border areas as possible.

Now, one thing I remember: my parents spoke no Polish, and so the mayor switched to German. We didn't wait around to be evacuated, we fled to the nearby wood, as we thought we'd only have to wait there a short time. During the night of 2 September we spotted a huge fire – our barn was ablaze. On the morning of 3 September we went back to the farm and put out the fire in the remainder of the barn which was still burning. Suddenly, some Polish artillery soldiers came over to us and told us we'd better get out of the border area as quickly as possible. Anyone disobeying this order would be shot as a spy.

So we headed off with a suitcase full of food along the road leading into Bromberg. Before we got there, we were stopped several times, and always the same question: Pole or German? Of course, we knew our way around, and my brother and I, acting as spokesmen, said almost automatically that we were Polish and were on our way to Warsaw.

What we saw when we got to Bromberg hardly bears repeating. We saw Germans rounded up from their houses, cellars or wherever they were accommodated – they were led in columns of 40–70 people to the corn market and shot. I remember one Pole saying to us: 'Hitler can have this territory, but he won't find any Germans here.'

We headed off down sidestreets until we reached a well-known blacksmith, called Altenburg, in Lindenstrasse, not far from Rinkauerstrasse. The smith told us his son had left, but he had some hunting rifles with him and he was going to defend his house until the end. The way things were, we thought it better not to stay with him and wanted to get out of Bromberg. Near the theatre we found a little cellar where we thought we'd be safe.

We were OK there until Monday 4 September. In the late afternoon we were found by some Polish soldiers who led us off in the direction of Hohensalza (Inowroclaw). We kept seeing a few Germans on the road making their way out of the town, but, eventually, we were taken into a slate quarry at the side of the road and told we would be shot.

We kept being handed over from one group of soldiers to another. We had almost resigned ourselves to our fate when my brother shouted out in good Polish: 'What are you doing? We are Poles – we were told to go in there by people on the streets.' They demanded our identification papers, but in the middle of all the confusion my father and I managed to escape into the woods. I don't know how we managed it.

I think we'd scarcely got ten metres into the woods when the first shots rang out. I only found out later that my brother had also made a break for it at the same time. I didn't believe we would be saved, I just didn't want to wait around to be shot. When I'd got about 60 or 70 metres into the woods, I dropped down exhausted behind a mossy bank. But I was soon startled by the rattle of machine-gun fire. So I carried on to the north in a wide arc until I fell into an exhausted sleep.

▲ Town after town falls to German lightning war tactics, which are tried and tested for the first time in Hitler's Polish campaign in September 1939.

I woke up in the first dawn light and went into the next village. I was starving by this time and frantically searched amongst the houses for a German name – I found one and stayed there until 6 Steptember. Late in the afternoon of the 6th the first German soldiers arrived and told me that since Tuesday morning Bromberg had been officially declared German.

So I went straight back to Bromberg, and spent the night at the smithy. On the morning of 7 September I reported my family missing at the *Gestapo* office, which had been set up on the Friedrichsplatz. From there I went to Mühltal. I'll never forget the feeling when the farm dog came running to greet me at the gate. He was so overjoyed he wouldn't leave my side. On the same day several Poles from the village came to offer me help. I was friendly to them and only accepted help if they let me pay them back in some way. **"**

▶ Warsaw capitulates on 27 September, devastated by the overwhelming German attack. The capital's streets are filled with the refuse of war – dead horses lie pathetically in the gutters, stripped to the bone by the hungry and defeated population.

1939

Leonard Witold Jastrzebski, aged 27, was a Polish engineer in Warsaw when the Germans invaded. He describes the period before the invasion, and his own desperate search to join the army after leaving Warsaw.

❝ I returned to Warsaw from a sailing holiday with friends one day before the Hitler-Stalin pact was signed. On the way back I had called to see a friend who worked for the Polish Foreign Ministry, and through him I found out that the invasion was imminent.

I lived in the centre of Warsaw, on the west of the Vistula river close to the southern bridge. The first bombs fell on Okecie airport. Every day there was bombardment of the city, but life went on more or less as normal. Then the ministries etc began to be evacuated, and by 8 September the situation was very tense. Blackouts had actually already started before I got back to Warsaw.

I cannot forget that period of optimism before the invasion. We were young people. We had grown up in what, for our country, was a relatively long period of peace. We were reborn after so many years of occupation and division by three countries – Germany, Russia and Austria. We were keen to build up our republic and make it strong.

Now, I had had an insight into the German military machine. I studied engineering, and we went to Berlin in the early Spring of 1938 to have a look at the Motor Show there. We also went to Mercedes Benz in Bavaria, and we took a trip into the Alps by car. Suddenly, as we were driving along the road we saw an enormous concentration of military vehicles of all types of construction heading towards us – many with caterpillar tracks on the rear wheels and heavy trucks for transport. We had arrived just at the moment when the German troops were beginning to mobilise to go into Austria. It was beautiful weather, snow and sunshine, and against this beautiful backdrop, we were confronted by a show of Germany's military might. We thought, 'Gosh, we have nothing like that in Poland.' We were very impressed, but we felt no fear. At that time we did not think that war was imminent.

I remember 3 September. We all sat around the radio and were delighted that the Allies had declared war on Germany. Everybody danced in the streets around the British and French embassies in Warsaw.

On 7 September, just before midnight, there was a special communiqué from the Polish Army that everyone available to bear arms should leave Warsaw and find regional offices where they could enrol. At the time I was working as an engineer at a factory making aircraft components. A lot of my friends got an immediate call-up. I did not get called up straight away, because I was a blue-card holder – my work was valuable to the war effort.

At that time things were very tense. More and more people were being evacuated every day. We were not sure whether we would hold Warsaw or not. On the morning of 8 September, I had made my decision: I went along to the university and handed in all the papers from my thesis, which I was still working on. I never got them back, actually, but no matter. I handed my notice in at my firm. They didn't object, they accepted that as a young man I was keen to go off and join the army. In fact, I learnt that a few days later the building was bombed and had I stayed there I would probably have been killed.

So my brother and I said goodbye

'BLITZKRIEG'

Blitzkrieg, or 'Lightning War', was designed to paralyse an enemy's 'brain' (his command capabilities) rather than destroy his 'muscles' (front-line forces). Using a combination of speed and surprise, the idea was to gain air superiority by catching the enemy air force on the ground in the first few hours of an attack, so giving ground units freedom to probe the enemy defences for 'lines of least resistance'. Once discovered, these would be exploited by armoured formations, using their mobility and speed to race for rear-area command posts, communications systems and supply lines. Dive-bombers would be used as aerial artillery to ensure a free passage, 'airborne' troops would be landed ahead of ground units to seize key road junctions or bridges, and enemy strongpoints would be left for follow-up infantry formations to mop up. With panic in the rear and no command being exercised, enemy front-line units would soon wither and die, surrendering to infiltrating forces.

German armour lays waste the land in the advance eastwards from west Prussia

to my father, and with three of my colleagues we left Warsaw on a long march to Lublin, which we reached in a couple of days.

The next day we went to the RKU (regional reinforcements office). I was the only one of the three who had already served in the army, so I did the negotiating. Just at that moment we heard German planes approaching and dropping bombs.

The building we were in shook at the foundations and the plaster was falling off the walls and ceiling. There was dust everywhere. Everyone was in panic. I told them, 'It's no good running away now, it's all over.'

Anyway, when all the panic had died down, the people were in such a nervous state, they gave us all the papers we needed without any fuss. My brother and two colleagues got papers to join an infantry regiment in another place. My national service had been in the Signals, so I got posted to a different place, but more or less in the same direction. We headed off for the train station. Well, as you can imagine, the trains were not exactly running to schedule, and we had no chance of getting a train to where we wanted to go.

We set off on foot again. It must have been about 10 or 11 September when we left Lublin. Two days later, I left my brother and the two others at their posting, and I tried to get a train to my posting in Dubno in the south east. I eventually managed to hitch a ride on a military train carrying equipment to the tank divisions.

The train would stop frequently and we'd all have to get out and take cover, as it was under regular bombardment from German planes.

On 17 September, just before sunset, someone came along the train, saying, don't wait around, don't wait, the Bolsheviks have entered the country. Boy, that was a shock – I can never forget that. Oh, that was

the end! We had no chance. Two armies attacking from both sides. How could we Poles survive?

I have to explain that I knew the Russians quite well. I was actually born of Polish parents in St Petersburg. I hated Bolshevik Russia. I had witnessed some of the Bolshevik crimes during the revolution, when I was only a young boy. So, it was a terrible shock for me to realise that we Poles were now being squeezed between two mighty enemies.

Anyway, we eventually decided to leave the train and took some bikes with us that I'd spotted on the train. There were three of us now, myself, the commander of the train and a corporal we had met on the train. I'd gone to check the trains behind us,

▲ The aftermath: the Polish campaign is fast and furious. Victorious Wehrmacht troops' faces relax, displaying the relief that follows a period of intense battlefield action. ◀ Over 120,000 Poles are taken prisoner by the time the country surrenders. Many of these were marched to their death by an unforgiving victor.

At dawn on 1 September 1939, German troops crossed the border into Poland on three fronts – in the north the Third Army aimed for Warsaw and Brest-Litovsk from its bases in East Prussia, while in the north-west the Fourth Army advanced out of Pomerania to link up and to clear the 'Polish Corridor' to Danzig; to the south and Eighth, Tenth and Fourteenth Armies cut through Polish defences towards Lodz, Cracow and Lvov.

The key to the campaign was speed, achieved by using the strategy of *Blitzkrieg* for the first time. As Polish aircraft were destroyed on the ground or in uneven dogfights, German armour probed for lines of least resistance – not a difficult task given the inadequate nature of Polish defences, strewn as they were along the border with few reserves.

On 11 September, the Polish commander ordered his men to withdraw to the south-east, but it was too late. Warsaw was surrounded and, between 16 and 27 September, the city was devastated by bombing, so forcing the garrison to surrender. On 17 September, the Soviets joined in, invading eastern Poland in accordance with a secret clause in the recently signed Russo-German pact; four days later, German and Soviet troops linked up on the River Bug. The Polish campaign was effectively over.

GERMAN SUCCESS IN POLAND

▶ **Poland's Air Force: most of it was destroyed before it could get off the ground – on day one.**

◀ **Bird of freedom: a pet canary is rushed to brief safety, through the rubble of Warsaw, by its worried owner. Its cage, still intact, is the only shelter left in sight.**

ganised their own summary executions, liquidating people they didn't like – people who resisted them. We realised the militia could search us, and we'd been concerned about the corporal who was with us, and what he might be carrying. He told us he was carrying some very secret documents in his pack and this was the time, we felt, to ask him to show us what they were. They turned out to

but everyone on them had fled.

Suddenly, we heard something moving – we hid in the bushes. A column of trucks came by – I could hear Russian voices. They had no guard escort. They must have got the all clear. So, now we knew it was hopeless.

The next day we decided the best thing to do would be to head for Romania. Romania had a peace treaty with Poland and so we felt we

would be safe there. But we never reached Romania. On the way there we came upon some patrols. They were wearing red arm-bands – local people, most of them not of Polish origin – you could tell by the accent. In the east of Poland there were a lot of Ukrainians and a large Jewish population. Many of these were members of the revolutionary militia, supporting the Russians.

I heard later that these groups or-be nothing more than documents concerning supplies of bridles for horses, but we discovered that the corporal also had a pistol with him. It was better for us to go unarmed than to run the danger of being taken captive by the militia so we buried the gun.

I never reached my posting and on the long trek back to Warsaw met up with my brother again, who had already been taken by the Russians. I managed to get him and a comrade out of the prison camp. We didn't reach Warsaw until the October, after the capitulation. "

Mrs Eva Bukowska (née Buterlewicz) was 24 in September 1939 and had just finished her teacher training in Warsaw. She volunteered for service in the Information Bureau of the Polish Army and got involved in clandestine teaching after the German clampdown in Warsaw.

" In the summer of 1939 I'd finished studying at the University College of Commerce in Warsaw, and had just completed a teacher training course. I joined the Voluntary Women's Service of the Polish Army. I remember telling myself as a student, look, there's no boys in our family, I'm still single, so I will do what I can for our country.

◀ The German general von Blaskowitsz (centre left) accepts the capitulation of the Polish capital Warsaw.

I was mobilised at the end of August and put in the Bureau of Information and Propaganda. I was trained to use a gun, but I never used it during the war. They put me in the telecommunications centre in Warsaw and I had to pass on messages and orders to the units in the field.

Until the Germans came in we had a radio, and I remember vividly hearing the news that England had declared war. We were overjoyed. We thought, 'We are not alone any more'.

I remember coming back from duty at the telephone office and I wanted to buy something to eat. I went to the grocer's and asked what I could buy. He said, 'We have only a few chocolate bars to sell,' and so I bought one. I wanted some bread, but I couldn't get any. It was really difficult.

But there were really some worse days – the last day of September, for example, they were really terrible. We were sitting downstairs in our three-storey house and the bombs were dropping all the time. The house was very old and it was shaking continuously.

The capitulation of Warsaw was, I think, on 27 September and the first time that I actually saw German troops on the streets was five or six days later. There was a formal entry parade through the streets. I was down on the street myself, because they had told us that we couldn't remain in our flats, because the windows were high above the streets – they were scared of snipers.

Warsaw was very very badly

▲ Hitler, flanked by some of his commanding officers, salutes his troops during a victory parade in the streets of Warsaw, when the city finally fell after an 11-day siege.

damaged at this time. I mean, there was no water, there was no electricity, no glass in the windows. We were very distressed, because we knew we were left alone – there was no help from outside, the Polish forces were overcome. We couldn't fight any longer.

As soon as the Germans came in they sent out very strict orders – there was a curfew. We started clearing the streets and repairing the windows. We tried to get ordinary life going again. About a month later, I remember my father told me to go out and get a teaching job. So I did. Germans ordered that there should be no grammar schools for the Polish people, only technical schools, teaching commerce, housekeeping and so on.

Of course, I was trained in commerce, so it was easy for me to get a job, but at the same time as teaching commerce, I would give lessons in forbidden subjects, like literature or history. This took place in private flats, not in the schools. In fact sometimes I would just sit in the room and keep watch, while another teacher taught my class – taught them something forbidden.

So, I suppose for me this was the beginning of my involvement in clandestine activities. Many of these clandestine teachers paid with their lives. They were arrested and taken away – you see, the German idea was that the Poles were to be workers for the new German authorities. They didn't need all the " old academic subjects.

AUGUST

7 Poland issues warning about the arming of its customs officers at the border at Danzig

20 During a speech to his generals in his mountain redoubt, Hitler announces that 'the destruction of Poland will commence on Saturday morning'

23 Hitler and Stalin conclude non-aggression pact – general lines of partition of Poland are drawn up

24 Poland mobilises her forces for war

25 Signing of mutual assistance agreement between Poland and Britain

27 The Heinkel He-178, the world's first jet-powered aircraft, makes its maiden flight

29 Hitler gives Poland an ultimatum on the question of Danzig and the Polish Corridor

30 Britain begins evacuations of civilians from London

DUEL AT SEA

British and German naval men remember the bitter contest for supremacy in the Atlantic. The first round is won conclusively by the Royal Navy at the battle of the River Plate.

B ritish naval strategy in 1939 revolved around one vital requirement – maintaining free passage of the world's sea-lanes so that supplies could be brought in from the Empire and Americas. Without that, Britain would quite literally starve. By the same token, German strategy had to include an element of denying the sea-lanes to Britain, either by U-boat warfare or the actions of surface ships.

The U-boat campaign began straight away – the loss of the liner SS *Athenia* on 3 September 1939 showed what was involved – but it was the surface clash that had the most immediate results for Britain. Once it was known that the *Graf Spee* was at large, stalking merchant ships, the Royal Navy had no choice but to destroy her and, although the Battle of the River Plate in December 1939 ended with the *Graf Spee* being scuttled rather than sunk in action, the result was a vital boost to British morale.

▲ Jim Goodson, pictured later in the war in air force uniform. So incensed was he by the sinking of the *Athenia*, that he swore allegiance to the King and joined the RAF.

James A Goodson, an American citizen, heard the news that Britain had declared war on Germany in the third-class lounge of the Athenia *as she prepared to set sail for America from Glasgow. Among the gathered passengers the feeling was that in leaving, they were well out of it.*

❝ By the evening we were off the Hebrides. The strong west wind was cold, the sky cloudy and the ship was pitching and rolling slightly on the ocean swells.

I had just mounted the staircase and was moving forward to the dining room when it struck. It was a powerful explosion, followed by a loud crack and whistle. The ship shuddered under the blow. The lights went out. There were women's screams. The movement of the ship changed strangely as she slewed to a stop.

We all knew the ship was mortally stricken – it was beginning to list. The emergency lights were turned on. I went back to the companion way I had just come up. I gazed down at a sort of Dante's Inferno – a gaping hole, at the bottom of which was a churning mass of water, on which there were broken bits of wooden stairway, flooring and furniture. Terrified people were clinging to this flotsam and to the wreckage of the rest of the stairway, which was cascading down the gaping hole.

The blast must have come up through here from the engine room below, past the cabin decks and the third-class restaurant and galley. I clambered and slithered down to the level of the restaurant. I started by reaching for the outstretched arms and pulling the weeping, shaking, frightened women to safety – but soon I saw that the most urgent danger was to those who were floun- dering in the water or clinging to the wreckage lower down. Many were screaming that they couldn't swim.

I slithered down the shattered stairway, slipped off my jacket and shoes, and plunged into the surging water. One by one, I dragged them to the foot of the broken companion- way.

When there were no more bodies floundering in the water, I turned to those who were cowering in the openings of the corridors which led from the cabins to what had been the landing at the foot of the stairs, and which was now a seething, lurching mass of water. Most of them were women, many were children and some were men. I went first to the children. They left their mothers, put their small arms around my neck and clung to me. They clung as we slipped into the water – they clung as I climbed the slippery wreckage, and they clung as I prised their little arms from around me and passed them to members of the crew at the top.

◀◀ *Revenge, Royal Sovereign* and *Ramilles* in line ahead.

◀ Britain's fleet at Scapa Flow.

Finally there were no more left, either in the water, or waiting at the openings of the corridors. I was at the base of the broken stairs. For the first time, I was able to pause and look around. By now the ship had listed much more, the water had slopped into the corridors on the down side until it was waist-high. The corridors on the upper side were out of the water.

I pushed off into the lurching water and swam to the opening of one of the half-flooded gangways. The water in most of the cabins was too deep and the light was too dim to conduct any kind of search. What was worse, as I stumbled through the water and darkness, there was a movement of the ship as it listed further. The water sloshed higher, and there were deep rumblings in the bowels of the ship.

There wasn't anybody there. The feeling grew in me that this deck was already at the bottom of the sea, as it would be for hundreds of years.

The ship was listing quite a bit now. We headed up the sloping deck to the higher side and found them launching one of the last lifeboats. It was crowded. Members of the crew were holding back those for whom there was no more room and telling them to go to another boat. Meanwhile, the two seamen fore and aft in the boat were desperately trying to lower it. But as the heavy boat lurched unevenly down as the ropes slid through the pulleys of the davits, a problem arose which was apparently not forseen by the designers of lifeboat launching systems. Because of the listing of the ship, when the lifeboat was lowered from its davits, and as it swayed with the slight roll-

◄ Survivors of the *Athenia*, the first British ship sunk in the war, *en route* back to Glasgow after their ordeal in the icy Atlantic. Inset: the news breaks of the outrageous attack on a passenger liner.

GERMAN HIGH SEAS FLEET

Hitler was not a naval strategist. His plans for the expansion of Germany involved land campaigns in Europe, in which his navy would play only a minor part, weakening Britain by attacking her sealanes, principally in the Atlantic. This would necessitate the construction and use of U-boats, but the idea of creating a Grand Fleet, capable of confronting and defeating the British Fleet in battle on the high seas, was never part of the plan. At best, capital ships such as battleships, cruisers and (if completed) aircraft-carriers, would emerge from German bases after the U-boats had succeeded, to finish the job of destroying British trade.

As a result, by 1939 the German High seas Fleet was weak. Some excellent ships had been launched, including the small battleships *Scharnhorst* and *Gneisenau*, the 'pocket' battleships *Admiral Scheer*, *Graf Spee* and *Deutschland*, and a number of heavy cruisers, with others under construction, but as a force they were grossly inferior to the combined Anglo-French navies. As the war began, moreover, two of these ships – the *Graf Spee* and *Deutschland* – were at sea, vulnerable to British attack. The destruction of the *Graf Spee* off Montevideo two months later did nothing to persuade Hitler that his land-based strategy was incorrect.

◄ Admiral Raeder, left, inspects the German warships with Hitler, 1936. Already the navy is expanding, ready for war.

▲ The British warship *Royal Oak* is an early victim of the marauding U-boats. Inset: the brutal headlines tell the story of U-47's victory – and announce the loss of over 1,000 men.

▶ Günther Prien, submarine ace and captain of U-47. The *Royal Oak* was his first war victim, sunk in Scapa Flow on 14 October 1939.

ing, it fouled the side. Although the seamen were playing out their ropes as evenly as possible, the forward part got caught against the side of the ship. The seaman continued to play out his rope. Suddenly it slid free and dropped – but the other rope hadn't played out as much. The front of the boat dropped, but the rear was caught by its rope. Soon the boat was hanging by the after rope and the screaming passengers were tumbling out of the boat like rag dolls.

There was nothing we could do. I helped the crew to shepherd the remaining group of passengers to the other side of the ship. Here there was another problem caused by the same list and the same swell – the boat was hanging on its davits, but swinging in and out. On its outer swing, there was a yawning gap between the lifeboat and the ship. Most of the passengers were women or elderly – or both. Crew members were trying to persuade them to make their leap in when it was close to the ship, but many of them waited too long, and the boat swung out again.

Finally the lifeboat could take no more passengers, and was lowered away, leaving a small group of us on the deserted, sloping deck. One of the ship's officers took command.

'That was the last of the boats, but the Captain's launch will be back for us soon.'

I went to the higher side of the ship and looked down the sloping side to the dark, rolling sea. There, just about 100 yards from the ship, I saw a lifeboat. Hanging from the davits were the ropes which had launched the boats.

In the dark, I couldn't see if they reached all the way to the sea, but

they went far enough for me. Soon I was going down a rope, hand over hand, fending myself off the side with my feet as the ship rolled . . . For the first time, I wished I'd been able to get to my life-jacket. If I passed out, it would at least have brought me to the surface. Just as I felt I could hold out no longer, I got to the surface. I gasped for breath. The sea was choppy and I got a mouthful of water. It was colder, rougher and more brutal than I had expected. I looked for the lifeboat I had seen from the deck. I could only see it when I was lifted by a wave – now it looked much further away.

I struck out in the direction of the boat, but it was a struggle. Eventually I got close enough to see one of the reasons. They had a few oars out, and were trying to row away from the ship. I knew that was in line with instructions, because of the danger of being sucked down with the ship when she sank, but I did feel they could at least stop rowing until I

caught up with them.

Fortunately their efforts were badly co-ordinated, and I finally reached them and grabbed the gunwale. I tried to pull myself up, expecting helping hands to lift me into the boat – instead a dark young man, screaming in a foreign language, put his hand in my face to push me away. A frantic middle-aged woman was prising my fingers off the side of the boat and banging on my knuckles.

Dimly I realised they were panicking because they felt the boat was already over-crowded. I heard the voices of the seaman in charge, yelling for them to stop – but help came from another direction, and it was much more effective. The diminutive figure of a girl appeared. In a flash she had landed a sharp right to the face of the young man and sent him sprawling back off his seat. In the next second, my other tormentor was hauled away and the strong young arms were reaching down to help me. **"**

◀A German mine-sweeper flotilla sets out, the crew of the anti-aircraft gun at battle stations to fend off air attack, November 1939.

1939

Ordinary Seaman Reginald Fogwill (Len to his friends), was in a good position, from his lookout post on the deck of HMS Exeter, *to see the action on 13 December, when the* Graf Spee *hove into view off the estuary of the River Plate in Uruguay.*

❝We were the South American squadron – there were four ships, the *Exeter,* the *Achilles,* the *Ajax* and the *Cumberland.*

For action stations and for cruising stations, my job was as a lookout, in the after control of HMS *Exeter.* This was right by the main mast where the after control position is, and on top of this is a position for lookouts and Lewis gunners. I was P1 lookout and Lewis gunner.

The *Graf Spee* had been raiding around the world, and it was anticipated that she would be arriving off the Plate, which was one of the lifelines for this country for the supply ships from Argentina and Uruguay. She had never, up to that time, made an attack on that route, and it was anticipated that she would be at that spot around that time. It was the anniversary of the battle of the Falklands in 1914 – that was the thinking which anticipated her move.

As it happened, she turned up there on the 13th December. It wasn't directly in the estuary – it was well out to sea and out of sight of land.

I had the middle watch the night before, from midnight to 4 o'clock in the morning. I turned in to my hammock after the watch to get a couple of hours' sleep before the day started. Then at about 6 o'clock the bugle sounded actions stations and we all closed up for action.

I went to my station and was informed by the fellow I took over from that there was a ship sighted on the after quarter, or port half quarter. I put up the glasses right away and looked at her – you could see the fighting top of the ship and just at that time, the challenge went out from us to the *Graf Spee.* I had my glasses on the ship and I saw a flash, which at that moment I thought was answering us. But then I heard the BOOM, and then the splashes of falling shot, and we knew then that we were in action.

We were ordered away to intercept – because we were last in line and were steaming line ahead with the *Ajax* first, the *Achilles* and then the *Exeter.* We were ordered away from the line towards the *Graf Spee* and we couldn't open fire because we were out of range at about 16 miles.

We closed the range, getting up speed as we did, and the *Graf Spee* was firing at us all the time. Quite early in the action her firing was very accurate and she hit us early. A turret got put out of action and the shell landed on the forecastle, causing the paint locker to catch fire, so there was smoke coming up from there. It looked worse than what it was, though.

We'd opened fire by that time, but the fire from the *Graf Spee* was still very accurate and kept hitting. I think altogether we were hit by 11 or

NAVAL BALANCE

When war broke out in September 1939, the German Navy was markedly inferior to that of the British, its major rival in the North Sea and Atlantic. Despite an intention to increase the size of the *Kriegsmarine* (Plan 'Z') so as to produce a force eventually capable of dominating sea-lanes already disrupted by successful U-boat attack, Hitler could only call on two small battleships, three 'pocket' battleships, two heavy and six light cruisers, 34 destroyers and torpedo-boats and 57 submarines at the start of hostilities. By comparison, the Royal Navy was huge, deploying (with the Dominions' navies) a total of 12 battleships and battlecruisers, six aircraft-carriers, 35 modern cruisers and 23 older ones, 100 fleet destroyers, 101 escort destroyers and 38 submarines. Admittedly, not all were in the Atlantic or home waters, but the balance was clearly in favour of the British. It was not to alter dramatically as the war progressed.

▲▲ **The new German flag is hoisted over the U-boat fleet at Kiel, 9 November 1935 – a flagrant infringement of the Versailles Treaty.**

▲ **British naval armament production is stepped up at the Woolwich Arsenal.**

◄ **Heroes of the River Plate battle march victorious through Admiralty Arch, London 1940.**

12 11-inch shells, and one of the salvoes, just after hitting A turret, hit B turret, and the explosion and the shrapnel from that went through the bridge killing or wounding all the bridge staff, including the captain and navigator. The steering control position was put out and the steering was then carried on from the after position by the sail-maker, and of course, he was receiving no orders because we had a shell come through on the port side and explode just above the 4-inch magazine, killing or wounding all the damage-control parties at that position. This also put all the communications and power out of action.

When the sail-maker took command of the steering, he was steering a zig-zag course, and I think that must have put the *Graf Spee* off, because they started missing us then – although it was reckoned that one of our shells had hit their control top, and damaged them so that they couldn't retaliate properly.

By this time the only guns we had in action were the Y turret, which had no power at all and they were just in local control. The gunnery officer had gone aft to Y turret – he clambered on top of the turret and gave sighting instructions from the top, calling down through to the guns – a very brave man.

The action, as far as we were concerned, was pretty close – I reckon we got to a range of about 5 miles – we were so close that it looked as if you could throw something on to the *Graf Spee*. At one time the captain had it in his mind to ram the *Exeter* into the *Graf Spee*. A good job he didn't – we would all have gone down.

About the time I went down to give orders to the torpedo officers from the captain, to get rid of the torpedoes. We started making smoke. Then for some reason or other, the *Graf Spee* drew away from us. We thought she was running away and had had enough. She must have been hit pretty badly.

The shells were passing right through the ship and it was only when they hit the armour-plating around the magazine that the shells would explode. There was one shell which passed right through the bridge and exploded on the other side of the ship. This caused a lot of deaths and damage by shrapnel.

We had 61 killed in action and four died afterwards. There were over 120 wounded, so we did suffer. The ship was in a pretty bad condition. The wounded were everywhere and the doctors were doing their best and getting help from the stewards to look after the men.

Inside the ship the sickbay was wrecked and the wounded had to be laid out on the deck. Towards the end of the action, we were ordered into working parties to clear the wreckage.

Although the shells were flying, you carried on doing these things. You didn't take any notice of the action, because you were so immersed in your work. When we went into action we always had the thought that we would come out alright – we were a pretty crack ship, you know – one of the best ships in the Navy. We were getting a bit old, but our record of gunnery and seamanship had top marks. I don't think anyone, when you go into action like that, has any thoughts but just to do their work, and that was what we did. There were quite a few feats of bravery, as the medal lists show.

It was the job of the cruisers to intercept and chase raiders, and it was in our line of duty to do that, so

◄ The German battleship *Graf Spee* raids the oceans freely until her brush with the British South American squadron. The Battle of the River Plate would seal her fate.

▼ Buenos Aires, December 1939; the crew of the *Graf Spee* is at leisure as repairs are attempted on its crippled battleship.

when we came across a pocket battleship, there was no thought of their being better – we went into action.

After the excitement, everyone was talking at once, telling each other what they saw. It wasn't everybody who saw the *Graf Spee* – you could reckon about 80 per cent of the ship's company were below decks and saw nothing. "

Frau Elizabeth Heinz was a secretary in her early 20s in the German embassy in Montevideo. Her account, written at the time of the scuttling of the Graf Spee, *took the form of a letter to a friend in Germany dated 21 December 1939.*

"It was the eve of my birthday – that's why I can't forget it – we suddenly heard on the radio that a battle was raging between German and English cruisers at Funte del Este and Piriapolis. One news announcement followed close on another. First we were told that the English cruiser *Exeter* had been destroyed by the battleship *Graf Spee* – and we were astonished by this – we couldn't believe that a German battleship was here, off our coast. When I came home from the office and heard the news on the radio, the battle was already taking place in Uruguayan waters. At 9.00 pm we were told that shots had been exchanged, then the cruisers had disappeared in the fog. One cruiser was heading full steam for Montevideo and if it held the same course and direction it would reach Montevideo in 90 minutes. Apparently it was a German cruiser, but the nationality could not be confirmed – two other cruisers

were following it. The radio announcer was practically tripping over himself as reports flooded in. Ten minutes later it was confirmed that it was a German cruiser, followed by two English. Ten minutes later: German embassy officials had gone to see the Uruguayan government – then a few minutes later – they were asking permission to dock in Montevideo. Then another announcement: they were asking for a certain number of beds to be made available at the military hospital. The reports became more and more frantic.

Shortly before midnight it was announced that the German cruiser had dropped anchor in Montevideo harbour and was unloading its dead and wounded – we were told not to go to the harbour as it had been cordoned off. How proud we Germans were of our 'boys in blue', of the beautiful ship – my tears are welling up again, for the burial of the commander is just now taking place in Buenos Aires. The next day, Friday 15, the 36 dead men were laid to rest. The English did not relent – they pushed and pushed and all the entreaties by the German embassy officials and the commander of the warship were to no avail.

In the meantime, a whole fleet had assembled off the La Plata estuary, waiting for the *Admiral Graf Spee* to leave the harbour: various heavy and light cruisers, an aircraft-carrier are on their way, and a French battle-cruiser – in other words a huge mousetrap was set. And the Uruguayan government is under intense pressure from the English minister, who is tightening the thumbscrews. They are wriggling like worms, but they have to do the bidding of Millington Drake, the English minister. The labourers are working day and night on the cruiser. On Saturday, from early morning until late into the

night, everyone was asking: *saldra* or *nor saldra* – will she leave or won't she? It was all in vain, even the efforts of our German ambassador. Even the right granted to every country to have the time to patch up the ship again was denied to him. He was told she had to leave port by 8 o'clock on Sunday evening. She couldn't even leave before this (the night of Saturday to Sunday was foggy and the weather was bad – this would have facilitated her escape), for according to the law, a given time must elapse following the departure of the last ship until any cruiser is allowed to leave. The English had been very cunning about this. A small English vessel left the harbour and by 6.15 on Sunday evening the time was up – which left the German cruiser with only 105 minutes in which to leave port. The tension and excitement amongst the population rose to breaking point. The harbour was packed with people as the time grew closer and closer.

Everyone was at the harbour and always the same questions: will she leave – to a certain death with all those brave young men on board? There must be a way out – a loving God would not wish this to happen. Then around 7 o'clock the anchor was raised and the ship began to move. The whole crowd froze. They couldn't believe their eyes, they didn't dare breathe. The women fell to their knees and prayed – the Uruguayans have different blood in their veins, they are more easily excited than we cool Germans – they prayed for the blond boys, for the *marinos rubios*. We Germans were white as a sheet. No, they couldn't be led off to their deaths, they must have something up their sleeve, but what? The ship slowly left the harbour one hour before the deadline. The crowd was dumbstruck and then gradually regained their senses and began waving and shouting. The ship left the dock, flying a massive German flag. We rushed back home to listen to the

radio. Then a few minutes before 8 o'clock, we heard a dull blast. The sun had now gone down, it didn't need to shine any more. Giant flames and explosions. Reports spread like wildfire, the captain and crew have been saved. Then others, the propaganda stations, reported, 1,000 young men in the bloom of youth have been sent to their deaths by one solitary man, who only needed to say one word. That man sits in Berlin' – Hitler! Then we could see *Tacoma*, the German steamer, which had been in the harbour a long time, and the whispers went round: the crew had transferred on to the steamer during the night and now they had been taken by Argentinian tugs which were waiting nearby. **"**

◄ **B Turret of HMS *Exeter*,** soon to be the target of the *Graf Spee*'s heavy guns. In the River Plate action, both guns were smashed from their mountings and the shield completely disappeared – many lost their lives.

▼ **Finally asail in open waters off the Plate Estuary, *Graf Spee* pre-empts any British attack. Captain Langsdorff's scuttling of his ship makes front-page news in Britain.**

Daily Express

The Pride of the Nazi Navy commits suicide

GRAF SPEE BLOWS HERSELF UP

Scuttled to escape fighting it out

FLAMING WRECK SINKS 2 MILES FROM HARBOUR

British Navy look on

61 died in the Exeter

1939

NOVEMBER

1 Danzig and the Polish Corridor officially pass over to the German *Reich*, plus all the territories ceded to Poland under the terms of the Treaty of Versailles in 1919

3 US neutrality bill amended to allow Britain and France to obtain arms

8 Hitler escapes Munich beer cellar bomb attack

12 First ENSA concert is staged for troops in France, featuring Maurice Chevalier and Gracie Fields on the bill

23 The armed merchant cruiser HMS *Rawalpindi* is sunk by German warships *Gneisenau* and *Scharnhorst* in the Atlantic

29 Russia breaks off diplomatic relations with Finland

30 Russia invades Finland

STORM WARNING

Vivid eyewitness accounts of Britain after the declaration of war. Contrary to expectation, the sky does not instantly rain bombs. A tense, seemingly endless period of waiting follows.

T he transition to war is never easy, particularly if the armed forces involved have not been prepared for conflict. In September 1939 the British Army was not ready for a long conventional war, having suffered economic constraint throughout the 1920s and 1930s. Despite the 'scare' of September 1938, calmed by the Munich Agreement, and the dismemberment of Czechoslovakia, equipment was in short supply and strategy had largely reverted to that of 1918.

But at least the army was expanding. In May 1939, two months after Hitler marched into what remained of Czechoslovakia and war suddenly seemed inevitable, a form of selective conscription had been introduced. Young men were expected to serve in the Regular Army for six months – in the event, most conscripts served until 1945/46. By September 1939, they had undergone four months' training. They were going to need it.

James Palmer was called up to the Royal Tank Regiment at the age of 18, in mid-July 1939, and was one of the many who would be 'home before Christmas'. His girlfriend Muriel and widowed father waved him off at the station in his home town of Hulme in Lancashire – and a new life began.

" It was with mixed feelings that I sat on the platform bench, awaiting the train. Dad, and Muriel had come along with me, and both looked terribly upset. I felt both excitement and anxiety, and was really at a loss as to what was happening. I knew that I would not like being in the army, yet I felt a little pleased at being one of the first to go. The militia men had been the sole topic in the newspapers for the last few days, and

in a way I was looking forward to the experience. It was only for six months, so the papers said, and I would be home before Christmas.

The train puffed to the platform and we walked through the turnstile. The moment of departure was here, and Dad was very emotional and upset. I know that he was thinking of another such occasion, 20-odd years ago, when he had stepped on such a train, taking him to some benighted camp.

Muriel was in tears and clung to my arm, and Dad turned away when she kissed me. It was all so dramatic, and a lump in my throat prevented me from saying much. I remember a woman crying as she spoke to a young lad about my age, who was waiting to board the train, and I thought that my Mam would have been doing the same thing if she had been there.

Two young lads were in the com-

[...] partment, but didn't say anything. They just sat [looking] out of the window [...] did the same, but I think our thoughts must have been exactly the same. We didn't feel like talking and were all busy with our own thoughts. The train had left Manchester, and the green fields were scurrying by the windows when the dark lad in the corner broke the silence with the blunt observation that he supposed we were all in the same boat. I liked him from that moment, and did not realise at that time what we would have to go through together.

His name was Joe, and he lived in Ancoats and had been a trolley boy with Manchester Corporation. He soon enlightened me that he was going to the Tank Corps at Warminster and that he hoped he would be home for Christmas, because they had promised to train him as a bus driver when his service was finished. The other lad was quiet and seemed a little shy, but he perked up when the Tank Corps was mentioned because he was going there too. It was good not to be alone, and fags were soon passed round.

Things happened quickly when we eventually arrived at Warminster. It was a dark and lonely station, and we could see that it was not very big. No sooner had we tumbled from the train, when a couple of cheery blokes pounced on us and asked were we for 'the Tank [...]'.

Our reception was [most pleasant] when we [arrived at the camp with] [...]

huts scattered [...] tarmac. The first thing [we had] was a [good hot] meal and I was favourably [impressed]. Nothing else seemed to [matter] except that we were [shown beds] and given blankets for the night.

In charge of our hut was a corporal named Jock (I never found out his full name, but he became a good pal of mine). It appeared that the regulars had been given the honour of training the militia, and had been instructed to try and behave like gentlemen with us, on the assumption that we 'civvies' were all gentlemen ourselves. There was to be no bullying, and discipline was to be mild. It looked a cushy set-up to me, and my first thoughts were that it was not going to be so bad after all. Our beds were quite comfortable and the meals were good and ample. We had been asked if we wanted any more plum duff! The corporal gave us a little lecture and I first heard the phrase 'You play ball with me, and I'll play ball with you'.

The corporal had turned out the lights when a bugle sounded, and I lay in bed thinking about the day's events and Muriel. Everything had happened so fast, it was hard to realise that I was in the army. George was in the next bed to me, and in the dark he seemed to want to talk more freely than he had done all day.

He chattered on and on, then someone at the other end of the room started to tell jokes. At first it was a low mumble of sound in the hut, but it soon developed into pandemonium. The corporal, who was sleeping at the top of the room, raised his voice to quell the noise, but no-one took any notice. At last he could stand it no longer, and his army training asserted itself. Never have I heard such a blast. The very walls shook as he told us what he was going to do if we didn't shut up. I cringed under the blankets, but one bright lad from Liverpool shouted to the corporal, 'Get stuffed.'

That did it – before I realised what was happening, the corporal was out of his bed and the lad from Liverpool was on the floor with his bed on top of him. The corporal held him against the door with his left hand. 'Did you say something?'

The poor lad from Liverpool stood wobbling at the knees, but tried to bombast his way out of the situation. Then it happened. I don't think the blow travelled six inches, but it was straight to the chin, and I saw a man knocked out cold for the first time in my life. He slithered to the floor and the corporal picked up a bucket of water and threw it all over him.

The corporal turned and, in a [frightening] bellow, gave us to understand that the next man who moved [out] of his bed would find himself in a [hospital] bed for a month. We all believed what he said, and Liverpool was left dripping on the floor. The corporal climbed back into bed and, in a voice that echoed round the hushed hut, said 'Now lads, let's get some bloody sleep.'

It was when the corporal thought that we were all asleep I heard him creep out of bed and go towards the crumpled body, and then I listened, amazed. The corporal was apologising to the lad and was helping him into bed. 'I didn't mean to hurt you, lad, but you shouldn't have said that. You'll be OK in the morning, so try and get some sleep.' I couldn't believe my ears! How could anyone be such a two-sided character? He was as gentle to 'Liverpool' as a mother, and yet ten minutes before I had seen him pole-axe the lad.

About two o'clock in the morning, I was still awake, and could hear drunken singing in the distance. The sounds came nearer until I could recognise the words. The song was about a troop ship leaving Bombay and the chorus finished with, 'Cheer up my lads . . . 'em all'. This song seemed to follow me about in later years, and it will always bring back memories of my first night in the army. **"**

◀ **The very first air-raid warning of the war in an empty Strand in 1939.**

▼ **'Wish me luck' – a Highland soldier with two gas mask-equipped friends.**

DECEMBER

2 The British steamer *Doric Star* is sunk by the battleship *Graf Spee* in the Atlantic

13 *Graf Spee* is sighted off the River Plate estuary near Montevideo

14 Russia is expelled from the League of Nations

17 Damaged in the Battle of the River Plate, the *Graf Spee* is scuttled by Captain Langsdorff, just off Montevideo harbour

23 A number of Latin American countries protest against the violation of their countries' neutrality by warring nations

25 Hitler visits and inspects his troops on the Western Front

George Rhodes was 23 and working in a mill when the news came that Britain was at war with Germany. It was no surprise to anyone – everything which had happened in the previous five years seemed to lead to this.

1938 was a rather peculiar year. In the cinema, where we learned all the news via the newsreel, they started 3D pictures. They gave you a pair of glasses when you went in and you put them in a large box on your way out after the film show. Everybody in the cinema used to sing with the organist, who played before the film started, in the interval, and also at the end of the film.

What used to happen went like this: there would be two 'houses', as it was called, 6 pm to 8pm and 8pm to 10pm. You sat down and waved to various people that you knew. The organist would finish playing, lights would go down and the first thing would be the newsreels, then a comic cartoon – Mickey Mouse or Popeye the Sailor Man – then a song-sheet would appear on film. The organist would play the tune and a small white ball would move over each word, and move on until the song was finished. So everyone learned the latest and the old songs as well.

After the interval you would settle down for the big picture and, if you were lucky to be with a girl, you would have a quiet snog. Sometimes they would have auditions, and if you could play an instrument or sing, you would be up there on the stage to do your stuff. The audience would

applaud and cheer – it was a happy time, even though at the back of your mind was the thought that one day war would come.

One knew that a war was impending, because the Government ordered the militia to be formed. The nearest to us at Shipley was a huge camp at Harrogate. We in the TA looked down on these militia boys, the same way the regular army chaps looked down on the TA. On the wireless, songs were being sung in praise of soldiers, such as *There's Something about a Soldier* and *Kiss Me Goodnight, Sergeant-Major, Quartermaster's Stores* and *When the Soldier's on Parade*. You could sense that England was priming her people in readiness for war.

Every day in the newspaper there would be all the doings of Adolf Hitler and his friend Mussolini – and trying to turn the British against these two countries you had the newsreels at the cinema, going at it pell mell. They tried very hard.

1939 . . . what can I say, but the fact that all the people in England were now resigned to face the war that in a few months' time would happen.

That year I went to camp – to Redesdale on the Scottish border. While we were there, rumours flew thick and fast that we were not going home after the camp but would be called up . . .

We had orders to be on parade, fully dressed, for Sunday morning at 9 am, on 3 September 1939. We were then told to stand at ease after a full kit inspection, and that the Prime Minister would speak to us all at 11 am. Loudspeakers had been placed on the roof of the barracks. The sun was shining. It was a lovely morning. At 11.15 am the Prime Minister, Mr Chamberlain, spoke on the radio for all to hear.

'This morning, the British Ambassador in Berlin handed the German Government a final note, stating that unless we heard from them by 11 o'clock, that they were prepared at once to withdraw their troops from

◀▲ George Rhodes, centre, pictured later in the war.

▲ With webbing and equipment from World War I, sappers from the Royal Engineers prepare for the next war.

◀ A dapper news vendor displays the grim news.

▶ These two girls filling sand bags in Hampstead on 5 September 1939 show the more glamorous face of going to war.

Poland, a state of war would exist between us. I have to tell you that no such undertaking has been received and that consequently this country is at war with Germany.'

After the Prime Minister, Mr Neville Chamberlain, finished speaking, another voice came on the air, telling the nation to carry gas masks at all times and to obey the orders of the Air Raid Wardens to take cover in the shelters that were being built in the streets and parks, and that subways could be used. Also, not to hoard food, as this would only make it scarce. After this pep-talk, the colonel called us all to attention, said 'good luck' to us, and then he and the officers went off. The regiment was then marched inside the barracks, just as the air raid siren went off. It was just about 12.15, Sunday dinner time.

We were told to draw from the

stores water bottles, mess tin, knife, fork and spoon, and queue up for dinner – a stew. After having this slop, we went on parade again to draw from the stores rifles (303), plus 50 rounds of ammunition, tin hats, gas masks, gas capes, gas goggles, ground sheets, three blankets and one palliasse. Then we were told to set up on the floor in the barracks (which was a huge hall) our bedding ready for inspection.

Then came the inspection. First, the sergeant, then the sergeant-major, then a second lieutenant, who passed it on to the captain, then the major, then the colonel. After various things had been corrected, he said, 'You are now going to sleep, eat and live here until further orders. No-one is allowed to go home. A guard will be mounted, and a fire piquet. Kit inspection will also be carried out daily. Any problems regarding home life, see your No 1 first, and he will make the move for you in the right direction. Tomorrow we will be able to tell you what is expected of us. Carry on.' With that, all the officers scarpered to some hotel for a binge.

It was a peculiar first night – totally different to what we were used to at the training camp. In fact, by 9.30 that evening most of the chaps were in bed. Some chatted until 10 pm, when the orderly sergeant and the orderly officer came round, and all the lights were doused.

Monday morning, 6 am, 4 September 1939. We of the 70th Field Regiment Royal Artillery, 49th Division, were asleep on the straw-filled palliasses in the drill hall of the barracks at Valley Parade, Bradford, Yorkshire, when reveille was blown by a bugler, who was standing by the stables. Well, the effect of this deafening bugle-call in such an enclosed space was electric, to say the least. Bodies were being forcibly ejected from their flea-ridden palliasses by the sergeants – and especially the orderly sergeant who, with his cane, seemed to delight in giving any recumbent figure a mighty whack.

After ablutions, we all lined up for breakfast. The time was now 7.30 am. The cooks had done to the fried eggs something which no person of sound mind would have done. They had obtained a huge metal tray, which was supposed to be used under the lorries to catch the drips of oil, and in this container they had cracked God knows how many eggs, and had fried them to a frazzle. Then they tried to separate them to give each man an egg in his mess tin. I must say, they tasted like a piece of leather. I'm sure that I would have done better to eat my gas mask!

I caught sight of my father standing near the door, and with him stood my sister Jessie. She was in the ATS. In fact, Jessie was one of the very first girls to join up in Bradford as a volunteer for the ATS in 1937. For my mother's sake, Dad, Jessie and I had a photograph taken of all three of us together.

The colonel then gave us all a pep-talk, including the ATS, and told us that we would, in the near future, be moving from Bradford, just as soon as the War Office had decided where to send us. It could be France, but we should all be home with our loved ones by Christmas, as that was about as long as the war with Germany was expected to last. Little did we know that six years would slip by before we would be back with our loved ones – and that many would never return. He then gave us a run-down of the total strengths of the armed forces opposing each other. From our side, the picture looked rosy. **"**

FEAR OF BOMBING

By 1939 many commentators were predicting that in the event of war enemy bombers would be able to fly unmolested over a country to destroy vast urban areas. In Britain, which had suffered such a strategic bombing campaign in World War I, these fears were particularly strong, despite improvements to air defence in the late 1930s. According to some estimates, the Luftwaffe would bomb London as soon as war broke out, dropping high explosives and gas to kill up to 100,000 people in the first raid. Thereafter, casualties would continue to mount at the rate of 20,000 dead per attack. Small wonder, therefore, that everyone was issued with a gasmask for protection, children and young mothers were evacuated to the countryside and over a million cardboard coffins were stockpiled for issue to local authorities. It was a frightening prospect.

Josephine Harcourt, as a young woman working in London, recalls her feelings towards the news that war was breaking out in Europe, and Britain had joined the fray. She remembers how it disrupted her work in the film industry and what her response to being called up was.

▲ The *drôle de guerre* for the French, or Phoney War for the British, is exemplified by a sedate French soldier 'on guard' with a light machine gun.

▼ Josephine and friends from the film set (centre, Stewart Granger) enjoy a peaceful picnic.

" The news, on that first day of September, was that Germany was bombing Poland. At the time I was working on a film at Islington Studios with Arthur Askey, called *Band Wagon*. On that day the production was called off – just temporarily, while everybody got themselves together and prepared for what might be the worst: nobody knew then whether it might be flights of bombers coming over or what.

Then, of course, came Sunday the Third: the ultimatum to Hitler had expired, and if he didn't withdraw from Poland, we would be at war. At 11.15, Prime Minister Chamberlain came on the radio and declared in a solemn voice: 'We are at war'.

We had all been standing in the sitting room, it chokes me even to think of it now, and one or two of us wept a tear – we thought it was the end of our lives, and especially we were thinking of all the children. Anyway, that was it.

Meanwhile, my younger sister was already 'evacuated' down to Bourne End on the river. We went back to Edgware, where we lived, to pack up all the things we thought we might need if we were going to evacuate down to Bourne End. I then phoned the studios at Islington and was told that the production was starting up again. Everybody had drawn a second breath – nothing had happened.

The Islington Studios were very ancient and it was very difficult to create any shelters around there. But they were an offshoot of Gaumont British which was at Shepherd's Bush, where the BBC Centre is now, and so we transferred the whole production from Islington to Shepherd's Bush, and in two days we had started production again. We were called at 7.30 in the morning, because the idea was to get in as much as we could of daylight hours, so that everybody could get home by night, because the bombers might come by night. Transport and everything else was organised so that people could get home in daylight. There was this terrible threat in the air that you never knew what would happen.

On 22 September, petrol rationing caused us to give up hurtling down to Bourne End using up valuable petrol, so we retired back to Edgware, which was not exactly a town house, but anyway, a suburban house, and continued to work from there. I think the next event was the call-up. People were called up by their age/class; it is always the young men who go first.

I have always been more or less a pacifist, although not a very active one, ever since my school days. I remember reading the war poems of the First World War and being absolutely shattered by seeing a production, *Journey's End*, which was about the First World War and the ghastly trench warfare. It actually

shook me to the core. I had a feeling this is such a crazy way for humans to behave, that I was naturally pacifist, although I have never been a very great activist – I didn't demonstrate or do anything like that. Indeed, I would have preferred to work in hospital services or something like that; I wouldn't have been against doing some social work, but I didn't want to be involved in the aggression.

So when time for call-up came, and I got my papers, I chose to go to a tribunal where I was interviewed; I had to explain why I didn't want to go into the services. Armed with letters from Sir Anthony Asquith, for whom I was working at the time, and Terrance Rattigan, who was the script writer, I went to this tribunal and I explained that I thought it was crazy to put me into the services where I would have to learn new skills and to bring somebody else into the film industry who would also have to learn what I knew already. Why not keep my experience going in the film industry? Anyway, they seemed to be convinced, and I stayed in the film industry – all through the war – which was quite hazardous because, of course, later on in the war we did all sorts of propaganda films that were very important: I went out on a submarine to make *We Dive at Dawn*. Another time I was based on a disused airfield up in Catterick in Yorkshire to do *Way to the Stars*, that was with Carol Reed. They're still quite popular, these oldies, I mean – they had a great message to tell.

It became difficult travelling to work from Edgware when the bombing started, then it became quite dramatic, because going by tube was OK, except, of course, the Underground was absolutely packed with people who had slept there all night. All the platforms were stacked with bunk beds. Anyway, you could get through on the tube, but the buses would probably take quite irregular routes to avoid the bomb craters that had occurred overnight, with buildings down all over the road.

I think what influenced our social lives largely was who was going to be home and when were the menfolk going to be on leave. Having this little country house down Bourne End was an absolute target for jollifications when the men came home on leave. We were all in our twenties then and we used to have some wonderful evenings if we had enough money. On a Saturday night we used to go to Skindles in Maidenhead for a dinner dance – well, I think we used to buy the minimum drinks and the minimum food, just whatever would get you on to the dance floor. But we did have " some good times.

1940
BRITAIN ALONE

Memories of the fall of Europe and the battle for Britain

For the first three months of 1940 little happened – the Soviets finally overwhelmed the Finns, and U-boats continued to attack Britain's North Atlantic shipping – but elsewhere the Phoney War persisted. With the exception of the Czechs and the Poles, few people suffered unduly from the conflict.

In early April Hitler attacked Denmark and Norway, drawing Anglo-French forces into a hopeless campaign in Norway's inhospitable terrain. A month later came the long-awaited attack on France, taking the Allies totally by surprise with classic *Blitzkrieg* tactics. Highly mobile panzer divisions advanced through the 'impassable' Ardennes towards the Channel coast, paralysing the Allied command system and cutting off the BEF in a pocket around Dunkirk. While the evacuation of over 330,000 Allied troops may have gone down in history as a 'glorious defeat', the reality was catastrophic. Hitler looked set for a complete victory. To cap it all, on 10 June, Mussolini declared war on the Allies, thus extending the conflict to Africa and the Mediterranean.

Britain now faced the real threat of Nazi invasion head-on. The Battle of Britain during the long summer months caused postponement, then cancellation, of Hitler's invasion plans, but led directly to what the British people most feared – an aerial 'blitz' on their cities. The foundations had been laid for what was clearly going to be a fight to the death.

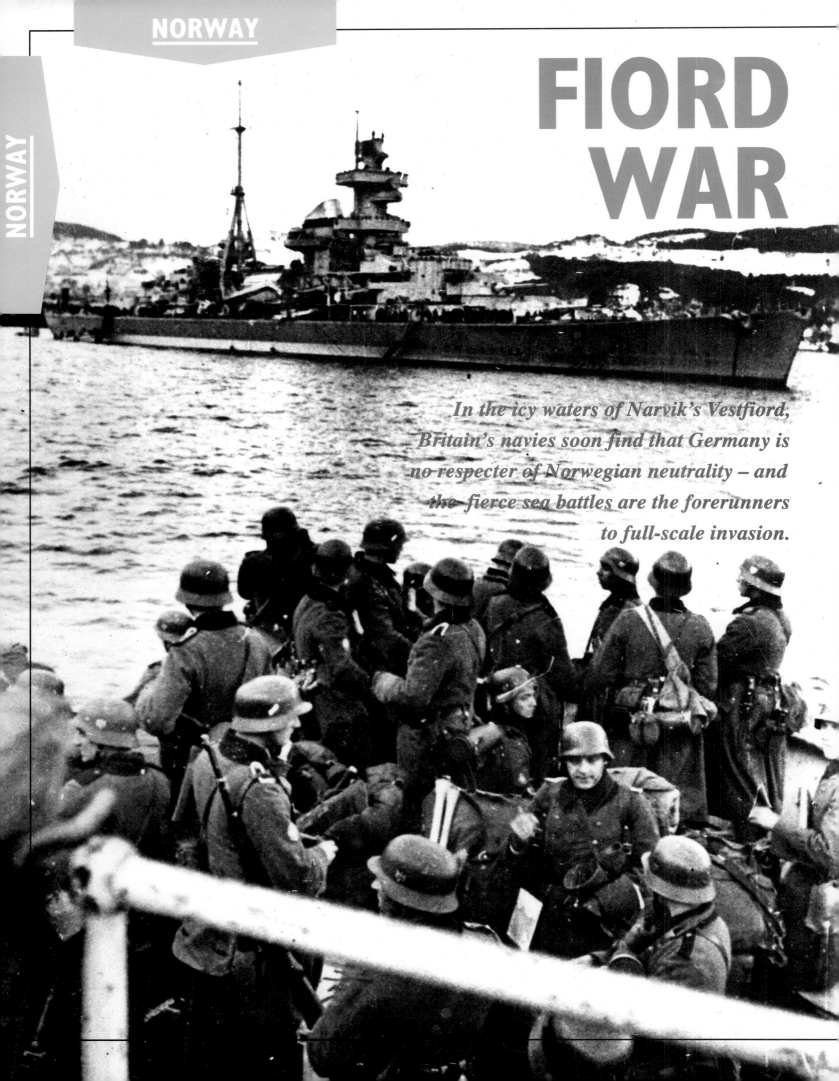

FIORD WAR

In the icy waters of Narvik's Vestfiord, Britain's navies soon find that Germany is no respecter of Norwegian neutrality – and the fierce sea battles are the forerunners to full-scale invasion.

On 8 April 1940, British warships approaching the coast of neutral Norway, intent on laying mines to disrupt the flow of iron-ore to Germany, clashed with elements of a German invasion fleet. This uneven fight was the start of a disastrous campaign for the Anglo-French allies.

Early on 9 April, the Germans made five landings – at Narvik, Trondheim, Bergen, Kristiansand and Oslo – and although their naval losses were significant, Norwegian defences were quickly overwhelmed. By the end of the day, most of Norway had been effectively lost.

The Royal Navy fought battles in the approaches to Narvik on 10 and 13 April, sinking ten German destroyers, but the enemy still held the town itself. Further south, Allied landings failed to retake Trondheim, although Narvik was liberated on 28 May. By 8 June, as the last Allied forces were evacuated – Norway fell to German rule.

Cyril Cope, a torpedo-man, was on the middle watch as his ship, HMS Hardy, patrolled the icy waters off Narvik. On 9 April, ten powerful German ships and 3,000 Alpine troops stood ready in Narvik, but ignorant of this, Hardy's captain decides to attack the six destroyers and one U-boat in Narvik's Vestfiord.

" Before the dash up the fiord we were to be given a mug of neat rum. We mustered at the galley and my messmate Tony Hart and I drank ours. Just in time. The officer of the watch told the cook to stop serving rum. The attack had been put off until midnight. We then headed out to sea, out of sight of land, so that anybody watching would think we had departed for good.

We entered Vestfiord near midnight. It was very cold, snowing hard. We closed up at action stations, only the engines running. We could not move about to keep warm, we could only speak in whispers and the only light visible was a blue one on the after mast to guide the following ship. We had now to rely solely on our navigation officer to guide us and our four other ships up the fiord to Narvik harbour – a feat hard enough in daylight, but in complete darkness it seemed impossible.

However, despite some near misses with the cliffs on the port side of the fiord, we arrived off the entrance to Narvik harbour at 0345. (A U-boat, U-51, was submerged at the entrance of the fiord on the star-

board side and she had reported seeing us head out to sea earlier in the day, so in Narvik they didn't expect the attack which was about to take place.)

It was still snowing, but dawn was about to break. The German sailors, except for sentries on watch, would be asleep. Our captain detailed two destroyers to check another fiord close by – the other two stayed outside the harbour, on guard alone as we went in. On our port side was a large British iron ore ship which had

been captured by the enemy. Two German sailors were on guard on the upper deck. When guns were pointed at them, they scampered down a hatch without giving any alarm.

We were alongside this ship with a few feet between us. The engines were just turning over slowly, and away on our starboard, not far away, I could see several ships, mostly transports, but also five German destroyers.

The order to fire torpedoes came from the bridge. Because my tubes were already trained on the starboard side, their four torpedoes were the first shots fired in the first battle of Narvik. The first one hit and sank the *Wilhelm Heidkamp*. Commodore Bonte and the majority of the ship's company were killed or wounded.

The second torpedo hit the *Anton Schmitt* in the magazine, when this ship blew up the explosion severely damaged *Hermann Kunne*. Our third torpedo hit *Anton Schmitt* and the fourth a large transport.

The captain had ordered full steam ahead on the engines and we turned to starboard towards the entrance of the harbour. On our way out he signalled the other ships to go in and attack with torpedoes only. This they did, then the four ships followed us down the fiord, not very far though, because on my headphones I heard the captain say, 'We have done a good job, but we must go back to do some more.' We turned back on our course, into the harbour, moving very fast. We began firing all our guns, doing much damage to the destroyers and enemy transports as well as the iron ore

◀ Cyril Cope, who fired the first torpedoes in the Battle of Narvik.

▼ Fatally damaged and grounded, HMS *Hardy* lies in the fiord off Narvik after the first sea battle.

◀ Following preliminary sea battles, Hitler's troops arrive by ship to continue the invasion of Norway by land, 17 April 1940.

▲By 12 April the German invasion is well under way. Here specialised mountain troops make fast progress in the foothills of Norway's snow-covered mountains.

▼Vidkun Quisling, a shameless supporter of his country's Nazi oppressors, found that he had backed the wrong horse when, later in the war, his so-called allies, the Germans, turned him out of prime-ministerial office.

ships taken over by the Germans.

We did not stop, but made our way out of the harbour. We sped down the fiord to what we thought would be the open sea – but it was not to be. Once again, I heard the captain say that we did a lot more damage, but that we must go back. This time we would be staying. All the men selected for the landing party should get ready.

We could not get into the harbour – there was oil on fire on the water. Ships were on fire, some sinking, so we fired all our shells through the entrance at the enemy. *Hostile* fired four of her eight torpedoes and then we turned to get on our way down the fiord. As we cleared the entrance we could see three enemy destroyers bearing down on us from Herjangsfiord.

The captain ordered a speed of 30 knots, which would have taken us well clear of these ships and out to sea. Through the heavy mist and snow, two large ships were sighted passing across our bows. The captain and others on the bridge thought they might be two of our small cruisers, coming to assist us, so he sent a signal. They didn't reply, but began to fire full salvoes at us. *Hardy,* being the leader, came in for a lot of heavy punishment. We turned to port and at this point the fiord opened out into what looked like a lake, which gave us a bit of room for manoeuvring, then a full salvo hit our bridge, killing or severely wounding all the personnel. A shell hit the chief coxswain who was on the wheel, killing him. The ship was momentarily out of control. His body was holding the wheel hard over to port, so we circled, the other four ships following in our wake, partly covered by smoke from our funnels.

Lieutenant Stanning, who had

been wounded in the foot, took over the wheel, then at that moment, a salvo hit on the starboard side below the wheelhouse. One shell went through the canteen then into the TS from where the guns were controlled. On its way it hit my messmate, Bill Pimblett, who was standing outside the door leading into the TS. It then chopped off the legs of two of the TS operators, who were sitting on high stools at the console.

Shells had also hit our two forward guns, killing or wounding some of the guns' crews, but the one which took the worst of the shelling was the gun between the two funnels. This was completely wrecked and all the crew killed. One shell hit the main

steam pipe in the boiler room and this cut off the steam to the engines. As the ship lost speed, Lieutenant Stanning gave the order to steer for the shore.

The ship drifted to shore until it grounded, the Germans still firing. I knew we were being hit forward, but nothing had come inboard from the after funnel to the stern. My mate Bill said he was going forward to get

NORWEGIAN TREASON

When Germany invaded Norway on 9 April 1940, it was with the open collaboration of Vidkun Quisling and his *Nasjonal Samlung* fascist party.

Quisling, a Norwegian army officer and ardent fascist, planned to take over his homeland in a German-supported coup. Hitler, meanwhile, maintained that Scandinavia should remain neutral, while covertly preparing for invasion.

When this became a reality, Quisling proclaimed himself ruler of Nazi-occupied Norway, hoping vainly that his countrymen would acquiesce on the grounds that his was better than an all-German government. Most of the government officials refused to serve under him, but undeterred, he instigated a massive persecution of Norwegian Jews, sending some thousand of them to their deaths in German concentration camps.

When Norway was liberated in 1945, Quisling was tried for treason and executed. His name has since gone down in history as being synonymous with treason and national betrayal.

a cup of tea, 'I'll bring you one.' I said, 'With all that stuff coming in-board forward, you had better be careful. Crawl on your belly along the deck until you reach the canteen flat.' He did so, but as he stood up outside the canteen he was hit by the shell, which went through his back and out through his stomach. I learned of this from a survivor of the TS when we went ashore.

I could not get any response from the bridge on my headphones (there was nobody alive up there to answer me), so I decided to go to my next action station in the engine room. I was with the engineer commander and the warrant engineer for about five minutes when the engines

▲ Back in England, *Hardy* survivors greet Churchill in London's Horse Guards Parade, 19 April.

◄ Crewmen from HMS *Hardy* aboard HMS *Ivanhoe* leave Norway for home after their icy ordeal in the fiord.

packed up. We all looked at each other. The commander said, 'This is it. We've had it.' The ship was then gliding towards the shore. Then I met the First Lieutenant, who said, 'Tell the Engineer Commander it's every man for himself. Abandon ship.'

The Germans were still firing, but only one of our guns was replying – the crew just would not give in. Our

chief stoker, Styles, was helping to launch a small boat in which to take the captain ashore. A shell hit the boat and exploded, wounding the men trying to launch it. The Chief Stoker was severely wounded but he and the captain and other wounded men, were towed ashore on stretchers.

My petty officer had joined me at the guardrails. 'It looks as if we will

have to swim for it, Cope.' I climbed over, ready to drop into the water. I had taken off my cap, overcoat, gloves and scarf, leaving them with my pack which I had kept near the tubes, ready for the landing. I dropped into the water and I swam to the whaler and Jack Walters pulled me into the boat. He then turned to pull the petty officer in, but at that moment it turned over, throwing us into the water. There were seven or eight of us, cursing and thrashing about, trying to get from underneath. Then it turned over again, just after we had managed to get across the keel to get our breath. It did this a few times, and each time we lay on the keel, one or two men left to swim ashore.

Eventually I decided to slide off and swim and as I did, I heard a shout for help from the direction of the ship. I looked back to see Tony Hart in the water with a lifebuoy round his body. He was a non-swimmer, so I swam back to him, grabbed the lanyard attached to the lifebuoy and started to swim, pulling him to the shore.

I could not use my legs – I could not even feel them because of the coldness of the water. Slowly but surely we got nearer to the shore. Lieutenant Hepple passed me twice, towing non-swimmers and the second time he shouted, 'Keep going, Cope. You will soon be able to stand up and walk ashore.' Very soon I could although I could not feel my feet – there was no feeling left in them. "

Bob Leonard, at just 17, was senior cadet aboard the tramp steamer Umberleigh. In early April 1940, on a convoy to Narvik and Immingham from Glasgow, Umberleigh found herself in Narvik's 'neutral' fiord, surrounded by rather too many German vessels.

▲ Bob Leonard, rear left, in cap, later in the war, this time after a shipwreck – but that's another story

▶ 13 April 1940. Wrecked ships litter the harbour at Narvik after two major naval battles.

" We got to Narvik to find, to our surprise, a number of British ships already in there, although this traffic went on day after day.

What we were even more surprised to see was five or six German ships, anchored close inshore and apparently with very little interest in getting a cargo. As the days went by, not only did they not move into the tips, but they were added to by ships, some with coke as deck cargo with chicken wire over the top of it – but some of these so-called coke-carrying ships were not deep enough down in the water to be fully laden, yet they apparently had deck cargoes.

This led our captain, Evans, to call the boat crew together and row round a number of ships, putting the point that we'd been expecting a cargo every day, and no cargo materialised, and now it was clear there was something afoot.

A decision was made that if no cargoes were available by daylight, the ships that were not alongside the tips would get the hell out of there.

We and five other ships got a cargo during the night. Four ships, of which the Pennington Court was one, elected not to leave without a cargo. You must remember that at this time merchant ships were still very much commercial enterprises. They were paid so much per ton mile by the Ministry of War Transport, but were still expected to make profits.

The rest of us set off, one after the other, with the Umberleigh in the lead. Captain Evans had taken his 45 calibre service revolver, and placed it ostentatiously on the shelf in the front of the wheelhouse. He said to the pilot, 'If by any mischance or accident, this ship touches a rock anywhere between here and Bergen, I shall blow your bloody brains out and dump your body in the fiord,' or words to that effect.

The next morning, in heavy weather, we get to Stavanger where there purports to be a naval control, where surely instructions of some kind were to be had. You understand that this is at a time where we're supposed to have got a Naval Intelligence, and all this is being carried out on the initiative of one captain, aged at that time 34, sadly never to reach 35. We pulled in to Stavanger into the fiord and rowed

War Stories

T he submarine Spearfish became trapped in shallow waters off Norway, and her crew underwent a seemingly endless ordeal as depth charges went off all around her every few minutes. To while away the time, the men held a sixpenny sweepstake among themselves – the subject was the time of the next explosion, and the bets were to be settled the next pay-day. In the hushed atmosphere, no-one dared speak, but a crewman walked softly about the craft to take the bets, all of which had to be agreed to in sign language!

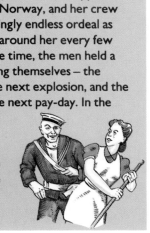

ashore. The place is like Amford on a Sunday night – not a goddam soul around. We tied up, the old man goes ashore with the instruction that if he is seen running back along the jetty, we start to row and he jumps the last bit. As he was a solidly built individual, we decided perhaps this was a joke.

It was very clear that the Harbourmaster's office is manned, and he comes back very quickly and says, 'Let's get the hell out of here,' or words to that effect. We then get our very first instruction, which is to head to muster at Bergen – nothing more and nothing less than that –

which we would have done in any case, because this is where the east-bound convoy for the east coast iron ore ports mustered anyway. That piece of news we needed like a moose needs a hat-rack. We would have done this if nobody had said anything.

So we headed for Bergen where we found a whole gaggle of ships of all sizes and nationalities, a couple of British destroyers and two Norwegian frigates. There was clearly a case of confusion, and clearly no direction.

We now had the first indication that hostilities had broken out in Norway and that the Germans had attacked in the south and were bombing the ports.

The escorts, slightly immorally, round up all the neutral ships, the Dutchmen, the Belgians, the Danes, the Swedes, and herd them out in front of the British ships, of which there are probably seven or eight. It was like the charge of the Light Brigade – to call it a convoy is to have an imprecise knowledge of the English language! But they were all driven out in front of us, at speeds varying from about seven to 12 knots, which added greatly to the confusion.

However, seamen being what they are, once clear of the land, we formed up into a passable imitation of a convoy with the British ships now in the front and everybody else fitting in where he was able – really, with every fire door and stoke hold hooked back open and every ship belching smoke and making speeds they hadn't made since their trials.

We were just clear of land when we came under heavy air attack. It was surprisingly inaccurate. Only the British ships were armed with anti-aircraft guns, and these of the 120-pounder variety. If you had a couple of ex-poachers or game-keepers as gun layers and trainers, you stood a sporting chance of hitting something. Otherwise you stood more chance of being struck by lightning.

Fortunately there were only two and a bit hours of daylight left and two or three ships were hit, despite the fairly heavy attacks.

It got dark and the weather deteriorated fairly rapidly. By the next day it was clear that no air support, other than reconnaissance for submarines, was going to be around. The Germans had failed, for reasons various, to muster their submarines early enough to attack the convoys. Remember that most of the large ships were loaded either with iron ore (which would have meant that they would become instant casualties), or with timber. So the attempt to hold the ships at Narvik was in an effort to capture them intact and use them.

The weather got progressively worse and the convoy became little more than a rabble by dark on the second night. We did not have the submarine attacks that we expected, and we fondly imagined that our air cover would keep them at bay once it got daylight. By daylight we were scattered like chaff and three or four ships were in sight, but there was now no longer any semblance of a convoy. It was every man for himself.

The *Umberleigh* had a strange quirk. She was a 10,000-ton ship with the boilers of a 6,000-tonner. I think she was built in what would be known in parlance as 'on the cheap'. She was a good sea ship – a shelter-deck ship with no well decks, but she had a raised foc'sle head and a shelter deck. This was my fourth voyage in her and apart from the cow being too slow to get out of her own way (which wasn't all that of a disadvantage in very heavy weather, where

▶German invaders examine a Gloster Gladiator of the Norwegian Air Force at the Fornebu airfield in Oslo. The speed of the invasion prevented any really effective mobilisation on the part of the Norwegians.

you were only seeking to make as much speed as would give you steerage way), she was as slow as the second coming of Jesus Christ, especially when she was deep laden. So we steadily fell behind the pack in typical north-east weather.

So it was we pulled into Methyl, which was a convoy marshalling port down the river from Edinburgh, and we had now had another of our disasters. In order to try to keep the speed up, we had been running the ship flat-out. The tides through the Pentland Firth, that northern area, are very severe, and it's difficult to

were not required, as they were later, to take any First Aid training at all, and yet they generally mended the cuts and bruises – anything short of a broken arm or leg. There was a call for First Aid from the boiler room and this steward goes down and puts cotton wool on this poor bastard. When we get into Methyl, the first launch comes out bringing a naval doctor. I've heard my fair share of invective in my long and varied career, but I have never, before or since, heard the invective poured by this naval doctor on to this chief steward. **"**

down there in our thin clothing, without canvas or winter equipment.

We were flying at less than 150 m above ground over Dombas, through fierce anti-aircraft fire and machine-gun fire. Sergeant Goncherowski's group in the machine to our left were shot down. Two dead and 11 wounded were carried from the machine, which was buried, nose-first, in the ground.

At around midday on the second day of the operation (15 April) 61 paratroopers from the company were still fit to carry on.

Independent of me, Sergeant

▼In uniforms apparently designed to keep out the cold, German ski troops tackle the hostile Norwegian terrain. Although some Norwegian units won significant battles against the invaders, they were no match for their superior training and weight of numbers.

keep steerage way in a heavily laden, low-powered ship, and we'd been running on full fan on the boilers. All British ships are fitted with a safety device which was when you open the fire-box door, the process of lifting the latch shuts the fan off, but when you are trying to make your best speed, there's a trick of wedging the fan-catch open. The effect of this is, as you throw a shovelful of coal into the fire, you have to duck as it blows back a sheet of flame, three or four foot long, which would flay you to the bone if you were caught in its way. This was a ploy which you could only safely use in relatively calm weather.

We had a young West Indian fireman, not quite as experienced as his peers. The inevitable happened and she took a big lurch, just as he fed a shovelful of coal into the fire. It blew back and hit him full on and knocked him over. It flayed every ounce of skin off him.

Tramp steamer ships stewards

Lieutenant Ernst Mössinger, with the Stendahls 1st Company of the German 1st Parachute Regiment, was ordered to drop over the town of Dombas in central Norway, as part of the invasion plan. Mössinger was unimpressed by the German planning.

"We were flying behind Lillehammer, deep into woodland again – deep snow as far as the eye could see. The freezing cold gnawed into us through the open door of our machine and it began to dawn on us what it would be like

Bobrowski had held back from leading his 28 paratroopers blindly into the heavily defended Dombas. In the first dawn light he had cunningly marched his men past strong Norwegian divisions into the Gudbrunst Valley, following the maxim, 'if

► In a slit trench, German infantrymen crouch with their guns at the ready. For the first time, the Germans employ a concept of total war, using the navy, army and air force to overwhelm their chosen victim – Norway.

there's shooting, that must be where our comrades are'.

Some 6 km before Dombas we began hastily to build a fortified position in a suitably narrow part of the valley.

We didn't have to wait long for the enemy. They arrived in a broad front with forces in strength, and in their snow clothing, and through the dense rows of trees, we could only make them out when they got very close.

This otherwise tranquil valley resounded for days with the bitter defensive battle against an opponent vastly superior in numbers. Our young soldiers, with absolutely no experience of a winter battle, defended themselves valiantly over a period of five days and nights and endured the most terrible hardship in the cold and wet. Without their magnificent *Unterführer*, who were masters of improvisation, these 18- to 20-year-old soldiers would never have been able to pull through their first encounter with an enemy. We managed to carry the company commander and the other wounded into a semi-protected wooden hut and they were looked after magnificently by our medical orderly, Rachold.

In this first battle we were relatively successful. But we were still very short of ammunition – the food situation was reaching crisis point. It improved only slightly when a JU-52 appeared and, under heavy anti-aircraft fire, dropped some crates containing rifles ammunition, and two sacks of food.

During the night of 17 April, Bobrowski managed to deceive the enemy so perfectly that we managed to move south to a new position with all our wounded and prisoners, all without suffering new casualties.

We were very soon having to defend our position again. The Norwegian commander, Major Arne Sunder, had twice asked us to give ourselves up, but we refused – and yet our ammunition and food were nearly all gone, and we knew we could not resist much longer. At about midday on 19 April we ran out of ammunition and we surrendered – 34 paratroopers in all, who had fought to the final end a battle which had lost all sense.

The Norwegians, who had shown themselves to be a well trained and fearless enemy, immediately arranged for the wounded to be taken to the nearest hospitals, and, for the critically wounded 1st Lieutenant Schmidt, it was not before time.

We were eventually taken to a camp, but it wasn't long before we were freed by a motor-cycle company of the General Göring Regiment, so we were now back under the command of our own Wehrmacht. Two days later we were taken to Oslo and two days after that, every one of the so-called 'Dombas Fighters' received the Iron Cross II Class from the very hand of the same *Fliegergeneral* who had dumped us four weeks earlier into the terrible chaos that was Dombas.

In the course of the Dombas operation, our 1st Company lost 15 men – 20 were wounded in the fighting and 15 sustained injuries when their planes were shot down. Of their 15 Ju-52s, only five returned to Fornebu, heavily shot up and carrying many wounded. Two machines reached Trondheim and one machine landed in Sweden. The other eight planes were shot down or had to crash land – most with all crew lost.

The whole episode should have been examined again before an internal Luftwaffe court. The operation was rushed and inadequately prepared and too many men died without even encountering the enemy in direct combat. **"**

JUNE

1 Rescue operations at Dunkirk continue amid heavy German artillery and aerial bombardment; four British ships are sunk in the process

3 The city of Paris is bombed by the Luftwaffe

4 Holiday camps are banned within 10 miles of the east and south-east coast of Britain
Operation Dynamo, the evacuation of BEF forces from Dunkirk, is completed. A total of 338,226 men have been lifted, leaving behind most of their arms and equipment
Speaking at the House of Commons, Churchill declares that Britain will continue the fight: "We shall never surrender"

5 The Battle of France begins with German attacks on the lines of the Somme and Aisne
In France, General de Gaulle is appointed Under-Secretary of the Ministry of War

7 British and French troops begin their withdrawal from Narvik in Norway
The French Air Force bombs Berlin

8 During the evacuation of Narvik, the British aircraft-carrier *Glorious* and two destroyers are sunk by German ships *Gneisenau* and *Scharnhorst*

9 The German Army occupies Rouen and reaches the rivers Seine and Marne. France is virtually defeated

10 Italy declares war on Britain and France

11 Rheims falls to the German Army
With the Germans 50 miles outside Paris, the French government leaves Paris for Tours

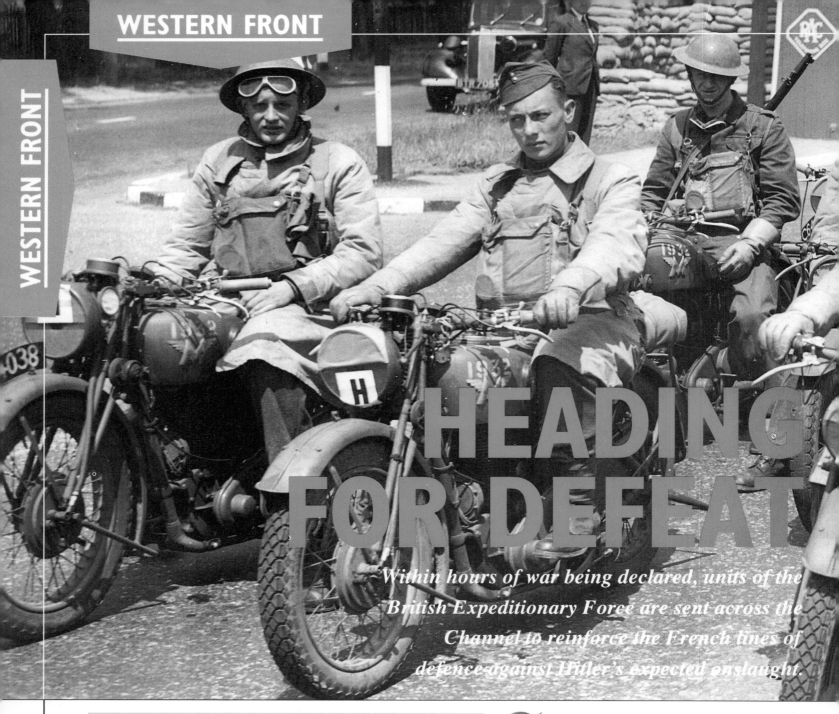

WESTERN FRONT

HEADING FOR DEFEAT

Within hours of war being declared, units of the British Expeditionary Force are sent across the Channel to reinforce the French lines of defence against Hitler's expected onslaught.

Between 10 May and 22 June 1940, the Germans achieved one of the most stunning military victories of the modern age. The German attack into the Netherlands and Belgium fooled the Allies into believing that the assault was merely a repetition of 1914 – an immense right-hook, aimed at Paris – whereas, in reality, it was an elaborate feint, designed to divert attention away from the panzer advance through the Ardennes. The Allies fell into the trap.

German superiority was also apparent in combat. They gained air supremacy on 10/11 May, allowing well-integrated ground forces to seek out and exploit lines of least resistance in the Allied defences. But the German victory was as much psychological as physical. This was reflected in the experiences of the soldiers involved – on the German side, euphoria and on the Allied, a mixture of confusion, frustration and anger.

Walter Hardy, one of seven Hardy brothers in the services, was with the 5th Battalion, Border Regiment and, as such, found himself in France, serving with the BEF, and, as it turned out, within some few hundred yards of three other Hardy brothers.

" The British Army held fast at Tournai, but the enemy, supposedly equipped with cardboard tanks, broke through on our eastern side and Joe's battalion was ordered to retire to Lille. My battalion, however, had lost the greater part of our transport and ammunition in the Tournai shellings, so our orders were to get back to Armentières. By this time the Germans had infiltrated our

▲Members of the British Expeditionary Force mount up, ready to be shipped across the Channel. Little did they know at this stage about the rigours they would have to face trying to counter the German *Blitzkrieg.*

lines and we were sniped at from all directions, shelled on stretches of road that we thought were miles away from the front line. The whole British Expeditionary Force was in extreme danger of being cut off, so the order was given to make for Dunkirk.

Chaos reigned. No-one of the lower ranks had the faintest idea what was going on, but as my unit approached the town of Dunkirk, I, with four or five others, was detailed to form a rearguard and hold on to a position on the eastern side of the town, and to hold on as long as they possibly could. This sort of order at a time like that was tantamount to being told that the place we were to hold was also the place where we could expect to die.

As the enemy closed in, one of us was so badly wounded in the leg that it was obvious that the leg would have to be amputated if we ever did get out – but we fought on until we had only about five rounds of ammunition left between us.

We were captured and herded on to the side of a slight hill above the road along which the Germans had advanced. We were ordered that we must remain in a group and that we must not look in the direction of the road. Under these sort of circumstances we very much wanted to do exactly as we were told and, shortly after the order, we heard the sound of about ten sets of jackbooted feet marching along the road behind and below us.

The normal strength of a firing squad, if there was ever anything normal about it, would be about ten men, and as we had been told to turn our backs to the road, there was

something very frightening about the sound of what could be a firing squad approaching from the rear. We were all more than a little apprehensive about what we thought might be about to happen, so I sneaked a glance towards the road. It was a firing squad, there was no doubt about it at all, but marching in front of the ten men there was a very frightened German soldier, who had been unlucky enough to have lost his nerve at a time when a German soldier was not allowed to do that.

The squad marched on past us for perhaps a hundred yards or so, lined up, then fired the volley that put an end to the life of a very young German. Minutes later, the firing squad came back along the road. It seemed that the Wehrmacht's form of justice was very, very quick – and very much to the point.

The same day, another German officer started screaming at us in what sounded extremely like abusive language, but as none of us could understand German, we just had to do what we thought he was demanding of us and hope that we got the thing right. We did what he wanted, and things finally quietened down. When the shouting died down and things became a little bit more settled, the same officer wandered over to us and said in perfect English, 'Take no notice of my shouting, you fellows – have to put on a bit of a show, you know.'

He then added that if one of us was to go over to a certain place, he would find some bread and some margarine to share amongst us, until such time as the Germans were sufficiently organised as to be able to supply them with food. We did just that, and it was fortunate that we did. That was to be the last chance of eating anything at all for a very long time, and we had already been suffering the agonies of hunger for longer than we cared to think about.

It was a party of about 12 German soldiers who'd taken us prisoner. One of the younger Germans, probably wanting to demonstrate just how tough he was, grabbed hold of my rifle by the muzzle and swung it round to crash the butt against a tree. I know I should have explained to him that the rifle was loaded but then he didn't ask. He ended up losing the greater part of his stomach – a rifle-bullet at about eight inches' range makes a dreadful mess.

We were made to march for four or five days without any supply of food at all. We were then embussed and moved to Trier, where, much to the delight of the German people, we were endlessly paraded through the streets of the city. The next move saw us on our way to Poland, Stalag XXID. **"**

Joe Hardy, one of seven brothers from Northern Ireland, five of whom were in France with the BEF, was on his way to Dunkirk. As chaos broke out, the point of his mission was soon lost – though he was to hear some fateful news about one of his brothers.

" I was detailed to do convoy work for the battalion on a motorcycle. The convoy quickly became a shambles. There were thousands of refugees on the roads and it seemed that every time we hit a cross-roads, Franch cavalry would tear through the column, first going in one direction, then at the next intersection travelling in the opposite direction.

My column became so mixed up that I had no idea where they were, where I was, where we were going or even where we had come from. Chaos supreme!

I rode for about 16 hours until I was absolutely flogged out, then decided that the British Army could all go to hell, that the German Army could all go to hell, that the French Army could all go to hell, that all refugees could follow whichever of the three units they fancied following and that I, Joe Hardy, was going to dump my motorcycle on the side of the road and go to sleep.

What time it was when I collapsed, I do not know, but it was dark. It was dark when I woke up! The road that I slept beside was a main road of some sort – four or five lanes of traffic, all heading in the same direction and all of them stopping and starting every few yards.

I had woken up very suddenly, and the degree of light was such that I could just make out the signs on the side of the truck that had stopped momentarily straight in front of me. Remember that it was, at its best, only half-light, that there were thousands of trucks in four columns passing the place where I was, stopping and starting, travelling a few yards and then stopping again. Whatever it was that woke me, I do not know, but the moment my eyes became adjusted to the light, I could see that the truck in front of me was Frank's [Jock's] truck. It could have been one of two thousand others!

I shouted to the driver, 'How is Jock Hardy?' The answer came back, 'He was killed at Louvain.' The driver changed gear and moved forward into the darkness. The answer was so complete, that I did not – probably could not – make any attempt to follow the driver. I felt that in this odd sort of way, things were arranged to get the news of his death to me. "

Robert Holding, with the 4th Battalion, Royal Sussex Regiment, had survived a series of seemingly inescapable batterings by the advancing Wehrmacht. His company nearly wiped out, he is among the stragglers who arrive in war-torn Dunkirk, hoping for a passage back to England.

" From all sides now I could hear the roar of enemy artillery, and in many places the chatter of machine-gun fire was almost continuous. Over the town hung a pall of black smoke, above which enemy bombers, flying in close formation, wheeled, dropped their loads and departed, unchallenged and quite

OTHER 'DUNKIRKS'

Operation Dynamo – the evacuation of Allied forces from Dunkirk – ended on 4 June 1940, but the recovery of the other manpower from Europe was by no means over. Significant British forces were south of the panzer breakthrough and were, therefore, still intact. They withdrew towards the western Channel and Atlantic coasts.

Some of the attempted evacuations failed, but others went well, despite the loss of badly needed equipment. Over 30,000 men were saved from Cherbourg, 21,000 from St Malo and 32,000 from Brest, while from Nantes and St Nazaire a further 57,000 made it back to England. It was a remarkable achievement, but largely forgotten in the shadow of the main evacuation.

◄ After the agonising wait on the beaches, these BEF men have made it home – to a welcoming cuppa.

▲ Messerschmitt Bf-110s over France. Used initially as long-range fighters, they were found to lack power and were later converted to night fighters.

▲ Northern France, May 1940. In the wave of the German advance, many towns suffer heavy bombing.

▶ Robert Holding of the 4th Royal Sussex Regiment – one of the lucky ones who were evacuated in good time.

unhindered.

On the road, our pace was now reduced to a crawl. The reason for this soon became apparent in the form of a road-block manned by military police. As each man reached the barrier, he was asked the name of his unit, and then directed to the area allocated to his division.

My road lay straight ahead through the suburbs leading eastward. The streets were lined with military vehicles of every kind, some overturned, but most of them immobilised. It was an incredible sight, particularly to those of us who had marched so far for so long and had seen so little transport – it was difficult to believe that the British Army possessed so much mobility.

The sun had now set, but the town was lit by a fiery red glow from the burning dock area, and from landward by flickering gun flashes and the deadly white glow of flares. On through this eerie ghost town we continued our weary way, stopping at intervals to be checked and redirected by police, 'til I finally found myself once more outside the town, still heading eastward toward the unmistakable sound of bursting shells. After a while we were directed off the road down a sandy track where quite suddenly I was confronted by an extraordinary sight.

There before me, lit to an almost daylight brilliance by a large passenger ship that blazed from end to end just a few hundred yards out to sea, was a long sandy beach that stretched as far as the eye could see. To the landward of the beach, acres of grass-tufted sand dunes seemed to move like an ocean as their shadows shifted in the flickering light of the burning ship. But it was the men that riveted my attention. They lay in their hundreds, huddled along the edge of the dunes or in long columns stretching down to the sea. Most were sleeping the sleep of sheer exhaustion – many were sleeping their final sleep.

I wandered around for a while, trying to find someone that I knew. Unsuccessful in that quest, I made my way to the dunes to find a place to sleep. In a depression between these sandy hillocks I came upon the bodies of three French soldiers, probably all killed by the same shell or bomb. Among the equipment that lay scattered around them was a large cavalry cloak, complete with hood. Gratefully I picked this up, found myself a sheltered spot, wrapped myself tightly in its ample folds and lay down to sleep.

I awoke with a start in the chill light of dawn. Cold and bemused, I lay trying to collect my wits. Slowly, I recalled that I had lain down here to sleep wrapped in a cloak – but now I had no cloak!

All along the beach orderly queues were forming, seemingly by common consent, for no-one appeared to be organising them. The sea was completely empty of shipping of any kind. I looked in vain for any sign of the ship that had been burning so fiercely the night before – nothing remained of it. It might never have existed. Nearer the shore, small pieces of wreckage and a number of bodies floated, moving gently on the flat surface of the unbelievably calm sea.

I was soon dozing off, only to be awakened by the sound of approaching aircraft. A flight of Stukas, followed by a second, then a third, passed overhead. One could almost feel those hundreds of men holding their breath. The aircraft passed on, heading for the columns of smoke that hung over the docks. The sound of their screaming sirens and thundering bombs came rolling along the beach toward us. One could not help but shudder at the sound – and be thankful that we were not the target.

We were not, however, to be left in peace for long. From somewhere

inland, the sound of gunfire heralded the commencement of an artillery barrage. Soon the shells came screaming in, sending up great clouds of sand as they burst among the dunes – which fortunately absorbed a lot of the blast and shrapnel. We pressed hard against the soft sand and rode out the storm 'til it stopped as suddenly as it had started. The guns turned their attentions to other targets. The dead and wounded were collected and carried back to the dunes, where makeshift dressing stations had been organised.

Our attention was now riveted upon a smudge on the horizon which, in due course, was revealed as a destroyer, heading straight toward our beach. It came to within a few hundred yards of the shore, turned broadside on and began to lower its boats. Unhurriedly and calmly, the boats plied back and forth, carrying as many men as they could safely cram aboard, but never seeming to make any impression on the endless queue which edged forward continuously.

The evacuation continued unhindered, save for the arrival of a group of Stukas which, on being greeted by a hail of fire from the destroyer, moved further down the beach, seeking a softer target. I was now chest-deep in the sea, and estimated that two more journeys would see me safely aboard. The boat returned, took on its load – I was now at the head of the queue, with the water lapping around my chin.

I watched intently as the boat drew alongside the destroyer. This time, however, the soldiers did not climb up the scramble nets to the deck. Instead, there before my disbelieving eyes, the boat was attached to its davits and was hauled inboard. This procedure was followed by the other boats and soon the destroyer

began to move. At an ever increasing speed it headed for the open sea.

I cannot remember what my feelings were at that moment. I just stood there. Perhaps it was never intended that I should be taken off – perhaps at that moment I no longer cared.

The Stukas were back. Wheeling into the sun, they came screaming down. I stayed where I was in the water – there was no point in moving. Their work completed, the aircraft went on their way and I slowly made my way back to the beach and up into the dunes where, soaked, indescribably hungry and mentally and physically exhausted, I fell asleep.

So the night dragged on into a misty dawn. Once more, the orderly queues began to form. I joined the one nearest me in a repeat of yesterday's tableau. Slowly the mist cleared, revealing a sea empty of any kind of vessel.

The enemy, spurred no doubt by the sight of so many of his quarry getting away, started the day with renewed urgency. From the land and air he was pounding the town and the beaches. Our column scattered with each attack, to reform immediately the danger had passed.

I was again knee-deep in water when, as yesterday, in an almost carbon copy, the shape of a destroyer hove into view, steamed towards us, turned broadside to the shore and began to lower its boats.

Once more, the queue shuffled forward, deeper into the sea. As

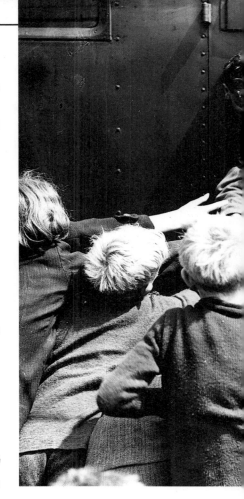

▶ Back from their ordeal, rescued BEF troops receive a heroes' welcome from London's children, who hand out cigarettes, refreshments and food to the men.

▼ The crammed deck of a troopship taking exhausted BEF troops back to England. Most would soon be sent abroad again as the conflict expanded.

▼▶ In the knowledge of a safe passage home, this Scottish soldier has found himself a quiet niche in which to find some sleep after the trauma of evacuation from Dunkirk.

before, the wounded were brought down to be given priority of place in the boats, and again the unwounded, unhesitatingly and without complaint, gave up their places to accommodate them. This in spite of the fact that the sound of enemy machine-gun fire was now so ominously close that it seemed certain that this destroyer represented the very last opportunity to escape from these beaches.

The time dragged interminably and, as I got nearer to the head of the queue, the boats seemed to my anxious eyes to get slower with every journey. I was again chest-deep in water. I counted the men in front of me. There were six. I could hardly believe it. Next time, I would make it – or would I?

With bated breath I watched the boat ease up alongside the destroyer, where to my relief, the men began to scramble up the nets. The oars dipped into the water, the boat was on its way back. Slowly, oh so slowly, it came nearer. I suddenly felt some life returning to my body. The numbness started to leave my brain.

I reached out my hand and touched the boat. At the same moment, a large formation of Junkers 88s came roaring in along the beach. They swept overhead, on toward the town. I breathed again. A sailor leaned over, grabbed my belt and unceremoniously hauled me **"** over the side.

AUGUST

1 In his Directive No 17, Hitler orders the Luftwaffe 'to crush the British Air Force by every means possible'
   Foreign Minister Molotov reaffirms Soviet neutrality and Russo-German pact

2 The Vichy Government sentences de Gaulle to death in his absence

5 Bad weather forces the Germans to postpone their intended air offensive against Britain
   Hitler and Mussolini meet in Rome to discuss future strategy now that France has been defeated
   German government announces that, in future, citizens will need an *Ahnenpass* (Certificate of Ancestry)

8 Heavy air battles over the Channel – Britain claims 80 German losses in a week

10 U-56 sinks armed merchant cruiser HMS *Transylvania* off Northern Ireland
   Vichy French offer Germany 200 pilots to help fight the Battle of Britain

11 The Battle of Britain begins in earnest as 400 German planes attack coastal areas of Britain, including Dover and the radar stations at Weymouth and Portland

12 Luftwaffe attacks Portsmouth, Isle of Wight and Kent and Sussex coasts

13 Luftwaffe makes 1,485 sorties on 'Eagle Day' (*Adlertag*) – dogfights continue all day from the Thames Estuary to Southampton

14 Germany suspends Luxemburg's constitution

On 12 May 1940 Sergeant-Major Hillion was commanding the 3rd platoon of the 4th Squadron of the 2nd Regiment of Cuirassiers. This regiment, equipped with Somua 35 and Hotchkiss 39 tanks, was involved in the first big tank battle of the campaign, in the Hannut region in Belgium.

On the evening of 12 May, my tank, H39, was positioned to the left of the village of Crehen. Around 8 pm, two enemy tanks came into view. I waited until they were within range to open fire. My first shot was a bull's-eye, and completely destroyed one of the tanks. I immediately took the second tank in my sights, but my shot was aimed too high and the shell passed just above the turret. My second shot was a direct hit.

Through the vision slit, I could see German infantry approaching, accompanied by four tanks. I opened fire with a machine gun and the group disappeared rapidly. No sooner had we gained that small victory, than a shell hit the back of our tank, immobilising it completely. We had broken down 300 metres from the enemy! Then a shell suddenly flew past the turret, splintering into shards and wounding me in the head

and left arm. Covered in blood and seeing only out of my right eye, I took aim again – but before I could open fire, I felt a violent explosion behind me. This time I was seriously wounded. Despite the smoke which obscured the tank, I continued firing randomly at the enemy.

By this time I was bleeding profusely, so in order to stop the blood, I went below to fetch a dressing. At that moment a new explosion shook the turret and my cannon pivoted to the left. Setting it up again I could see through the breach that the end of my cannon was torn. Only the machine gun appeared intact. So I decided to continue the struggle on foot. With my driver I took off the

machine gun, and we were about to set ourselves up behind a tree when two simultaneous explosions shook the tank. The air became unbreathable, but somehow I managed to struggle to the tree, then lost consciousness.

I was woken by a violent pain in my leg. A German tank was just in front of me and its commander was observing the positions of the first platoon. Soon, the tank disappeared. After its departure, the area was ploughed by the artillery. Clods of earth showered down around us and I was injured in the left hand. I lost consciousness again.

When I came round, it was pitch dark. I called out for my driver, but in vain. I later learnt that he had been killed. I managed to crawl for about 50 metres, but two Germans armed with machine guns came up.

For me, the war was over. The agreement between the French and the Germans meant that I was treated in a military hospital, rather than being left to die or sent to a concentration camp. **"**

Leo Keys, an office worker in the City of London, joined up at the 61st (Finsbury Rifles) Anti-Aircraft Regiment, Royal Artillery early in 1939. By 16 May 1940 he was in Cherbourg, but soon his company, along with the rest of the BEF, was in retreat. He tells of his capture and the long march to Germany.

We were followed around on the Abbeville front by heavy German artillery fire. This was in reply to a barrage we had put up to force the Germans to stay on their side of the Somme, but in fact the Germans advanced under our barrage. We retreated along the road with the German artillery following us on either side – but fortunately

found a clean pigsty with three other fellows, and fell asleep. In the morning, as we looked through the small holes in the door, we saw German soldiers and British soldiers wandering around. The truth was that the French Army, to which we had been attached, had capitulated.

It slowly dawned upon me – here I was, a Jewish POW of the Germans. Being a POW was bad enough – but a Jewish one? I walked up the hill as directed and disposed very carefully of my identity cards and papers. I really thought that we were to be shot. I was too tired and exhausted and disspirited to care. We were, however, led into an area surrounded by guards and machine guns. That night we were marched

◀ **Leo Keys, who joined the BEF in 1939, donning the uniform of the 61st Finsbury Rifles, finds himself in France a year later – a prisoner of war of the Germans!**

▼ **Surprised by the speed of the German advance, French civilians trying to escape get caught up in the wheels of war.**

some food, but the French civilian was on to a good thing and did not come back. The toilet was in the middle of the field in open view – a board over a big ditch.

Every day, the Germans would say, 'Tomorrow we will have transport,' but it was only a way to get you to walk on and on, into Belgium and Holland. We slept in open fields and I remember waking up and becoming momentarily unconscious from weakness. A little water, which was scarce, revived me, and I carried on marching throughout the day. We slept in a barracks in Tournai, where the stores compartments were turned into bunks. Unfortunately the whole thing collapsed and some did not survive.

While travelling through the streets in open-top cargo rail carriages, the Dutch threw food and drink into the midst of the prisoners. Some fellows ganged up and collected the food and then split it up amongst themselves. Anyone on their own or who did not catch any of the food themselves did not do very well. After about 21 days from St Valéry, we reached Walsorden, a town in Holland, and it was here that we were each given a small loaf for a two-day journey on barges. It was to be four days before we reached Emmerich in Germany. **"**

🪖 *James Palmer, having joined the 3rd Royal Tank Regiment in the summer of 1939, finds himself in action on his very first day in France – but soon he must make his way back.*

not hitting us. We drove on via Dunkirk towards the coast with towns and houses burning all around us.

At St Valéry en Caux we were told to immobilise all vehicles and throw away all mobilising parts of our armaments. We had seen the sunken vessels in the harbours on the way, and followed our instructions in good faith. We were now told that we would be boarding on vessels that had still to arrive and, on top of it all, we were surrounded by Germans who were firing into the already burning town.

We were led to the beaches to await embarkation, but at dusk were told to go and take cover off the beaches, which were vulnerable.

The roads we travelled on were full of refugees, at first travelling against us and later with us, and many dead and bloated cattle and horses littered the fields.

That night of the 11th June, I

out to a nursery garden where I fell asleep on broken flower pots.

The first full day we marched to Rouen, a distance of 25 miles, with very little food. There appeared to be miles and miles of captured French and English forces, marching with guards on either side. The Germans were not prepared for feeding such numbers, and the French did not have much to offer in the villages *en route*.

Food on the march was very scarce, and to go off the road to find something in a field was dangerous. Even to answer the call of nature could be a final event – the Germans took no chances. At Bethune I queued for seven hours for two mugs of horse peas (three and a half hours a time). My feet by then were raw, as my toecaps had bitten into my toes, so I was permitted to rest two days in a medical area. I tried to trade a few French francs with a local civilian for

It was evening when we pulled into Neufchâtel. While we tumbled out of the train, a siren wailed. Out of the sun came a group of small planes and the bombs began to fall – a mad dash ensued. As a farewell gesture, the planes circled slowly and then came along the length of the train, their machine guns chattering.

Although our casualties were only 15 wounded, we needed no coaxing to get away from the station. Our tanks were in a wood three miles from the village and in no time we were scrambling up the hill. It was with some relief that we entered a deep wood and came upon the tanks.

But our jumpiness returned when a whistle blew giving the signal that aircraft were approaching. The planes circled round the wood and we knew we had been spotted. Their departure only meant that they would come back later. The next hour was spent digging slit trenches, and as soon as they were finished, the order came to move. Our job was to make for Abbeville and prevent any crossing of the Somme – or at least delay the German advance. As we left the woods, the planes came over and blasted it to hell.

The next day we woke to the muffled sound of activity and one by one the tank engines roared to life. The sky was becoming mushroom coloured as we moved towards the river. Rifle shots were becoming more frequent, machine guns were chattering, and guns in our rear began to open up.

The squadron was now almost alongside the river, protected by a slight rise in the ground where we stopped. Tanks were seen on the opposite bank and suddenly the field seemed full of little men scrambling towards the river. The enemy were crossing to the accompaniment of a terrific gunnery salvo. The squadron went up the rise to get full fire on the river crossing.

It all happened so quickly: as we topped the rise, anti-tank guns hit us from the right flank and four tanks were ablaze before they had gone ten yards. The squadron commander was trying frantically to rally the tanks, but engines had stalled, men were struggling to get out of blazing tanks and some men were dragging their mates through mud away from the burning tanks. The casualties that day were 20 killed and 23 injured.

Several days later the Maginot Line had been bypassed. The French Army was making a tactical retreat and the German Panzers were on a *Blitzkrieg* and we were in danger of being surrounded.

Panic was the word and frantic orders were given that we get moving to the low ridge to the west of a small farm we could see about a mile away, but the shells screamed as soon as we were in the open. Armoured troop-carriers were dropping small groups of little grey men, but they were digging in and making no effort to advance forward. . . . The day progressed into a 'shoot-and-duck' operation.

For two days this situation continued, but then the news began to filter through. The entire BEF had been virtually driven into the sea from Dunkirk. We were ordered to move south and get the hell out.

All night we travelled along country lanes in strict black-out. The roads were clogged with refugees.

◄ These British sailors are safely home, the last ones to leave Dunkirk on completion of the Allied evacuation.

▲ British Bren-gun carriers in Arras, where heavy fighting took place against Rommel's panzers.

Rouen was strangely silent and seemingly deserted as we passed through in the early morning light. Planes came over as we rumbled through the square, and we were strafed and bombed.

About 20 miles south of Rouen we stopped at a village called Catanai, and there we pulled up and met the regimental supply column. Each man was told to keep as much ammunition as he could carry. We were bundled into the three-ton lorries and all other surplus vehicles were blown up with hand grenades. Just after midnight we were on the move.

At noon we halted and the news of Dunkirk was then given to us – that the evacuation had been completed. No more troops could be got out of France! At about 8 o'clock the convoy moved off into the night and we all felt resigned to our fate. Dawn came and still we kept moving. Towards sunset the column came to a halt. We were told that we were a couple of miles from Brest and that it might be possible we could get a boat from there. We were told to try and get some sleep.

We woke in the early hours shocked to find that everyone had gone in the night and we had been left behind. We all scrambled up and began to follow the trail of carnage, topped the rise and looked down on Brest.

The streets were deserted, but as we looked towards the harbour we saw a small steamer chugging out to sea. Another boat was against the jetty and we jogged down the road, laughing and shouting deliriously. The boat at the quayside was crammed. We scrambled up the gangplank as they were pulling it up and collapsed in a heap beside a life-raft. "

AUGUST

15 Biggest air attack by Luftwaffe on Britain so far in the Battle of Britain

16 Further Luftwaffe raids on southern England

17 Germany announces 'total blockade' of Britain
Germany withdraws its Stukas from the attacking forces as they have proved too vulnerable

18 Heavy daylight raids by Luftwaffe on airfields in Kent, Surrey and Sussex

20 Churchill reviews progress of war in the Commons: 'Never in the field of human conflict was so much owed by so many to so few'

22 Britain promises help by sea and air forces in case of an attack on Greece
German batteries in France shell Dover

25 26 First RAF night attack on Berlin in retaliation for attacks on London

26 Eire government protests to Berlin over bombings in County Wexford which killed three girls

28 Vichy Radio announces that laws protecting Jews in France have been dropped

29 Germany apologises to Eire for Wexford bombing

31 RAF Fighter Command loses 38 planes in Luftwaffe attacks on its operational headquarters
Malta is attacked by Italian bombers

SS *Herbert Brunnegger, aged 18, was in a communications unit of the SS Totenkopf (Death's Head) Division in northern France in May 1940. A merciless battle took place around the La Bassée Canal, and there were accusations from the Germans that some of the British soldiers had used dum-dum bullets. What ensued in the little village of Le Paradis has gone down in history as one of the worst atrocities on the Western Front.*

"" On the evening of 26 May 1940 we were ordered to advance across the La Bassée Canal, which we did during the early hours of 27 May. We had been told to expect heavy resistance from British élite forces and this proved to be the case.

After the capture of the village of Le Cornet Malo (2 km from the canal), we moved our battle headquarters into the village to attempt an assault on the village of Le Paradis (5 km from the canal).

The terrain immediately before Le Paradis was broad and flat, which gave the British defenders an excellent field of fire. Had our *Kradschützen* [motorbike and sidecar machine-gun units] not launched such a bold assault, our losses would have been considerably higher.

While we were regrouping, I saw a large group of British soldiers who had been rounded up and put against a wall. Those who were not wounded were standing – the wounded men lay on the ground in front of them. As our platoon marched past, they held out to us, imploringly, pictures of their womenfolk – wives and girlfriends. I thought to myself, 'What a sad bunch.'

As I took a closer look at the scene, I saw two heavy machine guns being set up in front of them. My first thought was that it was an odd thing to take two precious machine guns out of combat to guard these prisoners, why didn't we just lock them up in a cellar where we'd only need one guard for the whole lot. But then a horrific thought occurred to me. I went back again and asked one of the machine-gun operators nearby what was going on here. 'They are going to be shot,' he said.

I couldn't believe it, and thought that this must be a bit of black humour. So I asked the question again. 'Who ordered that?' *'Hauptsturmführer* Knöchlein,' came the reply. Now I knew that he was being totally serious. I ran on ahead of my unit, not because I was in any greater hurry than them, but because I had to get away from this place. I didn't want to see the execution.

First the Tommies' slaughtering with their 'special ammunition' and the malicious killing of our men, who actually wanted to spare them, and now this massacre of prisoners.

Any soldier who uses dum-dum bullets steps out of the ranks of decent soldiery and should expect nothing but the harshest condemna-

▲ **A German panzer unit rolls through a French town which fell to *Blitzkrieg* tactics.**

▼ **Villagers from Le Paradis tend the graves of the 97 British prisoners shot down on 27 May 1940.**

tion. But did all these men use such terrible ammunition? Probably not. It was impossible, as far as I could see, that all these prisoners could have been searched and interrogated in such a short time. Secondly, I could see no other group of prisoners, who had been separated off the rest as innocent of such a crime.

As I walked on, I was hoping that the gruesome execution would not be carried out. However, it was confirmed to me later by men who had witnessed it. The man who issued this murderous order, not only did he allow 89* defenceless soldiers, some of them wounded, to be slaughtered, but he also trampled the honour of our young division in the dirt. ""

* The memorial at Le Paradis cites 97 victims of the massacre on 27 May 1940 – all members of the 2nd Battalion, Royal Norfolk Regiment. There were two survivors, William O'Callaghan and Albert Pooley. The remaining eight men, Brunnegger claims (based on the testimony of one of his comrades), were part of a group of ten commandos who came out of the farmhouse, hands raised in surrender, prior to the execution.

The Germans allegedly held fire, but as they did so, machine-gun fire erupted from inside the farmhouse, killing almost all of the attacking German company. A German machine gunner, believing they had been tricked, gunned down the ten commandos as they ran for cover. Brunnegger's claim, then, is that these men were killed 'legitimately'. This is his claim, not ours.

IN ENEMY HANDS

From bombed-out Warsaw to Paris' untouched splendour, the people of occupied Europe face the vagaries of life under Nazi rule.

In 1940 vast areas of Europe came under German occupation, in most cases with a speed that left the civilian population stunned. Existing governments disappeared, with political leaders either fleeing to Britain or falling into German hands, and although in most countries it took time for Nazi rule to be applied (especially in rural areas), the people could hardly avoid feeling humiliated and bitter. Some collaborated from the start, but the vast majority just tried to pick up the pieces of their shattered lives and make the best of the situation.

Such a picture is hard to reconcile with the view, often put forward after the war, that Resistance groups sprang up more or less spontaneously. It did not happen like that. Many young men – a logical source of resisters – had been killed or captured in the opening campaign and ordinary life had been disrupted by the fighting. It was to take some time for an active and effective Resistance to emerge.

Philippe Ordinaire was 12 years old and living in St Helier, Jersey, when, shortly after the Dunkirk debacle, the Germans invaded the Channel Islands. A foster child since the age of 18 months, he found himself torn between his real mother and his foster parents in the rush to leave the island.

❝ Although I was only 12 years old I knew what was happening. As soon as we heard about Dunkirk, we knew the Germans would be here within days. The local newspaper announced it and many people were evacuated. The local garrison was taken out quickly, but some of them got stuck there throughout the duration of the war.

Actually, my real mother fled before they came and she wanted me to go with her. I refused, because I was happy with my foster family. They were like my real parents. I'd only seen my mother two or three times in the last ten years. I suppose, looking back, I resent what she did. She should have **told** me to go with her, not **ask**.

When we first saw the Germans it was their professionalism that really surprised us. They turned up overnight in the town square, about two or three of them decked out in fine uniforms, on motorcycles and in trucks, with machine guns and rifles. They really looked like they meant business. As a child at the time, I'd naturally laughed and joked with the boys from the local garrison, and, to be honest, they were a bit of a joke, but this was a totally different kettle of fish.

I was very frightened, actually.

Threatening – they looked threatening, that's as much as I can say. We knew the date and the time when they were coming and I remember my foster parents saying, 'Come on, let's go down and have a look.' So we went down and stood around the cenotaph in the town square. St Helier had been declared an open town, all weapons were confiscated. They could just walk in. Unfortunately, they had decided to bomb the island.

I have to say, it was all very exciting really. I was a child, I didn't know what was really going on.

I remember that the bailiff called a meeting in the town square and told us not to run away like rats, but stay and carry on as normal. Amazing thing was that people went running for the boats as soon as they could, saying 'Wanna car? wanna bike? Here, take it, we're off'.

Now, the houses they were living in were all locked up, and my foster father did a decent little trade in transporting their furniture and possessions from the evacuated houses and storing them in warehouses. There was quite a bit of pilfering going on, actually. I got friendly with one young lad – he went with his parents to his neighbours' house, who'd left for England. They took one or two towels and a few things from the bungalow. And do you know what? They all got done, after the war – slung in prison. Now, that seemed like a bloody injustice to me. I mean these people had hopped it, and left all their things for five years, and they were expecting to come back and find it all there. Ludicrous. ❞

▲German air power has arrived at Guernsey's airfield – and British services must assist them.

◄In Guernsey, the German Commandant takes over.

►The end of the line in France – the surrender of all military power.

DER DEUTSCHE KOMMANDANT DER BRITISCHEN KANALINSELN

⌐✠⌐ *Kurt Müller, age 19, was with a fully-mobilised Luftwaffe unit of 12 aerial observation groups, based at a central command station. As part of the occupying forces, his duties inevitably involved a certain amount of mingling with the locals, for which his French was a great asset – not all Germans made such firm local friends.*

" Our task was to follow the advancing army units and to alarm our air fighters in the event of an impending aerial attack. Our equipment was very rudimentary. We watched the sky with binoculars and radioed anything we saw to our company's HQ, which would in turn pass on our message to the nearest fighter squadron. Radar was still unknown to us at this time.

Our squad reached the Channel coasts not far from Abbeville towards the end of May. Our first lodgings were quite luxurious. Nestling behind the dunes was a little *château*.

To enter it we had to drive around the building on to a lawn surrounded by thicket. Without suspecting anything peculiar, we parked our van in front of the main entrance in order to contact the central station. Two of us had to mount guard and I was one of the two. We looked around rather casually, and suddenly, in the thicket we saw a multitude of French helmets. There were only 11 of us – ten rifles and one pistol – and here before us was an enemy unit of company strength, fully armed. They could have wiped us out in minutes, but they were unaware that no other German units were in the vicinity.

We had to bluff them. Quick as a flash, we cocked our rifles and pointed them in their direction. I am a fluent French speaker and I shouted: '*Haut les mains! Avancez doucement l'un apres l'autre!*' . . . And they came, one by one, leaving their weapons behind. We made them sit down on the lawn and asked them if they were hungry. They told us they had not eaten for days. By chance, there was plenty of food in the *château*, which, as we found out

▲ Kurt Müller with his 'adopted' French family and local girlfriend.

later, belonged to a French branch of the Rothschild family. There was bread, cheese, cakes, sausages and meat – enough to give each of our captives a substantial snack. They were anxious to tell us what their units were – I told them, I didn't want to know. 'Don't worry,' I said, 'You'll come to no harm. For you the war is over; for us it goes on.' Later on, some of our infantry came and took them away.

In the autumn of 1940 I was transferred to another little seaside village north of Boulogne, where I was to be trained on one of the first German radar stations for aerial reconnaissance. The village was located between Cap Bleu Nez and Cap Gris Nez at one of the nearest points to the English coast. On a clear day we could see the cliffs of Dover. There wasn't much aerial combat for us to report at this time, as the real fighting was taking place further north in the area of Dunkirk.

I should say something about my state of mind at the time, and how it felt to be occupying another country. I was brought up in a German conservative family and I had to fight for my country whether I liked it or not. As far as I was concerned at that time I was fighting to defend my country against an enemy which had declared war on it. I also had a very idealistic conviction that this was a fight for a united Europe under German leadership. Not one which would be united by consent, but by force, like Napoleon had tried to do. I was totally behind Hitler's war aims, but you must understand that at that time we were all victims of a remarkable propaganda machine. I did not imagine at this time that the French would be hostile to this.

Anyway, getting back to my posting in the village in northern France. There were a lot of German Army units in the area and our air force uniforms were rather a rare sight. Our relations with the local population were correct, even cordial to some extent, but it was understand-

able that most mothers kept their daughters indoors with so many young soldiers around. There were a few bistros where we could go. Two of them had very pretty barmaids and were enjoying an excellent trade. The girls were friendly but un-approachable. But on one beautiful autumn day at sunset I had an en-counter with one of the local girls, while I was on my way back to the radar station. She had brown hair and bright grey eyes, a beautiful young girl. I could hardly hide my amazement – all I could say was: 'Bonsoir Mademoiselle.' To which she replied: 'Bonsoir, Monsieur.' I walked on, but after a short distance I stopped and looked back. She did the same. I waved. She waved back. We were already too far apart to speak to each other, and I was late for duty. With quite a heavy heart I continued on my way. After many tedious weeks in this dreary little vil-lage I saw her again.

I needed some alterations to an overcoat. One of the barmaids dir-ected me to the village blacksmith and told me that his wife did some tailoring repairs. I knocked at the door and when it opened, to my sur-prise, there was the pretty woman I had encountered on the road a few weeks earlier – Yvonne Pierret was her name. She was the blacksmith's daughter. I was quickly invited into

▼ **German soldiers guard French POWs taken in the Marne region.**

the kitchen-diner and asked to wait for her mother, who was out. I was treated meanwhile to a sweet French coffee with cognac. We quickly fell into an animated conversation until her mother arrived. Her mother wasn't exactly pleased to see a Ger-man soldier in her kitchen-diner, but she was friendly enough. She took my coat and said I should come back in a couple of days. So, I did. And when I came back I brought a pres-ent. I can't remember what it was, but it was gratefully accepted. I could entertain them, and it was fas-cinating for them that a German sol-dier could speak their language flu-ently. Every second or third evening, when I was not on duty, I went there. They made dinner for me, I brought them presents – I even got them a Christmas tree.

Yvonne was 17 and I was 20 at that time. For both of us it was our first love. This is my story of 1940 in France. It was probably a much harder situation in the cities, but I never saw any of this. 〞

Hubert van Eck was conscripted into a Dutch medical unit which was dispatched to the border area between Holland and Ger-many in anticipation of the Ger-man invasion. He recalls the changes from civilian to soldier to prisoner and back to civilian again – in the now Nazi-occupied Netherlands.

〝 In 1939, the Dutch Army was mobilised. I was 35 years old then, and had last been in the army in 1926. In August 1939 a call-up letter arrived from the Minister of Defence – I was instructed to go to Utrecht. This was a shock to the Du-tch people. After the First World War, people thought, this cannot happen again.

However, I was sent to a little vil-lage to the north west of Ede and, as I was a pacifist, I was deployed with the medical troops. I spent nine

▲ German troops roll into Amsterdam to a deceptively friendly welcome – soon to be replaced by fierce loathing.

months in this village living with a family, and, for the whole time, did very little.

In May 1940, I remember, early one morning, I was in bed and we heard many planes passing over us. There were hundreds of them filling the sky. They were German planes – many of us couldn't believe the Germans were really here.

On 10 May 1940, we had to go to Amersfoort, a town five kilometres from our village near the Utrecht Hills. Land had been reclaimed here, and there was a dyke. We went there with our old-fashioned, outdated weapons and our horses. We were supposed to shoot the Germans when they arrived. It was such a shock, they arrived so suddenly, and there were so many of them, the next day there were even more. As the land was dry, they were able to travel quickly.

The Dutch Army had no fighting spirit, as I said, we had not been trained at all. None of us were familiar with fighting. Nevertheless we had to defend the hills.

After two days, we heard the Germans had broken through, and we had to leave. We travelled towards the west, some on horseback and me on my bicycle! There was some shooting about 10 kilometres outside Amersfoort, I still don't know who was shooting at us – whether it was Dutch traitors or German paratroops.

The main road between Utrecht and Amsterdam in the north was full of troops fleeing from the Germans. There was a dyke further north near Amsterdam, and it was hoped the Germans would be stopped there – then we heard that Rotterdam had been bombed.

Later we heard of the capitulation. General Vingleman had decided it was impossible to defend Holland. We could only hope that the British and the French would come. The British did not come, but the French did. There were French troops in the south of Holland. They had not been there for very long, but at least they were there.

Then we heard that the Queen had left us on the first day of the war and she was safe in England. Many people tried to escape to England, boarding boats in Amsterdam, the Hook of Holland and Rotterdam. There was great disorder. There was real fighting in some areas, even though our troops had no idea what to do. In the north and east of Holland, there were small numbers of very brave men who continued fighting. But almost everywhere the Germans beat them in a very short time. We were made prisoners of war.

We were taken to a vegetable market where we had to sleep on straw.

After that we lived in a big Dutch barracks in the centre of Utrecht with German guards. We were then moved to an old military camp called Austerlitz. We were there for two or three weeks and then, suddenly, the Germans said we could go home. As you can imagine, we were very, very surprised. At that time, the Germans were very kind to us. They said, 'You have been misled, you are not that bad really, you are of German origin.' So by June 1940 I was at home again and very happy to see my wife and little daughter.

After the summer holidays – I became a teacher in a high school in Amsterdam. The High School was for Jewish pupils only – the only such school in Amsterdam.

In 1940 the Germans were still tolerant. But anyone who knew about National Socialism knew this would not last. **"**

SEPTEMBER

27 Tripartite Pact signed between Germany, Italy and Japan, recognising a 'new order in Europe and the Far East'

26 US imposes embargo on export of all scrap iron and steel to Japan

28 First US destroyers arrive in Britain Luxemburg is 'incorporated' into Germany

30 Casualties of the Blitz during September: 6,954 killed and 10,615 injured

THE DUTCH FIGHT ON TO VICTORY

▲ A poster tribute to the courage of the beleaguered Dutch.

◄ In occupied lands, no private citizen is safe from the fear of sudden arrest or searching.

OCCUPATION POLICY

Nazi attitudes towards the countries they occupied varied according to the racial 'purity' of their populations. To Hitler, Nordic peoples were 'Aryan kinsfolk' – close to his ideal of the 'master race'. As a result, they were treated with some care, at least in the early stages.

Against less Aryan peoples, policies were progressively more severe. In France, the 'occupied zone' in the north and west came under direct military control, while the Vichy government in the rest of the country quickly became a symbol of collaboration. In the Netherlands, repressive measures were introduced from the start. But in the eastern territories (especially Poland) the people were regarded as subhuman, fit only for work or death.

Marc Sawicki had graduated from the Polish Armoured Corps Military School and been commissioned 1 September 1939, but was soon taken as a POW by the Russians. After escaping, and a long walk back to Warsaw, he put all his efforts into the anti-Nazi activities of the Polish Home Army.

" I stayed under occupation for a year, then, because of my activities, I had to leave Warsaw and either join the partisans in the forest or go abroad to join the British forces.

It was a time of organising with the Home Army. There was a number of units which were organised by more active elements, and these were later unified into the Home Army. But at the beginning, it was a fairly spontaneous reaction to occupation. After the defence against the Germans for 28–29 days, Warsaw was ruined and life was very difficult.

According to the rules imposed by the Germans, all officers had to report to the authorities and were to become POWs – to be sent into camps, *Stalags* or *Oflags*. Most of us decided not to report – probably 90 per cent or something. The rest started living and working to take some actions against the occupying forces.

I was informed by my commanding officer that information was needed about the German armoured corps. They suggested I join the German workshop to get in and to keep getting information for intelligence.

I applied as a mechanic to a German unit in Warsaw and was accepted as a mechanic, repairing cars. I was soon promoted to leader of a group repairing cars which were used by *Gestapo* units from Alia Schuhar – the interrogation centre.

In the summer of 1940, after the disastrous end in France, they brought to Warsaw a lot of French cars and lorries. We had to repair these for German use, and so I got acquainted with French equipment. There was also a certain amount of military cars and equipment. One of them was from French headquarters. It was a command car used at a command post, and this was locked. Nobody had access to this, but we were working beside it, and, during these repairs, I found that it had a hatch underneath for people to escape in case of fire or whatever.

We managed to open it and get inside and got a lot of information. It was late information, so it wasn't very valuable, but it was interesting because there were maps of attacks – this was near the Paris area.

We sealed back the hatch, but they somehow realised that someone had been there and started interrogations. Two people were taken from the unit, whom they suspected. They were tortured to death and their bodies were given to their families, stating that they died of heart attacks – but they were badly beaten and their bones were broken. This was a warning for me.

We had some restrictions on leaving Poland, but the Polish Air Force and the Armoured Corps were given the choice of going abroad and joining British forces to continue the fight. I finally got out and arrived in Palestine in February 1941. After some time I managed to convince the authorities of my identity and I was then attached to the Polish Carpathian Brigade – then we were sent to support the Libyan desert campaign. "

▲German soldiers watch as Luftwaffe aircraft batter a Dutch city, entirely unopposed.

◄Marc Sawicki, seen later in the war after his escape from Poland to fight on with the Allies.

▼Ready to invade, a giant German telecamera watches the English coasts.

THE CHANNEL ISLANDS

One of the more incongruous photographs of World War II shows a British policeman, talking to a German officer in the Channel Islands – the only part of the United Kingdom to come under Nazi occupation.

A German invasion of the islands of Jersey, Guernsey, Alderney and Sark had been expected as soon as the fall of France became a reality. Attempts were made by the British to evacuate the population – many thousands, including men of military age, were successfully shipped to the mainland – but nothing could be done to prevent the German arrival. Starting on 30 June 1940, after unnecessary air attacks, German forces began to land on the islands, encountering no opposition. The population of nearly 60,000 people had little choice but to accept German rule, dispensed by a commandant through the normal administrative channels. The occupation was to last for nearly five years.

AGAINST ALL ODDS

Western Europe conquered, Hitler resolves to batter Britain into submission from the air. But the RAF and the people of the British cities prove more than a match for the mighty Luftwaffe.

The image of heroic RAF Spitfire and Hurricane pilots – the famed 'Few' – battling it out with superior German forces in the skies over England in the summer of 1940, has lodged itself firmly in the national consciousness. This is hardly surprising: without RAF victory in the Battle of Britain, foiling the Luftwaffe's attempt to destroy the country's air defences, invasion by German units would have been only a matter of time. It is easy to forget, however, that the pilots were not alone, that the Observer Corps, the radar and ground crews, and the aircraft plant workers all made vital contributions.

After failing to knock out the RAF, it was only logical that the Luftwaffe should try to crush British civilian morale and industrial potential. The failure of this bombing campaign against the cities in the winter of 1940/41 – the Blitz – can be attributed to a number of factors. The shift to night-bombing made navigation and bomb-aiming difficult, and moreover, the bombing was not concentrated enough: life in the cities was thus able to go on almost undeterred. But, above all, it was the dogged determination of the British not to submit which convinced Hitler to use his air power elsewhere.

Pilot Officer Geoffrey Page had flown Spitfires with 66 Squadron before the Battle of Britain. When the typing error – and therefore the misdirection – was discovered, he was sent to what should have been his original destination – 56 Squadron of Hurricanes at North Weald, in the front line against the Luftwaffe.

" It was a hot August day – ironically it was the day that grouse-shooting began, August 12, and we took off from Rochford airfield, which is now Southend Airport, and we intercepted a formation of about 90 German aeroplanes bombing Manston aerodrome.

There were ten of us – we attacked them and I got the cross-fire from all the German bombers. My aircraft virtually just exploded in flames. I baled out – if you don't get out within ten seconds, you're dead, because the temperature goes up from cool room temperature to 3000°C in ten seconds – so you've got to get out quickly.

I floated down into the Channel. Unfortunately my life-saving jacket was burned through, so that wasn't any use. I had to swim for it.

I found I was a bit annoyed about the whole thing. I had in my breast pocket a brandy flask which my mother had given me. As I swam along, I thought, 'I've saved that brandy for many weeks now, and never touched it in case there was an emergency.' I thought, 'This probably warrants an emergency,' so I endeavoured to get it out from underneath this useless life-saving jacket. My hands were very badly burned – but eventually I got it out and undid the cap on the brandy flask with my teeth. I held the flask gripped between my wrists – and just as I was about to take a long, welcome swig of it, a wave came and knocked it out of my hands. I must say, I was very annoyed then.

By the time a little boat came along, with two men in it, off a big ship, and they circled me and asked me questions – if I was a German pilot or a British pilot – I really lost my temper and I started using every rude word I could think of. They immediately knew I was an RAF officer, so they picked me up.

I was taken into Margate, to the hospital, and eventually I finished up in the RAF plastic surgery burns unit at East Grinstead. I had two years there and went back flying after that.

It was a little frightening at first to

▲ G Page's first squadron, No 66, based at Coltishall.

▲ Geoffrey Page's squadron insignia during the Battle.

◄ RAF pilots study the shapes of enemy aircraft. The time taken for recognition in the air was often the margin between life and death.

▲ Luftwaffe air crew make the final flight checks on a Dornier Do-17. A middle-range bomber, the Do-17 was better in a ground support role than in the strategic one given it in the Battle.

▲ **Pilot Officer Geoffrey Page** who, after a horrific crash into the sea and sustaining severe burns in 1940, rose from the ashes to fight again.

fly again, but I got used to it. I got used to it – I got shot down twice more, so it started to become a habit!

McIndoe did all my plastic surgery – he was rather like an elder brother to me – a magnificent man. I got to know him very well. I was one of the very early ones to be treated by him, but certainly not the first, I think.

He was experimenting, really, so that's why we formed this club, the Guinea Pig Club, because we were, in a way, guinea pigs – in no nasty sense, but there was a lot of trial and error in plastic surgery in those days. You say he did a remarkable job – he was a remarkable man.

I remember my first encounter with enemy aircraft vividly, almost as if it were yesterday. We took off from Manston, here in Kent, and we had to intercept a formation of bombers and fighters who were attacking shipping convoys in the early stages of the Battle of Britain. There were six of us and as we climbed up, the controller said there were 20 bombers and about 60 fighters above. So three of us went up to attack the fighters and the other three went down to attack the bombers. There were so many German aeroplanes it was unbelievable, so I just fired at everything in sight and, ironically when I landed, I put in a report that I had fired a lot but didn't see anything hit – then 17 years later, in a German magazine, there was a photograph of a German fighter pilot by the wreckage of his burned-out Messerschmitt. He had just made it back to France, and he said he had been shot down by a Pilot Officer Geoffrey Page of 56 Squadron – so I'd got one!

Our training for fighting was instinctive – that saved my life when I got shot down the first time. You carry out natural drills to bale out –

you didn't think about it, you just did it. It was superb Royal Air Force training. The thought of whether you would or would not jump when the time came, didn't occur. When it gets that hot, you jump. The first thing then, is to look up above to see if the parachute is on fire. You were up at 15,000 feet, and if it was on fire, it wouldn't put itself out. *"* You'd be a dead duck.

✠ **Leutnant** *Ulrich Steinhilper was based with the Third Squadron of* **Jagdgeschwader 52,** *flying Bf-109s out of Coquelles, opposite Folkestone across the Channel. He was in the thick of the fighting in English air-space, and saw much to find fault with in the way the Luftwaffe was led.*

" I consider I lasted quite well – right up to the 27 October. In August we were mainly trying to hit the British fighters and their airfields, but on the whole they wouldn't come up and fight. This is where Dowding was so damned clever, he wouldn't release the fighters unless we came with bombers . . .

We weren't told there had been a change of tactics but when on the 15 September, we escorted a mass of bombers in two waves to London, it was obvious that things had changed. Now we didn't attack the airfields any more, but just tried to keep the people of London in the shelters. Even though the fighters did their best, there were huge losses to the bombers and by October the daylight use of bombers had been

virtually stopped. Instead they concentrated on the use of fighter-bombers, Bf-109s which had a single underslung 250 kg bomb. This was to have far-reaching effects for us because the pylon which was fitted to the under-side of the 109 to carry the bomb was the same as that which should have been employed to carry long-range fuel tanks. Because of Hitler's insistence on the reprisal bombing of London, this valuable equipment was given to the fighter-bomber wings instead of the fighters. It was a decision which cost us dearly.

On one mission some 35 109s were lost on the way back home, mainly because of lack of fuel, 19 of whose pilots drowned in the Channel.

So in October we started the so-called 'Waves'. The idea was that if bombs fell on London every 20 minutes or so then the whole population would stay in the shelters. One day we flew from Coquelles to London and back seven times.

My last flight, then, was on the 27 October. It was Sunday morning at 9 o'clock and it was very cold. My new aircraft was having its first overhaul so I opted to fly my old aircraft, 'Yellow 2', which had become a spare. It had been sitting around on the ground for two or three weeks and in the cold evenings and nights condensation had begun to build up in the grease around the mechanism of the propellor.

▼ *Leutnant* **Steinhilper** at his French base – carefree days before he was shot down and captured.

When we were approaching London I could see the moisture in the grease was beginning to freeze. I should have returned to base but there was so much talk at the time of *Kanalkrankheit* (Channel sickness) – that people were returning to base with faults which 'cleared up' on landing, or not being able to fly because of 'sickness' – and I didn't want to be counted amongst them. So that's why I didn't turn back.

In the turn over London we got into trouble very high. Spitfires were diving through us and I couldn't act as usual with very high revolutions on the engine and a coarse pitch to gain speed. Instead . . there was a bang and I thought the supercharger had exploded, but the engine was operating well enough. So I started the usual gradual descent towards home and passed through some cloud. I came out above and behind some Hurricanes and decided to shoot at them. Taking my oxygen mask off I realised the cockpit smelt like a steam locomotive – the engine was boiling. In the brief dogfight [with the Spitfires] I had been hit in the radiator. I soon forgot the Hurricanes and climbed back into the cloud before they saw me.

From then on I had to switch off the ignition and glide until the oil had cooled and then restart the engine to gain some height. On the third try I was very low because the oil temperature had not seemed to come down much and when I pushed the throttle forwards I could feel the

►The view through the nose of an He-111 bomber flying over England. Slow and poorly defended, it made an easy target for fighters.

▼Anti-Aircraft Gunners train on a Lewis gun.

ACK-ACK

The Spitfires and Hurricanes of the RAF were not the only means of defending Britain against air attack in 1940. Referring back to the lessons of 1917-18, British planners put great emphasis on anti-aircraft guns, organised in belts to protect the major targets.

Seven divisions of Anti-Aircraft Command existed by 1939, manned principally by Territorial Army infantry. Equipped with 4.5 in, 3.7 in and Bofors light anti-aircraft guns, the divisions – covering London; the Eastern Counties and East Midlands; Scotland and Northern Ireland; North-West Counties, West Midlands and North Wales; South Wales and South of England; South-East Counties and North-East Counties – played their part in both the Battle of Britain and the Blitz. Between July and October 1940, for example, the South-East Counties division claimed 203 aircraft destroyed by day and a further 18 by night.

engine was going to seize – and it did. I was in radio contact with Co-quelles and they said they would send the air-sea rescue, because I had said that if the engine stopped I would have to bale out.

I had real trouble getting out. Normally when the canopy release is pulled the whole unit, including the back part, comes off. This time only the lever came off in my hand and the canopy stayed in place. I had no option but to open the centre section which tilts and the slipstream tore this away but the back part stayed in place. When I tried to get out, my parachute got stuck under the rear section as the wind bent me backwards. I took a chance and just somersaulted backwards and my left leg was injured when the main chute deployed. I was so low when I got out that I saw the aircraft crash, right in the middle of a herd of cows.

A Home Guard man was the first person I met when I was testing my leg. A shot was fired and I saw a man with a shot-gun aiming at me. He didn't know it but I didn't have a weapon. New orders were that we could not carry side-arms any more because the bodies of aircrew had been recovered from the Channel with gun-shot wounds to the head. It seemed some pilots, half-drowned, had taken what our High Command had considered to be the 'easy' way out and shot themselves. ”

◉ *Wilf Dykes was a flight rigger at Hawkinge, a forward airfield just outside Folkestone. His job was to service the aircraft as they came in and get them ready to scramble again. His account underscores the fact that, without the highly dedicated ground grew, RAF pilots would have had no planes to fight with in the crucial battle against the invaders.*

▲ Flight rigger Wilf Dykes and his wife pictured in Folkestone during the war.

❝ It was very hectic at Hawkinge. When the Hurricanes or Spitfires came in, we automatically guided them in with our hands, into the right positions on dispersal. The next thing we were all over them, getting them refuelled, rearmed, ready again for take-off. It was quite fast working to get them off. I think the recognised fastest time was seven minutes to get six aircraft refuelled and rearmed, from the time of touch-down to take-off. It wasn't always for the same pilot – in fact it was different squadrons coming in all the time. Hawkinge really was an advance fighter base. The planes came to us during the daytime and we operated them right through the day, then they went back to their bases at Kenley, Northolt, Biggin Hill, Gravesend, West Malling – and if they went up on a scramble, they would probably be up for a half hour or three-quarters of an hour, then come back in to us for refuelling and rearming. We'd probably work the same squadron, perhaps, until about 2 or 3 o'clock in the afternoon. They would probably go back to base and another squadron would come in. There would be Hurricanes and Spit-

fires and also we had 141 Squadron, which was a Defiant squadron operating from Hawkinge, but I'm afraid they lost nearly all their aircraft.

When the aircraft came in, the first thing we did was check their petrol, oil and oxygen bottles. Naturally the armourers checked the guns and the wireless people checked the radios. They all did their very quick check, then we had to get them off again. We got the starter trolleys in position to get them away again. At that time there would be about 40 of you on a dispersal, of the trades. You had all the ancillary staff, the petrol bowser drivers and so on, but there would be about 40 of the trades.

It certainly happened that we got machine-gunned and bombed with them on the 'drome. If they were coming in, the pilots would scramble straight away and try to get them off the ground. Most of the time we had already got them refuelled and they were waiting to go. It was just a matter of starting them up. It was not like today, when you have a push-button starter – you had the trolley jack, which had to be operated by the fitters and riggers.

There were quite a few crash landings – it was a grass strip, as it is today, and when they took off, they didn't take off singly, there were six of them at a time, right across the field.

The squadrons were not only fighting the aircraft, they were protecting the airfields as well. Personally, I didn't like bombing, but I hated machine-gunning across the 'drome more than anything.

If the squadrons had scrambled and we came under fire, the station used to put a call out, 'Station under attack,' and they'd try to get something back round us.

▼ He-111s set off on 'Eagle Day' (13 Aug 1940), the massive strike against RAF bases which cost the Luftwaffe 45 aircraft.

NOVEMBER

1 Turkey declares itself neutral in the Graeco-Italian war

3 The first British troops arrive in Greece to combat Italian aggression

5 Roosevelt is elected President of the United States for a third term
Armed merchant cruiser *Jervis Bay* is sunk by battleship *Admiral Scheer* in the Atlantic

7 8 The Krupp factory in Essen is bombed by the RAF

11 12 Fleet Air Arm attacks Italian naval base at Taranto, claiming three battleships, two cruisers and two auxiliaries

12 Soviet foreign Minister Vyacheslav Molotov arrives in Berlin for talks with Hitler

14 15 More than 400 German bombers attack the city of Coventry
Greek troops push Italians back into Albania

19 Luftwaffe bombs Birmingham during the night for nine hours

20 Hungary agrees to join Tripartite Pact

23 Romania joins the Axis alliance
Southampton suffers heavy night raid

24 Slovakia joins the Tripartite Pact

26 The Jewish ghetto at Warsaw is sealed off from the rest of the city

31 British civilian casualties during November amount to 4,588 killed and 6,202 injured

▼ *Leutnant* Eric Schmidt of *Jagdgeschwader* 53, flying Bf-109s, describes the dogfight in which he chalked up his sixteenth 'kill'.

▲ Adolf Galland, one of the Luftwaffe's highest scoring fighter aces during the Battle, relaxes between sorties. He shot down 94 Allied planes in the period extending from midsummer 1940 to spring 1941.

Sometimes the first thing we knew was the bombs landing or the machine guns going – they used to come in so quick you didn't even get a warning. But, naturally, if they knew, they would get the sirens going.

They bombed the strip quite a few times, and they smashed the hangars and a lot of the buildings.

One day there were three Messerschmitts came round. They were very low and, I think some of the guns had to pack up firing because they were so low that they were firing across one another. I think all three would have landed if there had not been so much fire directed at them, however, one of them landed - and he had no hope of getting up again. The plane was intact, and they captured him. Whether he came in because he thought he'd been damaged, I don't know – but the overall impression you got was that all three would have landed. Maybe it was to get out of the war, or perhaps they had lost their direction and thought that it was the occupied coast – I don't know.

The pilot can't have been any more than 18 or 19 years of age. He handed over his revolver, got his little box out of the cockpit and they waltzed him off to the guardroom.

 Margaret Holmes, a vicar's wife living on the Isle of Dogs in east London, vividly recorded the effects of the Blitz in a letter she wrote after the first onslaught of bombings. She shows the imperturbable spirit of the victims of the war against the civilian population who, undaunted, carried on as ever.

❝ All last week we had dozens of warnings – six or seven in a day, and often lasting all night. Most people around us were frightened and went to shelters for every 'raid', taking their beds there at night. The planes only seemed to be reconnaissance flights and no bombs were ever dropped.

Then last Saturday evening at 6 pm, Arthur [the Vicar] was out visiting (the warning had gone an hour ago) and I was watching from our front door for any signs of activity, when I saw a formation of planes coming over. They were mostly huge black ones with four engines. I'd never seen any of this kind before, and they were much lower than usual. Our guns battered them, but they kept beautiful formation until they seemed to be overhead, when they spread out fanwise – and then came a long, big whistle and *crash*. Then another and another. By this time, I had grabbed Dodger (the dog) and was under the stairs. Arthur came rushing in. He had been on *the roof of the church*, watching the planes when the bombing started, but he soon shifted. He said the church swayed like anything. He had seen the nearest bomb fall 100 yards away on a paint wharf. It had hit a container of ammonia and the fumes made us think it was gas. Everybody put on their gas masks – our first experience of them!

We could see fires that had started all round. Ours was a good one. Oil poured in a river down the street and there were great clouds of black smoke. The Germans' idea was to light up the place with fires to guide them in on the night raids (to follow). But our fire was put out before dark. Arthur came back with a message to help with people from a block of flats which was bombed to bits just over the bridge. The people were safe, having been in shelters, but were homeless, of course. I got there after explaining my mission to several soldiers and being passed over an oily plank, over an oily river by several oily air raid wardens. We fed the people on biscuits by candlelight – all else had failed. When we went home we retired to our bed under the stairs. It was an awful night, lying down under that stair, listening to bombs near and far, and wondering when one would come for us! We soon got to know the whistle and crash of the high explosive, the long whistle and awful shaking (but no crash) of delayed-action bombs. Then at 3.15 am, we thought ours had come. The crack was terrific. The front door burst open, broken glass crashed on the pavement and dust and stones rained down everywhere. We looked out and could see nothing but dust, so we waited. I went through to Dodger, who was in his chair in the scullery. The back door had burst open too, but Dodger just shook himself and wagged his tail.

The dust settled and we looked

▶ Winter 1940: Londoners asleep in the Underground, then the deepest and most extensive subway system in the world, to escape the Blitz.

◀▼ The Rev. and Mrs Holmes did not have the shelter of the Tube during raids – only the stairs.

out. The street was carpeted thick with dust, bricks and glass. Arthur ran round the corner and met Firemaster Ayre, who said, 'Was anybody in the church?' Arthur said, 'No – why? Has it gone?' 'Yes.' Arthur said, 'Oh dear. Unemployed.'

Then Arthur took me round to see the church. What a sight! A crater, I think about 15 feet deep, took up the width of the road. It was floodlit by a 12-inch gas main burning nicely, the water was pouring in from the water main. All round the crater was spread half the church. The altar end was left standing and you could look up to the altar.

Windows and ceilings were broken for hundreds of yards along the street, where pieces of church had flown about. The pub at the next corner had all the ceiling down and all glass out, and yet the landlord was selling beer at 5 am.

Peter Wood was living in Tulse Hill in south London and working in the City for a shipping company. On 7 September, just before the Blitz, he was playing football near Crystal Palace when he heard some unseasonal thunder. He looked up to see the sky full of German bombers – but the game went on.

" Literally dozens of Germans, accompanied by smaller aircraft which I took to be fighters, were going over at about 500 feet. There didn't seem to be any gunfire from our defending forces at all . . . Fortunately for us, they overflew us, because they were obviously heading for the docks, for what was, as we know now, the first bombing of the docklands at that time. We shrugged

GINGER ACE

J H Lacey, known for obvious reasons as 'Ginger', had joined the RAF's Volunteer Reserve two years before war broke out, and in May 1940 he began a spectacularly successful pilot's career by shooting down five enemy aircraft over France – for which he was awarded the *Croix de Guerre*. Back in England, he shot down his first Battle of Britain victim, a Bf-109, in July, earning the DFM. That summer he cut a swathe through the Luftwaffe, becoming, with 18 'kills' to his credit, the highest scoring RAF pilot in the battle. Lacey went on to lead a squadron, chalking up a grand total of 28 confirmed 'kills' in the war.

'Ginger' Lacey in the cockpit of a 105 Squadron Spitfire.

◀ Peter Wood, pictured later in the war. During the Blitz, as a civilian working in the City, he found, like millions of others, that life could be worked around the Blitz and its dangers.

▼ A tea kitchen set up for Londoners bombed out of their homes. Tea was not the only solace dispensed in such places – here the victims of Hitler's 'total war' could compare notes and stiffen each other's resolve.

our shoulders and carried on to finish our game of football.

After that the bombing of London increased in volume and the routine was to sleep in a reinforced cellar where my wife's family lived in Tulse Hill, and when the all-clear went in the morning, you just got up, washed and dressed and went to work.

After just over a month of this, I remember the all-clear going, and it was still dark. We came up out of the cellar and went out into the street and I literally walked up a hill. A 500-lb bomb had peeled the road up about 50 yards from the house where I lived. This was, I suppose, the nearest thing to bombing that we got – except that about a month later I was walking my wife to her place of work, and we saw a hole in the gutter. We both peered down it, wondering what it was, then when we came back in the evening, that road was all blown up. It was an unexploded bomb, which had gone off during the day, and a bus had actually gone into the hole – that was how big the crater was.

Like all of us still living and working in London, we were members of the ARP and did our stint of firewatching and generally helping the fire brigade and police as best we could.

When we were in the shelters we played pontoon or poker most of the night and drank tea or cocoa. We didn't sleep very much because the anti-aircraft guns were going constantly. We could feel the shocks in the ground from the bombs hitting the area. The extraordinary thing was, when the 500-pounder came so close to us, we didn't actually feel much from it. We must have been so close to the epicentre of the explosion that we didn't actually feel it. That was why it was a shock when I came upstairs [in the morning] and went into the street.

Working in the City, sometimes you had a normal run through on the bus or tram – we had trams in those days – sometimes you would be diverted and you wouldn't get to the office for four or five hours. Or even, on some days, the damage was so bad that you just gave up and went back home because you couldn't get to the office.

Our area was not as badly affected at this time as later on, in '44 when the V1 and V2 attacks were going on. That was much more devastating than even the [Blitz] bombing – although that was very bad. The incendiary bombs were serious because they would start the fires going, then they would drop high explosives into the fires to stop you from putting the fires out.

Life went on as normally as possible. People got to the stage where, as soon as they had had tea or supper, they would take their bedding and go to the Anderson shelter – it became a way of life.

The extraordinary thing was that people were not badly demoralised – the more they suffered, the more determined they seemed to be that they would beat this thing. **"**

1941
THE WORLD ON FIRE

Fighters from all fronts recall a year of global conflict

When 1941 began, Britain stood virtually alone and, although the threat of German invasion had receded, the Luftwaffe was bombing Britain's cities almost nightly. The ravages of U-boat and warship attacks against British shipping led to stringent rationing in what proved a long, hard winter.

On a brighter note, Major-General Richard O'Connor's Western Desert Force in North Africa defeated the numerically superior Italian armies, and at last, in early February, Britain could claim a success.

But Hitler was obsessed with invading the Soviet Union – and to secure his southern flank, he was forced to help the Italians in North Africa. The arrival of Major-General Erwin Rommel and his *Afrika Korps* in Tripoli

in mid-February soon drove the British back, leaving Tobruk surrounded and besieged.

Operation Barbarossa opened in June, with a massive German assault to take Leningrad, Moscow and the Ukraine by winter. However, the Blitzkrieg overreached itself, and with the onset of the Soviet winter, supply-lines crumbled. The climate on their side, the Russians dug in for a long slogging match.

It was not until December that the last major protagonists showed their hand. On the 7th, the Japanese attacked the US Pacific Fleet at Pearl Harbor, following up with attacks on Malaya and the Philippines which left the Allies reeling. However, Germany and Italy then declared war on the USA. Now Britain no longer faced the conflict alone.

THE CAULDRON

Allied troops ship out to North Africa to counter the Italian threat in the Libyan desert – but before long the Germans too have landed and joined the fray.

By 7 February 1941, Major-General Richard O'Connor's 30,000-strong Western Desert Force had pushed the Italians out of Egypt (which they had invaded in September 1940) and across the whole of Cyrenaica (eastern Libya).

Because of Churchill's decision to divert British troops to Greece, no pursuit took place, and this allowed the Germans to send reinforcements. Commanded by Major-General Erwin Rommel, they drove the British back into Egypt, besieging the Libyan port of Tobruk.

It was not until November 1941 that the newly formed British Eighth Army was able to attack in strength to relieve Tobruk, but if it had not been for the fact that Rommel wasted his mobile units in an abortive outflanking move, it too would have failed. Despite a link-up with Tobruk garrison and Rommel's subsequent retreat, the seesaw war in the desert was far from over.

James Palmer, with the Royal Tank Regiment, was in the desert by late 1940. On 7 February 1941, news came that the Australians had taken Benghazi from the Italians. Palmer met the enemy in retreat at Beda Fomm. Later, in November, heading for Sollum from Barrini, Palmer entered the famous 'Cauldron'.

❝❝ The road south from Benghazi followed the coast and continued westwards towards Mers Brega and El Agheila. Some 500 miles to the west was Tripoli. We leaguered up behind a small hill which we called 'The Pimple' and looking down on to the Benghazi/Tripoli road, we couldn't believe our

▲ Negotiating a tricky mixture of rocks and sand, a British Vickers Light Tank takes part in its last campaign. First built in the 1920s, its 15-mm armour and .50-in machine gun were no match for German tanks.

▶ Under sparse camouflage, the crew of a 25-pounder gun prepares to go into action in the desert near Acroma.

►Crew from James Palmer's tank leaguer up for the night, having prepared a rough tent in which to sleep. The desert nights were often cold, and any shelter was welcome against the ravages of a sandstorm.

eyes! The whole of Graziani's army was retreating from Benghazi. They were sitting ducks.

By this time we only had 14 tanks left and everything went mad. The ammunition lorries were called up and every tank took on as much ammo as it could carry. Petrol was topped up and we prepared for attack. The Italian light tanks were at each side of the column like destroyers escorting a convoy and we came round the Pimple and hit the road. Straight alongside the column we crashed, firing into the column as we went and as fast as we could. Trucks burst into flames and within minutes the road was blocked with blazing lorries. The Italians were in complete panic and men were jumping out of the trucks, firing blindly at anything. Machine guns spluttered and we could hear the pinging of bullets hitting the side of the tanks.

The Italian tanks were scattered all around us, firing away – but in absolute panic. They were even hitting their own lorries and, on some occasions, their own tanks. Dusk was thick and at times we couldn't see more than a couple of yards. Everything was burning and there was a horrible sound of screaming and dying. Tanks were blazing and ammunition was exploding in the Italian tanks when they were hit. Some of our tanks were hit and the crews were scrambling out of the blaze to seek shelter in the rocks. The air was full of the whine of bullets and metal shrapnel was raining down. Smoke swirled around and explosions rent the air. The noise was unbelievable. Two or three of our tanks pulled out to replenish ammo behind 'the Pimple' and they were back again as if stricken with a blood lust. The whole operation was over in less than two hours – then there was nothing more we could hit. All the convoy was burning, all the tanks had been hit or abandoned and the remaining troops were lying beside the road, waving white flags. All the wounded were crying, screaming and dying. For two hours we had gone berserk, but now we were dazed, confused and sickened.

Italian medics and ambulances sorted out the mess and collected the wounded. Our casualties had been minimal but to this day I think that the carnage will be forever a scar on the minds of all those tank crews.

The next day we went out to the road to recover what Italian tanks we could. There was a smell of burning flesh amid the smouldering ruins. Men were hanging half out of the tanks with their legs blackened and these dropped off when we pulled the bodies free. Heaps of gooey black stuff were inside the tanks and these heaps had been men. It was a sight that I shall never forget and I know that my soul will be damned for having been a part of it. Graves were being dug by the Italians and no-one said much. Tears were trickling down many a face and both sides were mumbling that they were sorry it had happened. We sat amid the carnage and gave the Italians fags

▲ ▶ A halt in the desert for Palmer's crew, one of whom uses a sun-compass – a navigation aid based roughly on a sundial – to work out the direction in which to move.

▼ A couple of Tommies saunter down a ruined street in Tobruk after it has been cleared of Italian occupiers, early in 1941. The Italian POWs, the war now over for them, face a long detention.

but the war was over for them and they were just waiting patiently to be taken away. It had been a victory for us – but if that was victory I didn't want any more. I was stunned by the atrocity of war and bloodshed. I had experienced the ultimate degradation of human life.

As we rumbled on towards the Sidi Rezegh area we came under very heavy fire from the German 88 mm guns and smaller anti-tank guns. The screeching, rumbling, grinding and gunfire reached a crescendo. Smoke shells were landing all around us to confuse our sense of direction and the light panzers came out to meet us. Tracer shells were streaking towards us and the shell fire became more concentrated. We could see the guns far away to our right and there would be a puff of smoke, a screeching wail, a cracking explosion, the sound of whirling white-hot shrapnel raining down as the ground shook. Black smoke was pouring

from tanks to our left and right and the incessant chatter of machine guns was all around. Tracer shells were arching through the air and mortar shells were plonking in front and behind us. Everyone was firing at anything that moved in front of us and we stopped, started, veered to the right, veered to the left, crashed away and bumped and crunched into the inferno of blazing tanks, screaming of dying men, thick black smoke and the pungent smell of burning flesh. Tank crews scrambled out of burning tanks and tanks were exploding with a thundering crack. We were all in a jumble, German tanks alongside our light cruisers, infantry firing and throwing grenades at anything moving towards them; and all the time our artillery were firing salvo after salvo over our heads. The area was rightly referred to as the 'Cauldron' in later days. Everything was boiling into a massive area of explosions, crumping of shells,

screeching of tank tracks, fire, screams, the whine of engines and pathetic moans of terror. We could see very little and the inside of the tank was full of smoke and fumes. Empty shell cases were rattling around and the guns were firing as fast as they could. The breach-blocks were red hot. We could hear the pinging of bullets against the hull then there would be a tremendous thud and we would lurch over after a near miss. It seemed that the noise would itself burst us to kingdom come, then as quickly as it started there was a deathly silence. Tank engines stopped and there was a chilling quietness and the smoke swirled away. We had gone right through the 'Cauldron' and were in the open with only about twelve tanks intact.

We moved to a small wadi to our left to hole up for a while, but as we approached the wadi we came straight face to face with four light Italian tanks that had come up from

WAR IN EAST AFRICA

When Italy declared war on Britain in June 1940, it was inevitable that the conflict would spread to East Africa, where 250,000 Italian troops stood poised in Ethiopia. After attacking border posts in Kenya and Sudan they seized British Somaliland.

Initial British counterattacks failed, but in January 1941 two divisions advanced out of Sudan into Eritrea. The fighting was hard, especially around Keren in March, but in April Massawa was taken, opening the way to the heart of Ethiopia. Meanwhile, another British contingent, under Lieutenant-General Alan Cunningham, seized Italian Somaliland and invaded Ethiopia from the south, while other units from Aden liberated British Somaliland. After a final battle at Amba Alagi, the Italians surrendered.

▲ ▶ The Camel Corps of the British Army prepares to take on the Italian invaders in Abyssinia.

the south and the Ariete area. We pulled up and the Italian tanks panicked and tore away to our right, straight into a German minefield. We watched as they realised where their panic had taken them. Like big slow black bugs they swerved, left, right, left, right, seeking a way out of the minefield, but one by one there was the inevitable shattering roar and thump as the tanks were blown to eternity. **"**

Within a few seconds we had left our vehicles, grabbed our weapons and ammo and followed the commander. We managed to avoid the artillery fire pretty well, in fact. Immediately behind us was a wall of fire, dust and exploding earth. The tanks withdrew and turned round, drawing the artillery fire to themselves. Everyone just ran, stumbling forward, as best they could. The wall of fire came down upon us again and it became imposs-

meant death or serious injury

We couldn't make out the enemy. His positions must have been well camouflaged. It almost brought you to tears to have to watch comrades die, or wounded men stumbling back behind the lines.

In this inferno of artillery, machine-gun and anti-tank fire, we could see our medics binding up the wounded and dragging them off behind the lines. Would the hardly re-

First Lieutenant Eric Prahl, age 29, was adjutant to the 8th MG Battalion of the 5th Light Division, later to become the 21st Panzer Division in the Africa Corps. The following extracts are from the battalion diary, which Prahl kept during the campaign, before the attack on Tobruk.

" After a 2-km drive, we suddenly came under fierce artillery fire from the fortress of Tobruk.

ible to move forward. Now we came under anti-tank and machine-gun fire. We dug ourselves in with our hands and feet, and anything we could get our hands on. However, many of my comrades were hit before they could finish digging their foxholes.

In little jumps we managed to get a few metres forward, until we came under machine-gun and anti-tank fire again. We dug little holes in the stony ground with spades, rifles, hands and feet, building little stone walls in front of us to protect our heads. We came under gunfire. The slightest movement might have

cogniseable red-cross bandages be any use? Many of us said a silent penance that in peacetime we had looked down our noses a little at the medics . . .

Once more, we got the order to attack. Tobruk had to be taken. We had no artillery support, since they had run out of ammunition. So, we had to try to force a breakthrough with the help of the tank regiment. Unfortunately, the Division was unable to inform us exactly where the enemy positions were.

At 11 o'clock our tank unit rolled up at full speed. It came immediately under artillery fire. The tanks came

Marc Sawicki, forced to leave his native Poland by the dangers of his anti-German underground activities, made his way via Czechoslovakia, Hungary, Yugoslavia, Greece and Turkey to Palestine. Here he joined the Polish Carpathian Brigade en route for the Libyan desert and Tobruk – to see action at last.

" I was attached to the 2nd Battalion Infantry in the Brigade and was commanding officer of a

they were mostly Italian, but there were German units as well.

There were a lot of minefields, so the idea was to keep our patrols always at night, in close contact with the enemy front line, to prevent them from investigating us.

Then, after the patrol, which was usually after midnight, we had a very brief rest, then I had to write a report of the patrol and plan the next patrols for the following day. The report was sent to Brigade Headquarters and they communicated the report to the commanding officer (at the time it was General Morshead, then later there was General

charging through our own positions. Now we not only had to take cover from the enemy artillery fire but also from our own advancing tanks.

We leapt up and got in close behind the last tanks, pressing forward behind an army of tanks and a wall of fire. Then, suddenly, the tanks turned round and came at full speed through our lines, still under fierce artillery bombardment.

Everybody dug themselves in frantically. The earth was softer here, thank God, and so it went quicker.

Once the dust had cleared, we could see ahead of us a wide barbed-wire obstacle, with here and there a few little piles of stones, and now and again you could see the heads of the defending soldiers popping up. In the distant background you could see high poles, with observation nests at the top – we could clearly see the heads of the observers. But we had to get our heads straight down again – we were immediately hit with precisely-aimed machine-gun and rifle fire. We even had to pee lying on our bellies.

13.4.1941. Easter Sunday. We'd completely forgotten. It appeared that the enemy had received reinforcements overnight. After first light we could no longer raise our heads out of our foxholes – we came under machine-gun and rifle fire immediately. The artillery continued to fire on us uninterrupted, precisely guided, apparently, by the observer in his observation post about 1000 m away. As quick as a flash the 2nd and 3rd MG companies threw up one machine gun each over the covers and the observer was picked out of his little 'crow's nest'. This did not stop the continual artillery bombardment, however, which remained as intense as ever. We were under fire from about six batteries. At 11 o'clock, the order came again " to attack Tobruk.

◀▲ **Marc Sawicki with the crew of his Bren-gun carrier, serving with the Polish Carpathian Brigade.**

▲▶ **Their faces and clothes showing signs of wear and tear, two Tommies man a Vickers machine gun.**

Bren gun-carrier platoon – but in Tobruk there was very little chance of manoeuvre, so our Bren-carriers were dug into the ground and acted as defence strongpoints with machine guns and anti-tank guns. So I had a lot of time on my hands and was appointed intelligence officer.

This involved me in taking part in night patrols, two or three times a week, leading them to obtain information about enemy lines, minefields, defences. If possible we would also find out who the enemy were –

Scobie).

There were three kinds of patrols – one where people were sent into the area of the enemy lines, and they were left there as listening and observing posts, recording movements of enemy ammunition or supplies. Another was investigating the lines and mapping out the minefields, if possible disarming mines and marking possible access into the enemy stronghold. The third one was acting as so-called 'scorpions'. Here we had to go through the lines, through the wires into the enemy strongholds and try to get an enemy POW. This was the main source of information we could obtain. We hadn't the benefit of the army – being besieged, we had only photographs taken once a month by reconnaissance planes which were flying from Egypt over Tobruk. Then we could compare the photographs of minefields and formations – but this was on a higher level. I was on a lower level, which was affecting the tactical side, not operational.

I took part in two scorpion-type attacks and in both we were successful and got five prisoners each time.

► Wash day in besieged Tobruk. British and Indian troops get to grips with their laundry in front of a building which had formerly served as a school during the Italian occupation.

▼ Rommel's advance gets under way. The men of the Africa Corps, arriving with their Mark II panzers, would have their work cut out to regain the territory lost by the retreating Italian Army.

They supplied us with a fair amount of information.

In Tobruk the supplies came mainly during one week, on a moonless night, when the Royal Navy was able to deliver to us, but this was mainly to take out the wounded. Supply was very infrequent. We had large stocks of food which was basically corned beef and biscuits – no vegetables. Water was limited to semi-salted from wells near the sea. This was fairly bitter, but was used for tea or coffee – we were allocated one pint of water per head for drinking, and the rest was salt water for washing and so on.

The conditions varied on different sectors, of which there were three. The worst sector was called Ras al Madaur, which was a salient, which means the Germans managed to break into the defence perimeter and we had to contain them within a very short distance – in some cases we were only 60 or 70 yards apart.

There were three rows of mine-fields here, sometimes five – so this was one of the most difficult sectors in Tobruk.

Our General, Karpinski, decided the Polish Brigade should be in this sector. And to illustrate how difficult it was to stay there, the Australian unit from 9th Division (which we replaced in Tobruk), the longest period they managed on Madaur was 17 days. We, however, stayed there for 72 days.

Morale was extremely good. One thing that was uppermost in our minds was to stay a day longer than the Germans. We had no retreat – we were told there was only one thing, to attack and go forward, or go into the sea. There could be no escape.

I think we acquired this attitude from the Australian troops, who stopped the Germans so effectively – and we wouldn't want to do any worse. **"**

◉ *Flying Officer James Hepburn, an air-gunner with 216 Squadron of the RAF, arrived in the desert in 1940, but his navigational skills soon came to the fore in the featureless terrain, and it was as a navigator that, in 1941, he operated in the 'Maid of All Work', from a base near Cairo in support of ground troops.*

" When I first went out we were at Heliopolis, which is on the outskirts of Cairo. Of course we were always operating in the forward areas from wherever we happened to be. We used to get a large hole dug in the ground and put a tent over the top, so your head would be below

▼A motley bunch of tank crewmen gather round for a tot – it certainly doesn't look like gin, but any sort of improvised spirit is a great morale booster in the desert!

▼▼A convoy of German supply trucks weaves through the rough terrain of North Africa. The longer the lines of communication, the harder the job of the supply men.

ground level – it was no good if anything fell on you from above, but if anything fell a little way away, you wouldn't get the blast of it.

The squadron I was with was out in that area before the war, and they had worked out how to cope with the conditions there fairly well. There is no doubt that there are problems, because you get these sandstorms which blow up quite unexpectedly. They are more likely to happen at certain times of year, of course. You get the *Khamseen* wind blowing, which goes over the desert at about 80 mph – you can imagine what conditions that produces. There is sand everywhere. One doesn't know whether one is in the air or on the ground.

Ours was a peculiar squadron because it was a bomber transport. In the early days it was one of the main bomber arms, then as the reinforcements came out, we concentrated more on the transport role. We used to do things like landing behind enemy lines and depositing the various forces, or refuelling aircraft which hadn't got the endurance. We actually fuelled a fighter squadron once, to go and attack a force which was coming in to Tobruk, which Intelligence knew about. The Germans weren't anticipating that they would meet any fighter resistance because our fighter aircraft were too far away – but we went and refuelled them.

It was a marvellous war, really. It was more like a naval situation. We were operating on a completely open flank. You had the Quattara Depression, through which not even tanks could operate, and then you had the sea on the other side. You had these vast open spaces in between, with a couple of oases where the Long-Range Desert Group used to operate. You've probably heard of them – they were commandos really, the beginning of the SAS. Our aircraft was called 'The Maid of All Work' and we used to operate as it was considered the situation demanded.

Cairo was great. One had the Turf Club and the Ghezira, which was the most marvellous country club in the world, really. One had Tommy's Bar – one even had an air-conditioned cinema. You see, this was when we were operating from a landing ground. It was uncomfortable when you were there, but one always had to bring the aeroplanes back after 30 hours' flying. You might only come back for a day and a half, but then when we brought them back for major maintenance, one might be back for a week. Then you could stay at the Continental Hotel overnight – and arrive in the barber's shop to get rid of your seven-day stubble. Operating from a desert airfield, water was very short – one certainly didn't have enough water to shave, and what water there was was very salty. It actually used to spoil the taste of the whisky, so the problem was to get some decent drinking water up from the delta to put in one's evening libation – which was very necessary in that climate. One didn't, literally, take a drink until the sun was on the way down, and then a little whisky was very helpful!

 Karl-Heinz Böttger was an acting staff aide in the logistics branch of the 15th Panzer Division, part of the German Afrika Korps. He arrived in North Africa in the summer of 1941, and here describes the enormous difficulties in supplying the German forces in the desert right up until November 1941.

" Every serving soldier, from both sides, if I may say so, experienced that the North African theatre of war was a tactician's paradise, but a logistics nightmare. I was posted to Africa in the summer of 1941 and became an aide in that part of the military which had to keep the frontline troops supplied with all their day-to-day needs, be they food, petrol, ammunition or medical help,

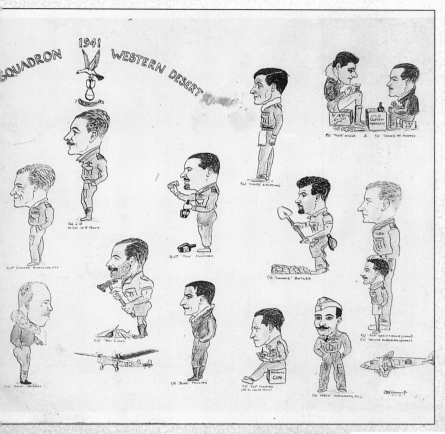

and the Tobruk by-pass road had to be tackled mostly in darkness, because nearly every movement on that bloody stretch was observed by the defenders.

During early autumn we had strengthened our position, so as to be able to withstand a possible onslaught by the British Army. In all considerations of operational command it had to be kept in mind that each 3-ton truck arriving at the frontline, east of Tobruk, could transport only two tons of goods, due to desert sand tracks, and the need to return to base. It was our task to get the columns through to all forward locations and get the wounded and sick back to field and base hospitals, regardless of enemy action.

Our enemy in getting our tasks carried out were mostly British strafing fighter planes or scout cars, who had intruded by stealth into our area, or harassing artillery fire from fast-moving columns with 25 pounder guns. Vital for the survival of our troops was strict adherence to security, radio silence of moving columns and a field routine which would save blood and supplies for future contingencies."

postal services and the like. Transport of troops and material from Europe to Africa, along the stretch of water from Naples to the Libyan ports proved enormously difficult.

Secondly, the long road transport from the unloading points, more than 1,000 km to the front on one single road, exposed us to possible sea or air attacks, not to mention the open southern flank, from which long-range raiding parties could hit at the supply and other columns. A third major difficulty was resupply on the actual battlefields, and this is where I was most closely involved, bringing provisions to the area around the Tobruk perimeter and to the area east of that fortress up to the frontier with Egypt.

In summer 1941, the Germans in North Africa had not achieved their aim to capture Tobruk, which remained a hard nut to crack. Together with our Italian allies, we had taken up 'fortified' field positions in a perimeter of about 40 km in length,

▲216 Squadron of the RAF in the desert, portrayed in caricature. James Hepburn, bottom left corner, would be among the first to extol the virtues of stopovers in Cairo to lift morale when the squadron's aircraft were undergoing major maintenance.

▶Italian troops lend a hand to the newly arrived *Afrika Korps*. The German assistance had come in the nick of time to prevent a complete loss of Axis gains in the Western Desert.

RUNNING THE GAUNTLET

An island nation, Britain depends on freedom of traffic across the Atlantic for vital supplies – but now her merchant convoys are an easy prey to the lurking menace of the U-boats.

Throughout 1941 Britain faced a threat of imminent starvation, caused by German attacks on Atlantic shipping. Despite the introduction of new weapons and, by the end of the year, the involvement of the Americans, the outcome of the Battle of the Atlantic hung constantly in the balance.

The greatest threat came from U-boats, operating in wolf-packs against merchant convoys. Escort warships were in short supply and a vast area of the mid-Atlantic was devoid of air cover. Long-range bombers and flying boats and the first of the escort carriers, had little impact.

A more optimistic picture emerged as far as the threat from surface warships was concerned, chiefly because the German battleships were deployed piecemeal, while the dramatic sinking of the *Bismarck* in May 19 deterred further German warship sorties.

Captain W Eyton-Jones was skipper of the merchant ship Benrackie, *sailing with a convoy across the North Atlantic. In May 1941, a U-boat torpedoed and sank the ship, leaving the captain, crew and passengers to take their chances in a life-boat praying to be picked up.*

I was still sitting on the overturned bridge boat when I saw the submarine surface. He went round picking cases out of the water – generally, possibly spirits, food and so forth. After a bit, he backed down through the wreckage towards us – and that is where we get into trouble.

Four men came out on the conning tower. The man who took was a commander – a youngish bloke, looked down on us. Then he shouted, 'What ship?' One of my crew, unfortunately, to my mind, shouted, 'The *Queen Elizabeth*.' I thought, 'Well, this is probably where we get shot up or in trouble.' He said again, 'What ship?' and somebody gave the true name of the ship – *Benrackie*. They looked at us and circled round for a bit – they laughed at us and went away to the north east. They never asked us if we had any water – if we had any damage or anything else. They just cleared out to the north east and we were left just floating amongst the wreckage in one boat.

We went round the wreckage and picked up the people we could, to get what gallons of water we could – a few tins of biscuits. Then, after having a good look round, as far as we could, we said, 'Well, there's only one thing for it – we try to get out of this if we can.' Halfway between Brazil and North Africa! The only thing I could think about was to try to get to the nearest land possible – so I set the course as near as I could to the north east. All we had was the one lifeboat which was made for 48 people – we picked up 58. There wasn't really enough room for people to sit down. The boat was leaking badly – it had been on the chocks for some time and you had quite a bit of trouble getting the crew to move so you could bail – and you bailed for nearly two days until the wood of the boat started to swell and tighten up. After that it wasn't so bad.

The worst days were when there was no wind – absolutely becalmed. The sun was terrific. We cut up a lifeboat cover which was in the boat for the men to put over their heads with their life-jackets to keep the rays of sun off them.

We started off by giving four ounces of water – two in the morning and two at night, and one biscuit. Well, that went on for some time and then we got a couple of squalls at night time and we were able to save a little bit of water – but not very much – and that was only by spreading the

◄A British battleship comes under attack in the Atlantic, June 1941. Although well able to compete against Germany's single capital ships, Britain's navies were ill-equipped to take on wolf-packs of U-boats.

▼Entering into her last battle, *Bismarck* engages HMS *Hood* in the pitch black of an Atlantic night.

mainsail out flat. You could hear the men underneath sucking it with their lips, trying to get them a bit more moist.

However, they behaved remarkably well – really they were damn fine men. On the second day we saw a ship in the distance – but they didn't see us. About the tenth day we saw an aeroplane – but they still didn't see us. On the morning of the 13th day I used to sit on the water barrel to make sure no-one could help themselves. 'Hey, captain, we see lights – green lights.' 'Oh,' I said, 'You're dreaming.' And I looked around – and I saw some green lights which looked to me like Brighton Pier. I couldn't make it out. So we burned a flare – then a few minutes later another flare. After a bit I saw the green lights getting closer, more visible. Then after a bit I saw a red light above the green – and it dawned on me that this was a hospital ship. Shortly afterwards they came alongside us.

On board, they put all our men, 56 at that time, into bunks and they were all whistling, shouting – almost in hysteria. Then some of the sisters from the hospital came round with cans of tea and buns. It was the most wonderful drink we had ever had – we were practically dehydrated. In the 13 days you didn't perspire. Nature completely stopped. You just became dehydrated and the average loss of a man's weight per day was about two and a half pounds. How long we could have survived I don't know. We had steamed and sailed 530 miles – the sun raging and squalls and so forth, and survived to be within 100 miles of Sierra Leone – and all I had to go by was the Pole Star, using my finger to think how high it was above the horizon. We had nothing but the boat compass.

In the wreck we lost one out of every three men. Without them, this nation wouldn't have survived more than three or four months. They did a wonderful job of work – they were wonderful men and I can't praise them highly enough. 🙶

 Otto Kretschmer was commander of U-99, on patrol in the North Atlantic in March 1941, when his submarine came under attack by depth-charge. Apart from the lasting memory of the struggle to survive the wreck, he remembers the horror with which U-boat men were viewed by the Allied seamen.

🙶 Knowledge, of course, is the basis of everything – and in peacetime training in seamanship tactics or whatever it is, you must know your job.

You must also be in the position to know what's going on on the battlefield – and that which you don't see – or which you see only at a glance, either when you're submerged or when you are on the surface. You must try to find out what your adversary, say the aircraft commander, for instance, is thinking, and what the crews of the ships are doing – whether they have come from America with a long sea voyage behind them, or from England to the West of Ireland, when they are waiting for the change of the watch, and what the weather is like – if the lookouts have got the wind in their faces, or the moon is shining at night. You must think about all these little things and store them in your mind, so that you have everything ready when you have to make a decision.

It's a bit difficult for us now, trying to get some insight into what was going on in the battle of the Atlantic,

 ▲▶Crewmen of a U-boat come out on to the deck to inspect the damage inflicted on an Allied transport ship which they have just torpedoed.

 ◀Survivors from the wreck of the *Bismarck* hang grimly on to any floating thing in the water as they waited to be hauled aboard HMS *Dorsetshire*, May 1941

because during the war the role of the U-boat sailor was a much despised one. They were thought of as pirates and that sort of thing, but when we talk to people on both sides now, naval officers on both sides, I mean, it's almost as if they were talking about a football match. Everything's very jolly and very friendly, and they're all marvellous chaps together. It's hard to realise that all those years ago these same people were at sea trying to kill each other.

Oddly enough there was no hatred on our side – at least on my side – and it was a pity to sink those ships. They were, some of them, very beautiful – but we never worried so much about the men because, well, I always thought they had time enough to go into the boats and on many occasions, I helped them.

U-BOAT TACTICS

When the Battle of the Atlantic began in September 1939, U-boats carried out independent operations, searching alone for likely targets before attacking, usually at night and on the surface. It worked well: between July and October 1940, in what U-boat commanders called a 'Happy Time', 217 merchant ships were sunk.

The British responded by improving convoy protection, deploying escorts armed with ASDIC detection gear and depth-charges. U-boat losses increased, forcing the Germans to alter their approach. By 1941, if a submarine sighted a convoy it would send a signal to U-boat Headquarters in Lorient, from where other U-boats would be directed to the target. Attacks were still chiefly at night on the surface (particularly as this undermined ASDIC effectiveness), but now entire 'wolf packs' would concentrate on the convoy. Escorts would be unable to cope and, as the convoy split, targets would be easier to hit.

◀Two lookouts keep watch from the deck of a U-boat, ready to give the word to submerge.

When I found a sailor on a raft, I took them on board and put them into a lifeboat to go and get safely home, and told them which course to steer and so on. I gave them food and what they wanted, so we didn't worry so much about the men. It was the ships we had to go after, and the most precious ships first of all – the tankers, to create a bottleneck, then the fuel – then that was that.

Well, when I was depth-charged, I had to go to the surface because the water was coming into the boat. I couldn't move and was lying in a large oil patch, listing to starboard and being fired at by two destroyers from portside (without success, I must say), so water spouts were coming up all around the boat – however, their 40-mm pom-poms had fuses against aircraft, so they didn't harm the boat very much. Only the paint was off, that was all, but still the aft part of my boat went under.

The boat was sinking by the stern and that part of my crew which was on the afterdeck was thrown into the water. I couldn't do anything about them. My own thinking was for the crew – I wanted to give them every chance to be picked up and get into captivity, and this I could only do by asking the one destroyer which was in the vicinity (the commander, Donald McIntyre, would later become my friend). Passing through during the night, about 4 o'clock in the morning, my morse lamp getting the signal that part of my crew was floating in the water, I asked him to pick them up. I couldn't do anything about them and afterwards he drew alongside the people in the water and put on his search lights so I could see their heads through my glasses, how they went aboard. At least half the crew got to safety.

Three were completely lost. One officer went down with the boat. He didn't get out in time – and two were lost in the water. I don't know why or how. One sick man we got safely aboard the destroyer. He had concussion and when I went aboard the destroyer which saved us, I couldn't see anybody left in the water. I was told on board that they couldn't see any more either. ▌▌

◀On the deck of an Allied cruiser, ASDIC has picked up the track of a U-boat. Crew on the deck start a barrage of depth-charges on the location indicated.

▲The gunners of a British destroyer go into action at full speed, manning the 4-inch after gun.

John Hughes was a subaltern in the Marines, serving aboard HMS York, *then with the 5th Cruiser Squadron of the Mediterranean Fleet. Regular duties of carrying out coastal bombardment and escorting convoys were uneventful until the night of 25/26 March, when he finally anchored at Suda Bay.*

MERCHANT RAIDERS

To supplement the activities of U-boats and surface warships, the Germans also deployed 10 armed merchant raiders. Fitted with guns, torpedoes and mines, their task was to loiter around the oceans, disguised as innocent vessels, ready to pick off unescorted merchantmen. In the early years of the war, they enjoyed some success.

One of the most effective was the *Atlantis*. Leaving Germany on 31 March 1940, disguised as a Russian ship, she sank a number of merchantmen. After a spell in the Atlantic in April 1941, she entered the Indian Ocean, crossed the Pacific and was heading home when she was sunk by the British cruiser, *Devonshire*. In a 20-month voyage, *Atlantis* had sunk or captured over 145,000 tons of shipping.

▶ **A British freighter falls prey to the ruthless tactics of Germany's Atlantic raiders.**

❝ I occupied a twin-bunk cabin right aft over the starboard screws. The two scuttles had been blanked off and sleeping at sea was quite an achievement, as I was competing against the vibration and the noise of the propellers and rudder.

Fortunately I did not have the second bunk occupied, and my only companion was a large black rat of whom I became quite fond. He used to sit on the wash stand and clean his whiskers, and carry on a quite intelligent conversation in squeaks.

As we were in the operational area and not back at base, I put on my sea-going sleeping rig, which consisted of a pair of trousers, an open-neck shirt, an inflatable rubber life-belt and a waterproof torch fastened around my waist with a lanyard. On my feet I had socks and a pair of gym shoes.

Somewhere around 2 am, nature called, and I padded up to the heads and looked out at the calm, quiet Mediterranean night. After a breath of air I went back to bed, and at 0430, the corporal of the gangway, complete with scarlet cap, knocked on my door and I remember him saying, 'Morning call, sir,' and a second later I was airborne, hitting the deckhead, but still very fortunately completely relaxed, and as a result, landed without injury.

The lights went out, but very slowly, leaving me time to get my torch switched on.

We had obviously been hit by some form of torpedo or alternatively there was some form of internal explosion which had affected the generators. The noise of the explosion was relatively small, but the damage aft was caused by the stern 'whipping'. There was no doubt that the ship was settling with a slight list to starboard and there were a num-

ber of injured in the after-flats.

I immediately made my way forward to the second bulkhead and closed the bulkhead door. Moving back, there was one commissioned boatswain with a broken arm, whom I got into the next flat where most of the casualties were, and again closed the bulkhead door and managed to get the temporary emergency lighting going in the flat.

Mobilising the corporal, I opened the escape hatch right aft on to the quarterdeck, and with his help succeeded in moving the casualties through to the quarterdeck.

Eventually, after a quick whip around to check that there was nobody left, I got out of the escape hatch and put the clips back on the hatch on the quarterdeck.

It was at this stage that I realised that we had a rail of depth-charges, all with hydrostatic valves. Still as-

▲ **The gunners of a British destroyer go into action at full speed, manning the 4-inch after gun.**

▶ **In calm waters, a merchant convoy makes good progress under the protection of Royal Navy escort.**

▲ ▶ **Good communications equal safety. A British sailor mans an Aldiss lamp on deck, making sure the convoy stays in touch by signal.**

sisted by the corporal, I shot aft and started removing the valves, which I heaved over the side.

Shortly afterwards, the destroyer *Anthony* came alongside on our port beam. Cables were very rapidly passed across and, proceeding at slow speed, the *Anthony* succeeded in getting the ship on to a beach which was about three quarters of a mile from our anchorage.

When daylight came, my marine team managed to get themselves into some semblance of order, and I sent a party forward to the marine barracks to collect clothing, until everyone had some form of footwear and body covering. I reported to Caspar John, the commander, who by this time had the immediate situation in hand. He told me that I was to assume command of the RM detachment and I should get the marines ashore as soon as possible and report with them to the naval officer in charge at Suda Bay. 〞

🇬🇧 *Mike Willoughby had just gone on leave from his previous ship, Elfin, when the Stationmaster at Oxford met him with a telegram. He was to report to the Forth at once, then join the patrol boat P38 as navigator: he was to sail the next day, 7 November – back to the icy Atlantic.*

〝 The first part of the patrol was uneventful, but then the weather got bad. *P38* was rolling alarmingly and we made great high speed surges on the crest of each enormous wave which was followed by a sickening wallow down into the trough. Then came the next sea – the stern dropped and it came roaring up, breaking high up on the aft end of the conning tower and a smother of white foam would fill the bridge. Occasionally the upper hatch shut and had to be pulled open quickly.

Neither I nor the three lookouts could do anything but just hang on and keep our fingers crossed, hoping that one of those seas wouldn't break over the bridge while we were up there. But the inevitable did happen.

I was off watch and was woken up to the roar of sea pouring down the hatch. I leapt out of my bunk into two feet of water. In the control room a green column of water was coming from the lower lid like a giant hose, and the voice pipe was hosing straight at the ERA's panel. Because of the wild rolling, it was like a maelstrom in the control room, with everyone hanging on like grim death. Then it stopped as though a giant valve had shut it off but not the main engines – they went on for another two or three minutes.

The vacuum, now considerable, was being reduced by air from the still open voice pipe and the shriek from it drowned all speech, but slowly the banshee noise died away and the barometer pointer stopped.

Meanwhile, the boat, now broadside to the seas and with an enormous volume of free surface water inside, would roll to about 40° and then stay there. I think most of us thought she was going to go over but she didn't. Finally the upper lid was opened, the water pumped out and we were off at full power.

Then it happened again – but this

time it was even worse, because *P38* literally lay on her side for half a minute or so, and even more water came than the previous time.

Finally, when the hatch was opened, there was a shout, 'Navigator on the bridge.' Hemmingway had the Aldiss on and was searching the sea. He just said, 'Christopher's gone. Get the other Aldiss and search on the starboard side.'

Pidgeon and I were four on and four off until I got ill, and finally Hemmingway took my temperature, which was well over a hundred, and he confined me to my bunk.

In Dolphin, the MO sent me straight to Haslar, where I fully recovered, but not before a surgeon had whipped out my tonsils, which restricted my eating and speech for a few weeks, and caused me to miss *P38* when she sailed, only to be lost soon after with all crew. 〞

JUNE

1 17,000 Allied troops are safely evacuated from Crete
British enter Baghdad; Regent reinstated

20 Manchester suffers heavy air raids
Greek government-in-exile formed in Egypt
Vichy publishes anti-semitic legislation based on German laws, Jews banned from public office

2 3 Ruhr industrial area bombed by RAF

4 Big air raid on Alexandria, 100 killed

7 8 First of five night raids on Brest by RAF as *Prinz Eugen* shelters there

8 Empire and Free French forces invade Syria and Lebanon with air and naval support; Allies offer Syria independence; Vichy protests

9 British advance 40 miles into southern Syria and Lebanon; Tyre occupied

10 Allied advance breaks through Vichy opposition in Syria

11 12 RAF raids Ruhr, Rhineland and German ports in first of 20 consecutive night raids

13 Russian news agency *Tass* denies German threat on borders; calls rumours 'absurd and obviously sheer hostile propaganda'
Russo-Japanese trade agreement announced in Tokyo

14 President Roosevelt orders all Italian and German assets in the US to be frozen

15 Operation Battleaxe begins in N. Africa to relieve Australian-held Tobruk

OPERATION REDBEARD

Named as it was after a notorious teutonic crusher of the Slav peoples, Hitler's Operation Barbarossa is calculated to bring Russia to her knees – before winter sets in.

H itler's decision to attack the Soviet Union was a turning-point in the war, not just in terms of its geographical spread but also because it introduced a depth of ideological conflict that could only be settled by total victory for one side or the other. Operation Barbarossa, elaborately planned, was designed to achieve that victory for the Germans in a matter of months.

But Hitler's invasion of the Balkans in April/May 1941 undoubtedly delayed Barbarossa and, with Leningrad, Moscow and the Ukraine as their objectives, German aims were ambitious. Despite stunning panzer advances and the destruction of huge numbers of Soviet units, Stalin used space to gain time, knowing that, as in the past, 'General Winter' would save the Russian people. It worked: the German advance stalled. Leningrad was besieged and the Ukraine was in Nazi hands, but Moscow was still tantalisingly out of reach. The Soviets would survive.

Lieutenant Ekkehard Maurer was with the German 32nd Infantry Division. Along with the rest of the German Army, he was convinced by the intelligence reports that the Russians were ill-equipped and unprepared. On 22 June, they advanced with confidence over the Russian borders unaware of the winter perils.

" Well, being as young as we were at the time, I think we had a lot of confidence in ourselves, as any young man would have. The second point – we hadn't lost a battle, so we were used to being victorious. We saw a tremendous concentration of German armed forces, and also got intelligence reports which seemed to prove that the Russian Army was not of a very high standard. We had some contacts with the Russians in 1939, when they advanced in Poland, and we met halfway. Our impression at the time of the Russian military as a whole was not very favourable. They were poorly clad, they were not very well equipped – they were hardly motorised until then.

All this led to some measure of confidence. On the other hand, I think we were quite conscious of the fact, even we young ones, that no army had ever conquered Russia permanently – that there was no final, eventual and lasting victory of an intruder into Russia.

We didn't admit it to ourselves, but there was this awkward and uneasy feeling that we may win battles in Russia – but we may not win the war. This, of course, is a personal opinion, which must not necessarily be representative of what the majority of German soldiers really thought at the time.

On the morning of June 22 1941, my battalion commander and myself (I was his adjutant at the time) were in our foxholes, very close to the barbed wire. Just before the artillery barrage began, he whispered over to me something like, 'Don't ever forget June 22 1941, at 3.15 in the morning,' then he paused for a moment and said, 'Well, I don't think I have to tell you not to forget it anyway! At this very moment, the worst decline – the worst disaster – of German history in many centuries, is going to begin.'

It was a beautiful summer with no problems, but right after an attack across the River Dnieper on, I think, October 1, we ran into very severe difficulties. It started snowing and becoming cold around October 10th and then we knew immediately that we were totally unprepared and unequipped for what was lying ahead of us. You might say it was a mistake to start this attack, and you could also say that, with regard to the human beings involved, it was a crime.

I felt terribly angry. We had no gloves, no winter shoes – we had no equipment whatsoever to fight or withstand the cold. We lost considerable amounts of heavy and light equipment, then, due to the cold, we lost a lot of people who got frostbite. We had not even the most primitive things to fight it.

We were cutting strips off our overcoats to wrap around our hands instead of wearing gloves, for example. As it became colder towards the end of November and early December, most of our artillery had become completely unusable. Guns didn't fire any more, even our wireless equipment didn't work properly any more because the batteries were frozen hard. So there was no way of communicating, even between the advancing lines and artillery batteries in the background.

We could hardly take care of our own wounded, not to mention dealing with the enemy. We were afraid to become wounded and become the prey of the very bad winter climate, as much as the prey of the enemy. We had seen enough of the enemy to know that in cases like that, prisoners were hardly ever taken, so a good many people, when it came to a decisive moment, opted not to stick his head out as far as he might have done otherwise. **"**

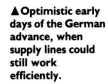

▲ Optimistic early days of the German advance, when supply lines could still work efficiently.

◄◄ German troops, trained to operate in the Alps, are faced with severe cold unimagined in their homeland – and not all are as well equipped as these.

◄ A victim of winter's victory over the invader.

✠ *Arnold Döring was a navigator with the Luftwaffe's Kampfgeschwader (Bomber Squadron) 53 (Legion Condor). On 21 June at 4 pm, the squadron leader announced a raid on Bielsk-Pilici airport, known to be full of fighter aircraft, to be carried out the next morning, as part of the huge German assault on Russia.*

❝ Hardly anybody could sleep. This was our first raid.

We were woken at 1.30 am, and a few minutes later we were running like madmen for the airfield. In the distance we could see a glare of fire, and a faint strip of light signalled the approaching day. Our group commander outlined the situation again, announced our targets and told us to 'break a leg'. He himself would be flying at the head of the squadron.

So many things went through my mind. Would we be able to take off in darkness, with fully-laden machines, from this little airfield, where we'd only been a few days?

We climbed in a wide arc to the left, getting into formation, and headed for the airport of Sielce to collect our fighter escort. However, our fighter friends were nowhere to be seen. That *is* rich, we thought.

So, after a slight change of course, we flew on stubbornly towards the target. At 4.15 am we flew over the Bug, the frontier. Quite relaxed, I made a few adjustments to our course. Then I looked out of the window. It was very hazy down below, but we could make out our targets. I was surprised that the anti-aircraft guns had not yet started up.

Then we dropped the bombs. Smoke clouds, flames, fountains of earth, mixed with all sorts of rubble, shots into the air. Blast it! Our bombs had missed the ammunition bunkers to the right. But the line of bombs continued along the length of the airfield and tore up the runway. We'd scored two hits on the runway. No fighters would be able to take off from there for some time, especially once the other bomber groups had blasted the whole of the runway.

As we climbed again, I could see that about 15 of the fighters on the runway were in flames, as well as most of the living quarters.

We were very soon engaged by Russian fighters from behind, but we managed to get back to base without losses. We'd been so successful that there was no longer any need to carry out the second raid we had planned on the airfield.

On 23.6.1941, we set off on our second raid, bombing tanks and motorised units on the road north east out of Brest-Litovsk via Koboyn up to the town of Breceza-Katuska. About ten minutes later, our group was in the air and heading for the target. We flew over Brest-Litovsk at a height of 800 m. Parts of the town were on fire. There was heavy fighting still going on around the citadel. Our fighter escort joined us, led by Mölders. There was heavy traffic on the road to Koboyn. Down below, the place was full of troops. Some of the units were travelling at the side of the road. Our advancing units were pressing on further into the country, the tanks at the head. In front of them there was a 2-km stretch of no-man's land, and then, enemy columns *en masse*. Bulky tanks of all sizes, motorised columns, carts pulled by horses, and artillery in between – all frantically making their way east. We'd reached our target. The squadron dove down and we spattered the road with machine-gun fire. We dropped the first bombs. We flew one behind the other directly over the road, some of us by the side of the road. Our bombs fell by the side of the tanks, guns, between vehicles and panic-stricken Russians running in all directions. It was total panic down there – nobody could even think of firing back. In order to leave the road intact for our own advance, we dropped the bombs only at the side of the road. The effect of the incendiary and splinter bombs was awesome. With a target like this there are no misses. Tanks were turned over or stood in flames, guns with their towing vehicles blocked the road, while between them horses, thrashing around, multiplied the panic.

▼ *Blitzkrieg* hits Russian airfields early in the operation – a Polikarpov I-16 fighter lies in ruins.

▲ Josip Broz-Tito, leader of the Communist partisans.

YUGOSLAV PARTISANS

When Axis forces overran Yugoslavia in April 1941, significant sectors of the population refused to submit, taking to the mountains and acting as guerrillas instead. Two rival groups emerged – one under the Serbian patriot Draja Mikhailovic (the Chetniks) and the other under the communist leader Jozip Broz, more commonly known as Tito.

To begin with, the Yugoslav government-in-exile supported the Chetniks, persuading the British to parachute weapons and supplies into their mountain bases near Belgrade. But Mikhailovich was actually using his forces, in collaboration with Axis officers, to root out the communists, who had bases around Uzice in Serbia. Not that this prevented Tito from harassing the invaders: by late 1941 German and Italian units in Yugoslavia were having to cope with mined roads, destroyed railway lines, ambushes and hit-and-run raids. Before long, the British, realising the extent of Mikhailovich's treachery, shifted their support to Tito and his partisans.

Professor Grigori Tokaty was a refugee White Russian, teaching at a leading military academy in Moscow when the Germans invaded. From a friend who worked in the Kremlin, he learned that there was panic at top level – Russia was not prepared to take on the German hordes.

" The Kremlin was worried and frightened. This care, although it would not be acknowledged officially, of course, was followed up by another event – a very fundamental event, hardly known at all. Namely, about one month after the war began, the government issued a secret order – well, I read it myself – which ordered the beginning of evacuation of the main strategic centres at once, and at any cost. Clearly the government did not believe that they would be able to stop the enemy, so we had the panic, the fright – the terrible feeling that we would be defeated.

I think the first panic, if it was a panic at all, was the fairly organised evacuation in July and August of 1941. It was fairly organised because the rear was still in good order, but in the second one, which started on October 16th, everything was paralysed. No transportation inside Moscow at all. The railroads were

▲ The Luftwaffe brings the blitz to Kiev, October 1941. Rubble fills the streets after an apartment block is hit by mines.

completely packed with trains of all kinds and the enemy was at the door. It was complete chaos. As to the state of Moscow itself on the 16th and especially the 17th of October, it was real panic. The few means of transportation that were available were exploited by those who were guilty – whose fault it was that we were in a state of panic. For instance, the security forces and government departments used them to move away their staff, families, archives, and so on.

People, ordinary people, lost any respect and any regard for the authorities, and the authorities themselves were probably utterly sure that Moscow would be taken by the Germans at any moment. But they were unable to do anything but just swallow lots of insults – sometimes direct attacks in the street on security forces' automobiles and things like that.

Yes, we hated Stalin. In fact, very many people began to speak openly against the party. We had reached, at that time, a stage in our history when everybody with a keen heart used to say, 'Never mind Stalin – number one is not to allow the Germans to take our town.' That was the supreme task. Nothing was allowed to interfere with that, and the secret services realised it and behaved accordingly.

There was some looting. I wouldn't say it was widespread, indeed, it's extremely interesting that the Soviet population displayed a highly disciplined attitude to the situation. There were occasions of looting, but on a limited scale.

On one occasion I remember a lady was conversing with a group of other ladies and said, 'We shall wait for the Germans. We shall stay behind and enjoy ourselves with the Germans.'

Then there were certain sections of the population which tried to begin preparing themselves to serve the new masters when they came. But this was on a very limited scale. I would point out that in those days of which I'm talking, literally hundreds of thousands of women and people with children and old men were digging defence lines outside Moscow. Now, if I state an example of a few cases, you can compare them with those hundreds of thousands of ordinary people, without even being mo-

bilised, who were there, being machine-gunned etc. Even children were defending, doing everything possible for their towns. Those were in the majority compared with the few cases where all moral fibre collapsed.

The people displayed a spontaneous unity. You see, when the country found itself face to face with the enemy, looking danger in the eye, the power of the government paled rather for a while. Something else appeared among us – a great Russian tradition, such as beat Napoleon. Then, too, there were the churches. You must remember that since the October revolution, as it were, we suppressed the churches. But then suddenly, religious feeling just appeared from the middle of nowhere, and it helped to unite people. Religion – the church – suddenly joined in the ranks of those who opposed the enemy and that was so natural that nobody even dared say a word against the church. The church became an ally in that awful situation we were in.

Once, after a dreadful night, as we were coming out of Moscow, we stopped and I walked along my train. I thought everyone must be fast asleep. Suddenly somebody was singing. They were singing a song which I had never heard, but had probably read of it before. I couldn't imagine how people knew that song. It was about the defeat of Napoleon – a very patriotic song which glorified the eternal values of Russia. And I suddenly heard it at night, in that dreadful situation. It shows that in that difficult time, the Russian people displayed something that

never dies. I don't think it will ever die – Russia is too big a place. Neither Stalin nor anyone else will ever be able to kill this spirit off for ever. They can suppress, but they cannot kill it – and we had an example of this in those days in Russia.

Stalin showed himself as the leader, the supreme leader, of the whole war effort when he made his first war speech to the public on July 1941. He addressed his countrymen, 'My dear friends and fellow countrymen . . .' very gently, very beautifully, I remember those words as if they were said only yesterday. I think he realised his mistakes by that time and tried to correct them. Then, in November of 1941 came the underground speech, and next morning, the Red Square parade; he showed the people of the USSR that, in spite of everything, his leadership was reasserted – that had a very important impact on the morale of the armed forces. **"**

▶ In some areas, notably the Ukraine, the Russians welcome the Germans as liberators – and the invaders are pleased to relax in female company. Inset: German troops make a base in a Russian church, an institution that was long outlawed by the communist regime.

SS *Konrad Mikulla, age 18, served with No 9 Company of the 3rd Battalion of SS Regiment* **Der Führer** *as the Barbarossa campaign began in June 1941. This was only his first taste of battle – as it was for most of his comrades – and by the time they neared Moscow, many of the more experienced men were already out of action.*

" A few days before the Russian campaign began, we were billeted in a big agricultural estate. Nobody knew why we were here, not even our officers. The rumours went round that we were going to be allowed to travel through European Russia on our way to the Middle East, and everybody wanted to believe this story. On the morning of 22 June, our commanding officer, *Hauptsturmführer* Hahn, set up instruction boards, indicating the different Red Army uniforms, ranks, planes as well as the arms they were using. We now realised what was in store for us. We were shown a map and told that our objectives were Smolensk, Moscow and, further on, a small town in the Ural mountains.

The next day, we moved on – we were the second wave of the advance. Any detailed account of the fighting action of an infantry regiment I leave to those who wish to glorify it. To me it was an inner struggle not to be afraid.

In the middle of October we lost our platoon officer. He felt nothing – a sharpshooter got him straight through the forehead. Our replacement was a greenhorn, straight out of the officers' school.

We now moved in on the defence line of Moscow. The place was called Jelingen, near Borodino. Late in the evening the company was taking cover in an anti-tank ditch. We all needed a rest urgently, as our group was ordered to make a reconnaissance patrol to the village lying about 2 km in front of us. We advanced as quietly as possible, hearing Russian voices, as we came under the crossfire of small arms. The platoon leader ordered me to return to the company's position and bring up an MG group to support us. I took the MG men with me and we set off back. Having entered the fighting again, I got hit in the back of the right knee. My comrades tied a rifle to my leg to stop it moving. They put me on a groundsheet and dragged me back to safety. This was the second time I had been wounded, and this time I was sent back to Germany. Three weeks later at the railway station at Brest-Litowsk, I asked for my bandages to be changed. The doctor had no anaesthetic, so he handed me a half bottle of cognac as he cleaned my wounds, which were already full of maggots. "

▼ **A group of Soviet soldiers is taken prisoner south of Kiev. The women would most probably be nurses at this stage of the war.**

▼ **Rows of crosses bear witness to the large numbers of German dead as an officer conducts a funeral service for more victims.**

Nina Yakovlevna Vishnevskaya lived near Kalinin, to the north west of Moscow when the German invasion began. In late 1941, although still at school in the ninth class, she and her contemporaries were keen to join up. So it was that she eventually became a medical orderly, a sergeant-major in a tank battalion.

" Soon the Nazi invaders came close to our town. They were only about 10 km away. So I, together with the other girls, hurried to the military registration and enlistment office. But they would not accept any but the strongest and the hardiest – and first those who were already 18. A captain was selecting girls for a tank unit. He refused to listen to me because I was 17 and wasn't tall enough.

'When an infantryman is wounded, he falls on the ground,' he

SUPPLYING BARBAROSSA

Operation Barbarossa was an immense undertaking. It involved nearly 3.5 million Axis troops, organised into three Army Groups, who were expected to seize objective up to 1,450 km (900 miles) from their start-lines in a campaign lasting less than five months. Keeping them supplied would be a nightmare.

Recognising that the assault would be spearheaded by motorised units, German planners concentrated their wheeled transport – up to 60,000 trucks, gathered from all corners of occupied Europe – behind the panzer divisions, leaving the follow-on infantry to make do with horse-drawn carts. But the roads in Western Russia were bad and a heavy truck-wastage rate had to be accepted: in such circumstances, it was essential that the railways take the strain. Unfortunately, the Russian rail gauge was different to that of the rest of Europe. Predictably, it created problems once the operation began.

▲▶ Horses, by now painfully thin from the strain of the advance, are still a major means of German transport and supply, in spite of the sophistication of the equipment on which *Blitzkrieg* depends for its speed and violence.

▼ For posterity and later study, a German cameraman records the steady erosion of Russian resistance from a Mark IV tank.

explained to me 'You can crawl to him and bandage him on the spot or drag him to shelter. But it's quite different with a tankman. If he is wounded in his tank, he must be dragged out of it through the hatch -- and you wouldn't be able to do that. Besides, when you climb up on to a tank, you're under enemy fire, with bullets and shell fragments flying all round.'

'But aren't I as good a member of the *Komsomol* as the others?' I asked, nearly crying.

'Of course you are – but you're short.'

He accepted my schoolmates, but I was to stay behind. I went to see the other girls off and they took pity on me and hid me in the lorry under a tarpaulin.

We rode up to the headquarters and the captain gave the command to fall in. We all lined up – I was last. Also, all the other girls had luggage – I had none. The chief-of-staff came out and the captain reported to him. 'Comrade Lieutenant-Colonel, 12 girls have arrived to serve under your command.' The chief-of-staff looked at us and said, 'Not 12 – 13.' The captain turned and looked at us and immediately came up to me. 'Why are you here?' 'I've come to fight, Comrade Captain!' 'Come nearer!'

My mother's pullover wrapped around my head, I walked up to them, handed them my certificate from the medical orderly's training school and said, 'I'm strong. I've worked as a nurse. I was a blood-donor. Please . . .'

They looked at all my documents and the lieutenant-colonel said, 'Send her back home by the first passing vehicle.'

Until such a vehicle came, I was temporarily attached to the medical platoon and was given the task of making gauze swabs. When I saw a car approaching the headquarters, I immediately stole into the wood and stayed there an hour or two until the car drove off.

It continued like that for three days, until our battalion went into battle – the 1st Tank Battalion of the 32nd Tank Brigade. Everyone set off for the battle and I was left behind to prepare the dug-outs for the wounded. It wasn't half an hour before the first wounded began to arrive – and dead men too. One of our girls was also killed in that battle.

They had forgotten about me, of course – they had already got accustomed to me.

What was I to do next? I had to be dressed in military uniform. We had all been given kit bags for our belongings. The bags were brand new, so I cut off the straps, ripped the bottom open and put it on. It looked like a uniform skirt. I found a tunic that wasn't torn too badly, put it on, fastened it with a belt and decided to show off before the other girls. Hardly had I finished my demostration, when our sergeant-major walked into our dug-out, followed by our unit commander. The lieutenant-colonel walked in and the sergeant-major addressed him.

'Permission to speak, Comrade Lieutenant-Colonel? The girls have created a problem. I've issued them kit bags to put their things in, but instead they've got into them themselves!' The commander recognised me and said, 'So it's you, Miss Stowaway! Well, Sergeant, you must fit out the girls.'

No one remembered about the car to take me home. We were all given issue clothing. The ground was half earth, half metal and lots of loose stones, so very soon we were again wearing rags, because we did not sit in tanks, but had to crawl on the ground. Tanks often caught fire and the tankmen, if they remained alive, were all covered in burns. We also got burns because, to get hold of the burning men, we had to rush right into the flames. It's very difficult to drag a man, especially a turret gunner, out from the hatch.

Soon, of course, when I had seen burnt overalls, burnt hands and burnt faces, I understood what war was. When tankmen jumped out of their burning machines, they were all ablaze. Besides, they often broke their arms or legs. They were serious cases. They would lie and beg us, 'If I die, please write to my mother or wife . . .' and we had already experienced something more terrible than fear. **"**

BOLT FROM THE BLUE

◄ The *USS Arizona*, blasted by bombs and belching smoke, settles down into a watery grave.

In the early hours of 7 December, the Japanese Navy launches a colossal air strike against Pearl Harbor, base of the US Pacific Fleet. America wakes to find itself at war.

C onflict between Japan and the USA was, in retrospect, inevitable. Throughout the 1930s, Japanese expansionism had developed, first in Manchuria in 1931-32, then in China after 1937: but it was the incursion into Indochina in July 1941 that tipped the scales. President Roosevelt, determined to curb their policies, imposed escalating sanctions on the Japanese, which antagonised and alienated them. No-one should have been surprised when the result was war.

Yet the Japanese did achieve total surprise on 7 December 1941, when their naval aircraft roared out of the sky over Pearl Harbor to hammer the US Pacific Fleet. The reason for this was undoubtedly American complacency - the notion that Japan was still a minor, undeveloped country, incapable of mounting attacks so far from home. Consequently, the initial American reaction was one of disbelief. It soon changed to anger.

Captain Mitsuo Fuchida was commander of the Pearl Harbor assault force, comprising 363 aircraft, and in direct command of the Akagi carriers air corps. Flying a Nakajima B5N 'Kate' bomber, his own contribution to the carnage included damaging the USS Maryland.

We should be nearing our objective. I strained hard to make out the shape of the islands through gaps in the cloud ahead. They were breaking up now – you could catch an occasional glimpse of the sea through these gaps in the cloud cover, then everything closed up again. Suddenly, just below my plane, a long continuous white line appeared: the northern coastline of Oahu Island. I changed course at once to starboard, guiding the entire force towards the west coast. The sky above Pearl Harbor was clear. Soon, across the broadening plain in the centre of the island, Pearl Harbor – at last! – came in sight. As we looked down, the morning mist hung over a strip of land. It looked peaceful scene, with wipsy trails from the cooking of breakfast lying across it.

I took up my binoculars, and gazed down. I could see eight battleships: *Nevada, Arizona, Tennessee, West Virgina, Maryland, Oklahoma, California, Pennsylvania.*

But however hard I looked, I could see nothing of the aircraft carriers. 'They're not there,' I muttered, disappointed. We knew already, from intelligence received the day before, that the carrier force had left port, but we still had the lingering hope that they would be back – we hoped and prayed for that stroke of luck.

At any rate the battleships were there, we were glad. I glanced at my watch. Just 3.19 am [Tokyo time]. I turned round to my wireless operator in the seat behind, and gave the order: 'Make TO!' He had been waiting for that moment and began tapping out the message to all formations: 'TO . . . TO . . TO . . .' This repeated signal was the abbreviated message TORA! TORA! TORA! [TIGER! TIGER! TIGER! – ALL UNITS ATTACK].

The first bomb dropped was on Wheeler airfield from a dive-bomber at 3.25 am. Leading the 25 dive-bombers in the attack on Wheeler Field was Lieutenant Akira Sakamoto. Fighters could be seen getting ready for take-off from Wheeler Field, all drawn up in orderly fashion on the aprons in front of the hangars. Sakamoto's planes spotted them, went into a dive and attacked in sequence, taking care not

▼ A huge pall of smoke billows from the airstrips of Ford Island. The Japanese destroyed 188 US aircraft in the raid, most of them on the ground.

◄ Scanning the skies – but too late. In the aftermath of the raid, men keep watch at a bombed-out airstrip on Ford Island. The engine cowling from a destroyed aircraft now forms part of their gunpit.

◄ Fireboats hose down the blazing wreck of the USS *West Virginia*, which had been hit repeatedly by torpedoes. Amazingly, she and two other badly damaged battleships, the *California* and *Nevada*, were later salvaged.

▼ ► Up with the sun: at dawn on the 7th, Japanese carrier crew cheer the aircraft bound for sleeping Pearl Harbor.

to screen the objectives of later aircraft by the smoke and flames from their bombs. A few minutes after the onset of the attack, Sakamoto had completely eliminated the possibility of any counter-attack by the most effective US fighter force in one clean sweep.

At the same time, 26 dive-bombers split into two at Wheeler Field and headed for Ford and Hickam [airfields]. Soon the smoke from their bombing rose up from both. Hickam and Ford were close to where the battleships rode at anchor in Pearl Harbor, and we were afraid that smoke from this bombing attack might interfere with the torpedoing of the battleships by obscuring them. So, Lieutenant-Commander Murata [leading the torpedo bombers] speeded up his attack.

He launched at 3.37 am, against the *West Virginia*. The torpedo smacked into the ship and a white column of water rose high into the air. Then there were two – then three – then four . . .

I watched these actions, keeping on course for my own high-level bombers. Our objective was the group of battleships which were situated on the east side of Ford Island. I sent the pathfinder in first, moving my command aircraft into second position.

We came into the bombing run – in the face of intense ack-ack fire. Some proximity shells burst just below us . . . No damage. But No.3's bombing release was cut, so he would have problems. In a five-aircraft formation, we [now] had four bombs.

The pathfinder dropped his bomb. I tugged promptly at my release, and watched the bomb's trajectory through the lower window. Four bombs nosed earthward. On the water, ahead, two battleships loomed up, one alongside the other. I looked at them, held my breath – they've been hit, haven't they? The bombs grew smaller and smaller and vanished from sight. From the port side battleship, two plumes of smoke rose up. Without thinking, 'Two bombs on target,' I yelled.

A deck-piercing bomb had a delay mechanism of half a second so that it should explode after it had broken through the deck armour, and penetrate into the ship. So the moment of impact was nothing special. Then two big plumes of water rose up in the air beside the battleship. The battleship *Maryland* had been squarely hit.

After finishing their job the bombers flew back to their carrier. I had to assemble the fighters for the next phase of the battle, so I stayed behind [over the harbour]. I observed the overall situation and calculated the results of the attack. The place was an inferno. **"**

SPIES IN HAWAII

The Japanese prepared for war some time before Pearl Harbor. In the 1930s agents were sent to the USA and native Americans were recruited to help: their primary mission was to spy on US naval bases along the Pacific coast and in Hawaii. In spring 1941 Takeo Yoshikawa, a retired naval officer, was assigned to the Japanese embassy in Honolulu. Using the cover-name Ito Morimura, he was in fact the Japanese Navy's chief agent, dedicated to discovering all he could about US defences around Pearl Harbor. Dressing up as a Filipino labourer or acting as a Japanese playboy, Yoshikawa built up a comprehensive picture. Only days before the Pearl Harbor attack, he hired a private plane from which to take photographs of Wheeler and Hickam airfields.

▶ The results of Yoshikawa's spying: a devasted airfield on Ford Island.

Lieutenant Graham C Bonnell, of the US Navy's Corps, was stationed aboard the USS San Francisco, which in December was undergoing overhaul in Pearl Harbor's Navy Yard. When the Japanese attacked, his ship was no more than a hulk: luckily for Bonnell, this may have made it an unattractive target.

❝ I awoke around 7.30 and lay in my bunk in a period of semi-consciousness as I often did when I first awoke in the morning. A few minutes later I heard the screaming dive of an airplane. I looked out of Ford Island, and saw a plane diving on one of the hangars. I saw the red balls on it clearly, but their significance did not register. I laid back in my bunk, assumed it was practice and thought, 'Navy bombers are the best in the world.' Then there was a loud explosion and I jumped out of my bunk again in time to see one on the hangars on Ford Island go up in smoke.

The general alarm on the ship sounded. My assigned battle-station was the communications room in the superstructure, and I got dressed hurriedly and made for [it]. Since we were stripped down, we could not engage the enemy in any way, nor could we get underway . . . The gun crews aboard were organised, sent to other ships in the harbour to help engage the enemy, and the boat crews were organised to help remove the wounded and trapped personnel from the ships being attacked . . .

I did not feel any fear. No-one seemed to show any. I could see the gun crews on the other ships. Every time a Japanese plane was shot down the men slapped one another on the back, and shouted congratulations. Being up on the superstructure and charged with getting the incoming information to the personnel aboard the dockside, I had a good chance to view what was taking place in the harbour. It was like a circus of horrors. There was something going on at each different point. The *Oklahoma,* a 33,000-ton ship, was hit. I saw it tilt, and then the *Nevada* attempted to get out of the harbour and was attacked by a dive bomber. By the time I looked back, the *Oklahoma* had capsized.

Time passed quickly. When I looked at my watch it was four o'clock in the afternoon. Rumours of all kinds were constantly flooding the harbour area. One was that the Japs were landing on various points of Oahu. Everyone became on edge then. ❞

William W Outerbridge was the captain of the destroyer USS Ward, whose task was to patrol the entrance to Pearl Harbor. On the morning of the 7th, just hours before the air attack, a Japanese submarine was spotted there. The Ward sank it, earning Captain Outerbridge the Navy Cross.

❝ We went to sea on the morning of the 6 December. We were prepared to open fire, we were prepared to drop depth-charges, we were prepared for any eventuality within the ship's capabilities. Everything went well. The harbour was a beautiful sight from the sea, and drifting across the buoys listening for submarines seemed a comparatively easy task.

On the morning of the 7th at about 0358 the minesweepers which had come out at two o'clock in the morning were on station sweeping the channel with their minesweeping gear. At 0358 a flashing light signal was received from the *Condor.* This said in effect, 'We have sighted a suspicious object which looks like a submarine. It appears to be standing to the westward of our present position.' The search revealed nothing. We did not locate the submarine. Therefore, I had the ship secured from general quarters, and told the Executive Officer, Lieutenant HT Doughty, to let the boys sleep in next morning.

I turned in, but about 6.30 in the morning Lieutenant O W Goepner, the Gunnery officer, awakened me .

◀ One of the 29 Japanese aircraft shot down – a Mitsubishi 'Zero'.

▼ The crew of the USS *California* swarm over her sides, after they have finally been ordered to abandon ship. During the bombing, desperate crewmen wielding kitchen knives had tried to rip away shade-giving canvas awnings, rigged for a church service, to free the after guns for action. The cloud of smoke at the rear marks the remains of another carrier.

. . He was rather abrupt. 'Captain, come on the bridge' – I scolded him for talking to the captain like that, but I did go to the bridge as fast as I could. We spotted what looked like a buoy, but it was moving. I looked at it and said 'Goepner, I believe that is a submarine. Go to general quarters and I told him that if it was a submarine we would attack.

So he went to his battle station, and had all the guns loaded. We had all the depth charges on 'ready'. . . We bore down on the object, all that we could make on two boilers which was a little bit better than 20 knots. As we bore down on it, I decided not to ram - I didn't know how big it was, I didn't know what it was, and I was afraid that if we hit it we would tear the bottom out of our ship. I decided to shoot and drop depth-charges on it.

We opened fire when within about

▲ US soldiers measure an unexploded Japanese bomb – providing US intelligence with too-late information.

75 yards of the sub. Gun one fired first, and missed, gun three fired next. The shell from gun three struck the submarine at the waterline, which was at the base of the conning tower where the conning tower joins the hull of the submarine. There was a light feather of water when the shell hit, and it appeared to us to have successfully penetrated the target. Several observers on board ship said that they saw a hole in the submarine.

We passed across the submarine's course so close that the men on the fantail and on gun four thought we were going to ram . . . In crossing ahead we dropped four depth-charges [which] exploded at the depth at which they were set to explode and the submarine then appeared to sink.

After we had completed the attack we noticed a sampan in the restricted area. This was a white fishing vessel, operated by the Japanese. We turned to the sampan and started after it. As we closed on the sampan, which was headed for Barber's Point, it hove to.

We went alongside and a Jap came out waving for the Coast Guard, and one of their ships came out of the harbour and escorted the sampan back to safety away from the restricted area.

We returned to our station, and picked up another sound contact which we bombed and reported. Executive Officer Doughty was standing on the bridge and we were considering securing from general quarters. It was then about 0750. Then we heard explosions, and Doughty said to me they were over on the beach. I said 'Well, that's probably that super highway that's being built between Pearl Harbor and Honolulu, they are probably blasting early this morning.' Then Doughty said, 'No, it's not. Look over there. There are some planes coming straight down. It appears to me that they're bombing the place.' And I said, 'My gosh, they certainly are.' And that moment was our first indication of the attack on **"** Pearl Harbor.

THE RISING SUN

Japanese imperial ambitions embrace vast areas of the Pacific and Far East. Following Pearl Harbor, their armies make a series of Blitzkrieg-like strikes which bring them hundreds of miles of territory.

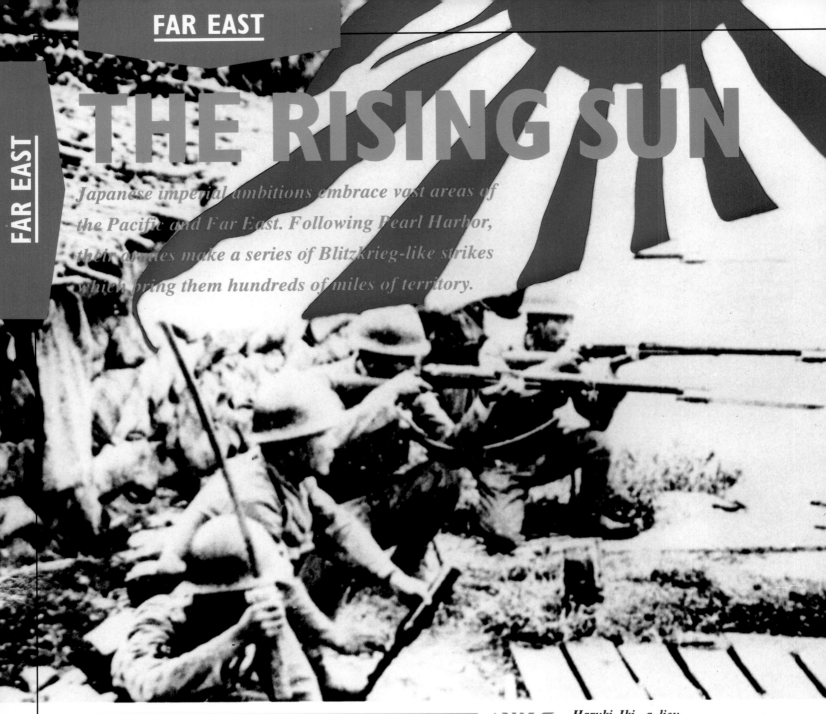

P earl Harbor was only the first (albeit dramatic) move in Japan's strategy of attack in late 1941. Japanese air and amphibious forces carried out concerted attacks in Malaya, the Philippines and various Pacific islands, designed to exploit Allied confusion. They were the first in a series of sweeping Japanese victories that were not to be stopped until mid-1942. In both Malaya and the Philippines, Japanese air raids took place at about the same time as the Pearl Harbor assault. Neither country was expecting attack, with the result that British complacency delayed a co-ordinated response. Not until Japanese aircraft had destroyed the battleship *Prince of Wales* and battlecruiser *Repulse* off the Malayan coast on 10 December did a realisation of the disaster in store begin to dawn. By the end of the month Japanese troops were well established in Malaya and the Philippines, while Guam, Wake Island and Hong Kong had been lost.

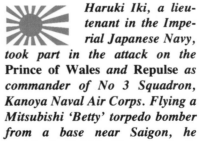 *Haruki Iki, a lieutenant in the Imperial Japanese Navy, took part in the attack on the* **Prince of Wales** *and* **Repulse** *as commander of No 3 Squadron, Kanoya Naval Air Corps. Flying a Mitsubishi 'Betty' torpedo bomber from a base near Saigon, he caught the British ships completely by surprise.*

❝ That day [10 December], after the reconnaissance planes had left at 6.25 am, the order to take off came to all assault units, and the 26 aircraft of our Kanoya Air Corps flew off to our objective, on the basis of intelligence that the enemy was sailing south and making for Singapore. We flew south for more than

▲ The Rising Sun of Japan billows above a group of heavily armed Japanese infantrymen in a posed photo, taken two years before the war broke out. Their years of preparation gave the Japanese an advantage of great power mixed with surprise when they finally launched their attack.

► Rallying to the defence of Britain's colonies, the stalwart Tommy, although kitted out for a tropical war, is largely untrained to face the jungle.

▼As time ticks away before the anticipated Japanese attack, troops shipped in to defend Singapore wait on board their transport for their ferry ashore.

650 sea miles without spotting the enemy, but on the return journey we had a signal from a reconnaissance plane, so we flew in that direction. The initial sighting was made at 11.45 am, and all units set off to seek out the ships and one by one arrived in the area.

When we finally reached the spot, we came suddenly out of the clouds and saw three destroyers ahead of us, then the *Prince of Wales,* then the *Repulse.* We estimated they were making 18 to 20 knots. Our plan as we came in was for No 1 Squadron to take *Prince of Wales,* No 2 the *Repulse* and for No 3 – mine – to take whichever remained undamaged. I tried to lose height fast. The *Prince of Wales* was heading south . . . We flew towards her, and at about 4,000 metres, the leading aircraft of No 1

Squadron made a torpedo attack and, without being hit by any of the ack-ack fire, struck the *Prince of Wales* on her starboard side, and a column of water suddenly shot into the air. Then I saw another torpedo hit her.

That's it, I thought, so I turned my attention to the *Repulse*; with nine of our squadron's aircraft we approached her on the starboard side, and she tried turning to avoid us but I think her rudder had been damaged by No 2 Squadron's torpedo attack . . . so all she seemed capable of was turning to starboard. The best thing was to launch torpedoes from around 1,000 metres at an angle of 30 to 40 degrees to the bow, so I reduced speed. I had a good launching point and released my torpedo – straightaway her rud-

der turned to port as she tried to take evasive action, but I turned too, and as an aircraft has a greater turning power, I flew right over her . . . and could see crew members falling down on the deck. I was so close I could see their faces, and they kept on firing until the very last moment. At this time, my observer shouted, 'Commander! We've hit her!'

At that moment the aircraft following me [hit by ack-ack] fell like a fireball in front of the ship's bow . . . then a second aircraft went the same way. I waited for the wing plane, at about 1,000 metres, out of range of the ack-ack fire, and watched the *Repulse* begin to sink, stern first. Then I let go of the control column and shouted for joy, 'She's going down! She's going down! We've sunk her!' We always carried wine in our rations and we toasted our victory.

About a week after the battle I flew back over the site dropped wreaths of flowers on to where the ships were plainly visible, lying peacefully under the waves – to express our condolence to the spirits of the dead. "

 Hugh O'Neill was a gunner with the 137th Field Regiment attached to the 11th Indian Division. He and his battery arrived in Malaya quite unprepared for jungle warfare. From the first, the 11th Indian Division was forced to fight a series of delaying actions, and in January 1942 were defeated at the Slim River.

▲ **The Japanese drive reaches Kuala Lumpur, the Malayan capital, deserted by the Allies in their headlong retreat south.**

" We sailed to Singapore on a ship called the *Dominion Monarch* in late September 1941. As soon as we had disembarked, they took us straight from the dock to a train station, and from there we went to Kuala Lumpur, then to Jitra, which was right on the border with Thailand. We waited about a bit there – they were waiting for the Japs to come to us.

Right from the start, we were in trouble the whole way. This was jungle warfare, and we weren't equipped for it. There was just a main road which we were on, and lots of rubber trees, which you

EMPIRE BUILDING

Only about a quarter of Japan is suitable for agriculture and the country as a whole lacks mineral deposits sufficient for industrial development. This helps to explain the pressures within Japan for expansion abroad before World War II, for if the country was ever to emerge as a major power, it needed raw materials. By 1941, the Japanese expansionism was a long-established policy. But once the USA began to react by cutting off vital imports, Japanese leaders faced a dilemma: if they submitted to US pressure, they would be humiliated; if they stood firm, war was unavoidable. The only way out seemed to be a swift attack to seize the resources of the western Pacific and Far East, creating a 'Greater East Asia Co-prosperity Sphere' to provide Japan with raw materials.

▶ **Japanese premier, Tojo (centre front with medals), with the Japanese War Cabinet.**

couldn't get through with the equipment. We had quads, which are gun-towing vehicles, and, of course, we were stuck with them.

We used our guns, which did quite a bit of damage. I was in charge of a 25-pounder. When we met the Japs, we would stop them so they couldn't advance. What they then used to do was to come round the back. They were prepared for it, of course. They used bicycles a lot, to dodge through the trees. The only thing you could do then was come back into your own lines, where you would fire at them. After a while, they would filter around us again. The trouble was, of course, that they just kept dodging. They would disappear. You couldn't see them, but you used to hear them, shooting at us all the time. They had longer-barrelled rifles than we had, but they were of a smaller calibre, so one balanced out the other.

The thing that a lot of people found difficult were the air attacks. They used to go in for dive-bombing – they weren't Stukas, but they were a copy. Their strategy was to dive down and spread panic amongst the troops – it was a very frightening thing. **"**

◉ *John Idwal Roberts (later MC) was coxswain aboard motor launch 328 in RAF's Marine Craft section based in Singapore in December 1941. Before the island fell in February 1942. Roberts and his little craft came face to face with a well-armed Japanese barge on a Sumatran river.*

" The Jap barge was a leader of the main fleet. I thought he was a Dutchman. He had been camou-

▲ A Gurkha wades through a stream on exercises. These troops were much respected for their courage and endurance.

▶ Men of the Manchester Regiment build what will prove entirely futile beach defences on Singapore Island.

NOVEMBER

9 Germans capture Yalta in Crimea

13 U-81 hits *Ark Royal* off Gibraltar; it sinks the next day

18 Operation Crusader, the British offensive in Libya opens

25 Rommel breaks out in Libya and attacks Eighth Army in the rear

DECEMBER

2 Germans five miles from the Kremlin

7 Japanese attack Pearl Harbor
 Malaya, Shanghai, Manila, Thailand and Hong Kong also attacked; Singapore is bombed

8 Japanese land in Thailand and North East Malaya
 Thailand surrenders

10 Siege of Tobruk finally ended
 British battleship *Prince of Wales* and battlecruiser *Repulse* sunk by Japanese off the coast of Malaya

11 Italy and Germany declare war on US; US declares war on both in return

17 Japanese are only 10 miles from Penang
 After strong resistance Rommel again retreats from Gazala area in Libya

19 Japanese land in Hong Kong, British evacuate Penang
 British take back Derna from Rommel

22 Japanese launch main invasion of Philippines
 32,000 Jews killed in Lithuania by Germans

25 Hong Kong surrenders after 17-day siege; British retake Benghazi
 Over 3,000 starve to death in Leningrad

flaged and there were flags waving on it so I got up on the coach roof and started answering it and our boat was steaming up. 'Christ, they're Japs!' I couldn't read the signals – and I was pretty good on semaphore – and obviously he couldn't read mine. I yelled to the lads, 'Duck, they're Japs, open her up,' – because I had been slowing her up as we got close to it.

As I say, we closed with them. We had noticed they had on the bow something like a three-pounder gun, much too big for our little Tommy gun, so all we could hope was that our speed could get us out of it — and it was a narrow river. The Japanese began firing this big gun at us, and the fourth shell hit us right amid ships, went right through the boat and killed two people.

There were a lot of machine-gun bullets – I was firing in the general direction of the Japs with the Lee-Enfield rifle, and Doc Markham, I remember, jumped up with his Tommy gun as we passed it – I thought 'You idiot! You're a big target there for them!', but he emptied a pan of bullets into the barge. The boat had been hit and there was no chance of it surviving, although she was still going. Then I went to the wheelhouse – it had been blasted.

An officer was dead and there was another officer – he wasn't touched. I don't know how he got away with it. My water bottle was hanging there – it was peppered with shrapnel, and it had been hanging in front of someone's legs and their legs were OK. Funny how things happen like that . . . Anyway we pushed the boat on to a bank . . . it was a nice greasy, sloping bank. She landed completely out of the water up this bank, and I jumped out of her. I was in the scouts when I was a boy and it was all coming back to me. We were going to survive . . . The lads were expecting any minute that the Jap would turn and find us. But we must have hurt him, he didn't follow us, anyway. We landed there and took all the gear we could. We pushed the boat – the bottom was really ripped. The prop shaft had come off her and right through a few planks beneath her. We locked the two dead lads together with an anchor chain, and thought we would bury them with the boat. That's all we could do. Then I played Tarzan for about three weeks! **"**

[John Roberts was captured near Palembang in late March].

▲ Just outside Singapore, men of the Gordon Highlanders demonstrate anti-tank measures – sadly to little avail once the Japanese attack began.

◄▼ The Japanese have arrived in the Philippines, with all going according to plan in their strategy of expansion. In 1942 they would continue in the same vein . . .

1942
TOTAL WAR

A year when the fortunes of war swayed in the balance

The year began badly for the major Allied powers – Britain, the Soviet Union and USA – in almost every theatre. In Europe the Germans had consolidated their hold on the occupied territories and, despite Soviet counterattacks around Moscow in late 1941, were poised for further advances – in North Africa Rommel may have been in retreat, but was about to resume an offensive that would take him back to Gazala and beyond; in the Far East and Pacific, Japanese forces seemed unstoppable and elsewhere in the air and at sea, Allied fortunes were hardly high.

Yet by Christmas 1942, a light had appeared at the end of the tunnel. Montgomery's victory at the second battle of Alamein in late October/early November had coincided with Anglo-American landings in French North Africa, and Rommel was potentially trapped. On the Eastern Front, General Paulus' Sixth Army was surrounded at Stalingrad with little hope of survival, but in the Pacific, American forces had won the Battle of Midway and were fighting to regain the island of Guadalcanal. In the air, the Anglo-American bombing of Germany had begun to gather pace, and in the Atlantic, despite horrific merchant-ship losses (particularly on the 'Arctic run' to Russia), the Allies were staving off defeat. No-one expected final victory to come early, but in 1942 the possibility of such a victory – albeit much later – was becoming apparent.

AVENGING FURY

The year in the East begins disastrously for the Allies, who lose Singapore, the Philippines and the East Indies to rampant Japanese forces. But they dig in their heels, and in New Guinea and Midway, hit back hard.

During the first five months of 1942, the Allies faced catastrophe in the Far East and Pacific. Japanese attacks proved to be unstoppable. By mid-February the whole of Malaya, including the vital naval base at Singapore, had fallen, and the Americans were under seige in the Philippines. By May the Philippines had been lost, together with Borneo and the Dutch East Indies, allowing the Japanese to thrust east into New Guinea and the Solomons, threatening Australia.

But the Allies did recover. In early June the US Navy won a major carrier battle at Midway. Two months later, US Marines landed on the island of Guadalcanal in the Solomons, triggering a series of hard-fought battles on sea and land. Finally, towards the end of the year, Australian troops blunted a Japanese advance on Port Moresby in New Guinea, operating in the extremely inhospitable terrain of the Kokoda Trail. It would be a long haul to victory.

Captain Cyril Wild, a staff officer at III Corps HQ, Singapore, was present at the conference at which Allied leaders discussed the surrender to the Japanese. Ammunition was running out, and the GOC, Lieutenant-General Percival, feared the effects of a siege on the civilian population.

"When details of the surrender were being discussed, Major-General Gordon Bennett, GOC 8th Australian Division, remarked, 'How about a combined counter-attack to recapture Bukit Timah?' This remark came so late, and was by then so irrelevant, that I formed the impression at the time that it was

▲ **Guadalcanal: a US soldier aims a captured Japanese light machine gun at its former owners. US troops there had to use any weapon they could lay their hands on.**

▶ **Lt-Gen Percival, GOC Malaya, in typically thoughtful – some might say indecisive – pose after the surrender. This Japanese photograph made good anti-British propaganda.**

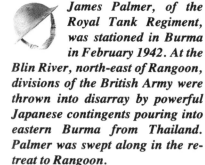

not made as a serious contribution to the discussion but as something to quote afterwards. It was received in silence and the discussion proceeded.

I returned later that afternoon to Command HQ, Fort Canning, arriving there shortly after 1600 hours. General Percival was seated at his desk and Brigadier Torrance and Brigadier Newbigging were standing beside it. I at once told Brigadier Newbigging, in the hearing of the others, that III Corps were still without definite orders regarding the time of the ceasefire and I asked that such orders should be sent to them. I received no reply whatever. I said, 'If I may express an opinion myself, it is that we should not cease fighting until after you have seen the Japanese commander at Bukit Timah.' I believe I added, and I know I thought, that even if the Japanese were annoyed when we met them at our not having ceased fire, this would be nothing in comparison with the risk of total disaster which we ran if our men disarmed themselves before the terms of any truce or capitulation were decided. Again, my remarks were received in total silence.

This was only broken when General Percival (I think it was) said, 'We ought to go,' and he and the two brigadiers walked out of the room and down to the two cars which were waiting to take us to the Japanese. I had no choice but to follow after them.

Astonishing though this may sound, it was not altogether so to me, as I had become inured during the past week to seeing General Percival's painful inability to give a decision, and, on three occasions, to make any reply whatever, when points of operational importance were referred to him. **"**

James Palmer, of the Royal Tank Regiment, was stationed in Burma in February 1942. At the Blin River, north-east of Rangoon, divisions of the British Army were thrown into disarray by powerful Japanese contingents pouring into eastern Burma from Thailand. Palmer was swept along in the retreat to Rangoon.

" In the middle of February the defence of the Blin River collapsed and the 17th Indian Division had to fall back towards the northern bridgehead at the bridge over the Sittang. We had moved our troops to the southern bank of the river near to Pegu and were expecting an airborne drop to be made by the Japs to capture the bridge from the southern end and so cut off the northern bridgehead. The position was hopeless!

Nearly all the 17th Division was cut off between the Blin and the bridgehead at the Sittang. If the bridge was captured by the Japs there was nothing to prevent them pouring into Rangoon. The decision was made to blow the bridge and hold the line south of the Sittang. This meant that nearly all the 17th Division would be abandoned between the Sittang and Blin unless the Jap encirclement of the northern bridgehead could be broken.

Then the final calamity occurred! As the 17th Division were fighting their way back to the Sittang, they were cruelly bombed and blasted by our own planes. This ended all hope of them ever getting across the bridge and breaking through the Jap encirclement. On the morning of the 23rd February there was no alternative but to blast the bridge sky high and leave the 17th stranded on the northern bank of the Sittang. Then an amazing thing happened. The Japs had no way of crossing the wide Sittang now the bridge had gone, and they broke off the engagement around the northern bridgehead and moved ten miles upriver to build a new bridge so that they could press on to Rangoon from the east. This was unbelievable and resulted in a large number of the 17th Division being able to swim across the river to the southern bank.

The situation was desperate and we knew that Rangoon could not be held, but would have to be evacuated and the remains of the army of Burma retreat northwards towards India and Assam. It was not going to be a 'tactical withdrawal', it was a full-scale retreat and we would have to live off the land.

There was no way that we could be

supplied to establish a defence line and we had to move fast. The docks and warehouses at Rangoon and all the port facilities had to be blown sky high. Nothing would have to be left so we took what supplies we could from the storage sheds.

Then we began the demolition. Everything that stood up had to be blown down. The whole of Rangoon was blazing as we moved out towards the Prome Road leading northwards towards Mandalay, passing the Swegon Pagoda, glistening in the sun.

Meanwhile the Japs had moved from the east, north of Rangoon towards Pegu, and our tanks had to move towards them to hold them away from the Prome Road, which was the only exit from Rangoon. Here we hit trouble. Around Pegu we were confronted by pockets of Japs who had infiltrated through and we came under devastating mortar and heavy machine-gun fire, but we couldn't see the little yellow men in the dense jungle growth. This was no place for tank warfare.

The jungle was a noisy place and the chirping of cricket-like creatures made a humming, buzzing in the air from morning till night. We used to lie hidden and watching when on patrol and the birds squawking and screaming were often a sign for us to be alert – something was moving and our guns had to be cocked. Sometimes, as we were crouched in the undergrowth, we would be startled by a loud cracking of fireworks, then a voice would come from the dense jungle. 'Tommy – give up. You have no chance and are surrounded. There is no point in lying there to die. Give yourselves up.'

The Japs seemed to be everywhere and were playing cat and mouse. It

▼ Survivors of the *Repulse*: Captain Tennant (left) and ship's chaplain, Canon Bezzant.

was nerve-wracking and demoralising. Planes sometimes strafed the road and dropped leaflets after the raids. The leaflets showed crude drawings of British women being raped by American soldiers and said, 'Go home and protect your loved ones.'

It was about this time that I had an accident with my foot, to add to my misery. A five-gallon drum of petrol toppled off a lorry when we were refilling a tank and crushed my foot. My infantry role did not help much and for the rest of the journey northwards I limped along. The big toe festered and my leg became swollen, but there was nothing I could do but get along as best I could. It wasn't bad when I went out in the scout car as a gunner, but during the most essential patrols I was a dead loss.

Most of us by now were covered with jungle sores caused by thorn scratches festering and bleeding. Dysentery and diarrhoea were rife and jungle fever hit everyone.

Excessive sweating and perpetual nausea drained us physically and we were becoming a sorry sight indeed. We were limping along and every mile seemed longer than the last. The damp heat of the jungle drained us even in the shade, and we all felt so tired and weary we just wanted to curl up and be let alone. Sod the yellow bastards – they wouldn't leave us alone, but followed us like a swarm of bees, stinging and taunting us. We couldn't get to grips and we knew they were letting us drag ourselves into the ground. 💬

►The Japanese outside Manila, early January 1942. By the 13th they were poised to attack US forces in the Bataan Peninsula with overwhelming ground and air superiority.

◄A Japanese tank unit in Burma, in hot pursuit of the retreating British. By the end of May British forces had been squeezed out into India.

Shiro Ishikawa was a petty officer in the aircraft carrier Shoho's *fighter unit. In May, the* Shoho *was sent with a troop convoy to take the strategically vital Allied base of Port Moresby, New Guinea. In the Coral Sea, Ishikawa watched helplessly from his aircraft as the* Shoho *was sunk by American dive-bombers.*

" At Port Moresby in East New Guinea there was an Australian air force and naval base. If we were to seize it, and make it a Japanese base, future operations in this area would go forward very advantageously. Moreover, if we could establish a defence line linking Port Moresby with Rabaul, the link between Australia and the United States would be severed.

For this reason, Imperial General Headquarters decided on a plan to seize Port Moresby after the occupation of Rabaul.

In accordance with this decision, the *Shoho,* together with *Zuikaku* and *Shokaku,* was sent off towards Port Moresby.

At the time, there were arguments between No 4 Fleet (a heavy cruiser force – of which the *Shoho* was a part) and No 5 Group (comprising the *Zuikaku* and *Shokaku*), who wished to use the three carriers as a uniform fleet. However, in No 4 Fleet, they thought it important to escort the convoy transporting the invasion force, so in the end, *Shoho* alone was sent as a direct escort to the slow transport convoy. This was one factor in the tragedy of the *Shoho* later in the Coral Sea.

On the *Shoho,* changes were made. We used 96-type carrier-borne fighters and then we were equipped with Zero fighters, but there were only six of these.

On 30 April, *Shoho* left Truk. *En route* she came up with the transport convoy carrying the Port Moresby invasion force, which had sailed from Rabaul on 4 May, and gave it an air escort. In this convoy escort, long-range Zero fighters were used. The Zeros flew off from the carrier at daybreak, and continued their anti-submarine and anti-aircraft patrols over the Port Moresby convoy, which was only making an average speed of six knots.

We pilots in our 96-type carrier-borne fighter planes acted as escort to the carrier. The direct escort watch was two hours, by two carrier-borne fighter planes and a number of fleet assault planes. So, we flew off the carrier at two-hourly intervals and circled over her, on the lookout for submarines or watching the sea ahead.

Before this, on 3 May, a landing was made on Tulagi, opposite Guadalcanal, and in support of that operation three Zeros and three fleet assault planes were despatched.

However, early in the morning of the following day, 4 May, a formation of US carrier-based planes attacked the Tulagi landing force and

MAJ-GEN BENNETT

When Singapore surrendered to the Japanese on 15 February 1942, Major-General Henry Gordon Bennett, commander of the Australian 8th Division, decided to escape. In company with two other officers, he managed to avoid the Japanese, eventually returning to Australia, where he expected to be welcomed as a combat-experienced commander who had ensured his availability for future operations. Instead, he received a decidedly frosty reception, being widely condemned for having abandoned his men.

Bennett was not given another combat command, being shunted sideways into Army Training for the rest of the war. After the war, a military court of inquiry found Bennett 'not justified in handing over his command or in leaving Singapore'. It was a controversial end to a promising career which had begun in World War I, yet to many who experienced his command in Malaya, where his inexperience at divisional level had been apparent and his relationship with British superiors poor, it was probably just as well. He had to make way for other, more tactful men to take responsibility.

inflicted great damage. As a result, it became clear that a US mobile task force had come up very close.

The fateful day, 7 May, dawned. On this day, too, from early morning, aircraft flew off for convoy protection of the aircraft-carrier.

It must have been shortly after 8 am, when suddenly the W/T (wireless telegrapher) began to tap out a message.

Normally in operations we observe wireless silence, but when I heard the W/T, I realised something out of the ordinary was happening.

I listened attentively to the dots and dashes, and got the message: 'Enemy aircraft approaching, direction . . .' The enemy was attacking – but I could not read off the number which followed, and as direction was given by means of a number, I did not know what the direction was.

It couldn't be helped, so I turned slowly, determined to discover myself the direction of the enemy attack. As I did so, I sighted them. In

▶ John S Thach, one of the US Navy's top fighter commanders. His job at Midway was to protect Devastator torpedo-bombers, such as these pictured on the USS *Enterprise*.

▲ Following action in the skies over Midway Island, a Grumman Avenger torpedo-bomber undergoes maintenance at its island base.

the sky, far off, a number of black dots were hovering. As I watched, those black dots became larger and larger. I could make out the shape of aircraft.

I saw three Zeros from the carrier flying off in great haste. Immediately afterwards, there were enemy planes everywhere, diving down at the carrier under my very eyes. The attack had begun.

As if in a dream, I turned to attack the dive-bombers. But what the Zeros could do, the first generation 96-types could not, and the enemy planes escaped. What's more, I saw a huge hole gaping open in the carrier. I altered course, and shot into the midst of the enemy aircraft, which were around me on all sides. I fired my machine guns – then all at once I was out of ammunition.

Black smoke was already rising up from the carrier, and it looked as if she were about to sink into the Coral Sea. This was the carrier we were to return to, and in a short while she was no more. I wondered how to proceed now. 🟥

Lieutenant-Commander John Smith Thach was air operations officer of the US Fast Carrier Task Force, commanding Fighter Squadron 3. During the Battle of Midway he was on USS York-town, *on which he waited with his fighter unit as part of the trap sprung against Nagumo's expected strike on 4 June.*

❝ There were 12 torpedo-planes for the attack on the Japanese carriers and our six fighters. I put two fighter planes just astern of the torpedo-planes, which were flying formation in the shape of a triangle. The two fighters were down at a lower altitude than the other four. We flew between 1,000 and 1,500 feet above the torpedo-planes. They were so slow, however, that we had to do S-turns in order to slow down and not run away from them.

We took off from the *Yorktown* by

▼ The Japanese carrier *Shoho* under US bomb and torpedo attack in the Coral Sea, 7 May. It later sank. The next day the Japanese responded by crippling the US carrier *Lexington*.

together. Nobody was going to be a lone wolf, because lone wolves don't live very long in the circumstances we were about to experience. Our primary job was, as I said, to protect the torpedo-planes and keep the enemy fighters engaged as much as we could, all the way in and all the way out.

We took off on a heading of about south-west. About that time, looking ahead, I could see ships through the breaks in the little puffy clouds. We had just begun to approach about ten miles from the outer screen of

large group that was streaming right past us and into the poor torpedo-planes.

Several Zeros came in on a head-on attack on the torpedo-planes and burned Lem Massey's plane right away. It just exploded in flames. And beautifully timed, another group came in on the side against the torpedo-planes. In the meantime, a number of Zeros were coming down in a string on our fighters. The air was just like a beehive, and I wasn't sure at that moment that anything would work. Then my 'weave' began

0900. Those on the *Hornet* and *Enterprise* started taking off a little after 0700. Before leaving, I had a last-minute briefing in which I told the people going with me and those standing by for combat air patrol, that I wanted the formation to stick together.

Then one of our planes was burning. He pulled out and I didn't see him any more. He was shot down right away. I didn't see the Zero that got him either. It didn't take me long, however, to realise that they were coming in a stream from astern. I was surprised they put so many Zeros on my six fighters – I had expected they would go for the torpedo-planes first. They must have known that we didn't have the quick acceleration to catch them, the way they were coming in at high speed in rapid succession and zipping away. But then I saw they had a second

this large force (Nagumo's Carrier Strike Force). It looked like it was spread over the ocean. A very short time after, Zero fighter came down on us – even before we got anywhere near anti-aircraft range. I figured there were 20 of them.

to work! I got a good shot at two Zeros and burned them. One of them had made a pass at my wingman, pulled out on the right and then come back. We were weaving continuously. I got a head-on shot at him and just then, Ram, the wingman, radioed, 'There's a Zero on my tail!' He didn't have to look back because the Zero wasn't directly astern. He was at about a 45° angle and beginning to follow Ram around, which gave me the head-on approach. I was really angry then – I was mad because my poor little wingman had never been in combat before. In fact, he had very little gunnery training. It was his first time flying from a carrier, and this Zero was about to chew him to pieces. I probably should have ducked under the Zero, but I lost my temper and decided to keep my fire going into him so he'd pull out. He did, and I just missed him by a few feet. I saw flames coming out of the bottom of his airplane. This was like playing chicken on the highway with two automobiles headed for each other, except we were shooting at each other as well. It was a little foolhardy, but I think when I hit him it pulled his stick back and his nose went up. The first reaction on being hit is to jerk back. I wanted him to pull out – I was going to force him to pull out. That is a foolish thing to do. I didn't try that any more. You really don't need to, because if you haven't hit by the time you get there, you can certainly afford to duck under, and then you'll get away.

The Japs kept coming in. By this time we were over the screen and more of our torpedo-planes were falling, but so were some Zeros. We thought at least we were keeping a lot of them engaged.

We could see the carriers now. They were steaming at very high speed and launching airplanes. And those planes looked like more fighters.

Now the torpedo-planes had to split in order to make an effective attack. We used to call it an anvil attack. They would break up formation and spread out in a kind of a line on each side of the target, the carrier. The reason a formation of torpedo-planes has to split is so that they can come in against a carrier

from various points around at least 180° of the compass.

We fighters thought we were doing pretty well until the torpedo-planes split. Then they were extremely vulnerable, all alone without any protection. Zeros were coming in on us, the fighters, one after the other. Sometimes they came simultaneously from above and to the side. We couldn't stay with the torpedo-planes except for the one or two which happened to be under us.

I kept counting the number of planes I knew I'd got in flames going down. I couldn't bother to wait for them to splash. But I could tell if they were flaming real good and there was something besides smoke. If you saw real red flames, why, you knew a plane had had it.

Then it seemed that the attacks began to slacken. I didn't know whether they were spreading out and working more on the unprotected torpedo-planes – but the torpedo-planes continued on. I saw three or four of them get in and make an attack. I believe that at least one torpedo hit was made.

Then I saw a glint in the sun that looked like a beautiful silver waterfall. It was our dive-bombers coming in. I could see them very well because they came from the same direction as the Zeros. I'd never seen such superb dive-bombing. It looked to me like almost every bomb hit. Of course, there were some near misses,

but there weren't any wild ones. Explosions were occurring in the carriers. About that time, the Zeros slacked off more. We stayed around and escorted two torpedo-planes out, one after the other, and tried to get them clear. Then we went back and picked up another straggler that we saw.

I could only see three carriers. I never did see a fourth one. And one of them, probably the *Soryu* or the *Kaga*, was burning with bright pink flames and sometimes blue. I remember gauging the height of those flames by the length of the ship. The distance was about the same. It was just solid flame going skyward and there was a lot of smoke. Before I left the scene I saw three carriers burning pretty furiously."

▶▶ The Japanese aimed to destroy all US aircraft on the ground in Guadalcanal – and in this they almost succeeded.

▶ Lieutenant Ferguson (cousin of Robert, who was also on Guadalcanal) standing by the wing of his Bell P-400 *Hell's Bell.*

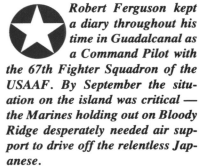

★ Robert Ferguson kept a diary throughout his time in Guadalcanal as a Command Pilot with the 67th Fighter Squadron of the USAAF. By September the situation on the island was critical — the Marines holding out on Bloody Ridge desperately needed air support to drive off the relentless Japanese.

" In the early morning darkness at the 67th's flight-line, Captain Thompson and lieutenants B E Davis and B W Brown started the engines of their P-400s and taxied slowly through the dusky darkness toward the end of the runway. At the first hint of light they were in takeoff position. The ground crew and other pilots watched as they roared down the runway and off, the dancing blue flames from their short exhaust stacks twinkling in the early-morning darkness.

They circled over the field and climbed to no more than 1,000 feet,

◀ A US light tank, supporting the Marines, rolls through jungle terrain on Guadalcanal.

was the first to receive a critical hit on his aircraft. With a punctured engine coolant radiator, he took advantage of the high speed from his strafing dive and pulled up toward the field, obtaining as much altitude as possible. He held on to a little power before losing all of his engine coolant and when he could reach the runway, he cut the engine and landed deadstick.

Lieutenant Davis continued to strafe the ridge until he was out of ammunition. The strafing by the P-400s was devastating and demoralising to the now-exhausted Japanese troops – it inflicted heavy casualties on their formations trying to marshal for continued attacks on the Marine lines.

In the face of this final turn of events, with 600 dead lying on the slope, General Kawaguchi finally gave the order to withdraw, conceding victory. "

swinging in a wide left turn to approach the ridge from the west in their first strafing pass. The entire time the planes could be seen from the work area of the 67th's flight-line and even better by the few who climbed to the top of the hangar, braving sniper fire, to watch the P-400s until they disappeared out of sight behind the treetops and the south slope of the ridge.

The target area could be seen by Thompson's flight when they passed over the field, swinging south to line up for their first pass at the south slope. On the ridge, the slopes were covered with Japanese troops, reforming for whatever action they were planning. Thompson's P-400s dropped to a little above treetop level. They came out over the treetops, taking the Japanese by surprise, dropping to about 25 or 30 feet above the heads of the troops on the slope with all guns blazing.

The concentration of fire ripped into the formation of Japanese troops as the planes flashed across the ridge. The chatter of their guns could be heard on the airfield while the men of the 67th and others on the ground cheered as the planes zoomed up for another attack. Strung out over the treetops, they dived for another pass at the ridge, knowing it would not be as easy as the first one. The Japanese officers and NCOs had quickly organised their troops for mass rifle and machine-gun return fire. The P-400s again showered devastating firepower on the slope.

In the hail of return fire from the Japanese troops, Lieutenant Brown

▶ Natives in New Guinea guide US soldiers of the 32nd Division during the victorious Allied campaign there.

serious and joking, 'I hope it will fire ONCE at least'. I took my pistol out, but I was not feeling very happy and just wiped it briefly before putting it away.

It was not that death was actually staring us in the face, but rather that we still had a few hours' or days' leeway, which made us think even more intensely about death. My life would be reaching its final showdown within three or four days.

Reflecting on my life, wondering about the meaning it may have had, I felt that I had done nothing at all – that it was completely meaningless. I seemed to have been living with concern solely for appearances and reputation, seeking praise and trying to avoid being blamed. I had neither core not content – no real self. My life of 20 or so years amounted to nothing. It might be described as empty or vacuous.

The next night we moved to the evacuation point and waited.

A launch with two or three cutters arrived at the shore. The wounded were taken aboard and they left. We waited as patiently as we could, not knowing how many warships were at sea, but knowing that at least by leaving the land we were escaping a death-trap. To us, this peninsula at the east end of New Guinea was a nightmare of a place. After waiting patiently we boarded the boats.

The pace was slow as the launch towed the cutters and we moved out over the black sea. They finally reached the *Tenryu* and I grasped a hand extended from the side of the ship and was dragged up on to the deck, where the previously evacuated were waiting, some lying and some seated. They were silently grouped in the darkness as if suddenly overtaken by exhaustion – they had the air of a defeated " force.

Lieutenant Chikanori Moji was an officer of the Japanese Special Landing Force, involved in the battle of Milne Bay on New Guinea. This was a crucial battle for the Japanese, but as the tide turned against them, some of the surviving officers met near the evacuation site towards the end of August.

" As the cutter withdrew with the wounded, we felt left alone at last, and sure that those remaining would die within the next few days, more or less. We could not imagine being able to hold out until the army came with reinforcements.

The chief medical officer noisily drew his pistol and as he wiped it with a rag, said in a tone between

FOX AT BAY

Rommel, 'the Desert Fox', and Montgomery's Desert Rats are locked in a see-saw battle – but Allied pressure at last begins to tell with victory at El Alamein and landings in Tunisia.

I n early January 1942, British forces entered El Agheila, having pursued Rommel's *Afrika Korps* across Cyrenaica. But their victory was short-lived and Rommel reached the Gazala Line by early February.

Delayed by the Free French at Bir Hacheim, Rommel nearly came unstuck, but poor British co-ordination let him break out to the east, seizing Tobruk on 21 June. It looked as if Alexandria, Cairo and the Suez Canal would fall.

The British were saved by a defensive battle on the Alamein Line in July, although this did not prevent the sacking of General Auchinleck, C-in-C Middle East, in early August. Montgomery took over Eighth Army and, after another defensive victory at Alam Halfa, he prepared for a decisive battle. This came in late October – the second battle of Alamein – when Rommel was forced to pull back. News of an Allied landing far to his rear in French North Africa (Operation Torch), made the Axis retreat inevitable.

Doctor Manfred Auberlan was a medical lance-corporal with the 2nd Mountain Infantry Company of Special Group 288. As the Germans attacked towards Tobruk on 26/27 May, fighting was heavy, but his job remained the same — bringing out the dead and wounded and burying or treating them.

"We had to bury the dead at night because it was assumed that there would be heavy air activity during daylight. As platoon medical orderly, I had to get, by fair means or foul, as much dressing material and morphine as I could lay my hands on. My main concern at the time was to ensure that no human

▲Brewing up in the desert. A Crusader III tank (right), the first British tank to be adequately armed with a 6-pounder gun to take on the German armour, inspects the damage inflicted on a German Panzer Mark IV after an encounter in the Libyan desert.

adjust dressings, give morphine and comfort the dying. I still hear the cries of those severely wounded men. Now and then they would fall silent, and I hoped that night would fall. Then we would unload the poor fellows' bodies, take one half of their identity discs, and their few personal belongings to be given to their commanding officer, and bury the corpses provisionally.

My medical vehicle showed white bands only, because the Red Cross flag was so torn, so we added some blood to colour the white, which soon turned brown in the sun.

Imagine what it is like, crawling 20 metres or more, to get to a fresh casualty, when he is still able to cry – and the shells are bursting nearby. The memory of it still robs me of sleep some nights.

On the attack of the 27th May, my tactics on our approach march were to stay within the cleared mine-lanes, within a good distance of the fighting vehicles, because British fighters would swoop down on them, strafing furiously, or those light Douglas bombers would unleash their loads, harassing us in area bombardments.

My orders were to stay close – but not too close. Our recent parties probing into enemy lines had to bring back not only the gen, but also preserved foods from the Brits. So when we got hold of a supply truck, we delighted in saving the good stuff such as canned rolled ham, orange marmalade, fruit preserves, tea, coffee etc. We had just sardines in oil, tuna fish, bacon, dry jam, cheese in tubes (we called it 'Rommel cheese') and some tinned meat called 'AM' (*alimentation militaire*), but we called it *Alter Mann* (old man), *Armer Mussolini* (poor Mussolini) or *Asinus morte* (dead donkey), and ersatz coffee from the field kitchen. Another famous army meal was dried vegetables, which we called *Draht-Verhau* (barbed-wire special). As bread we mostly had *Knackebrot* – a kind of hard bread which, when we spread our jam on it, attracted flies, which you had to chase away before eating.

At night we would look up to the sky and search for the Pole Star, to the north where Germany would be, and when we walked to the nearest radio set, we might hear *Lili Marlene* being played on the Belgrade military radio station.

On 8/9 June, while collecting casualties, I became a casualty myself. I got a bullet right through the lungs. Pulled out of action like this, you had time to wonder what would happen when the war was over. Despite the material superiority of the enemy, we had to fight on and do our duty. **"**

being had to die in great pain when his time came, and by that I meant our own chaps and the enemy. So, I pinched two boxes full of morphine from the stores and loaded them on to our vehicle.

The plan was that any wounded men would be looked after in the first instance by me and then gathered together in what we called a 'wounded-manhole', then to a forward collecting point. After that, they would be carried back to a casualty clearing station, then to a field hospital – the nearest one was in the coastal town of Derna. We were told that during the expected battle between Bir Hacheim and Tobruk, the moving of wounded would be very difficult because we would be virtually behind enemy lines. We were advised to take casualties with us on the trucks, so my task was just to

" *William James Ogden Hutchings, a platoon commander with the Essex Regiment in the Eighth Army, came back from Mersa Matruh to the Alamein area to form a defensive line in June 1942. At first, the enemy tanks were a matter of about half a mile away as the Allies dug in, but they crept nearer, day by day.*

" I was right at the front, with between a dozen and 20 men in my platoon. Gradually we got reinforcements and, of course, officers came up with them. I would be a Platoon Sergeant and then the officer could get moved somewhere else, and I would take command.

While the line was forming and being held, from June to October, we were going out every night on patrol, behind their lines. Night time is the active time – it's when you go out and you use your field craft and you crawl amongst them.

You never went out on your own – you used to take maybe a dozen blokes with you, or sometimes just two or three. You'd have somebody there who could speak German, and they would listen and you would ask what they were saying. Usually, they were only talking about home, and saying they'd got a letter – that sort of thing. The object was to get some idea of what you're up against. We always seemed to have the 90th Light Division facing us, wherever we went. We used to say, 'Oh yes, it's the Panzer Grenadiers again.'

It was up to you not to get caught. If a German spotted us and put up a fight, we killed him. It wasn't a gentleman's war, and they were doing the same to us. We used to catch them, coming into our lines – they'd snoop around and then go back. Another reason for our night trips was to find minefields. We used to use a bayonet to prod the ground.

We lost a lot of men at the beginning of Alamein, when the line was forming. The deaths were mainly through Stukas, but their artillery took out quite a few as well. We got dive-bombed and shelled. In the desert, you can't dig down – you've got to get bits of rock and build up to make yourself a shelter. You lie down in it, or kneel – it's not high enough to sit up in.

On the night of the battle, as it opened up, we felt as if we were doing something at long last. We had been there four months. The artillery opened up and this barrage went on all through the night. Then, on various sectors of the front, people made inroads into the German defences. **"**

◄ A house in Sollum already shows signs of fierce fighting, as two South African soldiers take cover in the ruins. Combat in any built-up area was rare – most battles took place in wide open spaces.

▼▼ Strange companions rove across the desert wastes. Camels wander among the tanks on open scrubland as the battle continues to hold on to territories won.

► Following the German breakthrough into Tobruk in June, Africa Corps trucks move into the town. The wall still bears the graffiti of a long period of Allied occupation during the previous year's fighting.

Robert Holding, having survived the BEF's initial rout in France with the 4th Battalion, Royal Sussex Regiment, found himself in the desert and, on the night of 4 November, in the middle of the Battle of El Alamein, a call came for volunteers to step forward for a Military Police duty. Hoping for a spell off the front, he volunteered.

❝ We assembled, six men and one officer, and made our way back to Battalion HQ, where a three-ton truck manned by two redcaps was waiting.

In the truck was a large number of shining petrol cans and large rolls of white tape. Here we were given the puzzling instruction that when the truck moved off, we were to follow close behind it on foot.

We followed slowly behind in a cloud of dust, scarcely able to believe that we were moving forward and not going toward the rear. Someone at the front of our little column asked the officer what we were going to do. His reply sent our already sinking spirits plummeting to zero. We were, he informed us, going to mark out the line of the night's advance. We were staggered.

The second battle of El Alamein had settled into a regular pattern, the tactics of which were dictated by the fact that the enemy held a solid line of entrenchments, protected by massive minefields and barbed wire that stretched unbroken from the sea to the sand sea of the Qattara Depression, some 90 miles inland.

After the huge barrage of 23rd October, waves of infantry assaulted the enemy positions. These were followed by tanks, hoping to exploit any breakthrough by the infantry. This process was repeated every night as our troops nibbled away at the enemy defences.

Thus, on any given night, the distance between the forward trenches of the opposing armies would vary at different points from a stone's throw to several hundred yards. On this particular night, the distance between our battalion's positions and those of the enemy were some six to seven hundred yards at the most.

The purpose of marking the line of advance was simply that in the featureless desert, one had no sense of direction and could, unless following a compass, walk around in circles. So, in order to keep the advance on a straight course, white tapes were laid from our own positions to a point as near as it was possible to get to the enemy. To guide the tanks, petrol cans were placed at intervals.

Now began the task of laying the markers. The officer, compass in hand, moved slowly forward while we laid the tape behind him. Every 20 yards a petrol tin was placed beside the tape. Slowly, yard by yard, we edged forward, the groaning of the truck in low gear seemed to grow louder every second. Every petrol tin seemed to clang like some monstrous cymbal. Surely the enemy to our front must be aware of us.

They were. Two flares sailed skyward – the night was suddenly turned to day. From both sides of the arc that formed the enemy front line, machine guns opened fire, the bullets whistled like angry hornets around us. I felt at least three tear at my trousers. We flung ourselves to the ground. The light of the flares died away and the officer was on his feet yelling to the MPs, 'Get those cans off and get the hell out of here.'

More flares soared skyward and the machine guns resumed their chattering, this time pursuing the retreating truck. We lay still until the flares had burned themselves out and the machine guns ceased firing, then resumed our task.

War Stories

Although the war in the desert between the Axis and Allied forces was very fiercely contested, the Arabs didn't care very much who won – indeed, both groups were fair game to them as a target for their special brand of stealthy theft. It was said that they could empty a kit-bag even when its owner was using it as a pillow! One RAF officer, a particularly heavy sleeper, woke up one morning to find all his belongings had gone, including the boots he'd gone to bed with the night before – and his tent!

Foot by foot, yard by yard, we moved steadily forward. We were now close enough to the enemy to hear their voices and the ring of their picks and shovels as they strengthened their defences. Some were singing as they worked, which showed a remarkable spirit, since they must have been aware that our barrage would soon be falling about their ears. Happily they seemed as yet unaware of our presence.

Slowly and with great caution, we inched our way forward until the penultimate petrol can had been placed in position and the last of the tape had been laid and weighted down with a stone. We were now left with one can, which we had been told to leave till last. This, for some

he said, 'one volunteer to go forward and place this tin just this side of the mound, open side toward us, place the hurricane lamp inside the tin and light it.' We stared at him in silent disbelief. Here we were within spitting distance of the enemy and he was asking one of us to go even further forward.

'Oh well,' he said, 'there's nothing like doing a job yourself. Now listen, I want no heroics. If I am shot or grabbed, run like hell back to our lines. No one is to come and help me, that's an order.' Consciences pricked. Suddenly there were six volunteers for the job. We saw him smile in the starlight. 'No. This is my job, and remember – no heroics.'

We watched with bated breath as

kicked a small stone. It made only a faint click but in that silence it seemed to reverberate like a thunderclap. From our front came a loud challenge followed by three random rifle shots, a flare soared skyward bursting above our heads flooding the desert with a brilliant white light. The officer froze to the ground where he lay till the flare burned itself out and then in the seemingly greater darkness, leapt to his feet and ran back to the shelter of our depression.

There was now no need for stealth – we were discovered. Three more flares turned the desert night into day. From our front and from both sides of the arc, machine guns began sweeping the area around us. We

reason, had one of its sides cut away. We had till then no time to speculate on the purpose of this or as to why the officer had, throughout the operation, carried an unlighted hurricane lamp in his hand.

The officer now called for our attention and motioned us to ease ourselves up to the rim of the depression from where he pointed out a small mound faintly visible to our front and near to the enemy line, 'I want,'

he crawled slowly forward, the tin with the lamp inside cradled in one arm. It was a slow and painful progress, but after what seemed an eternity he reached the shadow of the mound. The can glinted as he stood it upright, then came the match.

The enemy in front stopped talking, everything became breathlessly and frighteningly silent, the officer crawling slowly back toward us

huddled right to the ground trying to keep below the rim of the depression. The officer whispered to us 'Number off' We each in turn whispered a number from one to six, 'Now, turn and face our lines.' We crawled around until we had our feet to the enemy. 'When I call your number, get up and run like hell.' **"**

◀ **Men of the Eighth Army carve up the Christmas turkey.**

Second Lieutenant Jack Scollen, with the (Durham) 4th Survey Regiment, Royal Artillery, had been drafted out to the desert with a view to reinforcing the Alamein attack. After the assault, his unit advanced into former enemy territory to end the year and spend Christmas in the desert.

❝ On Christmas Eve, I took a party of men from the different troops in the regiment to a bulk NAAFI which had been established a few miles back along the road.

We were able to buy 50 cigarettes and a bottle of beer for each man as well as a small amount of whisky and gin for the officers and sergeants. Later in the day I found a mobile canteen and spent the afternoon buying more goods and in the evening I sat down to work out what stock I now had.

I wanted to arrange something in the way of a special Christmas offer and eventually decided on a free issue of the following to each man in the troop – 60 Players' cigarettes, a bar of chocolate, a bottle of beer and a tin of fruit or a packet of biscuits.

I suggested to Bryant, the Troop Commander, and Crowe, that in addition, we ourselves should stand the cost of a free issue of cigarettes on New Year's Day as a gift from the officers. We decided not to make any announcement so that it would be a surprise.

I went off to try to contact some chaplains or find out where and when there would be Mass or other services on Christmas Day. I had no luck so far as the non-Catholics were concerned, but fortunately a chaplain did turn up unexpectedly on Christmas morning.

Later in the evening of Christmas Eve, Bryant, Crowe and I were sitting chatting in the mess while they tried to repair an old army wireless set so that we could pick up the Christmas broadcasts. Presently we heard the sound of carols outside the mess tent. *Good King Wenceslas* first, beautifully sung in parts, then *Silent Night*.

It was very moving to hear it sung, quietly and reverently, by those soldiers, standing in a circle in the bright moonlight. We listened through all the verses and then invited the carol-singers into the mess. They were NCOs and gunners from

▲ **A German anti-aircraft gun fires from a well dug-in position in an attack on Allied tanks as they advance.**

S Troop, some of them old 'Terriers' of Gateshead days. We gave them whisky or gin and lime, and toasts were drunk to those at home, to old friends in the regiment now dead or POWs, and to happier Christmases in the future.

During the distribution of the Christmas issue news came that another canteen truck had been located and the Battery Commander came to ask me whether I had any money in our canteen fund with which to buy more goods. I gave him what I had and he went off to see what he could buy. The turkey, pork, Christmas pudding, cake and mince pies that we had ordered from the official rations had not arrived and we had been told that they might not reach us for two or three weeks – but as it happened, the ordinary rations we received on Christmas Day were amazing. Fresh pork and a double ration of vegetables and tinned fruit!

While we were sitting in the mess after the men's dinner, the major returned from his shopping expedition – with three 7lb tins of pudding and one and a half 7lb cakes. The cakes were magnificent, covered with white icing and 'A Merry Xmas 1942' in pink lettering. Instead of a biscuit and cheese or something equally meagre for tea, everyone had plum pudding and Christmas cake.

It was a dreadful night, bitterly cold, with a gale blowing and a torrential downpour of rain. We were very glad that our ramshackle bivouacs withstood the elements. The wind and rain, thrashing the roof of the bivvy, woke me during the night. The bivvy held, however. The next morning I filled my bucket with rainwater from the roof and had a glorious wash and shave. ❞

THE SAS IS BORN

In July 1941, David Stirling, a Scots Guards officer attached to No 8 Commando in the Middle East, received permission to raise a small force to carry out raids deep behind enemy lines. Known as 'L' Detachment, 65 men assembled at Kabrit on the Suez Canal for parachute training and, on 16 November, attempted their first attack on Tmimi and Gazala airfields. It went badly wrong, persuading Stirling that airborne deployment was too dangerous. Instead, he decided to use the Long-Range Desert Group (LRDG) for transport to and from their objectives.

More recruits were raised and the unit renamed the Special Air Service (SAS), carrying out more effective raids in December, when over 50 enemy aircraft were destroyed at Tamet airfield alone. Soon SAS jeeps, armed with machine guns, were ranging far and wide through enemy-held desert to hit supply dumps, ports and communications. A legend had been born.

◄David Stirling, right, with men of the Long-Range Desert Group – the pioneers of what would become the world's best-known specialised military squad.

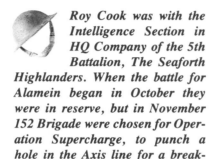

Roy Cook was with the Intelligence Section in HQ Company of the 5th Battalion, The Seaforth Highlanders. When the battle for Alamein began in October they were in reserve, but in November 152 Brigade were chosen for Operation Supercharge, to punch a hole in the Axis line for a break-out.

" This attack was to be under the command of Major-General Bernard Freyberg (2nd New Zealand Division), but without New Zealand Infantry. Instead he was given 151 Infantry Brigade from 50 Division and 152 Brigade from the 51st Highland Division.

We all lined up on the start line just after midnight on November 1st, and I remember we were all given an issue of rum to keep out the cold, as we were all in khaki drill uniform. We all suddenly moved forward behind our artillery barrage and soon all hell was let loose. We advanced steadily with our rifles at the high

port and visibility was soon obscured by the smoke from our bursting shells. Some of our men were hit by enemy fire and sank to the ground and very soon we overran the enemy's forward defended localities. In the darkness I distinctly recall seeing an Africa Corps Volkswagen rushing around and firing at will. Soon we met the first German prisoners and we directed them to our rear. Once on our objective, we were ordered to dig in, but this was sooner said that done, as below the shallow loose sand, we hit solid rock.

We did our utmost to get below the surface of the desert and when first light appeared there was a tremendous rumbling as our first Sherman tanks came up from the rear. We had to make sure we weren't all squashed flat, but it was most heartening to see our armour up amongst us, giving us the badly needed support we had all been hoping for. That day will go down in my life as 'the Longest Day', as we all had to lie out in the open desert, expecting every moment to be our last – we were right in the middle of a big tank battle and tanks were being hit all

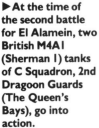

▶At the time of the second battle for El Alamein, two British M4A1 (Sherman 1) tanks of C Squadron, 2nd Dragoon Guards (The Queen's Bays), go into action.

around us!

Jerry had a screen of his anti-tank guns and all kinds of shot and shell were flying all over the place. Both our tanks and Rommel's panzers were being 'brewed up' and those of my battalion who were still alive were thankful when at last the sun began to sink behind Jerry's lines.

As my slit trench was so shallow, my haversack etc, had been left above ground, and I remember my mess tins were now useless, having been pierced with shrapnel. I had been slightly wounded and I applied my first field dressing, trusting that it would heal. Unfortunately my leg turned septic and I was forced later to be evacuated as far as Division for a few days. "

Major Vic Coxen of the 1st Parachute Battalion was one of Britain's new special assault force – an élite group of highly trained men. As the desert war progressed, Operation Torch landings were made at Algiers with the aim of beating the Germans to Tunis and Bizerta. Coxen's men were sent in in advance.

❝ We marched ten miles after we landed at Maison Blanche and pulled into some place for the night. In the morning I woke, threw off my groundsheet, looked up and there, hanging over my head, was a great bunch of bananas. I thought, 'I can stand this. This is alright. It's going to be a nice place to live.' Of course we'd spent the night in the Botanical Gardens, so it was the only bunch of bloody bananas in the whole of North Africa!

The next day we parachuted into Souk el Arba and found ourselves 400 miles ahead of Blade Force for the next few weeks. The French hadn't quite decided whose side they were on. We made it difficult be-

▲ With the start of Operation Torch – the landings in NW Africa – the Allies at last have the clout to secure the desert front for good.

▼ Men of Vic Coxen's company – an élite force of the 1st Parachute Battalion – after a successful attack on Kowshock Farm in Tunisia. Vic Coxen stands, far right.

cause we went and sat in the middle of them. The moment the Germans appeared we went for them. The Germans would then shell the French, so eventually they put their helmets on and said they were in the war.

One of our early contacts with French soldiers was when we dug in on some hills and found, when dawn broke, that we had dug in about 30 yards in front of the French positions. There behind us stood these huge seven-foot men with black faces and the old Lebel rifles. They were a regiment of *Tirailleurs* – the native levies of the French Colonial Army. We didn't stay long.

We were ordered to a place where a tank battle had taken place. It was at the end of a long valley. I was going to make the move with my company, but one platoon suffered badly from an attack by a Messerschmitt, then Alistair needed the other platoon, so I set out with ten men.

It was a moonlit night, so I decided that we would go beyond the farm and come in the back way in case anyone was there. It was slightly eerie with all these smoking tanks around. In the yard was an Italian tank with two blackened corpses. One of my soldiers stuck cigarettes in their mouths. The closer we got to the farm, the more my chaps began to cough.

I stopped them and said, 'Look, is

there any one of you bastards that isn't dying of pneumonia?!' I gave them each an acid drop and they shut up.

We were right up against the side of the house when I thought I heard some noise inside, so I said we'd do the normal drill. As I was a bit bigger than the others, I took a run at the door and wham – over it went with 'Titch' Stanley and the other men firing their Stens over my head. I shouted to them to hold their fire, because I landed on top of three dead Germans. There were seven of them laid out. This place had been a casualty clearing station, and these chaps had all been killed, or were shot and died there.

They cushioned my fall a bit, but it was a little eerie really, so Coxen's Farm, as it was called from then on, was taken by ten men, nine of which were asthmatic!

I got on the blower and Alistair sent up the rest of my company. We held the farm for some time – long enough to recover several tanks and blow up those that were beyond repair.

We had been going for some time – about six weeks or so – and I had run out of pants. They had literally worn to bits. I was rummaging around a few drawers in the farmhouse and found some clothes. I had a little boy's jersey, which I cut the arms off and opened it so I could pull my head through – it was rather like

▲ Hans Teske of the German 5th Parachute Regiment.

► Assisted by Italian allies, Germans set up an anti-tank gun in Tunisia.

a bust-bodice. Then I found this magnificent silk chemise and some bloomers, which were absolute heaven – and I wore them until Blade Force brought up supplies. I was very grateful to that woman, whoever she was, but of course, I was frightened to wash them and hang them out, in case anyone pinched them! "

 Hans Teske, a lance-corporal in the 5th Parachute Regiment – a 'trouble-shooting' unit, unattached to any division – was 18 years old when he dropped into Tunis. The controlling French forces in Tunis remained neutral for the first few weeks, but this would soon change as the Allies progressed.

" We arrived in Tunisia in November 1942 from France via Italy. Our purpose was to provide a secure back-up for Rommel's forces fighting in North Africa. We were told that, apart from the native Arab population, part of the inhabitants were French, and some were Italian. We were told not to alienate the French population, with whom we had had a good working relationship when we were in France. We did not know how sincere the offer by the French government was to allow us into Tunisia. We found this out once we landed. The French had tanks and fighter aircraft there, but they did not hinder us. They let us use all their facilities. In fact, when it came to setting up outposts on the outskirts of the city we could use the local trams, and the French army agreed with the local police force to give us a *gendarme* as protection on our journey there.

The French soldiers, learning that we had just arrived from France, asked if they could use our postal service, to let their families know how they were. And this we did, on an individual basis.

The French forces remained neutral for the first few weeks, and then sided with the Americans and British, though most of the French population of Tunisia remained friendly to the German soldiers. Most farms were owned by Frenchmen, some by local people of Italian origin. The local Arab population remained friendly with the Germans right until the end of the Tunisian campaign.

When we first arrived in Tunisia we were surprised to find how European the climate was, and the temperature was like a European spring. It was very peaceful, and the French and Arabs were trying to outdo one another in hospitality.

By 21st November, there were about 400 of us there. Our first camp was the Marshal Foch barracks, partly used by French troops. Some of our battalion were housed in the French police headquarters.

From our provisional front line we made further advances towards contacting the enemy, but normally the smaller party would give way to the larger party from either side. One example: we had a standing patrol near Bir Arada, and we were sent to pick them up. We had about six motor-cycle combinations, each with a machine-gun mounted on it, but we were ordered not to fire, because we did not want to give away the location of our standing outpost, as we wanted to use that position again. At this point the enemy troops were about 30 miles away. While we were travelling down a main road we saw a British motorcyclist coming in the opposite direction. He spotted us and threw himself down immediately into the ditch. We drove past him, ignoring him, and he lay there hiding from us. We looked back and he continued on his way, flogging the guts out of his machine. "

ALLIED RAIDERS

By air, sea and land, the Allies start to bring the war to Hitler with a mounting campaign to bomb German industry and a series of commando raids – which meet with mixed success.

T he German occupation of Europe was at its height in 1942. In December 1941, Hitler had authorised the *Nacht und Nebel* (Night and Fog) Decree, by which 'persons endangering German security' could be eliminated without trial.

But German occupation was not trouble-free, even under such repression. Throughout 1942, the British SOE (Special Operations Executive) continued to set up Resistance cells in Europe as part of the planning for an eventual liberation campaign. As early as February 1942, British parachute troops captured a radar set at Bruneval in northern France. A month later the dry-dock at St Nazaire was destroyed in a daring (but costly) commando and naval attack. The raids culminated in disaster at Dieppe on 19 August, when commandos and Canadians attempted to seize the port from the sea. The Allies were far from ready for a full-scale invasion.

◀ Nuremberg castle bears the signs of fierce bombing as citizens try to carry on life as usual.

▶ Aerial reconnaissance reveals the Bruneval radar dish on the path leading from the villa.

▶▼ Sergeant Cox, RAF, centre, who dismantled the Würzburg radar, recalls the mission to Group Captain Sir Nigel Norman, right.

1942

AUGUST

4 Germans begin final drive for Stalingrad

5 Churchill visits Eighth Army at Alamein, decides to replace Auchinleck

7 US forces land on Guadalcanal
Montgomery replaces British Army commander designate, General Gott, shot down *en route* to Cairo

8 Eisenhower sets up UK headquarters
Japanese naval counter-attack beaten off in Solomon Islands; US Marines take Henderson Airfield

9 Battle of Savo Island: Australian cruiser *Canberra* sunk off Guadalcanal. US lose heavy cruisers *Quincey, Vincennes* and *Astoria*

11 15 Operation Pedestal: vital convoy to Malta – five merchant ships get through

17 Rouen hit by Eighth USAAF in first all-American bombing raid

19 Anglo-Canadian disaster at Dieppe

22 US forces on Guadalcanal wipe out first wave of Japanese reinforcements
Brazil declares war on Germany and Italy

23 24 US forces beat off Japanese Combined Fleet (Eastern Solomans)

26 German success continues in Caucasus
Two thousand Japanese land on Milne Bay, east of Port Moresby

28 29 1,200 Japanese land in Guadalcanal

29 Japanese warships begin Milne Bay evacuation

30 31 Battle of Alam Halfa: Rommel sustains heavy losses

Major John Frost was selected by Admiral Lord Mountbatten, Chief of Combined Operations, to lead a daring raid to occupied France. The aim was to capture the Wurzburg radar unit from an installation near Bruneval and return with it intact. Operation Biting, 27/28 February, achieved complete success.

❝ I had been very busy prior to take-off, absorbing all the fresh intelligence that was coming to us each day. We knew the exact defensive position of the enemy, their weapons and even some of their names.

At last our 12 aircraft, carrying ten men in each, were off. We sat on our sleeping bags, but it was bloody hard to find a comfortable position. The noise inside the aircraft was considerable, but some played cards and we sang some songs. Flight Sergeant Cox, who had volunteered to dismantle the radar apparatus, gave a sentimental rendering of *The Rose of Tralee*.

I had a large water bottle filled with tea and laced with rum, which I passed around, so most of us were dying for a pee – which we did, the moment we landed! There was no wind and landing in snow was perfect. I would normally have travelled with Wing Commander Pickard (who took the first two sticks) to make sure they were dropped in the right place – but he was the only one who dropped his sticks in the wrong place!

The plan was that we should basically drop in three parties. the first, under John Ross and Ewen Charteris, would take the beach defences to the rear. The second lot, mine, were to capture the villa and radar equipment, while the senior sapper, Dennis Vernon, and Cox dismantled all the parts that were needed and photographed the rest. The third party, under John Timothy, were to interpose themselves between the radar station and the German-held village.

After we'd had our pee, we went straight for the radar. We could see the aircraft dropping our reserve party, so we knew we would have at least three-quarters of the force on the ground.

We had this very complicated plan which I didn't like because there wasn't proper control. I had been ordered to lead the assault on the villa, when I should have been free to command the situation. Instead, there I was with this bloody awful Sten gun, a most inaccurate and unreliable weapon, leading a charge on this villa. Fortunately, there was only one German, who was quickly dealt with.

After that I could assume command, but I had no proper headquarters staff or signals set-up. However, up to now all had gone well.

Then the enemy opened fire on the villa from *Le Presbytère*, a wooded enclosure 300 yards away.

They continued firing while Vernon and Cox began to dismantle the radar and take photographs.

With more firing and sounds of vehicles approaching, I ordered my party to take what they had of the radar and make their way to the beach. The sappers loaded the equipment on to canvas trolleys and off we went. Because I had no communications, I had no idea if John Ross was in control of the beach. As we made our way down to the hill in the snow, the Germans opened up with machine-gun fire from a pillbox. Sergeant-Major Strachen was badly wounded in the stomach. We got some morphine into him and slipped and slithered him down on his bottom. As we got closer to the beach, we heard someone call out that everything was clear. Then more firing started and John Ross called out, 'Don't come down! The beach defences have not been taken!'

I went to sort out the problem and found Ewen Charteris, who had been dropped by Pickard about a mile and a half short of the correct place. On their way to us they had fought a tricky little battle with a German patrol. He had dealt with the machine gun that had hit Strachen and, with great aplomb, dispatched any defender who tried to stop us reaching the beach.

It was 0215 and all we wanted now was the Navy – the signallers couldn't make contact. We tried the lamp, but there was a slight mist and we couldn't see more than half a mile. We had arranged a last-ditch communications, which was a Very light. We fired several of these, but there was no recognition. I'd almost given up hope now and was going to take up defensive positions and go on fighting for as long as we could.

We had just finished tidying up the perimeter when the signaller cried out, 'The boats are here, sir!' Unfortunately, instead of coming in two at a time so that we could make an orderly withdrawal in three phases, all six landing-craft came in at the same time. It was a bit of a shambles, and we were not able to check everyone in. On board the gunboat we heard from two signallers that they had been left behind. There was no way we could go back for them.

We learnt the reason for the Navy's delay. A German destroyer and two E-boats had passed within a mile of them, but thankfully had not seen them. It was little wonder they hadn't answered our signals. At a very early stage, the scientist who was on the motor gunboat with the radar was able to shout across, 'You've got practically every single thing we hoped to see!'

As we entered Portsmouth our flotilla of six destroyers passed us with *Rule Britannia* blaring out from their loudspeakers. We also had spitfires diving overhead, signalling success with their wings. It was a moment to feel great pride. We had suffered casualties, with two dead and five wounded, and those we'd left behind, but we'd carried out a most successful airborne operation.

The raid had been carried out when the country's fortunes were at a low ebb. Singapore had recently fallen and the German battleships had escaped up the Channel. The success of our venture, although a mere fleabite, did have the effect of making people feel we could succeed after all. We'd left our barracks on the Friday, and when we got back on the Sunday, their quartermaster was reading the Sunday papers with the news of our raid splashed all over the front. 'Good God,' he said, 'I wonder who they could have been.' **"**

 Captain R K Devereaux of C Company, 40 Commando Royal Marines, was ordered, on 19 August 1942, to move ahead into Dieppe Harbour, so he arranged to follow the landing craft of his commanding officer. Due to considerable smoke, he briefly lost sight of the leader, but finally spotted the craft on his port bow.

" The CO intimated that it would be impossible to make the harbour, and that we were to land on the beach, some 300 yards ahead. It was 'White' beach; we then became separated by the smoke again.

We were now coming under fire from a coastal defence gun and a number of machine-gun positions. About five to ten minutes later, the smoke cleared and I saw the beach about 12 feet away. The fire was still intense and there were many prone figures on the beach.

Away to the left, towards 'Blue' beach, were many who appeared dead or wounded. To my front was an MLC, lying broadside on the beach with about 12 figures stretched out on the beach to the seaward side of the vessel.

I then saw the CO standing in the MLC signalling to our landing craft to withdraw.

We then went half to starboard with an MLC carrying A Company colliding with us astern. Before we made this move, Marine Breen, LMC gunner in the bow of my ALC, fired on enemy posts ashore and one post in the Casino was neutralised.

As we went about again, through fresh smoke, I saw a TLC sinking, with some men in the water. I went alongside and took off two naval ratings, then searched for the rest. I found marine Corporal Ryan, who was slightly wounded, and we then moved about a mile out to sea. We were holed just above the engine on the port side, and were taking water fast*:* **"**

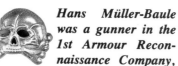

▲A Royal Navy motor launch with four landing craft stands off Dieppe during the unsuccessful raid, 19 August.

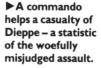 *Hans Müller-Baule was a gunner in the 1st Armour Reconnaissance Company, Reconnaissance Section 10 of the 10th Panzer Division. Having been on the Eastern Front, they had been posted to Amiens, they believed, to freshen up and take a well-earned rest. Then 19 August dawned at their camp.*

▶A commando helps a casualty of Dieppe – a statistic of the woefully misjudged assault.

▼Shocked locals stand among the bodies of FFI members, massacred by German occupying forces at Autun.

FREE FRENCH FORCES

When France fell to the Germans in June 1940, no recognised head of state fled into exile – indeed, the French retained their National Assembly, voting Marshal Pétain into power in Vichy. The only representative of the pre-surrender government in London was the relatively minor figure of Charles de Gaulle, and although Winston Churchill gave him full backing as 'Leader of the Free French', he was not immediately recognised as a political figurehead by those Frenchmen who had escaped to Britain.

The creating of Free French Forces took time. Those who rallied to de Gaulle, both in Britain and in the French colonies, were dependent on the British for arms, uniforms and equipment, at a time when such commodities were scarce. It was not until May 1942, when Free French units fought so effectively at Bir Hacheim in North Africa, that de Gaulle's command began to be taken seriously.

> **A** piercing signal, normally so familiar – the whistle of the duty NCO rang out through the high corridors of the barracks. We woke with a start, still a little drowsy. In our wire-mesh beds we – that was the six-man crew of the 1st Heavy Armoured Reconnaissance Unit – we didn't know what was going on. We had been pulled out of Russia so that we could freshen up and take reinforcements far away from the front.

And then, this incredibly piercing whistle again – interrupted for a moment by shouts of 'Alarm! Alarm!' To reinforce the effect of the signal, the door to our room was flung open. Quick as a flash, we were out of our beds, everyone diving on to his carefully arranged bundle of clothes and throwing on clothing out of a kind of instinct, cursing as we pulled on our boots and ran, as we had practised so often, out of the room, down the corridor, on to the courtyard and into the scouting truck.

The commander of the reconnaissance troop, Staff Sergeant Becker, was standing impatiently waiting by the radio-scouting truck, gesturing to us to get a move on with the most frantic hand movements. We had never seen him so animated – he usually radiated such calm. Seeing him like this woke us up to the fact that this was a serious alarm. The commander of our truck, *Unteroffizier* Hilker, from Osnabrück, who would take nothing less than 100 per cent, was in position. Dawn was just breaking, but every one of us, the driver, commandant, rear passenger and myself (the gunner) had practised this many times over and took our places quickly.

The rear passenger and radio operator, 'Sigi' Bolt, was having problems as usual getting his uniform and radio equipment in order. The commandant, as always, radiated calm and level-headedness. I was, to be honest, quite hyped up and thinking about how to operate the 2 cm cannon. In no time we were on the arterial road out of Amiens, heading for the coast, after our radio had picked up the news that an enemy landing was under way at Dieppe.

Looking at the sky through the gap in the tower, we could see that something like this was in the air. Bombers and fighters cut through the sky. We took cover for a moment under the trees at the side of the road, then set off again at top speed for the coast. There was a tense calm in the scouting truck. All my senses were on the alert and everyone, as much as the state of alarm allowed him to be, was deeply immersed in his own thoughts.

The nearer we got to Dieppe, the muffled rumble which we had been hearing at intervals on the way eased off – the unmistakable sound of ships' artillery fire.

About 20 km from Dieppe we were ordered to stop by military police. They told us there had been a failed landing operation – mostly Canadian soldiers. It had been beaten back for the most part, but we were told to proceed cautiously. When we arrived in Dieppe, fires were still smouldering in ruined houses. Other houses had suffered only light damage or none at all. The two reconnaissance trucks headed for the coast and there, on the beach, in view of our coastal fortress, we could see the aftermath of an obviously brief but intense and ruthless battle. In the water were the remains of landing craft, some totally destroyed. The beach was littered with corpses. **"**

 Frau Chantrain was a civilian, living in Cologne when it came under heavy air attack from the bombers of the RAF and USAAF. The city was very heavily hit and suffered extensive damage, while the citizens learned to live with the constant fear of sudden and violent death as the raids continued.

> **When** the sirens sounded, everyone went into the air-raid shelter, and on the 30th to 31st May it was a short attack. The sirens sounded at about 10 o'clock. I must say that in half an hour so much happened. Cologne lay practically in ruins. I came out of the air-raid shelter and Cologne was a wall of flame. I tried to get to my station. It was, of course, very difficult to reach it because Cologne was built with pretty narrow streets and the balconies were on fire and falling into the street. Meantime, though, the organisations – the Red Cross, the SHD and the Air Defence Organisation – had gone into action. We went through the ruins trying to find the way through them, and in parts we also had to dig.

You already knew if people were in a certain cellar and we fetched out various wounded people to bring them to our station post. We dragged them over the ruins and it was there that they got help for the first time. We took the seriously wounded people to transport points, from which they were ferried to the hospitals.

We took care of the wounded, some of whom could walk to us. In other case we had to carry them to the First Aid station where food was also distributed.

The digging parties hauled the

dead people out and laid them on the side of the road – those killed by high-explosive bombs were buried and propped up. Their skin was a grey, pallid colour. Their hair stood off their heads like wire nails. And of those who died of incendiaries you only found bits of bones which were gathered up in wash tubs.

Of course, the cruellest thing was when you had a friend in these houses; you saw the bones lying there and you knew they were underneath. That was unbelievably horrible. Even worse, when mothers came to me who had themselves very severe burns, with their children in their arms who were scarcely capable of life, and begged us for help. We

▲ A nightmare of mangled metal and broken landmarks makes Germany's bombed cities unrecognisable.

▼ Part of the work of the SOE is to recruit, train and equip local agents in occupied areas, and, where necessary, raise and arm secret forces with which to support regular operations.

saw it was pointless. The children were beyond help.

The soldiers on leave from the front came and asked after their relatives. Then you had to tell them 'Your wife is dead. Your children are dead.' I had to give the news to a soldier on leave from the front that he had lost many members of his family one night. And you mustn't forget the fear which one had oneself during an attack. I don't think I could ever really talk freely about that because it was really too horrible. You didn't know whether your own life was going to be spared and you waited with great fear. "

⌐┼⌐ *William Herget, aged 33 at the time of the RAF bombing of Germany, was a night-fighter pilot, flying Ju-88s, tasked with defending the cities of his homeland against the war of attrition waged by RAF Bomber Command. Often making several flights a night, the pilots needed intense concentration and stamina.*

" Once I was lucky. I was flying in one night and we were told the target may be Cologne. I was climbing up to 8,500 metres, about 25,000 feet, and then I saw under me, near Cologne, the search-lights going into the clouds. Then we could see from above all the planes moving along on the clouds. At night I always came up on the enemy aircraft from underneath, so as to come from the dark.

Usually I only had two successes in one night, and then I landed – but that night I really was in the middle of the bomber stream and I looked to the left and I looked to the right –

suddenly I was in the middle. I was flying through the wind stream and my plane was shaking and so I dived and I saw the first plane in front, the next to the right, the next to the left. Then I tried to attack – and on the first attack I did something I feel was wrong. I was shooting between the two motors – it was a Lancaster – and to the left another Lancaster. I shot again between the two motors, only a short time, though sometimes I needed only four to eight bullets until the plane was burning.

I shot between the motors, I tell you this because the first plane I attacked that night I shot in the body and that one exploded – but I never did that again. I knew the planes were flying now with bombs to a town, maybe Cologne, it may be Frankfurt, and I just had to do that. I saw the next plane was shooting and I was naturally proud I brought them down with bombs. I was sure they could jump out, the crew from the planes, because when the plane burns they could still jump out because I didn't touch the body.

I had another success with a bomber to Frankfurt and now on the way back I found another three. The last one was the hardest, because there was also a Lancaster and the Lancaster saw me. I knew how they had seen me because I came from Frankfurt that was all burning, it was a huge fire. So I want to the right, overtook and then I came from the right underneath, but again I was shooting the plane in the body because I knew they had seen me, so for their own defence – and please forgive me – again I was shooting at the whole body and the plane exploded and burned until it crashed into the earth. It was terrible, but it was self defence. "

SOE

On 22 July 1940, Winston Churchill's War Cabinet authorised the creation of Special Operations Executive (SOE), tasked with selecting, training and organising clandestine agents for deployment to occupied Europe. Once committed, these agents would set up Resistance cells, organise reception committees for air-drops of supplies, money and arms, and plan (and carry out) acts of sabotage. Secret radio networks would act as the link with London, liaising over future operations and relaying information.

Despite opposition from the more traditional intelligence services, recruitment was brisk. Those selected went through special training before being parachuted or landed by aircraft into enemy territory. By 1942, some success had been achieved, but the agents faced a lonely and dangerous existence – of the 480 SOE agents sent to France during the war, 130 were captured, and of them, only 26 survived.

ARCTIC ENDURANCE

Even though the U-boats have surprise on their side, life below the waves is fraught with dangers – not just from Allied attacks, but from the ocean itself.

By the beginning of 1942, despite the introduction of new radars, escort warships and long-range aircraft, the British were close to losing the Battle of the Atlantic. The entry of the Americans into the war should have tilted the balance, both in escort and shipbuilding terms, but this was not the case. Unescorted shipping close to the eastern coast of the USA was vulnerable and the 'wolf packs' retained the upper hand.

Germany deployed aircraft, U-boats and surface warships to Norway against Britain's Arctic convoys, culminating in the virtual destruction of Convoys PQ-17 and PQ-18 in July and September respectively. The 'Arctic Run' had to be suspended, to be resumed under increased protection. A British victory in the Barents Sea against German heavy cruiser *Admiral Hipper* promised long-term success, but there was a long way to go.

Lieutenant Werner Schüneman, age 22, was an engineer officer on U-606, which finally entered service in spring 1942. Kitted up in tropical uniform, they headed for the South Atlantic, sailing between Iceland and the British Isles – when something unforeseen happened and U-606's misfortunes began.

"All of a sudden there was a noise, and the commanding officer, whose name was Klatt, was found under the ladder situated under the conning tower, unconscious. He must have fallen down head first, but we had no idea what actually happened. Anyway he did not recover consciousness in the next two days. So under the circumstances, we decided not to proceed with our operation, but to find the nearest friendly harbour and get some treatment for him. We went into Bergen, which at the time was occupied by German troops.

By the way, our commanding officer did not regain consciousness for some time, even after being flown back to Kiel for treatment. In fact he suffered from the effects of this fall for some six months, but he did actually make it through the war.

Now there's an interesting point here, about doctors on U-boats. Essentially, what Dönitz had decided, based upon experience, was that to have one doctor on each boat was simply 'uneconomic'. To lose one doctor for just 50 men, if the boat went down – this was a bad ratio. So no doctors were placed on 'normal' submarines, as opposed to special missions, where the boats did have medical personnel.

Now, while we were sitting in Bergen, with only one thing missing – which was the commandant – a convoy appeared, heading for Murmansk. And we were sent out to attack it. We were given a replacement commandant – Van der Esch.

It was quite an adventure, our first mission with Van der Esch. There was a flying boat, which would fly around the convoy in a big circle all the time. Van der Esch, who had been in the Luftwaffe previously, was not sure whether this was a German or British machine. It took 45 minutes to complete a full circuit. All the submarines which were trying to get amongst the convoy had to dive, because, after all, this was a formidable enemy – they had depth charges, and they could easily detect a submarine. So, we had to dive, and then wait and dive again, but we would constantly fall behind. So after we had done this four times, I had to report to the commanding officer that we couldn't do this anymore, because our batteries were empty and we had no more air, because we used air all the time to pump out the water from the ballast tanks to be able to float again. So we had to stay on the surface. We had a little 2 cm anti-aircraft gun, not a very big weapon. So, when the flying boat got near, all we could say was: 'Shit!' We could now see that this was a British flying boat, not a German one. We had to take evasive action — we couldn't dive any more. We started to fire our machine gun, and we began to make a right turn. Now, of course, in a situation like this everybody gets very excited, and don't forget, we were a rookie crew. The man steering the boat made a left instead of a right turn. The gun started firing – and the people downstairs thought they had been given the order to dive. We were told to turn the engines up to full speed, which was what we did when we were about to dive. So they stopped the diesel engines and started the electrical engines, which meant we suffered an immediate drop in speed. So everything which could conceivably have gone wrong had gone wrong.

We had to endure nearly four hours of depth charges, and if you've seen the film *Das Boot,* you'll know what that was like. We had no air and an empty battery, but we knew if we could just hang on in there, the destroyers could not keep this up for much longer. We had a lot of damage, but we hung on, and limped back into port."

▲ Off-duty German U-boat crew in a none-too-capacious messroom aboard U-373. With no place to escape to, it was imperative that everyone got on together.

▼ Moored up at a home port, a U-boat takes torpedoes on board for its forthcoming mission against the convoys.

▼ A wireless-operator on U-373 in his 'office'. Concise and accurate signals could send a wolf-pack to meet a convoy – and the convoy to its doom in the icy Atlantic.

▼▼ The German battlecruiser *Prinz Eugen* – one of the ships which braved the British defences in the Channel Dash. This failure to contain the German capital ships was a major blow to British morale as they struggled in the Atlantic war.

for 30 minutes under water. The maximum time we could stay under water over all was about three days, but this was only in very special circumstances. Firstly the battery had to be on maximum charge, which in normal war conditions was very rare. Also the general conditions had to be perfect – the endurance could be affected by a change in the salinity of the water, which would make the sub difficult to handle.

So, it was not so that the U-boat in itself at this time was a very potent and agile hunter. Its weapon systems were what made it so potent a force.

The problem, though, was to get the torpedo under the target. The target never maintained a steady speed and constant course. Why then, did the U-boats have such great successes? The answer lies in tactics. The subs would be placed in a long row, and the distance between them would be such that each sub could be within sight of a convoy from either side. "

People have the wrong concept of submarines – at least before the snorkel came into use. They see them as formidable fighting machines, sitting under water, having a periscope, chasing surface ships and sinking them. This was what they hoped would happen, when submarines were invented at the turn of the century, but it never came about until the invention of nuclear subs. The submarines of the Second World War were quite a different kettle of fish. The subs were propelled by diesel engines and under water by electric motors. These electric motors had to be fed by electricity. Now we know today that it is difficult to store large amounts of electrical energy in batteries – look at the problems with the electric car – this is also the prob-

lem with subs. We had lead batteries of a gigantic size. The submarine had a displacement of 500 tons – of these 500, 120 tons was battery. Compared with the huge burden of weight in the sub from the battery, the energy that came out was pitifully small. The top speed from this battery when it was full would be 2 knots. A speed which is below walking pace, slow compared with a normal merchant ship which was normally between 8 and 12 knots. Certainly passenger ships were much faster. Destroyers had a speed of about 30 knots. On the surface the sub was a little faster, but not very much – about 15 knots. And the endurance of the sub under water depended on the speed it could maintain – we could only hold the maximum speed

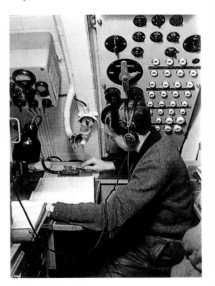

THE CHANNEL DASH

By early 1942, the German High Seas Fleet had achieved little of lasting value. *Graf Spee* had been scuttled in December 1939, *Bismarck* had been sunk in May 1941 and, although *Tirpitz* was posing a threat to Arctic convoys in Norway, the battlecruisers *Scharnhorst* and *Gneisenau* were holed up in French Atlantic ports under constant air attack.

In an effort to regain the initiative, Hitler ordered the battlecruisers, together with the heavy cruiser *Prinz Eugen*, to return to Germany – a voyage involving a move through the Channel, under the eyes of the British. The ships set out on 12 February 1942, catching British defences by surprise. Despite hastily organised air and naval attacks (during which Lieutenant-Commander Esmonde, a Swordfish pilot, won a posthumous VC), no damage was inflicted. By 15 February, the German warships were in Kiel, damaged by no more than a sea-mine.

Leading Stoker Len Horan was aboard HMS Unshaken, a submarine on patrol en route to the Gulf of Genoa via the Gulf of Lyons, when they ran into bad weather. It was 25 November and a period of winter storms was setting in – the worst conditions any of the crew could remember having to endure.

" Eventually the captain, Lieutenant Oxborrow DSC dived the boat to obtain respite from the weather and clear the boat up.

This was necessary because, even with the birdbath rigged, sea water was rushing down the conning tower and flowing over the birdbath, making the control room a miserable place to be in – as well as causing some gassing from the batteries.

The crew were quite exhausted – having to hold on hour after hour as the boat plunged and rolled in weather that only the Gulf of Lyons could produce. The prospect of diving, clearing up the boat and eating a meal in comparative comfort perked everybody up.

The boat did not stay down very long. A matter of an hour or so and all on board were most surprised to hear 'Diving stations' being called, much to everyone's disapproval. Being off watch, I was in the fore-end where all the seamen and stokers lived in the tiny 540-ton submarine. I started to go aft to my diving station in the engine room. Usually the whole crew would have been at diving stations before the

boat was surfaced, but I was again surprised to hear the air going into the ballast tanks to surface the boat. By the time I got to the control room, the boat was on her way up and was being thrown all over the place – as was usual in bad weather – but in this case it seemed to be even more violent. The red lighting which was switched on for some time before surfacing (to give lookouts time to adjust their eyes to the darkness of the night on the surface) intensified the feeling of chaos and abysmal discomfort.

The stench of sea sickness did nothing to alleviate the situation and even now, after 40 years, I recall the scene with horrific clarity. As the boat lurched I held on to a fitting and heard the captain shout down the voicepipe, 'Starboard five!' The next moment the sea poured down the conning tower and voicepipe, filling the birdbath and rushing into the control room. I recall hearing the coxswain shouting, 'She's slipping back!' Someone managed to get hold of the lanyard of the lower lid and pull it, the lid shutting under the weight of water pouring into the boat. The next order was, 'Check main vents!' It was discovered that No 6 main vent was open and that this had caused the accident.

The obvious question is, 'Why did the boat surface so soon in such atrocious conditions – and how could six main vents not have been checked out?' I feel the captain was so obsessed with getting to his patrol area in the Gulf of Genoa that he decided to surface the boat 'on the watch', but had then probably decided at short notice that everyone should be

▶PQ-18, one of the most heavily damaged convoys of the war, comes under attack. A British oiler explodes in flames as the rest of the group tries to stick together – the best hope for survival.

▼U-373 cruises on the surface, its lookouts cold, wet and miserable in the biting Atlantic gales.

closed up at their diving stations. I also think that as people were going to their diving stations with the boat rolling so badly and the birdbath rigged someone, thrown by the rolling, put his hand out to grab something grabbed six main vent lever!

It was realised that the captain and the two lookouts must have been lost, wearing as they were, Ursula suits and sea boots, as well as other clothing underneath this wet-weather gear. Pumping out the conning tower became something of a problem – with the sea breaking over the bridge and filling the tower up as fast as it was pumped out.

Eventually, after something like two hours, the lower lid was able to be opened. The first lieutenant called for two volunteers to act as lookouts, although there was a distinct feeling that they might follow the others over the side. "

◄**Another victim of the wolf-packs. It would be some time before Allied shipping could tackle the threat with advanced technology and superior tactics.**

►**Len Matthews, second from the right, with Commodore Melhuish, third from right. Serving on several ships with Melhuish, Matthews nurtured a growing admiration for his leadership and calmness in tight situations.**

Len Matthews had been Yeoman of a troop convoy which, on reaching North Africa to land troops at Bougie, was bombed and sunk. Back in Britain, he arrived in Liverpool by train at 5 am tired and dirty and was soon on his way to join the **Empire Archer,** *on a convoy under Commodore Melhuish.*

"It was the maiden voyage of the *Empire Archer* and I recall eight tanks on deck and a railway engine which subsequently partly broke adrift in the bad weather and caused much anxiety.

The 23rd was an uncomfortable day, pouring rain and the wind dead astern, which blew the thick black funnel smoke all over the bridge and made us all look like sweeps.

On the 24th the temperature started to drop and the sea grew calmer. We were sighted by enemy aircraft and submarines were about. Noon position 64N 05W. On the bridge that Christmas Eve it was crisp and cold with a bright yellow moon showing up the ships of the convoy. I smoked a cigar, leaning over the wind-breaker and ruminated on life in general. Exactly a year ago I was in the English Channel, running a small collier convoy to Southampton and we had 23 16-inch shells fall about us. I remember thinking it all futile.

The fourth Christmas Day of the war. Weather very mild and we had about six hours of half light as we were getting further north. We had an excellent lunch and everyone tried to be cheerful – but it was a bit forced.

On Boxing Day we passed into the Arctic Circle. Gradually getting colder. The only excitement was a mine that drifted by, five yards off. We counted its horns.

December 28th, the temperature still dropping – 24 degrees below. No real daylight, only about two hours of twilight. Water pipes frozen so unable to wash, unable to sleep and unable to keep warm. Inside bulkheads covered with ice. A very uncomfortable night, with a bad roll making sleep impossible.

December 29th. Another fearful night. I was repeatedly called to the bridge for ships signalling that their cargo had broken adrift. Trouble had broken out amongst the crew and the less said about this the better. They had broken into the hold and become fighting drunk on rum. Two had been knifed and one was seriously ill with broken ribs and later developed pneumonia.

December 30th. Soon after breakfast, P O Tel Stephens appeared with a garbled message he had intercepted over the W/T. 'Unidentified large warships sighted astern.'

At 0930 we observed flashes and explosions astern. We had some stragglers and were rather scattered after the bad weather we had experienced, but we were in reasonable formation.

Commodore Melhuish and myself went up to Monkey's Island. As he got to the top of the slippery iron ladder, he dropped his glasses and trod on them. This must have been the most frustrating thing, for throughout the battle he had to depend on my second-hand account of the fall of shot and what was going on generally.

Everybody obeyed well, with of course the incentive of the shelling to buck them up. Before one of our alterations I remember some argument about the direction to turn. We were being fired on from one side (port, I think) and it seemed obvious to turn away. I considered that a numerically superior enemy opposing our small force would have split forces, so we should turn into what might prove to be the lesser of two evils – and this we did.

From my vantage point on Monkey's Island there was a good view of the proceedings and, apart from occasional dashes down to the bridge to supervise the lights, I stayed on top. Our destroyer escort very gallantly took up position between us and the enemy, and by their persistence and tactics undoubtedly saved the convoy. It was my opinion at the time that if the positions were reverse and we, as Germans, were opposed by a British squadron, none of the enemy convoy ships would have survived.

Firing gradually died away astern as far as the merchant ships were concerned and this was the end of the battle. On the radio next morning, a report of the action had pride of place, and we claimed a destroyer sunk and a cruiser damaged."

WAKING THE BEAR

Slow to react after Hitler's initial onslaught, the Russian people are rallying. Not even starvation will deflect their icy resolve to eject the intruder.

German troops on the Eastern Front suffered appallingly during the winter of 1942-43. With temperatures down to −50°C, they faced the reality of the Russian weather, while encountering surprisingly effective counterattacks by soldiers more used to the harsh conditions. The Germans were lucky to survive.

Once the weather improved, Hitler resumed the offensive. The Eleventh Army cleared the Crimea, but the main attack aimed for the Caucasus. As units raced south to seize the oilfields, others marched east towards Stalingrad. Hitler shifted the bulk of his panzer force to spearhead an assault on Stalingrad itself, leaving the main advance weak. Both attacks failed. By September, General Paulus' Sixth Army was bogged down in Stalingrad, while the Caucasus advance had stalled. By November Sixth Army was cut off and, despite an attempted relief operation they faced Christmas in a nightmare of urban fighting.

Olga Rybakov was a housewife in Leningrad as, under German siege, the city ran inexorably out of food and necessary supplies. With nothing to sell, shops disappeared – the blockade left the city to face a winter of terrible hunger, cold and, eventually, starvation and death under German siege.

" The most terrible time was in December, because before, I think till August, we had commercial shops, so we could buy something. We could even buy caviar, but then the commercial shops were closed. The blockade began. And in September/October it was passable, although already in October a great friend of my mother's died. It was the first death that we heard of and in November it began to be cold and the rations were short – and were shortened.

In time there got to be less and less food. November, December and January were most tragical times. Firstly it was cold – minus 40 degrees – then the famine and hunger began to be felt and people began to starve and die from cold. Undernourishment and cold had their effects but the most deaths came at the end of February and March. Then, always when I went to find food, or when I went to the shops to receive the ra-

tion for my family and some friends living in our house I found I had to pass dead bodies – and then, on my way back, some more.

We would manage to live on these small rations only because we were rather organised people. We got them in, we put the bread in three little slices for morning, dinner and evening. Then we had something to make our rations a little more abundant – we had some gruel and preserves that were stored before the war. We had wood enough and we were warm so we could cook our meals. For the child I had milk and gruel from the district milk kitchen. Instead of white bread, which my child would not eat, I received biscuits. I think the most effective

thing was that we were rather optimistic people. My mother and I met four people that were in a dreadful nervous state and these people couldn't survive. And as I was very occupied and busy with all my duties in the house and in the family, I had no time to fret and I had no time to be ill. My mother was ill and all the time I was dealing with a family of five.

The force that kept us alive was our wish to live and to see the happy end – to see the victory and to see the punishment of the fascist regime. Another force that kept us alive was mutual help. We helped each other – and did for the old and disabled all that we could, bringing them water and rations. "

▲ With the retreat of 'General Winter' in Russia, spring floods set in, making progress difficult for the hard-pressed German troops as they resume their headlong drive.

◀ A Soviet observer on a roof scans the skies over Moscow for signs of German air strikes against his capital city.

◀◀ German troops advance on the city of Stalingrad – but here a tank has had to stop at the edge of a minefield. Sheltered by his tank, a *Panzergrenadier* takes a rest before pressing on towards the city.

Lance Corporal Maria Ivanovna Morozova had been working on a collective farm in the Proletarsky district of Moscow when war broke out. Not yet 18, she graduated from an accountancy course and took a rifle-training course as the Germans drew nearer to Moscow. By this time, national fervour was at fever pitch.

" Soon the Young Communist League Central Committee made an appeal to the young people to volunteer to defend their homeland, as the enemy was already approaching Moscow. Not only I but all the girls wanted to go to the front. My father was already there. We thought that we alone were like that . . . but when we came to the military registration and enlistment office we found there quite a few young girls. We were subjected to rigorous selection.

The first thing that was needed was, of course, hardy health. I was afraid lest I would be left out because I had often been ill in childhood and was rather weak. Besides,

NOVEMBER

3 Rommel decides to retreat in North Africa; Hitler orders 'stand fast'

4 Rommel issues orders for retreat: only 12 tanks left; 10,724 German POWs taken including nine generals

5 Allies attack Rommel's rearguard, now 100 miles to west of El Alamein

8 Operation Torch begins in NW Africa

9 German troops arrive in Tunisia unopposed by French
British successes in Egypt continue with capture of Sidi Barrani

11 French sign armistice in NW Africa

12 Eighth Army captures Tobruk

13 First sea battle of Guadalcanal
British Eighth Army clears Germans from Cyrenaica as First Army enters Tunisia from Algeria

14 15 Another night action off Guadalcanal costs US three destroyers for a Japanese battleship

16 US and Australian forces join up for assault on last Japanese stronghold in North Papua, the Buna-Gona bridgehead

19 20 Soviet counterattacks along Don River

23 Russian pincers meet west of Stalingrad, cutting off Paulus' 250,000-strong Sixth Army: 24,000 German prisoners claimed

27 German troops enter Toulon; French scuttle 72 warships docked there: four submarines escape

30 Battle of Tassafaronga: US lose one cruiser to one Japanese destroyer

girls were also refused if they were leaving their mothers alone. I had two sisters and brothers, much younger than myself but it still counted.

As we were in Moscow, we decided then to proceed to the Young Communist League Central Committee and debated for a while who was the bravest and would do the reporting. We thought that we would be alone there but it proved next to impossible to make our way through the corridor, let alone reach the secretary. Young people from all over the Soviet Union had come to the place, many of them from the occupied areas, seething to avenge the death of their near and dear.

We finally made it to the secretary in the evening and were asked: 'Well, how are you going to fight at the front if you don't know how to shoot?' We answered that we had already been taught that. 'And you know how to make a bandage, don't you?' And you know, during that very course at the military registration and enlistment office a district surgeon taught us how to bandage wounds. We had another advantage in that there were 40 of us capable of shooting and giving first aid. We were told, 'Go home and wait. You'll be given a positive answer.' And a couple of days later we had call-up papers.

We still did not know where we would be assigned, but it did not matter much what we were going to be – our only wish was to get to the front. It turned out we had been assigned to a women's sniper school. We began to study, learning garrison duty regulations, disciplinary regulations, camouflage, terrain and chemical warfare defence. We learned to mount and demount the sniper's rifle with closed eyes, to determine wind velocity, to evaluate the movement of the target and the distance to it, to dig in and to crawl. We could do it all. Upon graduation I got top grades in shooting practice and drill. I remember that the most difficult thing was to get up at the sound of alarm and to get ready in five minutes. We would take boots a size or so bigger so as not to lose much time when putting them on. We had five minutes to dress, to put on our boots and to fall in.

We eventually came to the front to join the 62nd Rifle Division outside Orsha. The commander, Colonel Borodkin, grew angry: 'They have thrust some girls upon me.' But then he invited us to have lunch with him. We would have been his daughters, as far as age was concerned. The next day he made us show how we could shoot and camouflage ourselves on the terrain. We were quite good at shooting and even did better than the men snipers who had been recalled from the front line for a two-day course. Then came the turn of terrain camouflage. The Colonel came and walked about inspecting the glade, then stepped upon a hillock but still saw nothing. Suddenly, the hillock under him begged, 'Oh, Comrade Colonel, I can't stand it any longer, you're so heavy.' What a big laugh everybody had. He just could not believe that it was possible to camouflage oneself so well. 'Now', he said, 'I wish I had not referred to you as "some girls".' We went 'hunting' (in the snipers' idiom)

CLEARING THE CRIMEA

German troops invaded the Crimea in October 1941, pushing Soviet forces back to Sevastopol which, by December, was the only area still going out, although a later Soviet counterattack out of the Caucasus gained a precarious foothold at Kerch.

In May 1942 General Erich von Manstein, commander of the German Eleventh Army, was ordered to clear the Crimea in preparation for the drive into the Caucasus. He eliminated the Kerch pocket with relative ease by 17 May – but Sevastopol proved more difficult. In early June, the Germans brought forward their 'super-heavy' artillery and began a systematic bombardment, followed by infantry assaults. The Soviets eventually succumbed on 3 July and over 100,000 of their men entered captivity.

▶ General von Manstein, left, with Colonel von Choltitz, prior to the Sevastopol breakthrough.

◀◀In the battle for Stalingrad, German machine-gunners take aim on a group of Soviet snipers who are positioned on the roof of the factory in the background.

◀Romanian mountain troops on the move towards Sevastopol. When it came to facing the harsh winter, these men had the edge over the Germans, who were ill-equipped.

side to side. The rear gunners and observers waved. Our unit, with our 20 tanks, spearheaded the attack.

The head of our attacking party was pressing on slowly to the south western outskirts of Rostov. From a nearby tank trench our infantry positioned themselves to attack the town from the south west. Commander Bünning, Sepp Fritz and myself followed the infantry and took cover in a ditch, when we heard a sudden burst of heavy fire.

We moved back and were surprised to see the men in the trucks standing up and firing from their vehicles into something in the grass. An order was shouted out: 'Switch off the engines.'

We now discovered what was going on. At the side of the road we could see a whole pack of Russian shepherd dogs, carrying strange packs on their backs. They continued to move steadily on towards us despite the gunfire. The firing grew more rapid. As the dogs went down, you could hear them howling

for the first time together with fellow sniper Masha Kozlova, camouflaged ourselves and lay in wait, me observing the terrain and Masha holding the rifle. Suddenly Masha said:

'Shoot, shoot! See, there's a German . . .'

'I'm observing. You shoot!' 'He'll be gone while we are arguing here,' she said.

'I have to make a fire map first,' I persisted, 'to designate the check points, locating the shed and the birch-tree . . .'

'Are you going to mount paper red tape, like they do at school? I've come here to shoot and not fiddle with papers!'

While we were arguing like that the German officer indeed gave orders to his soldiers. A cart appeared and the soldiers were busy passing some load along the file. The officer stood there for a while then said something and disappeared. Meanwhile we went on arguing. I noticed that he had already showed up two times, and if we did not do anything about it the next time he appeared we would miss him altogether. So when he appeared the third time, I decided to shoot. Then it occurred to me that he was after all a human being, even though he was an enemy. My hands began to tremble and a chill went down my spine. I was seized with inexplicable fear . . . I could not bring myself to take a shot at a human after plywood targets. Nevertheless, I braced myself up and pulled the trigger. He swung his arms and fell. I don't know if I killed him but I began to shiver knowing I'd killed a human being . . . **"**

SS *Alois Hedwig was with an armoured unit of the 5th SS-Division Wiking, an international anti-communist division within the SS, which, as part of the summer offensive, 1942, tried to retake Rostov. During this struggle, he and his men had their first encounter with one of the Russians' secret weapons: the mine-dog.*

" A wide terrain of steppes dotted with Russian field positions and tank trenches lay before the town. One after another, Stukas with their sirens blazing bombed the defensive positions both within and in front of the town. There was a hellish din. As the returning machines spotted our attacking forces, they flew down low and rocked from

▲Rostov partisans give themselves and their *Minenhunde* (mine-dogs) up to the Germans. The dogs were sometimes used to deliver mines under the tracks of advancing German armour.

▶▲Alois Hedwig of the SS Division *Wiking*, photographed during the Russian campaign.

terribly as they lay dying. It was an awful sound. Practically all of these beautiful dogs were shot dead before they reached anywhere near their target.

The dogs were laden with a pack of explosives around their haunches. Tied up with this pack was a piece of wood about 25 cm long. They would crawl under a vehicle and somehow dislodge the pin detonator with the help of the piece of wood – obviously blowing themselves to smithereens in the process.

I could see one especially large dog scampering away across the tank trenches. Sepp Fritz offered me his shoulder as a support for my rifle, and I shot the dog. I had no choice; I had to kill it.

Then, an *Untersturmführer* from the engineers ordered one of his platoons to follow him. I somehow got dragged along with this group of

◄ As the German threat moves ever closer to the capital, Moscow's defences are strengthened and anti-tank barriers are erected in the streets.

▼ Cold and hungry in the melting slush of early spring, Russian citizens go out in search of food.

▼▼ In the stark ruins of a Stalingrad factory, Russian snipers run to take up positions in inch-by-inch urban warfare.

SS *Herbert Brunnegger, with the SS-Totenkopf (Death's Head) Division, moved from France to fight on the Eastern Front. In the summer of 1942, having suffered heavy losses in the Demyansk pocket, they were now being topped up with raw recruits from all over the Reich who had little hope of survival.*

" During May and June 1942 our units were being topped up with young ethnic Germans and reservists from the *Reich*. Training in the rejuvenated units took place in areas close to the battlefields and under very realistic conditions.

Up until the end of July we had light security duties to carry out and in the following months we were thrust straight back into heavy fighting.

without even being able to go home first, were transported off and assigned to the *Waffen-SS* or the Wehrmacht.' I thought I'd misheard him at first and asked him to repeat the story.

So these were our 'volunteers'. But in spite of all this, they were magnificent lads, very determined to do their duty. But, they would soon find out that they had the raw deal, the 'lucky ones' had been put into the Wehrmacht.

On 13 July we went into battle again south of Demyansk, before being deployed a few days later as a 'fire-brigade' in a nearby area, where the Russians were trying with all their might to break through the pocket. On 17 July we came under a colossal barrage from heavy enemy guns.

Under the hurricane of fire from the Russian rockets and artillery most of our battlestations bedded in the swamp were blasted to pieces.

men. We were told to 'comb' the entire area ahead, looking for Russian field positions. Our platoon leader missed absolutely nothing, even when we had gone straight past very well camouflaged holes and bunkers. He was using heavy ammunition.

Suddenly in the distance we could see a shimmering silver strip. It was the Sea of Asov. On seeing the water, I suddenly realised how dry my throat was, and that since 5 o'clock this morning I had eaten nothing. It was at this point that we came up against fierce resistance and had to retreat, to be replaced by a whole company.

Our booty: a whole heap of dead dogs, and 13 Soviets, who still had a few of their dogs with them. They told us they had not wanted to send in their dogs against us. We gave them some cigarettes before they were taken off to the rear. "

I was given one of the young recruits as a dispatch rider to assist me with my duties. He was called Hugo Schrock and came from Timosoara (Romania). What he told me sounded almost criminal. One of his stories went like this: 'With many of the young lads from our village I was invited to a sports event in the neighbouring town. After this finished we were given a lecture about the brave struggle of the German Wehrmacht. We were told that we should all think deeply about this and that it was our duty to protect the German homeland from the *Untermenschen* (subhumans) from the East. Without more ado, we were then declared volunteers for the war effort, and

Our young lads' baptism of fire was horrific. Their limbs were crushed and they suffocated under the splattered bunker covers. The branches of the birch and alder trees, which had recently sprouted new leaves, were hung with human insides. We could hear the cries of the dying young soldiers all over the battlefield, and this drove even many of the 'veterans' to lose their wits. For days on end, the Russians pounded us with shells, pummelling us literally into the foul, stinking swamp.

After this terrible waste of human lives on both sides, there followed a brief respite. We then got down immediately to building new " bunkers.

1943
IN THE BALANCE

Fighting men remember a crucial year of sustained effort

Having halted Axis advances in all theatres in 1942, the Allies spent the following year pushing back the tide. The process was not easy – in most cases it entailed fighting hard against enemies who were still strong.

This was shown in the Far East and the Pacific, where Allied forces battled to clear the Japanese from eastern New Guinea and the Solomons, while compatriots further north prepared for a major drive through the Central Pacific. When that began in November 1943, at Tarawa in the Gilbert Islands, the heavy American casualties augured ill for the future.

Similarly, on the Eastern Front in Europe, Soviet advances following their victory at Stalingrad triggered German counterattacks around Kharkov and Kursk that were only blunted after particularly harsh engagements. Nor were things any better in the air over western Europe, where both the RAF and the USAAF discovered that the bombing of Germany was a costly affair.

Only in the Atlantic and North Africa were decisive Allied victorys achieved, for by May 1943 the U-boats had been contained and Tunis had fallen. The latter was followed by campaigns to seize Sicily and invade southern Italy. In the process, the Italians surrendered, but to little strategic effect – a swift and violent response by the Germans condemned the Allies to a hard slog north towards Rome in worsening terrain and weather.

CHALLENGING THE EMPIRE

As the Americans go island-hopping to drive the Japanese from the Pacific atolls, the British Allies pit their newly trained jungle forces against the Rising Sun in Burma

Once the Japanese had been halted in the Pacific, the Allies went on to the offensive to regain lost territory. In the South-West Pacific, General Douglas MacArthur masterminded a two-pronged attack on the island of New Britain, while other forces mounted an island-hopping offensive through the Solomons.

Meanwhile, further north, US forces under Admiral Chester Nimitz began a drive through the Central Pacific, aimed ultimately at Formosa. It was not a plan that received MacArthur's backing (he preferred an attack on the Philippines first) and the opening assault on the Gilbert Islands was far from easy – but by November it was clear that the Allies were on the move. This was less obvious in Burma, where British-Indian troops carried out an abortive attack in Arakan, while digging in on the Imphal plain of Eastern India, although a Chindit thrust behind Japanese lines proved the enemy could be confronted effectively.

Lieutenant Joshu Otomo was regimental flag-bearer in the Japanese 124th Infantry Regiment, 18th Division. By the beginning of 1943, the Allies were gaining ground – and the Japanese were short of supplies and had taken a heavy beating at Mount Austen on Guadalcanal. They now faced retreat or capture.

❝ I think it was just after 10 January 1943, I had gone out in front of Regimental HQ and was positioned near Mount Austen when

▲ The Chindits, Orde Wingate's specialised jungle troops, at last start to claim some successes in Burma after the original retreat. Here the men cross a river by raft.

▶▲ On Guadalcanal a US Marine pack howitzer squad fires shells into a Japanese stronghold.

ordered me to get back at once, assumed I wasn't coming back and had gone on ahead. I thought something must be badly wrong, and hurried on after HQ.

We were right at the rear, and when Regimental Commander Oka withdrew, the regimental flag was buried at Mount Austen.

We calculated that if we were taken by the Americans, the 124th Regimental flag would have to be handed over to the enemy. The final battles were so ferocious that if it came to an emergency, there might be no time to burn the flag – that's why it was done.

Because the order to withdraw was late in reaching us, we had to catch up with Regimental HQ, and in the end we were lucky enough to meet up with them after a couple of

days. It might seem miraculous, but the first evening something really odd happened. We were in the middle of this appalling jungle and came across a US forces telephone cable. We could hear a whistling sound. We crept up to it and we were able to break through the enemy position without being spotted. It was two days after that that we joined up with the Oka unit. Another battalion, was discovered by the Americans and completely wiped out.

As it happened, the order came from the army: '124 Regiment is to concentrate, with its flag.' 'That does it,' was Oka's reaction. He called together the officers of Regimental HQ and two or three NCOs – about ten in all — and they went back to Mount Austen where the flag was buried, to bring it back. I too, was summoned by the regimental commander at the time.

'Lend me that little Colt, the wo-

man's gun, that you carry,' Oka said. I'd got it, brand-new, in Borneo, and Oka must have heard from someone that I had it. 'Perhaps he's going to commit suicide,' I thought. I said goodbye to Oka and the others who were going back to Mount Austen to pick up the flag. It was about four days' journey. If you were very fit you might do it in a day, but they had almost to crawl.

Well, the regimental adjutant had a first-rate sense of direction, and in the end he found the flag and they dug it up. But on the way back, when they'd marched for about three days, they came to a river and took a break. While they were resting, the Americans spotted them and they were swept by cross-fire. All of them, regimental commander included, jumped into the river and

tried to escape, but only the regimental flag-bearer, 2nd Lieutenant Obi, survived. Obi put the flag diadem in a bag, wound the flag round his middle, buried the flag pole and then finally got back to the unit a week later.

I'm not sure, in the end, how we got the order to withdraw. When I look back, we were completely burnt out on Guadalcanal.

Part of 2nd Division was still fighting on, and we were told to cover its withdrawal. So I had to go back to the front. If you like, it was 'right about turn'. Then 2nd Division came away, and when there was no Japanese Army between me and the enemy, I got the order, 'Move on to Kaminbo.' So we marched along the sea coast by night and reached Kaminbo on the morning of February 7th. That night I was in time for the final withdrawal from Guadalcanal. At Tassafaronga, when we got down

suddenly the sound of fierce small-arms fire seemed to come from somewhere behind us. 'That's odd,' I thought, when an NCO came with a message from Regimental HQ. I was to return at once. The company commander had been killed and I had taken command of the company. I set off and reached Regimental HQ after half a day's march – but there was no one there apart from the casualties who had been left behind. I made enquiries and it turned out that the NCO who brought the message had malaria, and on the way had found he couldn't move, so he didn't arrive with me until a day later. So the regimental commander who had to the Bonegi River, I received another set of orders.

We made it by a hair's breadth – there was no-one left after that. Our platoon was down to 20 men. We didn't know there was a withdrawal from Guadalcanal – we thought all that was happening was that we were falling back on Cape Esperance. On the way there was a rainstorm and when I said, 'Take a break, then we'll go on,' an NCO called Kusunoki, a really splendid chap, said to me, 'Lieutenant, it's only a little further to Cape Esperance, let's rest when we get there.' So we went on without a rest and found a liaison NCO, Uesugi, waiting impatiently for us.

If we'd taken a rest, we would have missed the boat. That's when I first heard the phrase, 'withdrawal from Guadalcanal' from Sergeant Uesugi. 'I can't have 20 men straggling behind up to Kaminbo,' I thought, so we marched during the

Bougainville.

As we had gone along the coast for the last time, there were groups of men here, there and everywhere, without the strength to walk. And there were men who looked as if they'd fallen out and become separated from their units. Those men must all have died, or been taken prisoner. They were sick with malaria or amoebic dysentery, and many of them must have been on the point of death. They were given hand-grenades to kill themselves with.

I became a regimental adjutant in Bougainville, and along with the regimental commander who had succeeded Oka, I went to Saigon. Here there was talk of those who came back from Guadalcanal being sent back home to Japan, so I naturally thought I was going home too – but I was given notice by the regimental commander that I was to go to Burma. **"**

▶ Lieutenant Kenneth C Sparks, a US fighter pilot whose squadron made a total of 72 kills on Japanese aircraft over New Guinea.

▼ New Guinea natives play a vital role in transporting the wounded to and from dressing stations away from the battle zone.

▼▼ Supplies come to the Allies in New Guinea by outriggers manned by locals. These resources were invaluable in the tropical jungle.

about 200 rounds of ammunition.

At Buna, every Japanese position was difficult. These Japanese soldiers were crack troops. The army force was commanded by Lieutenant-General Tomitaro Horii. He had been lost in the retreat from Kokoda when he set out into the jungle, and so Colonel Yokoyama, commander of the 15th Independent Engineers, was senior officer in charge.

A key factor in the Allied success at Kokoda had been George Kenney's Fifth Air Force, which had broken up the Japanese supply system so that they had to retreat. Now the Allies were starting an offensive and the Japanese were setting up defensive positions at Gona and Buna.

As we later learned, the Japanese had established a whole series of strong defensive positions along an 11-mile front from Gona to Cape Endaiadere. It covered about 16 square miles. There were three major positions – Gona, the Sanananda Track, and the Buna area. They were all studded with blockhouses, made of coconut logs and concrete, sometimes with steel reinforcing. They were solid enough to bounce off mortar shells.

The defence consisted of these blockhouses, bunkers, trenches and many outposts. Those Japanese were masters of concealment. The air force flew over every day, but they never saw any Japanese, and so General Harding, the commander of the 32nd Division, did not think there were many in the area. He had suggested that his division would take

night. In the morning, when we reached Kaminbo, a great mass of troops was concentrated there.

However, the US forces had landed at Belahiu, about 10 km to the south of Kaminbo, and were making for Kaminbo – so if we'd been even one day late in withdrawing, we'd have been wiped out.

We came out on a destroyer. On 7th February we boarded landing craft, waiting for the sun to go down, so it would be about 4.30. If those landing craft had been spotted and fired on, it would have been all up with us, but they didn't see us, and we waited at sea for a destroyer to come from Bougainville to pick us up at 9 pm. We must have waited about four hours. It really seemed endless. The destroyer reached us without being spotted by the enemy, and we were able to make it as far as

George Weller was a war correspondent for the **Chicago Daily News**, *reporting on the Buna campaign in New Guinea in the winter of 1942/3. These are his observations of a particular battle where the Australians attacked the Japanese at Gona and, across the Girua River, the US 128th Infantry Regiment attacked Buna.*

" Our troops suffered from a shortage of everything – and particularly of artillery and transportation. General Waldron, the 32nd Division Infantry commander, had discovered an abandoned Japanese barge at Milne Bay and had commandeered it. He had two 3.7 inch Australian mountain howitzers and

Buna before November 1 1942 – in fact, as we learned, there were about 6,000 Japanese in the area.

Every treetop was a Japanese position. In those treetops would be one or more Japanese – a sharpshooter or a pair of soldiers with a .25 calibre Nambu machine gun. They had their own system of communications, using flashing mirrors or the waving of palm fronds. What looked like innocent jungle and sandy track was a fortified area, where one position led to another.

Everywhere fields of fire had been laid out, with distances carefully measured for mortars and knee mortars [rifle grenade launchers].

One Japanese position that proved the very toughest was located three miles south of Sanananda Point, where the track to Cape Killerton joined the main trail from Soputa. The land here was wooded but dry. The soil at the junction was sandy – and here the bunkers were built.

Two miles to the south, forward outposts commanded views of everything around them. One half mile to the rear another trail branched off from the Track to Cape Killerton. Here, the Japanese had another fortified position, and beyond that was a third fort.

These positions were all on dry ground – the only dry ground around. The American attackers would have to move through sago swamp four feet deep in some places, and they would have to fight in this muck, that got into their eyes and noses and mouths, rifle muzzles and breechblocks of the guns.

The attack began. The Australians were coming down the track from Wairopi to Gona. They were bogged down with malaria and heat prostration. One company moved forward to see if there were still any Japanese left in Gona. There were, in fact, about a thousand of them there in their fortified positions, centred on Gona Mission at the head of the trail.

Every approach was covered and the Australians ran into these defences. The Japanese had a very neat trick which they pulled time and again, until finally the Aussies and Americans got on to it. They would let a squadron or a platoon pass by the outposts in the trees and approach the blockhouse. Then, at a signal, the Japanese in the blockhouse would send out a rain of fire. The noise would cloak the fact that the Japanese in the trees were shooting the Allied soldiers in the back. They wrecked whole platoons that way, time after time.

At Gona one night, they pinned down 60 men of the Australian 2nd Battalion of the 31st Regiment. That night in the dark, the battalion lost 36 of the 60 men.

The Americans reached Soputa. They had the same lessons to learn. Major Bert Zeeff, executive officer, soon found himself in command of elements from four different companies, the casualties were so heavy. There were plenty of acts of heroism. One was that of Private Hymie Y Epstein, a medic. He crawled into an area swept by Japanese machine-gun fire to help wounded infantrymen. Major Zeeff told me about it. 'I was prone with a musette bag in front of my face. Epstein was in a similar position about four feet on my left. Private Sullivan was shot through the neck and was lying about ten feet in front of me to my right. Epstein said he had to take care of him. I said I wasn't ordering him to go – the fire was too heavy. Epstein crawled on his stomach, treated and bandaged Sullivan, then crawled back. He did the same for another wounded man. Next morning Private Mike Russin was hit by a sniper. Epstein went out to him – but his luck had run out. He was shot and killed. They buried him there.'

As for Buna, the Americans finally captured the place on January 5, 1943. **"**

![shield emblem] *Rear Admiral William Davis Irvin, at the time captain of the US submarine Nautilus, brought his craft away damaged from a mission to observe the beaches of Betio, Tarawa. His next mission was to help capture Apamama, landing Marines. After two days, the Marines signalled they needed to return to rearm.*

" We positioned ourselves that night and Jones came up in a rubber boat with two other men. One man had been badly shot by an

automatic rifle and the other had a hernia. Jones wanted ammunition badly, and more food. He said their progress was all right, and that he hoped he would make it around the south-east corner that night and up along the eastern shore. His men had made a reconnaissance up there and found that they had to get across a stream that ran from the ocean into a lagoon. They were pretty certain they could see Japs entrenched on the other side of this stream. There was a coconut grove and they saw the Japs under the trees. Jones' thought was that he would line his people up along this stream and face the Japs from the north side, because he thought they were entrenched there. He said that, if I surfaced off this point and opened up with our guns on this grove, our guns would be able to blast the Japs out.

Well, we were equipped with some superquick fuses that went off on palm fronds. We arranged a fire-control staff with a walkie-talkie. We were to work into a position just off this stream, as close as possible to the beach. After establishing communications we would open up and shoot into the palm trees – also shoot down if we could. We were close, however, and the trajectory of the fire was so high that it was extremely difficult to bring it any closer.

We opened up and fired. The shell hit the palm fronds and fell on to the ground below. Jones radioed back to me that that was fine, but to aim the next shell a little bit to the right, or lower, or to the left.

Both of our guns went off, but only one was working. They were made so that when they fired one would squat. The breech would go down and the brow would go up and the shell would go way over into the centre of the atoll. Our elevating mechanism had gone haywire on one gun – when it fired it would slip and throw the barrel up into the air and project the shell way out.

It wasn't very long before Jones thought that the blasts had combed out practically all the coconuts, and he didn't think there were any Japs left. He told us to cease firing. His men were going to try and get across the stream. In a very short period of time he called back and said they were across. There was nothing but debris and dead bodies – Japs all over the place, all dead. We had agreed that if he did succeed, I was to go off and do the next thing I was told to do.

In the meantime I had been told to withdraw to a particular spot south of Apamama, which was supposedly out of the action area. The surface task force command had become awfully leery of Japanese submarines. The US carrier *Lipscomb Bay* had been sunk during the action at Tarawa. As a result, practically the whole area was untenable for us. We would shoot first and ask questions afterwards. I had been screaming to Pearl Harbour to send somebody to take off the casualty I had on board. I also asked for a welder and some plates so that we could try and patch up the holes in our port side.

There was a salvage vessel that had been in the area between Apamama and Tarawa, and when the going had gotten rough with shells lying all over the place, the vessel thought the better part of valour was to get out of there, so she pulled down around the southwestern corner of this atoll. I thought this was the ship that was going to take care of my problems. I was on the surface, flashing my light and trying to tell the vessel to close. But instead she put her tail to me and ran to beat all hell. So, I began to chase her down. The more I chased, the more she tried to get away. Finally she did read my message and slowed down, but she kept her tail to us.

She put a boat in the water and sent a man over to us. I asked him if he had a welder and some plates. He didn't know anything about a welder and plates, I told him that we had a sick man we wanted to get to a doctor fast. He said he didn't have a doctor on board, so I shouted, 'What the hell are you doing down here?' His reply was, 'The Captain didn't tell me.'

◀ Captain of the US submarine *Nautilus*, William Irvin, later to become a rear admiral.

▼ Red Beach, Tarawa, where US Marines land after pre-bombardment has devastated the area.

⦿ *John Idwal Roberts was captured by the Japanese after a daring attempt to escape from the Palembang area by boat, soon after the fall of Singapore. By good fortune, a hardy man, he weathered the starvation rations and hard labour better than many others – even the more ingenious and desperate – in his camp.*

JUNGLE TRAINING

The British had not devoted a great deal of effort to training for jungle operations, believing that such areas were impassable to enemy troops. A Bush Warfare School existed at Maymyo in Burma, and facilities had been provided in Singapore, but resources and official support were in short supply. Small wonder, therefore, that in early 1942 British units suffered at the hands of the Japanese, who used the jungle for outflanking moves.

Improvements took time, and it was not until the first Chindit operation in 1943 that the British enjoyed any success in jungle warfare. Even then, disease, lack of clean water and the need to air-drop all supplies took their toll. Much more would have to be done, building on the Chindit experience.

▶ No matter how good training is, troops on exercises can only make the grade in the real jungle.

"It was hard labour. Working from the docks. I drove a truck. They formed driving parties. Ours was called Rambarra party. We were sort of attached to the Japanese equivalent of Royal Army Service Corps. We carried stuff around from the docks to their depots. Sometimes we profited by it because it was food. Our main interest in life was food. Wherever we worked we thought of 'can we eat it?' – whatever we were carrying, even weeds. We were for-

a square inch of soap, about a quarter inch thick. It was this hard, scrubbing soap – the sort we used to scrub decks with. We conserved our water allowance for drinking. Having said that, the dry season was a good time to smuggle back into camp. You were searched when you left your place of work, and searched again, but we would take these empty water containers with us to work – the Japs allowed this, as they knew we were short of water. They let us take wa-

Japs would do a body search and he would pretend to be all coy, like a sissy. The Japs used to laugh at this, but he didn't want them to touch his private parts because he had this chicken there. When he got back, he couldn't wait to get the bloody thing out – it was full of fleas.

That was the thing that went through my mind all the time – what is there here to eat? A man sank really low. If the Japs threw their dinner away – and they'd do it in front of us. Well, I never did this, but some lads did – they'd go and pick it up, no matter where they threw it. I just couldn't go that far. Men I knew pre POW days who had been respectable, honest – decent types – they were the worst. Some turned out to be the worst characters you could think of when things got tough. They would steal someone's rations. On the other side, there was Jock Monroe, he was a real tough Glaswegian – but he was the best of the lot. I wasn't well one day in the camp and he came to see me. He said, 'Och, I'll come to see you tomorrow' – and he brought me an egg. None of my RAF mates did that. It certainly showed you who was who – what people were made of, I think.

We had one chap who had been brought up in Japan – I met him in Singapore before the war started. He was a fitter on the boats. He looked like a Jap with his hair cropped. He was always on his own and he'd sit in a yoga posture on his bed. He was fluent in Japanese and he was an interpreter, but we often wondered if he was a fifth columnist. He was quiet and didn't talk to anybody. I don't know what became of him. I think he was taken aside and questioned towards the end of the war about where his feelings lay, but we never heard of him after the war.

There were some reasonable Japs – some of them were sympathetic, but on the whole they were sadistic. In the early days, before I started driving, we were working on an airfield and there was a burned-out, crashed Blenheim. They wanted it moving, it was in the way, and it took six men to move it. It had collapsed and burned out, and it needed breaking up. Six men with no tools would take maybe a week to move it – and this one Jap said, 'Two Japanese men could move that.' 'You'll be bloody lucky,' somebody said. He shouldn't have answered him back. He beat hell out of him. Made him stand to attention and slapped him with sticks, kicked him. We learned quickly that the drill was 'don't fall down'. If you fell down, they had no respect for you and would just trample on you. If you stood up you were likely to get off lighter. It was little

tunate we had a doctor, a lieutenant surgeon, with us, a voluntary reserve from Malaya, who had been in Malaya for about 20 years before the war started. He was well acquainted with native diets, native illnesses. We all suffered with beri-beri, dysentery, ring-worm and all the usual horrible things. Doc Reed, as he was known, if anyone deserved VCs, he did. He saved countless lives with nothing. Just patience and know how of native ailments.

We were issued with food – about 250 – 300 grams of rice for a working man, but if you were sick you didn't get anything – only those who went out to work. So we had to share ours with those who couldn't come out. Sugar – we had one tablespoonful every month. It was supposed to be 50gm, but it never was – more like 25gm. Same with salt – you got about 25gm of salt a month. You got about

ter back. This wasn't always water. There was water there, but we might have been somewhere the lads found tins of bully beef or tins of soup. They'd be in the can and the water was on top. You jammed the lid on tight and it was a job for the Jap to get it off – he couldn't be bothered.

I brought sugar back like that. I half filled a can with sugar and just topped it up with water. I know the sugar had mostly melted, but it was nice sweet water to make our coffee sweeter. The residue in the bottom could be dried out and it was still sweet enough to put on your rice.

There were a lot of survivors there – from the *Prince of Wales* and *Repulse* – the two ships which were sunk. Jan Whitman was one, and he brought back a live chicken in his crotch. He tied it up, lashed it, and it couldn't move a feather. He used to do a bit of a song and dance – the things like that.

Some of them did come across and give you a packet of cigarettes. There was this one prisoner who was an artist and they would come over and ask him to do a sketch of them. He'd get some tobacco or a bunch of bananas – some luxury. He didn't get any money, because money was no good anyway. They paid us 10 cents a day – I got 15 cents a day because I was a skilled man. They considered a fellow who could drive, skilled. Every ten days I got one guilder 50, and I could buy perhaps an egg, or tobacco or some sweets that the Malays used to make. Tobacco was the main thing everybody wanted – and food, of course. You could buy eggs and pineapples when they were in season. You could get a big pineapple for five cents – but you couldn't get any meat. They would say that a pig wandered into the galley today – and this was a piece of pork which passed through the big soups they made and there were 2,000

men waiting. All you got was a sniff – could just about taste it. In the mornings we had pap – a very wet sort of rice like porridge. Our next meal was outside – they used to bring it to our place of work – this would be maybe 100 gm of rice and so-called soup, which was just river weeds which were collected by the natives.

In the evening we had the remainder of the rice which was dry, and a better soup. This was where the pig might appear on the menu. It might be pork soup or some horrible fish – sea slugs. They looked terrible and tasted terrible too, but you ate it. Eating was everything and you made it last as long as you could. 'I can make mine last longer than you' – it made people think you'd got more. Even if you started eating well after the others, people liked to eat on their own, while everybody watched them. I used to eat like hell, in case anybody, by any chance, happened to ask if anybody wanted any more. They never said that, but you never knew. The rations used to come to each mess, with 20 of us in

each mess. Two men issued it, and there were two different men each day, so you couldn't work a racket – and there were rackets being worked there, believe me. That was where I first heard the name black market. The two men would be dealing out the food and all the plates would be down, in an order. The man who was first today would be the man who, if there was any left over, be it just a spoonful, he'd get it. Tomorrow he would be at the end of the queue. Number two would get anything left over. Sometimes we would issue it so that there were 20 equal portions, and there was enough for three left, perhaps – so the next three would have an extra portion. But the next day, those three would be at the bottom of the queue and they would have to wait a week until they came in for 'leggee', as it was called.

There was Tenko every morning, when we were counted. I'd be standing in line at the back, and the guy in front of me, I could see every bone in his spine and all his ribs. I used to say, 'I'm not like that am I?' You kidded yourself a lot. **"**

▼ **The Indian Mountain Battery uses Texas mules to carry the Burmese guns in the rugged, mountainous and jungle-covered terrain of the frontier regions of Burma, where wheeled transport is of no use.**

▼▶ **Air-drops of supplies help to keep the Allied drive in the Arakan on the move. While this was invaluable to the men on the ground, the pilots had to brave all weathers to keep the service going. Here, parachutes litter the dropping zone in a large clear area.**

◄

Brigadier Michael Calvert, nicknamed 'Mad Mike', had trained commandos and operated a jungle warfare school in Burma before commanding a column in Orde Wingate's first Chindit campaign. Under Wingate's positive jungle leadership, he led 77 Brigade in many successful behind-the-lines missions in 1943.

"I first met Wingate when I came into my office and there was an officer, a short squat officer sitting in my chair, and I said, 'Who are you?' And he said 'I'm Wingate.' I said, 'Well I'm Calvert and that's my chair and I'm the commandant here.' He said, 'I'm very sorry', and he got up and I gave him another chair – I didn't know who he was – I didn't know the name Wingate. Then he started to talk. I was training guerrillas and I had tried to learn as much as I could about this warfare from books, and from other men who had fought as such, then I came across Wingate. I found he was miles ahead of anybody else I'd ever heard of or spoken to. British Forces had never held a position under attack for more than three weeks. Morale was low, and we were confused, we were trying to take on the world.

Then here came Wingate with set ideas, determination and optimism. He had a tremendous belief in the British soldier – not quite such belief in the British officer, because he reckoned that often he'd been trained wrong. And he believed that with proper training and with his own zest and conviction, the British soldier could beat anyone in the world after good training.

The first Wingate operation took place in 1943 after the retreat from Burma. Wingate had been in Burma, I took him round before the retreat so he had knowledge of it. The first operation was initially to accompany a general advance into Burma, but this was cancelled. However Wavell wanted the expedition to go forward. It was a testing operation. We went in in seven columns crossing the Chindwin and, as official history says, we averaged about a 1,500-mile march. My column of Gurkhas plus British commandos got on to the main Japanese lines – of communication, their railway – and we blew up bridges in about five places. I blew up the railway in about 70 different places. My orders were to link up with another two columns and attack the Japanese headquarters.

Then things became difficult. We got surrounded, the Japanese found out what we were and of course we were on air supply all the time – and we were running beyond it. We fought a few actions, then we were given the orders to retire. We got back fairly intact but many other groups got caught and about one third of the force was lost.

This was a raid, its tactical and strategic effect was not great – its main effect was on the morale of the British and Indian troops. Our forces were not picked men, they were ordinary British and Gurkha battalions and the rest of the army said 'My God if those people can do it, we can'. And they could, as they showed later. We had been taught very well and very hard by Wingate in central India, so by the time we went into the jungle on the first operation we understood column drill and we relied upon mobility to prevent being ambushed by the very much stronger Japanese."

ROUND-THE -CLOCK ATTRITION

In a whirlwind retaliation to the Luftwaffe's attacks on Britain, 'Bomber' Harris's squadrons mount a massive, relentless – and costly – campaign against Germany's stunned cities.

Pilot Officer Tony Bird DFC, of 61 Squadron, had survived several narrow squeaks when, on 2 December 1943, he and his crew completed their sixth operation to Berlin, at the end of which British Movietone News visited the squadron to take a short interview with the crew, and provided his mother with a glimpse of her son at war.

"Close friends were made and lost in so short a time – and by the end of the war, over 2,000 aircrew were to die in operations over Germany from the two squadrons based together at the airfield.

As was the custom, as a newly arrived pilot, I was sent on an operation with an experienced pilot and crew, so that on this occasion there were eight of us in the aircraft instead of the usual seven.

The target was Berlin, which I was soon to get to know rather well, if only from the air. The first pilot and captain of the aircraft was Sergeant Strange, soon to be listed among those who failed to return from operations, but not before his commission to pilot officer was confirmed.

Our approach to the target – the wall of bursting flak shells ahead – looked almost solid and it seemed like suicide to attempt to continue towards it.

It was a great relief to discover that the objects which looked so daunting were large puffs of black smoke from shells that had already exploded, and we flew safely through or close by many of them with nothing worse than turbulence from the swirling air.

The thing to worry about was from shells about to burst in the vicinity – but there was no way of knowing of

▲ The opposition from the ground – German 8.8 cm anti-aircraft guns greet the night bombers.

◄ By March 1943, Bomber Command had 18 squadrons of Avro Lancaster B Mk I aircraft.

them until too late.

We were fortunate, however, and were able to avoid the dreaded searchlight fingers probing the sky, our only damage being slight peppering from the shrapnel of shells that had burst some distance from us.

We arrived safely back at our base for debriefing and the usual bacon and eggs early breakfast, having been in the air for almost eight hours. The conversation rarely strayed from details of our flight. In common with other returning crews, we had witnessed several of our aircraft going down in flames – a sad and frightening sight, visible for several miles on a clear night. We did not see any escapes by parachute, but it was no easy matter to exit a

steeply diving burning bomber.

At our operational altitude of about 20,000 feet, nearly four miles high, any physical activity became difficult in our unpressurised aircraft once the oxygen supply was disconnected, especially with our heavy flying clothes to hamper any movement.

Portable oxygen bottles, suitable for short periods were available, but connecting them in an emergency wasted precious seconds, which could make the difference between life and death for us.

I remember in my pilot's log book 23 August 1943 as the date of my first operation to Berlin, and on the 27th August, I was ready to carry out my first Lancaster operation over Germany as Captain with my own crew.

The target was Nuremberg and the bomb-load of 9,100 lb or about 4,116 kg. On a short flight, the Lancaster could carry well over 5,000 kgs of bombs, but the longer the journey, the more fuel that was needed, and consequently less bomb-load to avoid exceeding the safe permitted level. Our operation to Nuremberg was completed safely, as was one to München Gladbach three fights later.

Now that my commission had come through, I was expected to eat in the Officers' Mess, but continued to use the Sergeants' Mess, preferring to remain with my crew, who were all sergeants at this stage. Eventually I was ordered by the commanding officer to conform, but I was still a frequent visitor to the Sergeants' Mess.

On the 3rd September, a groan went up from the assembled aircrew at operational briefing. The target was Berlin – known to us as 'the Big City'.

Not only was the Berlin trip a long and arduous eight hours' flight, but we were over the most heavily defended area of Germany for longer

---

By 1943, the RAF's strategic bombing campaign against Germany – based on the principle of night area-bombing of entire cities rather than daylight precision-bombing of individual factories – was beginning to gear up. New and improved aircraft, more efficient radar aids to navigation and bomb-aiming, and a special Pathfinder force to spearhead the bomber streams all made Bomber Command a potentially formidable force. But when the RAF shifted to a campaign against Berlin in November 1943, many tactical and operational problems remained unsolved.

The Americans fared no better, particularly as they insisted on flying by day in 'self-defending' B-17 Flying Fortresses and B-24 Liberators. However, by the end of the year, P-51D Mustang escort fighters, capable of accompanying the bombers deep into Germany, had appeared. In time, their intervention would prove decisive.

▲ **Squadron Leader Millson DFC (with paper) and members of his crew who, between them, completed 228 missions over enemy targets – an amazing record given the usual high casualty rate.**

spite of that we still had to continue flying straight and level until the camera had taken the vital photograph of our bombs exploding on the target.

There was great rivalry amongst bomber crews to bring back a clear picture proving that they had hit the target accurately. The photographs were enlarged and posted up for all to see, and any crew whose picture was off target was the subject of some derision.

It seemed like hours instead of seconds during which I had to maintain a straight and level heading while flak shells were bursting all around us in a proximity much too close for comfort.

Suddenly the flak in our immediate area ceased, and almost as the camera shutter opened to take the picture, the fighters attacked. I was now able to take avoiding action and put the Lancaster into a steep dive on full throttle. With the four Rolls Royce Merlin engines on maximum power and with the help of gravity, the airspeed quickly exceeded 300 mph – twice our normal cruising speed – but still far less than the fighters were capable of.

We felt and heard the thud of the fighters' cannon shells hitting our aircraft as I twisted and turned, first one way then another, to make it difficult for the fixed-gun fighters to aim accurately.

We knew, then, why the flak had stopped so suddenly. It was a signal for the fighters to attack. The searchlight fingers were, by now, pointing almost horizontally in their effort to keep us illuminated – and suddenly we were in blessed darkness.

The port outer engine, which had been hit by the fighters' cannon shells, was now useless, and we had dived over 5,000 feet below our nor-

than on almost any other target. The worst part of the operation was the need to fly the aircraft straight and level on the bombing run to enable the bomb-aimer to take accurate aim at the target, and then to continue on until the automatic camera had recorded the bombs exploding on target. During all this time it was not possible to change heading or to weave so as to avoid attack from any enemy fighters or flak.

The Germans had started to use barely visible ultraviolet master searchlights, which were used in conjunction with a number of 'slave' normal white searchlights. Within a second or two of an ultraviolet beam shining on one of our bombers, all the white lights in the area would converge on to the unfortunate aircraft, forming a dazzling searchlight cone, several hundred yards wide from which it was difficult to escape. The bomber pilot and crew would be dazzled and quite unable to see attacking German fighters coming in from the surrounding darkness.

Just as we released our bombs over the target, we found ourselves caught in a searchlight cone but in

'BOMBER' HARRIS

Air Marshal Arthur 'Bomber' Harris was a firm advocate of strategic bombing as a 'war-winner', capable of destroying German industry and civilian morale without the need for land campaigns.

Harris' command was characterised by single-minded dedication to his task, shown as early as May 1942, when he mounted the first of the '1,000-Bomber' raids, even though it meant using every available aircraft. Thereafter, the campaign grew and, as techniques, aircraft and radar aids became available, almost nightly raids were carried out against urban targets. The costs to the RAF were high, and Germany did not collapse as a result of bombing alone – but Harris' role in the final victory could not be denied.

▶ **Arthur Harris, third from left, studies aerial shots of bombing attacks as part of future planning.**

▶ Their target obscured by thick cloud, B-17s drop a deadly raid of bombs during a daylight raid.

mal operational height.

Our navigator hurriedly worked out a revised flight plan for the return journey while I trimmed the aircraft to fly on three engines due to the damage.

There were no further sightings of the fighters, who had probably returned to the main bomber stream above. Due to the limited time that they could stay airborne, the single-engine fighters were reluctant to lose too much height for fear that they would not have sufficient fuel to climb back up again.

Our route back took us over Denmark and then over the North Sea to our base in Lincolnshire. We were an hour late in arriving back, limping along at 115 mph on three engines and had been given up for lost by our ground crew.

Our faithful ground crew were still waiting up as usual to welcome us back. 'We thought we would wait up in case you made it,' one of them said laconically – but the joy of relief on their faces needed no words. We had made it back.

The air battle over Berlin was starting in earnest and we were destined to complete six bombing missions to 'the Big City'.

On 2 December 1943, we completed our sixth operation to Berlin and British Movietone News visited the squadron to interview us and take a short movie film. The newsreel featuring us was shown throughout the country and was seen by my mother at a Croydon cinema. In her amazement and excitement, she jumped up and cried out, 'That's my Tony,' no doubt to the surprise of the surrounding audience. "

Werner Schroer was, by 1943, one of the Luftwaffe's more experienced night-fighter pilots, flying in defence of his home-land's cities. He and his comrades started to notice the extended range of the USAAF escort fighters – a new and serious threat to the existing defence set-up in Germany – when they came up close to them.

" When I met the first Fortresses in '43, I think I had some experience in flying, and I didn't attack them coming from behind in a direct way, but I tried to have my plane approaching in a way to give no chance to the rear gunner to get me. They started firing at one thousand metres almost with their tracer ammunition in order to frighten us, and

I told my younger pilot who had no experience to close his eyes attacking from behind. Naturally the best thing was to attack them when you were in a far higher altitude and you could transform your altitude into velocity and get right behind them. Behind them all of a sudden in order to surprise them. But this didn't happen very often. My most vivid memory was when I cruised down behind a Fortress which I hadn't expected to approach, and I was so close that I could really see the rear gunner – and saw him frightened as I was.

I finally got him. I had a very nice experience with him because he was shot down and wasn't wounded but he was captured and interrogated. And I met him and he told me he was a sergeant – he told me that he was very surprised that he bailed out and the pilot himself managed to make an emergency landing.

Any fighter escort – Mustangs or Thunderbolts – gave us much concern because of their quantities. They arrived with the bombers – they even came before the bombers showed up, and attacked our airfields. And we were very much astonished about their long-range capabilities. But we had nothing the same, and I think they frightened us quite a bit.

In one day once, we had three bombers and another time two Fortresses and one Mustang in two hours flight against a raid on Berlin. We managed to assemble more than a hundred fighters in one formation and attack the American bombers with strength – that had never " happened before.

★ *Sergeant Donald Chase of the USAAF's 44th Bomber Group had flown his first missions over Sicily before transferring to a Norfolk base. Already wise to the dangers and pitfalls of being in a bomber crew, he selected battlehardened men to accompany him in his B-24, Heaven Can Wait.*

" It was my duty as the radio operator to leave my regular position behind the co-pilot's seat and go to the belly of the B-24 where I would straddle the narrow catwalk off the bomb bay and activate a push-type lever which prevented the bomb doors from creeping, once the doors were opened preparatory to the bomb-run. Then I had to watch the bombs fall and, to the best of my ability, assess the bombing results as they fell.

So there I was on my first mission poised in the belly of our ship waiting for our load of 12,500-pound bombs to drop when I noticed the bombs of our sister ships plummeting earthwards. But not ours. Could it be my fault? Did the bomb doors creep in? I pushed the anti-creep lever as hard as I could. There was no creepage. So I returned to the cabin area and plugged in my headset and tuned into the intercom. 'Use the back-up release, Whit,' called the bombardier Harold Schwab. Our pilot Charles Whitlock nodded to the co-pilot William Phipps. Phipps reached down to the console be-

◀ Armourers of the USAAF 376th Bombardment Group prepare a bomb for a mission over the Ploesti oilfields.

▼ A Liberator skims low over the chimneys of the Astra Romana oil refinery at Ploesti. Despite good results, the refinery was soon restored to its previous level of production.

tween the pilot and co-pilot seats and grabbed hold of a T-shaped handle and pulled upwards. The bombs were still cradled in their racks. Phipps apparently didn't have enough leverage to activate the release handle.

So, I stood between the pilot and co-pilot's seats, tapped Phipps' arm and pointed to myself and I grabbed the handle with both hands and pulled with all my strength.

Immediately the plane lurched upward as 6,000 pounds of metal left *Heaven Can Wait*. The bombs of course landed far from the target area and splintered hundreds of trees. That was the event on my first mission. We had flown from Benina in Libya to attack the Cerbini air base in Sicily – we had on the whole successfully bombed the base and sustained only moderate damage. This was July 1943.

A particularly memorable event happened once when we landed. Two or three mechanics and armourers gave us the thumbs up greeting and hastily removed canteens of water from the bomb bay section. The water was still frozen from its five-miles-high ride and would soon be savoured by the men in the late afternoon heat. Water was tanked into base and very little was allowed for personal use. Each of us however, did receive an allotment of one can of beer a day. We often carried many cans of water and several of the men's hoarded beer, festooned to the bomb bay struts, on mission. A bomber cost about $300,000, but more importantly and personally grievous would have been the loss to more than 200 airman of the stashes of water and beer !

This was my last mission before reaching England and I was in a non-assigned state of limbo. Maybe it was guilt or pride or shame. Whatever, I decided to complete my tour of combat, 25 missions. But not if I could help it with an inexperienced crew.

My opportunity came towards

mid-December when the radio man of Lt James Hill's crew fell, or was blown from the foot-wide bomb bay catwalk during a bomb-run and ended up parachuting into France. This was a great crew to join as they had survived the 90 per cent group loss suffered by the 44th in just three missions and had several enemy aircraft credited to their gunners. John Pitcovick in the top turret had tallied six himself. It made me feel comfortable flying as radio operator with John in the turret above me. Fortunately I flew ten missions with this battle experienced crew. The first mission was my first for three months as we went for Bremen from the 'drome at Shipham in Norfolk. The flak was

'MEMPHIS BELLE'

US aircrew involved in the bombing campaign against Germany had to fly 25 missions to complete a 'tour', after which they were rotated home. Their chances were not high, but by spring of 1943 it was apparent that a number of aircraft and their crews were approaching the magic figure. Hollywood producer William Wyler suggested that a film should be made, both to commemorate the event and to act as a training aid for future crews.

The aircraft chosen was a B-17F, nicknamed *Memphis Belle* (after the pilot's girlfriend), serving with the 324th Bombardment Squadron, 91st Bomb-Group, of the Eighth USAAF. Stationed at Bassingbourn, it later transpired that this was not the first B-17 to reach the 25-mission total, but by then Wyler was already filming. The result – based on *Memphis Belle*'s final raid, against Lorient on 17 May 1943 and shot, unusually, in colour – was one of the best air documentaries of the war.

◀ Crew of the *Memphis Belle* prepare to fly back to America after their 25 successful missions.

intense and accurate and very frightening. Compared to Italy, the flak coming up was thicker, more intimidating and fired with greater accuracy. When we got back I downed my two ounces of whisky and it hit my stomach like an exploding star . . . mission eight, 17 to go!

Just before Christmas that year, it was 22 December, 22 aircraft took off to attack Münster, an important railway and waterway centre as well as an important garrison. Some of the other groups were met by enemy aircraft but we managed to get back without being engaged. We had bombed at altitude where the temperatures of 50-55° below were not uncommon. The aircraft's enclosed forward cabin, while not heated, did protect us from the wind. But after, especially at the waist gun positions, the 170 mph winds coupled with arctic-like mercury readings caused much suffering to the crew. Minor and severe cases of frost bite occurred. When we got electrically heated, snug-fitting flying suits (bunny suits) the problem was minimised.

The worst experience I had was when a wounded crewman was left unattended for just a few minutes while the rest fought off enemy aircraft. He died from exposure. Another time one was alive and in need of morphine, suffering extreme pain because syringe needles broke when attempting to penetrate hard, deep-frozen skin. But, conversely this cold temperature sometimes saved lives. A blood-spurting limb or severed artery would be freeze cauterised, so a life would be saved by bearing the injury to the icy blast. 🟊

▶ A damaged Messerschmitt Bf-109, caught by the gun camera of the American aircraft which hit it.

Staff Sergeant Russell D. Hayes was a radio operator/air gunner flying in a B-24 Liberator from Benghazi to occupied Europe. He recalls the terrible risks the crews were exposed to on daylight, low-level raids as crews gambled on outrunning the German fighters waiting to end their mission.

❝ My fifth mission was to the oilfields at Ploesti, Romania, the low-level raids, 1 August 1943.

But nevertheless, we did go on this mission and we were briefed to hit at low level – and we did. In fact we went across the target at 180 feet at 220 mph. You could look right down into those gunners' eyes and they were firing 20 and 40 mm cannons right back at us. I looked out of the window and I saw a big ball of fire coming. I jumped back thinking that I'm going to get it in the nose, but it

was gone behind before I could jump. It seemed like it was between the tail and the trailing edge of the forward wing but it did miss us. I fell backwards on the spent ammunition rounds and the waistgunner thought I had been hit and by the look on his face I thought I had been hit too, but I got back up again. By now we were over the target and you could see the previous planes' bombs lying down there. They were phosphorous bombs, burning through these big tanks and we were hoping that they would not go through until we had passed over them. One tank did explode, and the thing blew up like a soup can after you've put a firecracker under it. Everything was on fire. The bombs that were dropped had a one-and-a-half hour delayed action fuse and one of them hung up in the bomb bay, we had to cut it out with an axe. It was a 300 pound fragmentation bomb and when we did get it out we were about a-half mile from the target. I watched it roll down the main street of a small vil-

lage and while we were flying over those homes, at probably 30 to 40 feet off the ground, one man – he came out in his shirt sleeves with a gun and it resembled a guy shooting skeet. He just looked for one of the targets to take a shot at and then shot.

We ended up with a 32-calibre shell in one engine and we were never sure whether it came from his rifle or from another gun source. We flew on at about 15 to 20 feet off the ground and when we came to a hedgerow we'd kind of just raise it up. It was quite an operation for a 30-ton bomber flying that close to the ground. We continued on, and of course we were flying through the oilfields by then. The derricks were old, made of wood. We were told to fire at them with our incendiary shells and you would hit them with a couple of bursts and they would pop on fire.

As we had approached the target, right before the bomb-drop, the right wingman who had been flying to our right, had got a direct hit in the bomb bay which carried a bomb bay fuel tank full of fuel – 100-octane fuel. It doesn't take much to set that off. And the complete bottom of the airplane was streaming gasoline and fire and I'm not sure if they were aware of it or not. The pilot knew he was losing his altitude but the crew in the waist window were looking out.

▶ Flying officer D W Samson, an Australian, watches as ground crew put the finishing touches to his aircraft before flying escort to a daylight raid. The long range of the Mustang allowed it to accompany the bombers far over enemy territory.

We waved goodbye.

They waved back, it was all they could do. We watched him go down looking for a place to land – to go in on a belly landing. They came in trying to get to a dry river bed, but they went into a bunch of trees which were about 20 to 30 feet high. They were clipping off the tops of the trees, leaving a trail of fire and gasoline behind for many yards and then as the plane finally came to rest, it spun round and went off – poof – like a paper box that suddenly burst into flames. We thought nobody would survive that but later, years later, I heard that the top turret gunner was blown clear and is still living

somewhere in the US.

The plane on our left – we lost him. I never did see where he crashed. Another was hit just before the run but he dropped his bombs and then hit the ground and blew up, killing all on board – he got the Medal of Honour for that feat. We continued on at 30 feet. The German fighters were just like flies around us by then. They couldn't quite work out what our altitude was because they couldn't believe a four-engined bomber would fly only 15 to 20 feet off the ground and there was no way for them to attack. They would try to attack us and fly right into the ground. "

▼ Flying Fortresses return from the first USAAF bombing mission to Germany, 27 January 1943. Ground crew rally round to discover what the defences were like over Wilhelmshaven – and to look for any damage to the aircraft.

OPERATION FUSTIAN

A new terrain with buildings and trees opens up for soldiers straight from the desert war, as they land on Sicily – just the first step towards a major assault on Mussolini's mainland fortress.

I t took the Allies until May 1943 to clear the Axis armies from North Africa, despite General Sir Bernard Montgomery's victory at Alamein and the Torch landings in November 1942. Now the Allies had to decide on their next move. The American preference was for a shift to North-West Europe, but if Italy could be attacked, it would open up the 'soft underbelly' of Europe. Consequently, Sicily was invaded on 10 July 1943, helping to trigger the overthrow of Mussolini in Italy. In early September, the Allies crossed the Straits of Messina, attacking both Taranto and Salerno. Marshal Pietro Badoglio (Mussolini's replacement) sued for peace.

As Allied troops landed on 9 September, Field Marshal Albert Kesselring sent forces south to oppose them. Although the Allies eventually broke out, the weather had deteriorated and the Germans had been able to construct mountain defences. The Italian campaign was not easy.

Sergeant Joe Hardy had returned from Dunkirk then trained for a mountain campaign in Norway – only to be told that he was to retrain for airborne work. After training, victory in the desert seemed secure, so his first mission was to Sicily as Acting Lance Corporal, 1st Bn, Border Regiment, 1st Airlanding Brigade.

❝ After training, Sicily was our first major mission. Getting into the glider, I dropped my torch just inside the door. It went straight through the canvas and on to the ground below – I remember quite plainly thinking that if all the Italian Army is laying on a reception committee, I will still be very glad to get

▲ The American flank of the attack has reached Messina on Sicily – and far from getting a hostile reception, they are greeted with flowers by grateful locals, no doubt weary of the fascist regime.

back on to the ground.

As we approached the coast just below Syracuse, it seemed that all the Italian Army was trying to blast us out of the sky. The slow curve the tracer formed as it came up was almost nice to watch – but the speed at which it flew past the window was apt to make one wish the flying part of the affair was over. We were supposed to land a few hundred yards in from the sea, but most of us found that we were gliding some long time before we should have been. The moment that a glider releases the tow-rope, it must necessarily head downwards. Whether my glider pilot hit the release switch or whether it was the tug aircraft that cast us off, I shall never know. The tugs naturally wanted to get away from that flak as quickly as possible. It was decidedly unhealthy. Who was to blame, I do not know – I do know that the 1st Airlanding Brigade lost a terrible amount of its men through drowning.

My glider hit the water about 200 yards from the shoreline, the complete fuselage sank below water level, but the wings kept the framework from sinking altogether. My seat was near the door at the rear, and a split second found me completely in the drink. The tail end was completely submerged. An air-lock in the part of the fuselage connected to the wings left just enough room for most of the men to get a gulp of air. I managed to get the door open somehow, managed to get my fingers round the tubular steel on the upper side of the fuselage, release my equipment and pull myself out.

I immediately heard the voices of those trapped in the forward part of the fuselage, so I kicked my way along the top, tearing the canvas

with each kick. Two or three heads popped out, then the men started to tear at the canvas from the inside. To crash in the drink in the very early morning, black dark, is not a nice experience. If we ducked, there was a fair chance of getting drowned. If we didn't, there was a very fair chance of getting shot.

It was a fairly long swim to the shore, so I asked for volunteers to swim in with the object of trying to do something about the machine guns.

I was wearing a brand new pair of boots at the time, so I took them off,

tied the laces together and hung them round my neck, dumped all my gear except my revolver, and three of us slid quietly into the water. (In fact I lost the boots in the water.) To swim in the Mediterranean in the dark is an almost unbelievable experience. The phosphorus in the water is so concentrated that the arm movements caused what to us seemed like a million lights with each stroke.

When we made it to the shore, we found ourselves at the foot of a perpendicular cliff that was impossible to climb in the dark.

When it became light enough for us to scale the cliff, up we went, looking absolutely ridiculous. On arrival at the top we ran straight into three Italian machine-gunners. They were so surprised to see us appear a few yards in front of them, that they just couldn't decide what was best to do. I shouted in my very best mixture of obscene English, French and Italian, that 'La guerra finito. Mussolini kaput!' They were very willing to agree to that suggestion, so I immediately relieved one of them of his boots and then demanded that the rest of them should show us how to use their weapons. We took the weapons, explained to them that they were prisoners, to stay exactly where they were and they would come to no further harm. As to whom they were the prisoners of – they were perfectly happy with the guerra finito story, so that was good enough.

By this time, the CO had joined us

▲ As soon as they arrive, Sherman tanks move inland. Inset: men of the 2nd Bn Seaforth Highlanders embark on LCIs for the invasion.

◄ Bren-carriers land at Salerno on the mainland.

► Gun crew site a 17-pounder anti-tank gun for action.

and he suggested to me that he must get to where the regiment was supposed to be, to get command of whatever troops were available, so he and I set off. As the pair of us had to go through perhaps a mile and a half of what we presumed was enemy-held territory, I thought that his idea was extremely unfunny, but one does not argue with one's CO. Off we went.

Progressing down a hillside. I looked over a wall on the lower side of the land and found myself looking directly into a quarry in which there were something like 80 people, about 20 of them female. The remainder of them were Italian soldiers, all fully armed. I gave them the *guerra finito* business, and was then left with no other option but to go further down the lane, turn into the quarry, and walk up to the soldiers as though I was leading a thousand men, and explain that Mus-

solini was *kaput*.

I then got hold of one of the soldiers, made him lean his rifle against a very large rock, raise another rock above his head, and throw it down as hard as he could on to the rifle. The ladies and soldiers started to cheer.

As soon as it seemed to me that they had accepted the idea of destroying everything, I turned my back to walk out of the quarry. For the 20 or so paces that I had to take to get into the lane, I felt that my back was at least four yards wide, and that it was due to get the sharp end of an Italian bullet at any second. I was terribly pleased to get to the corner.

 Staff Sergeant TN Moore of the Glider Pilot Regiment was to bring in troops to capture vital areas near the port of Syracuse on Sicily. High winds began to foul up the plans, then the tug pilot dived to avoid searchlights. The glider followed the tug down and was soon flying just above sea level.

" We cast off at about 2,300 feet, a mile and a half from the coast. The wheels were smashed on landing and the glider came on to an abrupt stop as the nose hit a large rock. This penetrated the nose of the machine, broke my ankle and pinned my legs under the cockpit seat.

Within a few seconds of landing, the fabric top of the fuselage was in flames, caused by grenades thrown by the Italians. Flaming patches of fabric fell into the handcarts of ammunition in the centre of the glider and before all the troops could escape there was a series of explosions caused by the ignition of phosphorus grenades and mortar bombs.

Six of the airborne infantry managed to get out, but the remainder perished. Those who did escape took cover among the rocks and shrubs, but the explosions were so violent that one man was killed well over 100 yards away. I saw Garrett help one injured man from the burning machine and then stumble. A piece of flying grenade or bomb struck his left arm and tore away practically the whole of the elbow joint. I was unable to move and the cushion on my seat was beginning to burn.

Garrett struggled to the nose of the glider and with his right arm, lifted it a little. I knew this was my only chance. I threw myself forward and wrenched myself free. As I did so, I felt the bone break. Once free, Garrett and I tried, but without success, to pull another man from the wreckage. He was unconscious and already burnt.

During the night, Garrett lost a lot of blood – he was later given a total of seven pints – and he suffered from intense cold. I used a puttee as a tourniquet to control the bleeding, but by morning his forearm was completely black.

We heard a cry from some 50 yards away and saw someone propelling himself towards us on his back by the use of his elbows. We recognised him as the corporal from our glider. He had been struck between the knees by an exploding grenade. I ripped the legs off his trousers and tried to dress his wounds, but it was almost hopeless, for the hole in each knee was larger than a field dressing.

I dragged myself towards the wreck of our Waco and came across a dead Italian. I took his carbine and bayonet and found that together they would serve as a crutch. On

1943

reaching the beach, I lay there for some time, half-submerged in the sea. I dozed for a time and when I awoke, I found a large fish nosing about my legs. It had been attracted by the blood oozing from my trousers into the water. I though of tickling trout in the Cumbrian hills, but without the finesse that I had been taught there, I scooped it out of the sea on to the beach. I ate it raw with great gusto. I swallowed two Benzedrine tablets and set out to swim to the shipping. About a quarter of a mile out, I saw the corporal had reached the first apron fence and got himself a couple of wooden sticks. I could see a farmhouse about three-quarters of a mile ahead of the corporal, and near the beach, and I decided to swim along the beach and contact him there.

I scrambled ashore near the farm and hauled myself towards it along a wire fence. It proved to be completely deserted. The corporal followed slowly and was obviously in great pain as he pushed himself along with his sticks. By the time he reached the farm, he was obviously at the end of his strength. He lay down in front of a smouldering charcoal fire and proceeded to fortify himself with a piece of cheese.

We discussed means of getting Garrett under cover. The corporal had found a path which led quite near the glider and we made plans to use a couple of donkeys from the stable. I had made myself a splint for my injured leg and found that, with a stick, I could get along.

The corporal wanted some water from the well in the courtyard, and on his way, poked the smouldering charcoal fire. It immediately burst into flame and the glow must have been plainly visible for quite a distance, for the door was open. In a few moments I heard voices, so I hid under a friendly pile of beans. I heard the sound of approaching footsteps and someone stood in the doorway, silhouetted against the evening sky. For a few anxious moments there was silence, and then I realised that the visitor was wearing a British steel helmet. A medical officer and a stretcher party from an Indian division having spent all day searching for us had given up, and were returning to Avola when they saw the light at the farm.

Garrett lost his arm and the corporal found he would never bend his knees again. Garrett, by his bravery and self-sacrifice, had undoubtedly saved my life. **"**

After being present at the landings at Syracuse on July 10, HMS Aurora with Royal Marine Robert Porter on board was sent to follow the Eighth Army along Sicily's eastern coast, occupying every port. At first there was little opposition, even at Syracuse, the first port of call on his ship's occupying tour.

" After a couple of days in Syracuse harbour, we went ashore and we found the installations, everything, still intact. I met some of my Marine friends who were shore-based, and we all had a good time together. With the Germans retreating, there was no danger.

We left the rest of the ships at Syracuse and continued up the east coast. We were working with the Eighth Army and had to be on hand to bombard the shore, but we were never needed.

From our point of view, there was very little fighting. You can tell how easy it was for us, because while we were in St Augusta, we had swimming parities off the ship. The sea was lovely and warm. This was

Main picture: two American infantrymen pause for a cigarette as the town of Messina still smoulders from the invasion behind them.

◄**British troops open fire with a 305 mm gun captured from the Italians on the outskirts of Catania. This was the largest gun the Eighth Army had used to date.**

PRIMOSOLE BRIDGE

British troops were advancing quickly from Syracuse across the coastal plain towards Catania, but the road to Catania crossed a bridge – the Ponte di Primosole – which it was vital to capture. Brigadier Gerald Lathbury, commanding the 1st Parachute Brigade, was ordered to take it in advance of ground forces and hold it until relieved.

Lathbury's force – 113 aircraft carrying over 1,800 men – approached its objective late on 13 July. Some aircraft were shot down, but the main problem was one of concentration – only 295 men were dropped accurately enough to attack the bridge. They captured it, but were forced to withdraw by German paras. Within the hour, spearheads of Eighth Army linked up, and fought for two days to retake the bridge.

▶**Gerald Lathbury – photographed when Major-General Sir Gerald – who led the raid on the bridge.**

around July 12, only a couple of days after the first landings. I remember being on shore at Augusta, wandering around, drinking the wine. I went into a police station, where they gave me a Sicilian police officer's uniform with a funny hat. I used to wear it on board the ship.

The only opposition that we came across was further north, at Catania. We got in after a few days, once the Germans had left it.

Our troops were travelling up the east side, and the Americans were travelling up the other side of Sicily. I remember going into Palermo after the fighting had finished. It was a great contrast to the eastern ports which we had occupied. American flags and banners were flying and it was one hundred per cent American. Our Eighth Army chaps were much more low-key about everything. "

Lieutenant-Colonel Michael Forrester, DSO, MC, was appointed commander of the 1/6th Queens at the age of just 25, having undergone rigorous training with his brigade in Jordan. It was working as for a text-book operation that he captured the only remaining bridge over the Sarno at the town of Scafati.

" Everything just fell into place, really. Everyone knew what was expected of them, and I suppose it was the luck of the draw, really, that things were almost set up as we had hoped.

Part of every unit's training consists of practising what are called deployment drills, and in the case of Scafati, we had the advance guard of the battalion out in front, the forward body, as it was called. That was made up of infantry, tanks with artillery and Royal Engineers escort. They are the first people to make contact.

My role at the time was to receive back what information they were able to pass, because I was immediately behind them, as the commanding officer, with the rest of the battalion grouped behind me. So I could only act in the light of what information or intelligence I was getting from those out in front. That, of course, enabled me to make what further deployment decisions were necessary, but our order of march was such that we could react to almost any situation that the forward body found themselves confronted with. That is to say, we could produce companies with tanks, artillery support and engineer support on either flank, in order to follow up what success had been achieved, wherever it was achieved.

We realised quite early on, that A Company, commanded by Johnny Johnson, was making progress – in fact, they had reached the river – and that this all-important bridge, the only bridge over the Sarno, was intact. We didn't know, of course, how proficient the German demolition parties were, or how stalwartly they were going to react, but I knew from the reports I was getting back that the forward elements of A Company had reached the river and were working along the south bank towards the bridge. Were they going to be able to get across the river and get

round behind the Germans – or were we going to have to confront the Germans frontally across the bridge? Of course, that wasn't what we particularly wanted to do – it was the last thing we wanted to do, because that was going to give them all the warning and all the time. As it was, A Company picked up this friendly and knowledgeable Italian, who showed them to a footbridge higher up the river, which enabled A Company to cross the river and come

▼ An American sergeant shares his rations with local Sicilian children who are fascinated by the invaders.

◄▼ Tommies arrive in a small town whose church, miraculously, has avoided damage.

round behind the Germans before they realised that anyone was that close to them, and certainly before they realised anyone was across the river.

For some reason or other, the hand that must have been poised on the plunger to fire the demolitions and detonate the charges, failed. Although the bridge, as we subsequently found, was perfectly prepared for demolition, they never blew it. I do not know why – I can only say it was the very quick action of A Company. As soon as one realised that Johnny Johnson and his men were over the other side of the river and were coming round behind the Germans, we got an artillery observation post established in the high building overlooking the river, and the battery commander, Bill Fisher and I were able to join him, so we had an unparalleled command-post view of what was going on and were able to order the deployment of the rest of the force.

We knew exactly how each would react in any sort of crisis, and we had tremendous confidence. Bill Fisher, the battery commander and Harry Oulton – we were all together in this church tower. We suddenly thought, 'My God, we're going to capture this bridge!' This was too good to be true. Enormous elation. Then you had to temper that with care because you don't want to get carried away in a moment of elation. You don't want to forget something when you ought to be thinking of something else. All the time, the mind was concentrating on how we were best going to be able to support A Company on the other side of the river – should we send another company across by footbridge to support them? **"**

Friedrich August Freiherr von der Heydte, commander of the German 6th Parachute Regiment, had been fighting in North Africa when he contracted a mysterious illness. In January 1943 he was flown to Sicily for a thorough medical check-up, but soon found himself in Rome – chatting to the Pope!

" From Sicily, I was flown to Rome, where I was taken in by the sisters in Via del Olmata and looked after very kindly. Whenever I felt up to it, I took a stroll in the city, basking in the sight of all those wonderful places again. But I knew what I wanted to do above anything else. In theory, it was forbidden by order of the Führer for any member of the Wehrmacht to have an audience with the Holy Father. I thought to myself, 'Well, Hitler might be the "greatest General of all time", (a title which I had already had sufficient reason to doubt), but this does not give him the right to forbid a Catholic to visit the Head of his Church.' So, in my filthy and rather threadbare Africa Corps uniform, I went to the Porta Santa Anna to ask if I could join in on a large public audience.

Some of the more curious officials there asked me about my medals, which included the Knight's Cross, the German Cross in Gold and two Italian medals for bravery. The Swiss Guards presented arms before me, the halberds and the Noble Papal Guard lowered their swords. I was bathed in sweat as I entered the large reception chamber, hoping to lose myself quickly in the crowd. Some

hope! I had scarcely set foot in the room when a chamberlain asked me to come with him and let me into a little side room.

There were three German officers in civilian clothes standing there, together with a medical NCO, a sergeant from the Luftwaffe and an ordinary soldier in uniform. The Holy Father – Pius XII – had apparently requested to see the German soldiers separately.

Hardly had I stood in line next to the others when the Pope entered. We were all a little embarrassed – how should we greet him? Should we stand to attention or kneel? He soon solved our problem by starting up an immediate conversation with the nearest man. He then offered his hand to each of us and spoke a few words to each in turn, asking after our families and about our experiences in the war.

To me he expressed the wish that I might soon receive the Oak Leaf decoration to my Knight's Cross – which I did in fact later achieve. He asked me what North Africa had been like.

I could think of little else to say except to describe the vast expanse of the landscape in North Africa, which drew from him the following remark: 'The desert is vast; perhaps that's why your Führer chose it as a

▲ **Hidden from immediate view on a small road through a vineyard, Germans set up a formidable line of artillery against the invasion.**

◀ **In the town of Salerno, men of the 9th Royal Fusiliers watch for enemy action from an observation post in an abandoned house.**

▶ ▲ **The locals of the town of Militello greet the Brits with wine. The vehicles and men already show the signs of wear and tear from the desert war.**

▶ **General Gotti-Porcinari, Commander of the Napoli Division, and staff resign themselves to captivity.**

battle theatre. Europe is too small for him.'

Finally, he asked me about my uncle, Konrad Preysing, who was then Bishop of Berlin, adding the comment: 'He was, nay, still *is* one of my best friends.'

After he had spoken to each of us, he gave us all a rosary. He gave me two – one for myself and one to give to my wife, and then blessed us all. Now, of course, we knew we had to kneel. **"**

Alfred Otte was a paratrooper fighting with the Hermann Göring Panzer Division in Sicily in summer 1943. The Commander of his Brigade, Lieutenant-General Schmalz, was anxious to second-guess Allied strategy for the landings on the island and anticipate their arrival, wherever they had chosen.

" I was part of a 'special assignment' brigade of the division, Battle Group Schmalz, which had been assigned to defend against the British and Canadian troops of the Eighth Army, landing on the eastern coast in the area of Avola-Syracuse. Our job was to throw the enemy straight back into the sea. Since April 1943 our units had been based in the area of Catania-Misterbianco-Paterno-Belpasso. Under the scorching heat, we had been accommodated in tents, in olive groves, lemon plantations and on the slopes of Mount Etna.

In the event of a battle alarm we had positions at the ready on the northern edge of the Catania plain facing south, and close by Catania itself, facing east.

On 9 July, Schmalz was given an air reconnaissance report that the invading fleet was heading for Sicily. One section of the fleet was heading for the south and south-east coast. The Battle Group were on immediate alarm and took up their planned positions on the northern slope of the plain between Paterno, Gerbini and Catania. All this had taken place during the night of 10 July. Early next morning one of the radio reconnaissance units on the coast reported an enemy landing at Syracuse, Noto and Ispica! So the Battle Group had to go in alone for a counterattack at Syracuse.

Schmalz commented on his decision later in his memoirs: 'At the point when I left Catania with all my troops to go into battle at Syracuse, I was obviously leaving Catania free. The enemy's intention might have been to draw us out of our positions by a series of small landings – their spies had reported our positions very accurately – and then take us by surprise by pulling off the main landing at Catania, from where they would advance to Messina and go for a quick victory. In this sense then, it was a very risky decision to take on my part.

If all went well and the English landed only at Syracuse and not subsequently at Catania, my decision would be proved correct. If it turned out the other way, not only would the consequences have been incalculable, but of course everybody would have said: "Why the hell did he do that?"

This is the sort of decision a commander has to make all the time, often discussed and written about, and about which people on the outside enjoy passing judgment, but when you are there and the responsibility is yours, it is enormously difficult.'

As we saw it, it was the failure of the supporting Italian divisions to defend the coastline adequately, which made it easier for the Allied troops to break through our lines, as they did so successfully. On 13 July units from the 1st and 3rd Parachute Battalions were dropped on the island to support us. **"**

WOLF-PACK WAR

Stalemate reigns at sea. British ships are getting through, but losses are huge. The gadgetry with which to foil the U-boats would be some time in coming.

*Signalman Trained Operator Albert John Newcombe was aboard the American-built sloop HMS **Kilbride** on her maiden voyage. Her task was to escort a convoy of 32 ships from Halifax to Greenock in Scotland, a dangerous voyage across the Atlantic for a small craft.*

"We joined the Fifth Escort Group, which was led by a destroyer called HMS *Hotspur*, at Halifax. We left with about 30-odd ships and did a steady old run across the Atlantic at about 8 knots.

The weather was atrocious most of the way. When we started off, it was calm but misty, with a lot of floating small icebergs about. Then it really got up to blow. I have never seen anything like it.

I had seen 40-foot waves – well, these must have been about 80 on average! When I was standing on the bridge, I just hung on for dear life. I was terrified. When you were on top of a wave, you could see a couple of miles away, and then you went down into a big, deep trough. It was only a small ship, only about 170 feet long and 35 feet across – she hadn't even got a funnel. It was an electric diesel, with a little diesel exhaust on either side of the ship.

It calmed down after a few days – we never lost a ship. Then we had another scare. There was a ship at the end of the line – Tail End Charlie – and somebody had hoisted a flag. I told the skipper and we got in closer to have a look.

As soon as I got a look at the flag, it said, in international code, 'Your attention is drawn to bearing 270'. We looked around and couldn't see anything, because we were much lower than this ship. So, we steamed

The Battle of the Atlantic reached its climax in 1943. By spring, Admiral Karl Dönitz had concentrated his U-boat 'wolf-packs' to the south of Greenland, where convoys were unprotected by aircraft from North America or Britain. The U-boats struck in mid-March, and sank 120 Allied ships that month.

The Allies stationed 'very long-range' Liberator bombers in Northern Ireland, Iceland and Newfoundland, and deployed 'support groups' of warships, centred around escort carriers, to aid the convoys. The results were soon apparent – in early May, Convoy ONS-5 fought its way west from Britain. In five days, 12 merchantmen went down, but six U-boats were sunk. High May losses persuaded Dönitz to seek quieter waters. Later in the year, the battlecruiser *Scharnhorst* was sunk, while *Tirpitz* was attacked in its Norwegian hideaway. The Allies had the upper hand.

◀◀A Heinkel He-111 with an escort of Bf-109s. Based near the Breton ports, they could easily harry shipping in the Bay of Biscay.

◀Steam is used to thaw out anchor chains in the bitter Atlantic winter, aboard HMS *Scylla*.

▶▲Canadian destroyers shepherd a convoy safely into port after a successful Atlantic crossing.

Main picture: in spite of major improvements, many ships still fall victim to the U-boats.

back, flat out at 17 knots – that's all we could do – and after about ten minutes we spotted some masts. We went to action stations and I started calling on them to identify themselves. They acknowledged the code of the day. It turned out that they were three 'bird' class frigates – the *Pelican*, the *Snipe* and the *Curlew* – which had been detailed to join us, and had been going like the clappers to catch up! They were put into position in the screen and we carried on.

When we got just north of Ireland, we ran straight into another convoy. I don't know how it happened, because we had all got radar. You know how soldiers countermarch? Well, it was just like that. Everybody put their steaming lights on and they went through each other, just like that – and there wasn't one accident. There were about 100 ships involved. I remember one huge French ship – which I recognised as being the *Louis Pasteur* – passed us about 50 yards away!

We got into port and I was that tired. It had been four hours on, four hours off, and I was wet. I used to crawl underneath the chart table and sleep on deck. I slept for 48 hours after that trip.

Ernest North had served in the Royal Navy since 1934 aboard the Hood, Revenge *and* Antelope *when, late in 1942, he took some leave and waited for new orders. His new ship was to be the* Chanticleer. *After jokes from his mess mates, he joined what he found to be 'a neat little sloop but not exactly a fleet greyhound'.*

❝On the 18th November we joined a convoy somewhere in the vicinity of the Azores. It was a glorious morning and for reasons I cannot recall, I spent it in the main armament director. It was quite a large convoy, and included a large landing craft that had obviously been employed at Sicily and was on its way to the UK for repairs and maintenance in preparation for Normandy.

I think we were told that German aircraft and submarines were in attendance, but there was nothing new about that. At about 12.20 pm I went down to the mess, had my tot and dinner – I think there was a sound of depth-charging in the distance, but none in our immediate vicinity. The ship then altered course and increased speed, and as expected, the submarine alarm went almost at❞

▲ Survivors of the *Scharnhorst*, sunk on Boxing Day 1943, are taken on to the catapult deck of the *Duke of York* which had attacked her.

AA platform. The ship shuddered horribly and rolled to port, and then less quickly came upright and was moving most unnaturally.

I knew we had been well and truly 'fished'. I do recall the ghastly silence that followed, probably only a second or two. I ran to the quarter-deck, but I cannot hope to record the sequence of events after all these years. I do recall a young lad, he was the depth-charge telephone number, sitting on the deck by the starboard screen, his phones still on his head, and to me he looked in a bad way. As far as I could see, he was the only person alive on the quarter-deck.

The ship's rudder, which I suppose weighed between 30 and 50 tons, had flown up into the air and had come down like a butcher's cleaver, and was knifed into the upper deck a few feet from the lad on the phones. Both after Oerlikon power-mountings, together with all the upper deck, had gone and the cabins and offices below were open to the sky and sea. The propeller shafts were hanging out of the wreckage and loose depth-charges were hanging in various positions. By this time, others were arriving and I returned to the guns up forward. The upper deck was littered with debris from aft, and there were huge ridges and rents athwart ships in the vicinity of the funnel.

In various places also were the more horrible remains of our late messmates. A young officer was found alive – just – in the wreckage of the cabin flat aft, but he died within minutes. The ship was fairly steady but was well down, aft, and we were lucky in that the weather was kind.

All the boats were holed and even some of the carley rafts were damaged, but the damage-control

once.

As we had done literally hundreds of times before, everyone rushed to their action stations, hatches were closed, fans and ventilators shut, and within about a minute, the *Chanticleer* was ready to play her part in the defence of the convoy.

My action station was as officer of the quarters on the two foremost twin 4-inch mountings. I was informed by the gun's crew that a submarine had been sighted astern of the convoy and had been seen by those already closed up.

We could hear the HSD searching for the U-boat and the voice of the captain ordering the sectors to be swept by the ASDICs. We soon heard also the mournful sound of the set transmitting out into the ocean.

We also heard the contact when it was made.

A shallow pattern had already been ordered, and I was running aft along the port side of the upper deck, passing under the midship AA gun platform. The gunner, who normally positioned himself on X, had already moved on down to the quarter-deck to take charge of the depth-charge party, and as I neared X gun, the first charges were just exploding astern.

At this point, with a tremendous roar, it appeared to me that the whole quarter-deck just disintegrated upwards in a jumbled mass and a wave of pressure and heat hit me. I needed no-one to tell me that what goes up must come down, and I turned and got under the midship

BRITISH SUBS

Between 1940 and 1944, over 100 British submarines served in the Mediterranean, although operational strength at any one time rarely exceeded 35. They accounted for over a million tons of Axis shipping (about half the total sunk in the area) and on more than one occasion, they were the only Allied warships operational in the Med. Such a record is impressive, particularly in view of the problems of sustaining submarine operations. In 1940, for example, nine submarines were lost and their base at Malta had to be temporarily abandoned. Nevertheless, by late 1942, Rommel was suffering chronic supply shortages, caused primarily by submarine attack – between January and April 1943 submarines accounted for 220,000 tons of Axis merchant shipping as the noose tightened around Tunis.

Their submarine surfaced, British crewmen keep a lookout and make routine checks.

party amidships and the engine-room staff were shoring up the bulkhead between the engine room and the boiler room. It was damaged, but they did a good job, as did a lot of people that afternoon. At the guns, we remained closed up, but had no power, so any firing would have to be in 'local'.

The remains of one of the Oerlikon mountings was on the fo'csle and we ditched that and a lot of other wreckage over the side. I don't know if the ASDICs lost power at all, but soon after I returned to the mounting, we picked up another U-boat bearing on our starboard bow. A Sunderland aircraft then flew overhead, and continued circling the ship – I believe the aircraft asked if they could take pictures! I think they were politely told to look for U-boats.

One of our group, HMS *Crane*, then came to assist us and I recall that we prepared to abandon ship. The *Crane* was to take us off and then sink the *Chanticleer* with gunfire. The men were advised not to go between decks as she might decide to leave us at any moment. However, someone decided that we needed some fags and cartons of Churchmans No 1s appeared on the upper deck from the canteen. If the ship was to be sunk, who was to complain? The *Crane* was waiting off, until we were ready to leave – in fact, she attacked an echo at least once, when another torpedo was fired, I don't know at whom, but the *Crane* was obviously in danger and moved off again. She may have made another attack at this stage.

There were over 30 killed, and on a small compact ship, with a very close-knit set of officers and men, it was a crushing blow. "

Herrmann Wien was a warrant officer on U-180, which left Kiel harbour for its first mission in January 1943. None of the crew knew where they were bound for, but everyone was curious about the two strange passengers they were carrying – what was more, even the purpose of their mission was a mystery.

" Were we bound for Singapore or Japan, or somewhere else in the Far East? The only man who knew was our commander, Captain Werner Musenberg.

The evening before we set off I had watch duty and spent the night on board the boat. At about 21.00 hours the sentry guarding the boat reported a car approaching along the pier. A naval officer appeared, showed his identity pass and had a suitcase and some other luggage brought on board. We were all ordered to keep quiet. The next morning we got the engines ready for the open sea.

We were waved off by relatives and friends, the Admiral of the Fleet gave a little address. We raised anchor and headed out of the bay. Nothing unusual happened. Then, in the middle of the bay, the boat stopped, a motor boat came up alongside and two gentlemen got on board. We set off again.

We were all totally intrigued. Who were these two men, with foreign yellowish-brown faces, dark clothing, hats and dark horn-rimmed spectacles, giving them a very mysterious air?

By the time I'd finished my watch duty in the engine-room at 12.30 these men had been transformed into 'U-boat men', dressed, like all of us, in grey-green boiler-suits. Their black hats had been changed for officers' caps. One of them was strong and stocky, about 5ft 8in tall, while the other seemed small and slight.

We continued under escort past the Danish islands and Skagerrak, until we arrived at the German supply base of Kristiansund. Nobody was allowed to disembark when we arrived here.

The wildest rumours were going round the boat. One of the chaps said: 'That's the "Indian Adolf", he's just been to see Hitler. I've definitely seen his face not so long ago in a magazine'. Our commander then announced that these were two expert U-boat engineers, whom we had to drop off in Norway.

Around noon, the next day, we reached Egernsund near Bergen. Nobody left the boat, and our two guests were not making any moves to leave either. It was not until the next day, when we'd put dry land far behind us, and been travelling without escort for some time, that we were told of the identity of our guests and our destination.

The two men we had taken aboard in Kiel were none other than the Indian freedom-fighter, Subhas Chandra Bose and his Adjutant, Habid Hasan. Our task was to bring them safely to the waters off Madagascar, where they would be transferred on to the Japanese U-boat I-29 and taken to India or to the Burma Front.

Chandra Bose had fled India in 1941. With help from the Wehrmacht he had formed the 'Free Indian Legion' to fight British colonial rule in India. Hitler hoped that by fostering the resistance to the British in the Far East, he could divert them, and ease his own burden in the European theatre. Bose's only chance of reaching India was by sea. On 22 April 1943 we transferred the two men, as planned, on to " U-boat I-29.

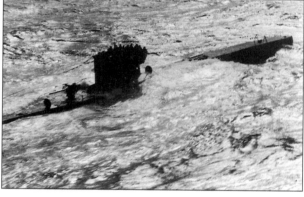

▲▲ German U-boat production goes on, in spite of heavy bombing raids on the shipyard.

▲ Lucky not to be stranded in the Atlantic or adrift in dinghies, the crew of a U-boat come out on deck to surrender.

▼ Subhas Chandra Bose aboard U-180.

CAUCASUS RACE

Only waiting for winter to end, Hitler sends his forces in a new drive to take the Caucasus. As the Russian war-effort consolidates, German victories, if any, are of little overall value.

Sturmmann Heinz Landau, *as a Transylvanian Saxon, fought with the Germans and at the beginning of 1943 had just joined the SS Viking Division. His unit was heading for the Don area, for an early spring offensive to the Caucasus region, when they took two Russian prisoners who then accompanied them.*

❝ We decided to take them back for interrogation. Their lorry contained rations, so we helped ourselves to as much as we could carry and loaded the backs of our two Russians who, by now, not having come to any harm, were grinning from ear

With the surrender of the German Sixth Army at Stalingrad the war on the Eastern Front entered a new phase. Before that time, the Germans had not been defeated; after it, they were to know nothing else.

Soviet forces swept westwards, seizing Rostov to cut off enemy units still in the Caucasus and, further north, liberating Kursk. Only a shortage of supplies, plus a brilliantly conducted armoured counterstroke by Field Marshal Erich von Manstein beyond the Donets River, saved the German effort from collapse.

Hitler insisted on a counterattack in the salient around Kursk, with forces thrusting simultaneously from north and south. It did not succeed. By the time Operation Citadel was launched in early July, the Soviets had constructed defences in depth, against which the panzers could make little headway. Germany sustained huge losses – now little could stop the Soviets who were poised for a series of decisive victories.

MOBILE DEFENCE

Tanks are normally associated with offensive operations; however, Field Marshal Erich von Manstein, commander of Army Group South, proved this to be erroneous – in response to Soviet advances in the aftermath of Stalingrad, he masterminded a form of warfare known as 'mobile defence'. He allowed Russian armoured spearheads to thrust deep into German-held territory, knowing they must soon run short of fuel and supplies. Their momentum would then falter, allowing the Germans to attack from the flanks, using carefully nurtured panzer reserves. By mid-March 1943, the Soviets were in chaos, having lost an estimated 600 tanks, 500 guns and 40,000 men – only the spring thaw, which stopped all mobility, saved the Russians from disaster.

▶ German soldiers inspect a Russian ISU-152, knocked out by their 'mobile defence' tactics.

to ear trying to please us. I could never get used to these Russians.

The next day, it was noon and we were still making our way towards our lines, tiredly shuffling through the snow. Our sergeant stopped suddenly, looking down at some footprints. We immediately crouched down, holding our weapons at the ready, carefully studying our surroundings. I pointed my MG at the two Ivans, touching the index finger of my left hand to my lips. Not a sound. After a while our sergeant started swearing, yet looking rather relieved. The prints were our own. Like Robinson Crusoe, we had come full circle.

'My bloody compass is *kaput*,' muttered our red-faced sergeant. 'It's a good thing there are some trees around.'

We searched the trees for moss, the moss-covered side being north, and started off again, hoping we were heading in the right direction. It was getting dark when we came upon a small cluster of farm houses.

We took over one kitchen, borrowed a large black frying pan, and I started making potato pancakes – a great favourite with the German Army. I was half way through when we came under artillery fire. Everyone took cover. I was determined to finish my frying. Holding on to the frying pan, I kept doing knees bend exercises, taking cover behind the massive peasant cooking range until I had all the pancakes we needed. The firing stopped and we had our supper in peace.

One of our sentries spotted something. We all rushed out, instinctively adopting the low crouch that had become second nature to all of us. It was a German patrol. The Wehrmacht sergeant thought our lot were to the north of his unit.

At dawn, we thankfully reached our lines, crawled into our dug-outs and I was fast asleep within seconds. 'Alarm! Alarm!' Someone was shaking me. 'Come on, Heinz, *Panzerangriff*!

We dragged our 5 cm anti-tank guns forward. I threw myself down between two guns, positioning my MG34, my *Schütze Zwei* helping with the chain of bullets which we draped

▲ Heinz Landau – as a Transylvanian, his dislike for the Russians was traditional.

◀ The Division *Grossdeutschland* plods on through the thawing snow of spring.

◀◀ Cautious and battle-worn, men of a panzer unit pause to survey their surroundings in the next town.

around our necks like scarves.

About 30 T34s were attacking. One of them blew up, even before we commenced firing. Our gunners were knocking them out at an incredible speed. The gun on my right was hit, literally disintegrating under the impact. The one on my left was crushed by one of these rattling steel monsters, grinding its way through our lines – heads, arms, legs, bits of human flesh and hair were all going round and round on its tracks.

Now I let rip with my MG at close quarters into the Ivan infantry crouching behind the tanks. One Russian fell across my back, having apparently lost his weapon in the process. He grabbed me by the throat and started squeezing. Someone shot him though the head at very close quarters, drenching me with blood and brains – some of it running into my mouth as I was gasping for air. I was violently sick.

The attack was beaten back and only a handful of Russian infantry got back to their lines. The tanks which overran our positions were destroyed by the second line of defence. One, however, managed to recross our lines, and looked like getting away with it, as all three of our guns were destroyed. There was a howl of rage, and three men charged the tank with hand-grenades. Two were shot, but the third reached the dead angle of the T34's armament and pushed his hand-grenade down the tank's gun-barrel. It blew sky high.

Now we came under devastating artillery fire, lasting about 90 minutes, then another determined attack. We beat this one back and chased the Ivans into their own positions and out of them, only to be pushed straight back again. They kept this up for two days, non-stop.

Where they were getting their men and tanks from, we just could not understand. Our numbers were greatly reduced, with no sign of relief or reinforcements.

One could hardly tell if it was day or night. A thick blanket of sulphurous smoke enveloped everything. I kept thinking if I do not get shot, stabbed, clubbed or torn to bits, I'll probably choke to death in this inferno. Many of the Russian tanks were burning fiercely and so were many of the dead – Germans and Russians. The stench was indescribable.

One man was crawling all over the place as though searching for something. 'What's the matter, *Kamerad*?' I asked. 'I must find my hand,' he said, in a dazed voice, holding up his right arm. The blood was pumping out of his sleeve. A couple of minutes later he was dead.

I could not locate my MG *Schütze Zwei*. A few minutes later I stumbled over a body lying across several others. It was that of my missing comrade. His left arm was stretched behind his head. Every five seconds, like some machine, it would raise itself, perform a 90-degree semicircle, slap loudly against the inside of his right thigh and straight back to the ground again with a forceful slap of the back of his hand. A couple of stretcher-bearers came, looked and moved on.

I looked more closely – his head was split open from the hairline to the base of his skull, but some nerve in his young body would not die. I pulled my Lüger and shot him through the heart. I put my 0.8 away and groped blindly for his possessions, which I later handed in to the sergeant major. **"**

Sisters Zinaida and Olga Vasilyevna, both in their early teens at the outbreak of the war, joined up and became medical orderlies in the 4th Cossack Cavalry Corps. During the bitter winter of 1942/3, spent in action in the mountainous state of Armenia, they witnessed fierce action and treated horrific injuries.

" After one attack, I had eight wounded. I dragged them above the village, up the slope. But we had evidently blundered in not cutting communications, and the German artillery began to shell us with long-range guns and mortars. I hurried to help my wounded into a cart. I got them in and off they went

▲ The Russian 2nd Cavalry Regiment in action. Casualties were high in this fierce hand-to-hand warfare.

▶ General Paulus (centre), with General Breith (right), plans Sixth Army's next move, Stalingrad, January 1943.

▼ A German infantryman cleans his rifle, the strain of the war showing clearly on his face.

– then a shell hit the cart before my eyes and blew it to pieces. When I looked there was only one man left alive and the Germans were already scaling the hill. The wounded man begged, 'Leave me, nurse. I'm already dying. I'm done for.' He was wounded in the stomach and it was impossible to move him.

I thought that my horse was covered in this man's blood, but when I looked, I saw that it too was wounded, in the side. The wound was the size of an entire first-aid pack. I got a few pieces of sugar I had with me and gave them to the horse. Firing was already coming from every side and it was not possible to tell where the Germans were and where ours were. If you went ten metres, you stumbled on wounded men. I had to find a cart and pick

them all up. I rode until I came to a slope, at the foot of which were three roads. Which way should I go? Perhaps I was prompted by an instinct of some kind and I had heard somewhere that horses can sense the right road – so I dropped the reins before we reached the fork and the horse went in a completely different direction from that in which I would have chosen.

It went and went, and by now I was sitting lifelessly in the saddle, quite indifferent to where the horse was going. It went on and on, and then became more and more excited, shaking its head, and now I lifted the reins and held them. I bent down and pressed my hand to its wound. It grew more and more lively and then it neighed as if it had heard someone. I was apprehensive – perhaps

Germans were nearby. I decided first to release the horse, but already I too could see fresh tracks – horses' hoofprints and the wheel of a machine-gun car – at least 50 people had passed by. And after two or three hundred metres, the horse bumped straight into a cart. There were wounded men in it and I saw the remnants of our squadron.

Help was already on its way to us – carts had been sent. The order had been given to pick everyone up. Under fire we collected our men amid the bullets, wounded and dead alike.''

Her sister, Olga, continues. "We occupied a village where a German field-hospital had been abandoned. The first thing I saw was a large pit dug in the yard, in which some of the wounded lay shot – before leaving, the Germans had shot their own wounded men. Only one ward was left – they had evidently not had time to get that far, or perhaps the men had been left behind because they were all without legs.

When we went into their ward, they looked at us with hatred – they clearly thought we had come to kill them. The interpreter said that we did not kill wounded men, but treated them. Then one man began to make demands – they had had nothing to eat for three days – and their bandages had not been changed during this time. I had a look and it was true – it was awful. They hadn't been seen by a doctor for a long time. Their wounds festered and the bandages had grown into the flesh.

I knew how cruelly the Germans treated our people. I experienced it myself. A driver and I were in charge of an ambulance filled with wounded. The road was bombed and although we were able to drag several men into the ditch, the aircraft

DECEMBER

1 Start of Fifth Army offensive on river Garigliano
Russians isolate Germans in Crimea

2 Conscription for active service introduced for Hitler Youth

2 3 Ammunition ship hit in Luftwaffe raid on Bari explodes, sinking 18 ships

6 Fifth Army takes Monte Carmino

8 Lt-Gen Spaatz made Chief of US Strategic Air Forces, Europe

10 British Eighth Army crosses Moro in Italy

11 Heavy US raid on Emden – 1,000 killed

12 Czech-Soviet treaty of friendship signed

13 At war crimes trial at Kharkov Germans accused of killing thousands in gas vans

18 Fifth Army takes San Pietro after ten days' fighting

18 Kharkov war criminals sentenced to death

20 21 RAF drops 2,000 tons on Frankfurt

21 Russians smash German bridgehead on Dnieper
Eighth Army in battle for Ortona, central Italy

24 Third Russian winter offensive in Ukraine
Eisenhower appointed Supreme Commander Allied Expeditionary Force; Monty C-in-C 21st Army Group

26 Battlecruiser *Scharnhorst* sunk off North Cape by Royal Navy
US landings near Cape Gloucester (New Britain)

29 30 Eighth 2,000-ton air raid on Berlin

31 Russians retake Zhitomir

CIRCLE OF DEATH

By 1943, the Soviet Air Force had recovered from the mauling received early in Operation Barbarossa. Out of the ashes had grown not only an efficient fighter force, but also an increasingly effective ground-attack capability, based on the Ilyushin Il-2 *Shturmovik* single-engined attack aircraft and the Petlyakov Pe-2 twin-engined light bomber. In a favourite tactic, the 'Circle of Death', squadrons of Il-2s and Pe-2s would appear, protected by swarms of fighters, to attack a German formation. As the Pe-2s attacked from medium altitude, the *Shturmoviks* would come in low, disrupting German anti-aircraft defences. Each *Shturmovik* would make an attack, circle round and repeat the process – as soon as the squadron ran short of fuel, another would take its place.

The Petlyakov Pe-2 in action. Manoeuvrable and fast, it played a major role in Russia's air effectiveness.

▲ A group of partisans, men and women, listen as their leader (toting the sub-machine gun), briefs them on their forthcoming raid. The rifles for the rest of the band are stacked in the foreground.

began to circle and rake us with fire and we could do no more. There was a ploughed field with a heap of stones collected in one corner. I dashed away from the road and lay down by the stones, I thought that if I was killed, they could cover me with them and it wouldn't be as terrible as lying in a ditch.

There were about six aircraft. Five flew away, but one remained and circled us three times. I could see the pilot shaking as he fired his machine gun. It seemed to me that he flew so low I thought he was bound to crash. He could see that it was a girl lying there, too. I had long blond hair. Well, why did he do that? Or take another example – once they set up a row of boots in front of their trenches, boots belonging to our soldiers with their cut-off legs still in them. **"**

Nicolai Sonderenko, a Russian by birth, joined a special detachment of the SS – Sonderkommando 10a, tasked with policing the eastern territories of his own country and putting down partisan operations with reprisal attacks. This activity, directed against his own people, could be unspeakably harsh – and final.

" Under the leadership of and with the personal participation of *Obersturmbannführer* Christmann, we went out into the area around the town of Mozyr, cordoned off villages, rounded up the population and had them forcibly removed to Germany. The livestock belonging to the local population was rounded up to provide food for the German troops. The villages themselves were completely burned down. One of these operations has remained deeply imprinted on my memory.

We set off during the night in trucks. In the early morning we came to the village of Koptsevich, which was about 40-50 km away from the town of Mozyr. On the orders of Christmann, the village was surrounded by sections of the police and the *gendarmerie,* as well as one section of the Special Detachment, so that nobody could flee from the village. Once the village was surrounded, some of the soldiers from our detachment who were not involved in the surrounding operation, interpreters and commanders of platoons and units, together with Christmann, moved into the village. I myself was in the encircling chain 70-80 m from the houses of an area on the outskirts of the village. The inhabitants could now see that the village was surrounded. There was panic. The people ran out of their houses, there was crying and screaming. Then, I watched as SS men, who had assembled with Christmann inside the village, went into the houses and drove out all the occupants, old and young. They rounded up the women, children and old men, who were running around desperately in all directions, and gathered them into groups. Not far from where I was standing was a well, to which the soldiers led off the villagers.

I could see quite clearly about 50 women, old men and children – some of whom were babes in arms. The whole crowd of people was highly excited – they were crying and shouting. Some of them tried to get away, but they were driven back into the pack. I then saw Christmann walk up to these people. He gave out some orders to the soldiers, shouting and flailing his arms about.

I clearly saw some of the soldiers grabbing the people and throwing them into the well. On Christmann's orders the SS men shot at the people from point-blank range with machine pistols. Some of the people fell to the ground. Some of them were killed on the spot, some wounded – you could hear shouts and crying from the scene of the violence. Now, on the orders of Christmann – I say orders, because I could see him pointing to the well with his hand – the SS men began throwing corpses and wounded people, including children, into the well. I heard that similar incidents had taken place in other parts of the village.

Then, on Christmann's orders, we rounded up all the livestock and led them out of the village. We then burned the village down. **"**

1944
THE TIDE TURNS

Memories from a year when Allied victory came in sight

By 1944, the Axis powers were on the defensive, fighting to survive rather than secure final victory. In Europe, Germany began the year facing enemies on two fronts – the Soviets in the East and the Western Allies in Italy – and the situation worsened as the year progressed, with Anglo-American landings in Normandy and Southern France leaving Hitler's forces in an untenable strategic position.

Although the fighting was hard on all fronts and the Germans were still able to spring surprises, notably in the Ardennes in December 1944, the Allies were squeezing in from all sides. At the same time, Anglo-American bombers were hitting German civilian and industrial targets by day and by night,

destroying popular resistance and morale.

The Japanese faced similar problems, although no-one expected their final defeat to come quickly. It took time to organise the wide, sweeping offences through the Pacific – against the Mariana Islands and the Philippines – each of which involved a full commitment of naval, air and land elements as well as heavy casualties. Even so, by October 1944, with US victory at Leyte Gulf, Japanese naval power had gone and the advance was gathering pace.

A similar pattern was apparent in Burma, where the British Fourteenth Army fought the Japanese to a standstill on the Imphal plain and then counterattacked towards Mandalay. The pressure was on – and getting stronger.

TURNING ON THE HEAT

Having begun the war with seemingly endless resources – and gained even more – Japan is now running on empty, both in men and equipment. Surely Japanese resistance must soon collapse under heavy Allied pressure.

T he Americans' first priority in 1944 was to complete the operations they had begun in the previous year, then seize the Mariana Islands, needed as bases for B-29 bombers in their campaign against Japan. In the process of this, Admiral Nimitz won the naval-air battle of the Philippine Sea in June, inflicting substantial damage on the Japanese. Four months later, General MacArthur's forces invaded Leyte in the Philippines, triggering a Japanese operation to destroy the US Pacific Fleet. It failed at Leyte Gulf, ensuring US naval superiority.

In March the Japanese mounted a full-scale assault on eastern India, halted by British-Indian forces at Imphal and Kohima. Outfought and short of supplies, the Japanese fell back, and General Slim counterattacked across the Chindwin and into Arakan. By then, Chinese units, supported by Chindits, had attacked in northern Burma.

Peter Cane, a Major with the Special Force, 3rd Indian Div. was dropped in, in command of two columns, to take part in the second Chindit campaign on 4 March 1944. Operating by stealth, he and his men were able to wreak havoc with the Japanese, who by this time were without the protection of any air support.

" I started off as a one-column commander and then happily took over both – the other one was led by a cowardly man but he went. Our objective was to ambush and

▲ Men of the 10th Gurkha Rifles rest after winning the battle for 'Scraggy' – a pimple on the Palel-Tamu road – another mound, Scraggy Pimple, is to the left.

▶ Chindits coax a mule into a transport aircraft to be part of the large airborne force sent in behind Japanese lines.

the things up, but what you want to do is to shatter the foundations. If you know your explosives – and I had done a lot in the desert – then it was easy. The big drawback for us was that you couldn't get enough explosives, as everything had to come in by air and then be carried from where it had been dropped.

We were right up in the hills where the road cut right into the hillside. The British had built the roads and were frightfully good at constructing hairpin bends round the promontories where bits of the hill would stick out. All you did was to drop that, then you could really get to work. If you got your explosives right, you drilled holes with explosives and then stuffed the holes with other explosives and BANG! The lot goes down the hill, and as the hairpin bends were only made by the wicked British, certainly not the Japanese, then that was the end. It really was fun choosing the place to blow up.

Once we saw this mass of 350 Japanese trucks, three-ton lorries, five-ton lorries, and we timed the blowing of the road absolutely right. We had prepared the explosives and camouflaged them. The Japs then drove a truck past. The trucks were full of second-class troops, generally with corks in the end of their rifle barrels to keep the dust out! We would find the rifles complete with corks after we had blown up the trucks. In any case we blew the road and then called in the air force. But they couldn't come – it broke our hearts. The trucks dispersed and we missed them. I sent a terrible signal back, as by then I thought I would be leaving the army, I just didn't care.

The whole thing about setting an ambush on these lovely mountain roads was that you could set one by just rolling grenades down that had a seven-second fuse. It wasn't the thing to fight where you stood. The idea was to do as much damage as you could and then disappear. You wanted odds of ten to one on your side – that's war. You want to play on a pitch where you know it and the other bloke doesn't and you have the umpire on your side too!

When setting an ambush, you would wait until they sent a truck up the road and then signalled back that it was OK. Then, at night, the rest would come. You would often let one or two through and then blow the road or bridge and put as much fire down as you could. After a while, I would fire a coloured Very Light, which would mean pull out, get the hell out of it, it's over. We didn't have the numbers or the arms to wait to daylight to fight it out against heavy odds. The Japs would pursue us but we would belt straight up the hill and then split at the top and they wouldn't know if you had gone right, left or centre. Occasionally it was very difficult. They would send first-class troops – but the joy was they couldn't call in the air force. But they would get some satisfaction, unhappily they would almost surely come to a village which we had been to at some time, and they would knock hell out of those people.

We were happily among the Kochin's which were a highland race, terribly pro-British and wonderful to us. The Japanese used to send spies to the headman's village. They would send in two at a time, but invariably we would capture them. But it was awful, the first five or so villages we went through the Japs would come to and take five to ten from one family and shoot them. So we had to pick up these Japanese spies and get rid of them otherwise the villagers would no longer help us. **"**

destroy the road from Bhamo to Myitkyina which linked with the Chinese and was a very important road.

It was a wonderful job – I was happy as a sandboy. We started our attacks quite by chance. I had a pre-war touring guide to Burma – an AA guide or something like that – which gave details of every bridge with the number of spans. It was a superb book to work from. We started off just blowing up the bridges and then it became obvious that that wasn't the way. The Japs could often go round them or whatever.

There was one very important bridge that happily we destroyed and they never rebuilt it again. It was the ideal job. Any bloody fool can blow

Lieutenant Susumu Nishida of 11 Company, 58th Infantry Regiment, 31st Division of the Japanese Army in Burma was with the vanguard company of the assault on Kohima, and in March 1944 his company stood ready in the jungle to cross the Chindwin to begin the offensive against the Allies.

" We have already been in the assembly area for several days, since X minus 3. As the sun went down, and rose again, we felt different from everything in nature which was around us, our tension was gradually increasing, until today – so long as they didn't change the date of X-Day – the long-awaited moment had arrived.

The men were preparing their weapons, inspecting their packs, distributing rations, unconsciously humming songs of home.

With great care I studied, once more, the plans for the crossing. Discussions with the platoon commanders to ensure there were no mistakes in details were at an end. There was nothing more to do. Yet I was sure we'd forgotten something. It seemed a very long day.

The distance to the crossing point was 4 km. When we came out of the jungle, the whole area was covered with miscanthus. Of course there was no road. Since we were expected to cross the river at midnight, we should be on our way by 10.30 pm. We wanted them to confirm X-Day as soon as possible.

The sun's huge red disc went down beyond the distant range of mountains. Seven o'clock. Nine o'clock. What had happened to our marching orders? Our tension and unease increased.

At 9.15 pm, 'River crossing begins at midnight!' As the runner came up with the long-awaited order, the men in the jungle switched from 'rest' to 'move'. They had waited two and a half hours, and were just about at the end of their tether.

I looked at the fingers of my watch as they moved on. In the darkness, preparations went forward in silence. The column – around 100 men – all its equipment checked, was formed up by 10.30 pm. The platoon commanders inspected their men, verified their weapons and kit. Quiet voices could be heard, confirming final details. Then everything was quiet again.

At the juncture, I had nothing to say. Everything had been accounted for. Slowly and deliberately, in the midst of the column, my steps came to a halt. For a moment, there was an oppressive silence. Then, in a low voice, summoning all my strength, my voice broke that silence. 'Let us now bid farewell to our mother country!' My beloved sword flashed, the moon's rays slanting down on it. I was about to raise the curtain on the invasion of India.

'Fix bayonets!' The clash of bayonets flicked from their sheaths, the blades locked on rifle muzzles. Then again, the silence.

'Present ARMS!' The thunderclap of hands slapping rifles, and the single line of steel points like the crest of a wave. For a moment, there was not the slightest stir in the ranks. Eyes filled with tears.

As the song says, 'If I go to the mountains, let my corpse become grass; regardless of death, I dedicate myself to the Emperor!'

It was the moment for the soldiers' hearts to swear unalloyed allegiance, to swear to die for our far-away motherland.

An hour later, the company was hurrying through the tough miscanthus, aiming for the crossing point. The noise of wild elephants trampling close by, the roars of tigers on the opposite bank, the distant sound of enemy planes bombing – all these sounds were outside our consciousness. We had only one mood, one idea – to do our duty.

Soon we came out off the tough grass and the river valley opened out before us in the moonlight. The Chindwin flowed peacefully on, reflecting the moonlight. "

▲Having found an enemy block on the Imphal-Kohima Road, an officer of the West Yorks Regiment reports back to HQ.

▶A group of US 'Marauders' patrols through thick jungle, on the lookout for Japanese snipers who might be concealed in the undergrowth.

THE INDIAN ARMY

During the war, British ranks were swelled by troops voluntarily recruited from the Indian martial races, as well as Gurkhas from the independent state of Nepal – Indian and Gurkha units fought in almost every theatre of war. Their first campaigns were in North and East Africa in 1940-1, but their primary responsibility was always the defence of India itself. Although Indian divisions continued to fight in North Africa and Italy, the bulk of the army was committed to Burma. There they formed the backbone of General Slim's Fourteenth Army, holding the line at Imphal and taking a major part in the advance to Rangoon. Characterised by toughness, adaptability and, on occasions, great bravery, they were respected and feared by the Japanese.

▶Indian troops, highly disciplined and trained, man a machine gun in a ruined building.

Torao Suematsu was, by October 1944, Staff Officer, Number 1 Special Attack Forces, in the Japanese navy. Trying to anticipate the US moves as their fleet swept across the Pacific towards Leyte Island in the Philippines, plans were made for Operation Sho 1 to stop the US in their tracks.

" The fact that the Combined Fleet tried to ensure the success of the Leyte operation, even by using a decoy force, certainly shows

enemy aircraft cannot be as active and because a simultaneous attack disperses the enemy's forces. As I've already said, it goes without saying that we must have the co-operation of our air forces.

The idea of the talks at Brunei was to explain the operation orders of No 1 Striking Force based on the orders of the Combined Fleet, the instructions from the C-in-C and so on, but nothing was said about direct co-operation with air units.

Separate orders had already been issued to the air units by the Combined Fleet, and it was not specially emphasised that this was a seaborne special attack unit. Afterwards,

Atago, *Maya* and *Takao*.

I was just below the bridge, and suddenly the collision buzzer went. This happened whenever there was danger, and you had to take collision measures, so I dashed up top. *Yamato*, in which I was sailing, was some way behind *Takao*, and when I looked, I could see the bow seemed to be listing to port. *Yamato* made a complete emergency turn to starboard, and *Takao* stopped, because *Yamato* had moved ahead. However, in the end, *Takao* didn't sink, but withdrew to Brunei. Then the flagship went down. *Maya* was 1,500 metres forward of *Yamato*. She must have been ahead to port at this time,

how important they considered breaking through into Leyte to be, but it is regrettable that direct co-operation with one more air unit was not considered. I wonder whether it wasn't necessary to throw in air strength as well as breaking into Leyte Gulf. In that way, the main object of the operation would be not to destroy the enemy mobile task force, but to break into Leyte.

In order to make the Leyte operation a success, it was most desirable for Kurita Force and Nishimura Force to act in concert and break through at dawn, according to plan. If that one element was lacking, we would be at a disadvantage. The reason is that dawn is a time when

when the *Yamato* was sunk during the Okinawa operations, *en route* for Okinawa, that certainly was a 'special attack' sortie. At the time of this Leyte breakthrough, there was no direct co-operation with the air units, and it undoubtedly was a self-sacrificing operation by the seaborne forces. Even so, even if it were much closer to death than the idea of 'saving one life from nine deaths', I don't think that we considered our chances of life to be zero.

The day after we left Brunei, we were attacked by enemy submarines in the Palawan Passage. US submarines were waiting for us, I think two or more were involved and three ships were torpedoed – the flagship

and I saw her make a complete turn to port. She appeared to be dead ahead, and I could see three or more torpedo-tracks ahead to port, with smoke rising up. *Maya* took evasive action well, but I think she was too late because the point of fire was from the optimum position. She went down at once. There may have been an induced explosion that blew up the magazine.

You either have to turn the ship's head immediately in the direction the torpedo is coming from, or you turn the ship's stern, depending on the point of fire. That is, you give the objective as narrow a width as possible – but in the case of *Maya*, this was too late.

JANUARY

27 Germans counterattack French at Cassino
Siege of Leningrad lifted

29 Luftwaffe penetrates to London
800 USAAF bombers pound Frankfurt; 14th night raid on Berlin by RAF

30 US Ranger battalion wiped out at Anzio
Russians attack toward Nikopol on the Dnieper

31 Land fighting begins in Dutch New Guinea

FEBRUARY

1 Polish underground 'execute' chief of *Gestapo* in Poland

2 US Marines complete capture of Roi and Namur in Marshalls
Stalin agrees to USAAF bases in Russia

3 Anzio breakout attempt ends
Japanese open counter-offensive in Arakan

4 Panzer drive to relieve Korsun Pocket
Japanese launch offensive on Arakan front
US forces take Kwajalein Island in Marshalls

5 US troops reach outskirts of Cassino
Chindits begin moving towards Indaw

6 Japanese force British retreat in Arakan

7 Germans begin full-scale counterattack at Anzio

8 Russians capture Nikopol; Germans asked to surrender in Korsun Pocket

10 Australians complete occupation of Huon Peninsula in New Guinea
Allies announce that southern Italy to be handed over to Italian government jurisdiction

◀With wings neatly folded on the deck of a US carrier, an Avenger torpedo-bomber and, at the rear, Hellcat fighters stand ready for action in the Pacific.

▶American sailors manhandle a tin fish – a torpedo – into a submarine. A small number of US subs made a major impact on the Japanese fleet in the Palawan Passage.

This was a terrible shock – *Atago* was in the C-in-C's flagship. Admiral Kurita transferred straight away to *Yamato*. The transfer was effected by a destroyer coming alongside. At exactly that moment, a small waterspout put in an appearance, and it looked just as if another torpedo was making for us, and everyone was petrified. But fortunately, it did not turn out to be a torpedo at all, so we could all breathe freely again.

Since the vessels are stationary during a transfer operation, if the enemy puts in a torpedo attack at such a time, there's nothing you can do about it.

The C-in-C was full of high spirits. He must have been thrown into the sea and had to swim for it, but he didn't show the least sign of fatigue, his movements were firm and decisive and he really inspired us. I think he must have had plenty of misgivings, because three out of his four cruisers had been sunk or damaged, but outwardly at any rate, you wouldn't have guessed he was perturbed at all.

This setback at the beginning of the operation was hard to take. We expected the enemy to spread a network of submarines, and that day, too, high-frequency signals were intercepted which we took to be WT signals from enemy submarines, and we judged that they must be close by, but our radar was not particularly efficient. In contrast, the enemy had not only radar, but echo-ranging equipment and hydrophones. In a 12-minute run, the exposure of his periscope was infrequent, so it was extremely difficult to spot him, and as dawn was the worst time for our lookouts, the enemy managed to hit us.

I don't think it can be denied that this loss had a tremendous effect, not only because of their material strength as a battle force, but also from the point of view of morale.

Derek Headly had served for seven years as a District Officer in Malaya, so spoke the language fluently, knew the people well. His specialised SOE training culminated in a dummy burglary and all-too-real interrogation before his departure for the familiar jungles of Malaya.

❝ The first course I attended was at Arisaig House on the west coast of Scotland, where we were instructed in all the skills required for active guerrilla operations. The most important of these was the use of explosives for demolition and sabotage, particularly of lines of communication. We also spent much time practising instinctive shooting with a pistol, Sten gun and carbine. We had two PT sessions every day and we negotiated the assault course.

Finally, we learned to kill silently with a fighting knife or bare hands.

We next went on to a stereo-typed parachute course, then on to the agents' course at Beaulieu.

The instructors continually stressed the absolute necessity of good security. For instance, a safe house must always have a back door. Safety must be positively signalled – an ornament on a windowsill, for instance. Lack of a signal spelled danger. There must be a known secret rendezvous if the group or circle had to go underground. We learned many unusual and interesting skills – they included ways of finding out if one was being followed, and if so, how to avoid the tail; picking locks; opening stuck-down envelopes with a knitting needle. We were told to practise reading upside down. This subsequently developed for me into an anti-social habit which sometimes yielded interesting results. The most ❞

exciting and ultimately frightening exercise began with a burglary in one of the houses on the Beaulieu Estate. Three of us had to gain access and find a specific item. Although we were sure it must be a put-up job, we took it very seriously because we were sure it would be monitored by staff.

We'd been told to concoct a cover story for the night of the burglary, and we had worked hard on this, using railway and bus timetables and our knowledge of the London Underground. A few nights later we were arrested, put in different rooms and interviewed separately. No violence was used, but a powerful electric light shone directly into my eyes. Some extremely hostile questioners were followed by a nice kind one,

▲13 July 1944, medics give on-the-spot treatment to an American casualty from the landings on Saipan in the Marianas. Japanese resistance remained fierce in spite of dwindling resources and lack of reinforcements.

who gave me a cigarette. They broke us down all too quickly. It was very unnerving, particularly when I remembered that we had only been incommunicado for two or so hours, and had only missed one meal. How much worse if we had been tortured and deprived of sleep and food? We were told that 24 hours was the maximum that any ordinary person could hold out. All clandestine groups must be so organised that they could go underground within that period if one of them was captured.

US PACIFIC SUBS

Japan depended for survival on imports, carried to the Home Islands by merchant ships. She started the war with just under six million tons of merchant shipping, to which she added in the course of the conflict, either through capture or new construction, a further four million tons; by September 1945 she had less than two million tons left. The rest had been sunk and 57 per cent of the total was attributable to Allied (predominantly US) submarines.

The Americans began the war with just 112 submarines, many of them old, but this number was increased to 370 as the conflict progressed. Operating in the Pacific from Pearl Harbor and Australia, they concentrated their attentions on the East China and Yellow Seas, reaching a peak of effectiveness in late 1944. Top scorer in tonnage terms was the USS *Tang*, but *Barb*, commanded by Lieutenant Commander Eugene B Fluckey, also did well, sinking 98,000 tons of enemy shipping, principally between May 1944 and January 1945.

We Europeans could not live overtly in Japanese-occupied Malaya; we must stay in the jungle and train local people as agents. After these three courses, I was confident that I had a realistic appreciation of the risks involved in, and the skills required for, special operations.

I was flown out to Ceylon and eventually dropped in April 1945, with four Malays, a British second-in-command, and a wireless operator. In Malaya there was a Chinese resistance movement, dominated by the Malayan Communist Party – but I was charged with promoting Malay resistance, and in doing so I received a very enthusiastic, courageous and skilful co-operation and help from all the Malays I met, as had my three friends who also led Malay missions. **"**

Petty Officer Sidney Woollcott had undergone years of training to become one of the élite submariners who, on two-man chariots, would sabotage and mine enemy vessels at anchor. On 27/28 October 1944, HM Chariot Tiny *left HMS* Trenchant *for an attack on the recently salvaged* Sumatra *in Phuket harbour.*

" The *Sumatra*, recently salvaged after resting on the bottom for some while, was awaiting towage to Singapore, and she was selected as the target for my number one, Sub Lieutenant Tony Eldridge, and me.

We were thankful we were going on a real job at last – but then my oxygen started playing up. That was another disappointment. I thought the operation was going to be scrubbed again – but I actually thought of the idea of going in on air. Off we went again. I was hoping we could catch up and not make the operation too delayed.

I was thinking on the way, 'I hope I come back. My mother will be rather mad at me if I don't.' Of course she didn't know a thing about what I was doing – I had told her I was just an ordinary helmet diver.

We got near the harbour entrance – we had been on the surface all the time, and when we got near the harbour, Tony Eldridge carried on the normal practice of starting long dives, coming up occasionally to have a quick look-see, then going down again.

When we got to within about 500 yards of the target, he had one final look, got a compass course on it, then dived and we passed under the target.

▶The way now open for the Americans to land at Leyte in the Philippines, army Alligators roll out of the shallows towards the Japanese lines of defence.

We went pretty deep. I saw a long, dark, cigar-shaped thing above me, and I thought it was a shark at first. It didn't move, so I decided it must be the ship. We went round and came up near to the bottom. It was a very dark night and the water was dark where we were, but under the ship it was even darker, so you knew where you were. Tony steered the machine towards the bilge keel. We knew that, having sat on the bottom for months, the bottom would be pretty badly covered with barnacles, so we decided that as well as taking the magnets, which were the normal way of fixing the warhead on the bottom, we had a couple of large G clamps made.

As soon as we came up against the bottom, I saw the magnets would be useless there, so I took the G clamps with me. I uncoupled my oxygen supply from the machine and went on to the bottle which I carried on my back, and felt my way along to the warhead, and clamped the two clamps on to the bilge keel. But the line from the clamp to the warhead

was a bit too short. I motioned to Tony to bring the warhead nearer the bilge keel. As he did so, the jack-stay which we used to put up to stop ourselves from going right up into the bottom of the ship, collapsed backwards and buried itself in the barnacles, and when he moved forwards it collapsed. The jack-stay didn't move, but the machine did, so he was cramped up against the bottom, fending it off with his hand.

I fixed the warhead and tied the lines to the rail at the top of the warhead, then I released it, set the clock for five hours and made my way back. I got to where Tony was sitting, and just said 'OK'. He put his hand over and got hold of mine and we shook hands. That was a wonderful feeling then. It was the culmination of years of work, all tied up in that one handshake.

I made my way further along to my own seat – I couldn't get in because the machine was jammed tight against the ship's bottom. I just hung against the side. Tony flooded the main ballast and we dropped off. We

►Two divers float a Mark I Chariot off the casing of a submarine. This is the type in which Sidney Woollcott, picture inset, did his training. The Phuket mission was carried out using a Mark II Chariot, which was larger and more powerful.

◄King George VI inspects two 'charioteers' in full diving gear – a far cry from today's wetsuits!

started diving away and I climbed back into my seat as I sat down, I breathed a sigh of relief.

I wish I hadn't breathed out so heavily, because when I went to breathe again, I couldn't. It was just as if somebody clapped their hands over my mouth. I had empty lungs and I couldn't get any air in. Apparently, when I was working under the ship, one of the shoulder straps of my breathing bag had slipped down my shoulder and allowed the bag to drop forward. Then, when I got back in the machine, the breathing pipe from my mouthpiece to the bag got tucked down behind the bag, so when I sat down and pulled the bag automatically against my chest, it flattened the breathing pipe out. I panicked for a minute – I thought I had torn the breathing bag on the barnacles at first. I felt around it and gave Tony four digs in the back which means, 'surface', and while I was still getting no air, I felt around the bag and discovered there was nothing wrong with it. I found the pipe tucked down below, pulled it out and gave Tony the signal to dive again. We were fortunate: we were on the surface and could have been seen. It took us about two hours to get back to the *Trenchant*. 🙶

RED FIRE

The Germans are in headlong retreat in Russia, pursued by Soviet armies resolved to blast the hated invaders out of their land.

During 1944, Soviet forces completed the liberation of their homeland, defeated Finland, swept into the Balkans and decimated the German Army.

The year began with the relief of Leningrad, besieged since 1941. At the same time, far to the south, the Red Army launched a successful offensive from the Crimea and liberated Odessa. But these were only preliminaries. On 23 June, Soviet forces struck at German Army Group Centre, reaching the gates of Warsaw and triggering an insurrection by the Polish Home Army. But for political and logistical reasons, the Soviets halted, allowed the SS to suppress the uprising brutally. Instead, the Red Army turned south, advancing into the Balkans. By the end of the year, Bulgaria, Romania and most of Hungary was in Soviet hands. In September Finland sued for peace, and the Soviets pushed towards East Prussia.

Nikolai Popel had joined the Red Army as a private, but rose to the rank of General by 1944, and was a member of the Military Council of the First Guards Tank Army which, in late July, was fighting its way towards the Vistula. He found that the Germans would not yield ground without putting up a ferocious contest.

" There was a hold-up. Above the road, like a horde of gnats, danced the sharp-nosed bodies of Me-110 fighters, trying to drop bombs into the column of vehicles, or sting it with low-level cannon and machine-gun attacks.

▲ A Red Army gun battery in action during the Soviet winter offensive of 1943-44. With huge artillery barrages, the Soviets annihilated serious opposition in the path of their armour and troops.

Behind the Messerschmitts flew the short-winged Junkers with their terrifying roar and stupid-looking snouts, bombing the stationary targets with their full loads of explosives. Somewhere in the front of the column, a stock of valuable fuel was burning beneath a column of flame. From time to time there was an horrific explosion that signified one fewer ammunition truck going forward.

Immediately beyond the culvert the marshes began. Bombs that fell on the swamp exploded in its depths, which saved us from fragments and blast. Tired, worn-out and dirty men were lying on the hillocks. After each explosion, a liquid wave was thrown up and rolled over their bodies. Then the black figures of the soldiers would get up and with machine guns, rifles and even submachine guns, fire into the sky at random.

Something had to be done. We got out from the armoured troop-carrier and went up to the recumbent soldiers. 'What's the hold-up?' 'Don't know.' 'Where's your commander?' 'Somewhere up in front.'

Then suddenly a voice, which sounded indifferent through sheer weariness but yet rang with inexpressible happiness, announced, 'We've shot him down! We've shot him down, Comrade General.'

Along the river bank for tens of kilometres there were dykes, and they only had to be blown up to let the water pour out up to a kilometre or more, in which case we would have to build a bridge a kilometre long. I never discovered why the German colonel left the dykes untouched. Possibly he feared drowning his own men, who were actually in the rear of our advancing tanks and who were hurrying to cross the Vistula. I pointed out to Katukov the boats, scurrying from one bank to the other, 800–900 metres upstream. 'The Germans are crossing.' Katukov looked through his binoculars.

'They're fighting on the water,' whispered the commander.

Two parallel streams of soldiers were firing at each other. The Germans, supported by guns and machine guns hidden on the dykes, were firing from their boats at our scouts crossing the river. Our men knew what was confronting them. The most advanced ones faced each bullet fired at the water and each mine in the minefield on the bank. They were fired at from the pillboxes, point-blank. The young soldiers threw themselves into the water, churned up by the explosions of shells and mortar bombs, and in which floated the bodies of their dead friends.

We made the crossing with whatever was to hand, by which is meant a hunk of timber on which a soldier could ride, a piece of wooden fence, and in general whatever could be utilised. The butts of sub-machine guns served as oars, although it was necessary quite often to pull them out of the water in order to deal with tiresome German riflemen. From each piece of timber, from each boat, from each steed, the soldiers aimed their fire at the enemy, only a few score metres away. **"**

SS **Untersturmführer**
Heinz Landau, a Transylvanian Saxon, returned to his SS unit after leave in Vienna in 1944. They had been sent to the Debrecen region of eastern Hungary, near the Romanian border. As he joined them, they were expecting an attack by the Soviet Army and were ready in their fox-holes.

" Two of our anti-tank guns had been knocked out during my absence and the third was out of order, so once again, we were amongst the infantry with our *Panzerfaust* and hand grenades.

▶ Heinz Landau, left, in 1942. Stationed in eastern Hungary 1944, he was witness to the struggle with the Red Army.

▼ Red Army Marines storm a height in the Crimea, which the Soviets fully liberated in May 1944. German losses here totalled approximately 110,000 killed, wounded and taken

▼▶ German soldiers captured in the Ukraine, May 1944. Like thousands of other prisoners, they are bound for Stalin's camps. Few would survive to return to Germany.

We were sandwiched between two SS units with large contingents of Transylvanians and Schwabs from the Romanian Banat. These men were members of some of the more recently formed, unnamed SS divisions, recruited mostly from ethnic Germans.

Our positions had been under constant aerial attack, alternating with devastating artillery and rocket barrages. All of us were absolutely terrified by the Russian rocket-launchers. The devilish shrieking, thundering noise in itself was paralysing. The accuracy of the Soviet artillery was, I had to admit, incredibly good.

I very clearly remember one particular case on the Donez, when heavy shells and rockets, fired simultaneously from about 1,000 guns, straddled our front lines. About 15 metres from my somewhat elevated position, the surface of the earth began to open in huge, endless cracks, as in an earthquake, then the soil, including our trenches, men, weapons, everything, started to lift, in slow motion, into the air. Terrified shrieks rent the air. It all lifted to a height of about 20 metres, hung

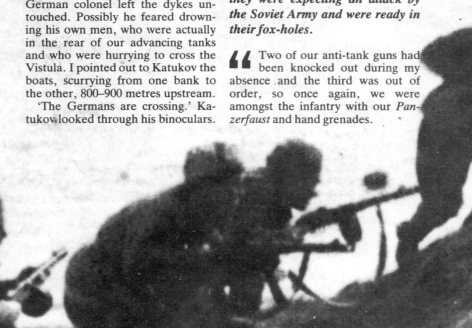

there for a second, then started to break up into small pieces, turning somersaults, crashing back into the huge empty, black gap thus created, burying a whole line of our defences, a minimum of 300 men. The Russians, unaware of this unbelievable bit of shooting, did not take advantage of the situation – it should have been a walk-over.

Well, here at Debrecen, this sort of magnificent target-practice had just come to an end, and on raising our heads, we could just discern the enemy approaching through the smoke and fumes. No tanks this time, just huge numbers of infantry. Suddenly, up went the cry, 'Romanians! The treacherous bastards!' The blood-pressure nearly lifted the helmet from my head. In a flash I remembered my childhood and youth: 'Speak Romanian – you live in Great Romania – you eat Romanian bread,' and I was obviously not the only one. One could easily believe every man on our side used a machine gun. The Romanians were withering under the murderous fire pouring into them, and their attack

was faltering. Our lads, without any orders, jumped up and clubbed, stabbed or shot the Romanians in a veritable orgy of frenzied, long-pent-up hatred and fury. I could not see more than a dozen of them reaching the safety of their own lines. Even the Russian commanders must have been stunned at the complete rout – nay, annihilation – of such a large force.

We then had several days of relative peace and quiet. Inevitably, the steamroller in the form of huge numbers of tanks, followed by endless numbers of infantry, started rolling again.

We steadily retreated, destroying Russian tanks by the dozen, every now and then assisted by our Stukas, which somehow still managed to fly and cause havoc amongst the Ivans. Russian casualties were astronomical and we never encountered Romanians again. Every square foot of ground was fought over desperately. We made a desperate stand at Tisza-Füred, to allow for the crossing over the River Tisza of troops, as well as an ever-increasing flow of refugees.

Just outside Tisza-Füred, having knocked out a large number of T34s, we got involved in hand-to-hand fighting. This was by now tantamount to suicide, as the odds were against us. Here we were outnumbered by ten or 15 to one. Russian morale was now at its highest, while ours was at its lowest. The Russians were now a well-fed, healthy lot, while we were a sorry-looking lot of flea-bitten, skeletal scarecrows. My weight was down to under nine stone, from 10 stone 5lb, and we were wheezing and tottering on our feet. Nevertheless, the spirit was still there and we still considered ourselves far superior to the Ivans.

A particularly vicious Russian bayonet attack was met by an equally determined counterattack. I was firing from the hip as I ran towards the enemy. An unbelievably

huge Russian cannoned into me, not even noticing, and drove his bayonet through one of our chaps. Not only the bayonet, but even the long rifle came out of the poor man's back, the impetus carrying them on, so that the man actually speared a second German before I, sprawling on the ground, literally shot him to pieces with my Schmeisser.

The Russians retreated in disorder, but we had no strength left to follow up. Just outside our trenches, something hit me on the back of my helmet, and I toppled forward into the trench. I did not lose consciousness, but the pain in my head was excruciating, and I was trying to remove my helmet, but found it literally nailed to the back of my head. A grenade splinter had penetrated my headgear like a dart, and was stuck in my skull. I was carried into Tisza-Füred to a first-aid station but lost consciousness. How they got my helmet off, I shall never know, but they did, and I was back in action within 48 hours, the damage being negligible.

Within the next three weeks I managed somehow to stop a number of small grenade splinters on my left hand, nearly ripping off my index and gold fingers; one small splinter penetrated my left wrist and stuck amongst the bone and gristle. A piece of shrapnel the shape and size of an old-fashioned battleaxe, became embedded in my left arm, just above my elbow. Eventually, with further injuries, I was ordered to a Roman Catholic hospital. ”

 John Green had been with a searchlight unit in the Royal Artillery when he was captured at Dunkirk in 1940. He had spells in various prison camps before ending up in a British POW camp within the Auschwitz complex. In summer 1944, a fellow prisoner, Charles Coward, hatched an unbelievable plan.

❝ Sergeant-Major Charles Coward actually introduced himself to the rest of us just after our arrival from Stalag B. Because of his rank, he had been given administrative duties within the camp and so was allowed out only rarely. It was immediately clear to us that Charlie Coward was the man with his finger on the pulse. He told us exactly what

▲ **Auschwitz in its 'heyday'. Prisoners are put to work building a new extension to the kitchen, to cater for the increasing number of inmates.**

◄▼ **Vengeance falls on the innocent: a woman and child murdered by retreating Nazis in western Russia.**

▼ **John Green pictured with his fiancée in 1939. They would have to wait six years to be married.**

to expect, as far as work was concerned. We worked amongst the inmates of Auschwitz concentration camp, which when we first got there, was a sight you would never forget until the day you die. You saw all these walking skeletons with shovels, brushes and picks, being knocked about by their own *Kapos* – they were the German political prisoners who were put in charge of the Jewish internees – knocked about by the SS, and not being able to do anything about it – it was the most distressing thing I've ever experienced.

Sometimes we would get an assignment of about 20 Jewish prisoners from the concentration camp to help us as labourers in the yard. Some of them were so weak, they couldn't lift a nut-and-bolt – you've seen the pictures. I got friendly with a Jewish draughtsman called Hans. He said to me: 'What have I done to be put in here, except be Jewish?' He had actually seen people taken away to the gas chambers and he told us about the method of selection. Everybody would get up in the morning to work at 5 o'clock. They were made to line up outside the huts. It didn't matter how cold it was, and it was sometimes 40 below zero there. The Germans expected a good number of them to fall down – and they were then taken to the gas chambers. The *Kapos* – they were worse than the SS. They would actually whip them. And it was they who selected which prisoners would go and work with them that day. The remainder of these were selected for the gas chambers.

This chap, Coward, he wouldn't accept some of the stories we were telling him about the concentration camp inmates. He would only occasionally be allowed out of our camp. I mean, we hardly believed what we were hearing ourselves, but Charlie Coward had to go and see for himself. So, he found a British POW who was the same height as him, same build, and swapped clothes with him. He saw for himself the state of the concentration camp internees and was so disgusted that he felt he had to see the inside of the

camp himself. He confided in about seven or eight of the British POWs about his plan and I was one of them. I had a word with Hans, and he was terrified. He said, 'Please discourage the man, don't let him do it.' He told me he wanted no part, and on no account should I get involved. When I came back that night, we had another meeting, and Charlie asked

me what I'd found out. I told him what Hans had told me. But he was determined. He went round the table until one of our group told him he'd found someone who could arrange it for a price. He'd found a Pole, a civilian employee within I G Farben, who said he would fix it for him to swap places with a Jewish prisoner.

It was soon arranged. A Jewish prisoner was found, with the same height and build as Charles Coward – Coward was a thin bony man, so he could 'get away with it'. On the day of the swap, Coward went out on a working party as a British POW, and then, in a toilet in the factory he shed his uniform and changed into the Jew's striped uniform, while the Jew changed into Coward's uniform.

The Jew came in with the working party and was immediately smuggled into safety within the camp. We gave him a good feed, and a good wash and brush-up. But he wouldn't

shave, in case, when he went back the next day they would see that he was clean-shaven and get suspicious. He cried for most of the time while he was in our camp, and he told us stories of what went on inside the camp, most of which we'd already heard from the other inmates. Believe it or not, these men still had hope. They all thought that the end of the war was near and they could stick it out. He knew there was no way we could keep him with us.

Meanwhile, Coward spent the night inside the concentration camp and had to get up at 5 o'clock with everyone else and stand in line. On this particular morning, a selection took place for the gas chambers. Not a selection of those who had fallen exhausted – this was a random selection. The SS man looked along the line and stopped at Charles Coward, stared at him full in the face, looked him up and down, then down and up, and passed on. He came that close. As he told us later, all the inmates knew what fate awaited them if they were picked out.

I remember him telling us this, he was shaking all over, his nerve had gone completely. He'd marched back 'normally', held his nerve, until he got in the camp, and as soon as he knew he'd made it, he went to pieces. He was never the same again. After spending just one night and morning inside Auschwitz concentration camp, he was a broken man. He didn't know whether it was night or day, or who he was talking to.

Now, what possessed him to do such a thing, I'll never know. Only Charles Coward would ever know that. The only thing I wanted to do was to get as far away from that place as I could. Charles **"** Coward was one in a million.

FALL OF ROMANIA

By the summer of 1944, there was considerable dissatisfaction in Romania with the war against the Soviet Union. Romanian casualties on the Eastern Front had been heavy and there was talk of a negotiated peace with Stalin to prevent a Soviet invasion. On 23 August 1944, King Michael organised a *coup d'état* against the pro-Nazi Military dictator, Marshal Antonescu, and two days later declared war on Germany.

The Soviets were not impressed. Having already opened an offensive into Romania on 20 August, they refused to talk terms and advanced relentlessly, capturing the oilfields and pushing the Germans back into the Transylvanian Alps. Soviet troops entered Bucharest on 1 September; 12 days later the Romanians signed an armistice with the Allies.

When the future looked rosy: Marshal Antonescu with his puppet-master in 1941.

THE SECOND FRONT

In four and a half years, Britain has cowered in solitary defeat, defended against invasion and, at last, gathered allies to her cause. Now, rallied and determined, the Allies are ready to liberate Europe.

A t the beginning of 1944, the Western Allies were bogged down in Italy, in the mountains around Cassino. It took until May for Cassino to be taken by frontal assault. Rome fell on 4 June. News of this was eclipsed two days later when the long-awaited invasion of Normandy took place – but it did not achieve all its objectives on 6 June, forcing the Allies to fight in difficult terrain to effect a breakout. Even so, Paris was liberated on 25 August and the Allies advanced to the Low Countries. Meanwhile, forces had landed in southern France, and in Italy the Allies reached the Gothic Line. With the resumption of the bombing of Germany, Hitler seemed doomed.

But in autumn stalemate set in, worsened by Montgomery's failure to cross the Lower Rhine at Arnhem. After hard fighting for little progress, on 16 December, the Germans suddenly counterattacked through the Ardennes, the situation looked decidedly worrying.

Major Dick Rubinstein volunteered for Special Operations work in France and went in as one of the three-man Jedburgh teams. These consisted of an officer native to the country, a British officer and a wireless operator and their task was to recruit and direct Resistance workers – and sometimes supply ammunition.

▲ September 1944: a *maquisard* guards German prisoners taken in the liberation of the Loire area.

" Throughout the clandestine years, I suppose the Brits had kept perhaps 50 to 60 agents at any one time in northern Europe, mainly in France. If you get into southern and eastern Europe – Yugoslavia and Greece, you can have a para-military phase for longer, due to the wild nature of the terrain.

The Jedburgh teams were formed for France, Belgium, Denmark and Holland, but nearly all the teams were for France – although four Jedburgh teams were used at Arnhem. The aim was that the team would represent the coming of the Allies, and not be just a continuation of this odd thing, the Resistance (which was made up of a lot of nutters, in a way – you had to be very hard, completely patriotic and prepared to risk not only your life, but also your wife, children, everything). At the time, I was disappointed at how little support for the Resistance there seemed to be in France, but five years later, when I got a house and we were planning a family, I wondered if I would have felt quite the same myself.

The native officer's job was essentially liaison with his own people. The Allied officer's job was to supply weapons training and, to some degree, to make sure that everything stayed on course and didn't become emotional – once arms appeared on the scene, there were often a lot of old arguments to settle. The Allied officer also supervised the wireless operator, who was generally a sergeant, and was responsible for the cyphering.

The Jedburgh teams were dropped in just before the breaking wave of the advancing liberation, so they had a few weeks to explain how the Resistance in the area could most help the military situation, then take what action was possible – call for arms and distribute them.

You couldn't give youngsters rifles and expect them to be a crack force immediately. The best they could do was lie in a hedge and try to lay an ambush. But generally speaking, we

◄ In a prelude to invasion, a US B-26 Marauder softens up the French coast with 1,000lb bombs.

couldn't attempt to do anything militarily, and of course, trained troops could turn round and crush these chaps, as well as taking reprisals.

In the wild areas you could have a *maquis* – a group of chaps who lived in the area and were used to the terrain. Although I talk of 'untrained' lads, because of the military training in France, there was always a stiffening of chaps with military experience, although a lot of them were sent to labour camps.

The Jedburghs by no means com-

▲ Major Dick Rubinstein who, after work with Jedburgh teams in France, was dropped into Burma.

manded operations – of course a strong personality would end up commanding, but generally speaking, you went over to win the cooperation and collaboration of the local people to do what was wanted in the area. At that stage in the war, the Allies had complete air superiority. As the Germans were pushed away, they wanted to move back their better equipment. They could only move it at night, so if you knew where it was in the morning, you could get an air strike out. It was very good for morale if, as a result of your signal, there was an attack.

I went in twice, once to the area around Lorient. The aim was to work with the French, essentially to establish a ring of about 3,000 lads around Lorient to contain the, by now, very deluded, but nevertheless fairly numerous, garrison that was occupying Lorient. Nobody was going to fight for it, we didn't need it – it was a bombed-out submarine base, as were Brest and St Nazaire, but we couldn't just leave a garrison free to sally forth as they liked. It was thought that it would be a good role for the Resistance to keep these garrisons in check.

Militarily we didn't do very much except assist in establishing the ring around Lorient. There was also a big French SAS regiment operating in the area and, in fact, they were working magnificently, getting in touch with other groups like us, and were more involved in the fight. The last thing we did when the area was clear was to organise a flight of three Dakotas to arrive at a nearby airfield to bring more ammunition for the arms which had been sent. This was a final flight in of British ammunition to keep Lorient people going. The flight went back through Normandy and picked up wounded at the beachhead – I must say it was a bit of a shaker to see all those lads coming aboard. **"**

 *Yvonne Farrow, known to the Special Operations Executive in France as Annette Cormeau, was in the WAAF and, being bilingual in French and English, volunteered for undercover work. After training in radio, photography, codes, cyphers and some parachuting, she was dropped into France in August 1943.*

ing around, and we didn't dare move, even to brush them away. Then their airfield telephone went and an adjutant got the message that he had to get back to his people or risk being overrun, so he let us go. That was really a stroke of luck!

I trained with Yolande Beekman and Noor Inayat Kahn – we were the first three WAAFs as far I can make out. Unfortunately neither of them came home. Noor Inayat Khan with her dark Indian skin – and not very security conscious was kept an eye on and was eventually given away.

We're not quite sure, but we think she was shot in Dachau at the end. Poor Yolande was caught too. As they got into the train, they recognised each other and they were transported to the final concentration camp.

I would stay three nights only in any one house, never stay longer than that, because the signals could be traced. This went on for quite a while. I had to be philosophical about the danger of being caught, it was no use having tantrums, and nerves and trying to do things too quickly. I had to be calm in all situations and that's how I got out in the end. A member of the team which received me on my arrival in France, gave us all away. But luckily the Germans never caught up with me. I needed a lot of places, as my area covered from the Pyrenees to the Dordogne, from Bordeaux to Toulouse, so I had several houses I could stay in regularly. French people were very helpful and the women were especially courageous. They never got the thanks they really deserved. They had to keep up appearances all the time, while the men could go off to work. The women had to be at home, and they had to receive the *Gestapo* if there was a visit, and quickly make excuses to be sure no one was caught.

If I was discovered to have been with any of these families, I would have endangered them – that's why I was so grateful to them. I go back every year. They not only gave me food (I could give them money, as I had no tickets for food), but they gave me a bed. And they knew, not only that I was English, but I had a radio transmitter. They were extremely brave and I know some of them got MBEs for it.

I thought it might be better to learn a little patois while I was there, I didn't use it very much, but I though it would be helpful if I was ever caught. I always worked alone as a security measure. I experienced

some of the major operations during D-Day. Everything was prepared for D-Day, we had little stocks of munitions and weapons, dotted around the area. We heard 36 hours before D-Day happened, and when we heard it had happened, I had to go and check everyone had heard their messages. After that I was on the air every day to let them know what we were doing – where we were located, for example.

I also organised for people to escape through the south of France, over the Pyrenees and down into Bilbao, where I told them to go to the consulate. If they were caught by the Spaniards, they were put into concentration camps run by the Germans. But having told London to expect them, if they didn't turn up in three or four days, consulate staff would go to camp and bail them out.

There were so many hairy incidents during my time in France, but on one occasion after D-Day, my boss came to the farm, and said, 'Come on, the Germans have traced you and are looking for you.' I picked up my radio set, and my code book, no clothes or anything and got in the car. He explained they were coming up the road to the west so we went along the middle road, as he didn't trust them not to be coming up the eastern road as well. We had travelled about 10 km on the middle road when up came a personnel carrier from the German Army, and they stopped us, and put us in the ditch. Luckily it was dry; we were back to back to start with and then two soldiers with pistols separated us. I could feel the pistol in my back, and the same was happening to my boss. This lasted about an hour under terrible July heat, with flies buzz-

▲▲The hated French *Milice* surround a home where they suspect there to be Resistance supporters - these police would suffer heavy reprisals after the liberation.

▲As the Allies advance, French locals in a liberated town show their appreciation by doing washing for British soldiers in the area. These people, at least, could show their support openly.

 Major Harry Despaigne was sent into the Toulouse/Castres area of France to work for the SOE in recruiting Resistance workers to be ready for the D-Day landings. He had volunteered for undercover work in preference to trench warfare. Being bilingual he was an ideal agent.

Our mission was to recruit people and create a private army for D-Day – a date which nobody knew. We had to organise drops of arms, ammunition and explosives and disperse the proceeds all over the countryside. We were to persuade people to join us as soon as we had notice of the day of D-Day, which we received around the end of

May.

We got all these people to come and join us at a certain spot with their weapons, food for several days, and transports. This became the basis of the *Corps Franc de la Montagne Noire* – our private army. We only wanted about 600 men but got 1,000 plus. As we could not arm or clothe so many, we had to send some home. From D-Day onwards, we carried on with what we were taught – cutting railway lines, telephone lines and so on, and stopping the occupying forces from moving north towards the landing beaches.

The people we recruited just stayed at home and lived a normal life, but when we told them to come, they came as directed bringing with them some of the local *maquis*. We all met on top of a mountain and it

was chaos for about two days, but eventually we got organised for the D-Day actions. To feed this multitude, we had to kill about three bullocks we bought, and go to about five or six bakers to get the bread made with the flour we supplied. We also had to rob a Pétain's Youth Centre

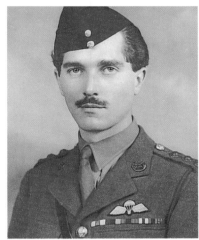

▲ Major Harry Despaigne, later MC. Working covertly, nonchalant behaviour became second nature.

store to get the cloth to make uniforms. The logistics of special operations are not always what comes to mind when you think of it.

You were there as a liaison man – a leader for the men. You suggested and ordered a few things, but underneath, you were not supposed to be in charge. Yet we were told at the time, by a man who is now a well-known politician, that our people were acknowledged as fighting but belonged to a friendly but foreign power, which could not be considered as French in its ultimate aim. This, until not very long ago, stopped any recognition from the French

government and de Gaulle.

It was quite difficult to avoid being noticed in the South of France, seeing my height, but as my papers said I was born in Normandy, it was alright. You behaved normally, and didn't look frightened or break into a sweat. I had so much confidence in my false papers that it wasn't until after the war that I realised I was not entirely safe. What SOE failed to realise was that all the documentation of births, deaths and marriages was kept in two places. I had mine from Cherbourg, where the town hall was burned down and all the records destroyed, but there was another duplicate set elsewhere. If I had known, I might not have been so confident.

On one occasion, I was given away by a double agent – a Frenchman. Some say he was working for another intelligence agency, bent on destroying SOE, others that he was simply working on German orders. The fact which confirmed to me that I was given away by him only became clear to me a few months ago, after reading part of the verbatim of his trial in France after the war. Looking back, it was obvious that I was followed from Angers to Paris and from Paris on my way to Arles. In Paris, arriving from Angers, I had to spend the night in a hotel near Montparnasse Station, although I had been expecting to spend the night in a safe houses. This had not been arranged, presuming we would all be arrested. The next morning I had a meeting with this man at a cafe near the Champs Elysées, when he started pumping me as to what was my mission – where I was going. I did not tell him anything and soon as I could, wirelessed London to voice my suspicions and complain **"** about my reception.

VERCORS

On 6 June 1944, coinciding with Allied landings in Normandy, 950 *maquisards* under Major Huet raised the *tricouleur* in Villard-de-Lans and declared the Vercors plateau, south west of Grenoble, a 'Liberated area'. It was part of the disruption carried out by French Resistance fighters throughout the country, designed to delay any German response to the Allied landings, but Vercors was more ambitious than most. Believing that 4,000 airborne troops were about to fly in from Algeria, Huet's followers saw themselves as spearheading a nationwide uprising against the Germans. They were sadly misled. No Allied troops (and insufficient airdropped supplies) arrived. Instead, German forces closed in, using artillery and airpower against the *maquisard* positions. On 21 July, SS troops landed by glider as part of a final assault, during which entire villages were destroyed. By 23 July, it was all over. Nearly 900 French patriots had died.

◄ The Resistance movement is always at risk - here the pro-Nazi Milice line up a row of suspects.

▶ B-24 Liberators of the USAAF's 93rd Bomber Group release their bombs over Magdeburg, Germany, 16 August 1944. The city was a centre of aircraft manufacture in the *Reich*, and so became the target of heavy area bombing by the Allies.

Pilot Officer Tony Bird of 61 Squadron had lost three members of his crew over Germany when, thinking he was dead at the controls, they bailed out in an attempt to survive. Soon these men were replaced and Bird (now Acting Flight Lieutenant) set out on a mission on 22 April from which he felt he would not return.

The presentiment of doom would not go away. The feeling was so strong that I wrote letters to both my parents and to my girlfriend, telling them not to worry if I did not return from this operation. Somehow, despite this feeling, I felt that I would survive. I gave Boris, my adopted dog, to one of my ground crew to look after – I had never felt the need to do any of these things before previous operations.

As briefing we were given a short talk to introduce us to the new 'J-type' incendiary bombs, which we were to carry for the first time. We were told that, once this huge incendiary device ignited, there was no known fire-fighting equipment that would be able to extinguish it. The thought of anyone attempting to extinguish one of our horrific 'J-type' bombs with a bucket of sand was ludicrous. We were told that the heat from them was so intense that no

fireman would be able to approach one, even with protective clothing. It was mentioned that the heat from these new bombs was so high that it would melt many metals – and within a few hours, I was to have verification of this at close quarters.

Just before we went out to our Lancaster on the 22 April for the operation to Brunswick, a strange chance event made the difference between life and death for me.

Two types of parachute were available – seat-type, which the wearer had firmly strapped to him by a harness, and which pilots usually preferred, and the clip-on chest type, which the remainder of the crew had little choice but to use, due to the confines of the aircraft.

When I joined the squadron in August 1943, I had been issued with a seat-type parachute which I subsequently wrote my name on, as evidence of ownership.

Shortly afterwards my parachute was either mislaid or taken by another pilot. As no further seat-type 'chutes were immediately available, I was issued with a clip-on type, which I used on every subsequent operation except the last one to Brunswick.

I had never been entirely happy with the chest-type parachute, knowing that those few seconds' delay in retrieving it from the fuselage and then having to clip it on might be fatal in an emergency.

When I called at the parachute store on 22 April, prior to the operation to Brunswick, much to my surprise, there was my old seat-type 'chute, lying on the floor.

Why it should have turned up – and who had been using it for the past six months, I did not establish, but I greeted it like an old friend. In a few hours it was to save my life.

At this stage of the war, German anti-aircraft defences were in many respects more advanced than our own, or so it seemed to us. Certainly the master ultra-violet searchlights were highly efficient.

Suddenly there was a tremendous thud as a flak shell exploded immediately under us, and within seconds, flames appeared, coming up through the 'Duralumin' aluminium alloy floor at my feet.

The special J-type incendiary bombs were on fire, and there was nothing that could extinguish them.

Even the metal alloy floor was burning and I instinctively raised my feet from the rudder pedals as the flames engulfed the front of the aircraft where I was sitting.

As I raised my hand to switch on my microphone and give the order to bail out, the aircraft exploded and I can vaguely recall shooting up through the perspex roof as everything disintegrated around me.

There was a terrific jerk as my oxygen supply tube and intercom flex were ripped from their sockets and one leather gauntlet was sucked off my hand.

Everything went grey from the sudden violent change in velocity, and I was probably unconscious for quite some time, partly due to oxygen starvation.

I was amazed that I was still alive and apparently still in one piece, but as I dropped to a less rarified atmosphere, my senses returned and I suddenly became wide awake. One vital action was necessary if I was to remain alive for much longer, and I reached across to pull the rip cord of my parachute. I had been rushing downwards at a speed of perhaps 120 mph, but had been quite unaware of this, and as my parachute opened, the sudden braking effect gave me the sensation of being pulled upwards.

Seconds later and without warning, I hit the ground, falling over backwards as I was dragged by my parachute. I had regained my consciousness just in time.

I released my 'chute harness and cleared my ears – suddenly I could hear the roar of the bombers returning to England and the German guns.

A feeling of great loneliness and sadness came over me as I thought of my crew, who I knew would not have

▼ Ground crew in Britain fit an auxiliary fuel tank to the wing of a USAAF P-51 Mustang fighter-bomber, giving it the range needed for its role as bomber escort over Europe. The fastest piston-powered aircraft of the war, the Mustang outclassed anything (short of jets) that the Germans could put in the air.

had time to clip on their parachutes to escape.

Having thoroughly hidden my parachute, harness, flying helmet and accessories in dense undergrowth, I opened my standard issue escape kit.

I knew that I was somewhere to

the west of Brunswick and that it would be impossible to walk the 130 odd miles to the Dutch border, but at least I would be heading towards home.

I removed my pilot's brevet, rank braid and DFC ribbon so that I was left with an RAF battledress. The tops of my flying boots were designed to rip off, leaving serviceable walking shoes.

I was soon in open country, but as dawn approached, I found a wooded area where I was glad to rest. I slept or rested for most of the day, but as it started to get dark, I set out, avoiding any main road and trying to find a suitable path leading in the right direction.

Resting for much of the day and walking at night, I had only the haziest idea of just how far I had travelled, as I had to make frequent detours to avoid buildings, or areas of population.

Eventually, weak from lack of food and with a suspicious growth of beard, I was accosted by a member of the Hitler Youth, who saw me before I had time to hide.

His opening words were, 'Are you *Engländer*?' and at my reply, '*Nein*,' he hesitated and I continued walking, only to be accosted for the second time. 'Are you *Engländer*?' Although the boy's English seemed rather limited, it was infinitely superior to my knowledge of German, which was almost nil. The boy was joined by two Wehrmacht soldiers, who pointed Lugers at me although, at this stage, they were still uncertain as to who I might be. (Some foreign workers wore British battledresses captured at Dunkirk, although these were more likely to be khaki colour).

I normally carried a revolver, but this had been lost in the explosion.

A Wehrmacht officer arrived and undid part of my escape kit which I had concealed in my battledress, then I was marched off at gun point to a nearby farmhouse.

The local *Gestapo* official and I had a mutually nonproductive interview as he spoke no English and I spoke no German. He was easily recognisable as the only official without a uniform, and after shouting at me for some time, he finally gave up, and I was taken to the local jail at Linden, then to *Dulagluft* at Frankfurt-am-Main – the centre for interrogating captured RAF personnel. On the way, I had a first-hand opportunity of seeing the devastation our bombing had caused. "

★ *Captain Edward McGuire Jnr of 409 Squadron, 93rd Bombardment Group, was on his fifth of an accredited 36 missions over Germany. On 17 October 1944 he flew in G George, loaded with 12 500lb bombs in icy weather and poor visibility, for which H2S radar had to compensate in navigation.*

" Several times we took off carrying our shaving kits and a blanket, to be informed after the target as to whether we would land in Scotland, France, Italy (once), Russia (once) or wherever! Also, nervousness or fear affects some men differently. Many are afflicted with a tremendous output of urine – I was a urinator, first class! After briefing, ALWAYS a bowel movement in the latrine near the briefing room, where there was always a long line. No constipation among combat crews!

The trucks would take us out to the hardstand. First urinate, then check the ship, then urinate, then wait, then urinate, then start the engine.

We were dressed so clumsily that the only place the flight-deck personnel could urinate was on the bomb-bay doors. On this particular trip it was very cold, and I was extremely active until we were well out over the North Sea *en route* for Cologne. Finally I ran dry.

We turned the IP and the lead opened its doors – which was our signal to do the same. This day, however, our doors wouldn't open. Frozen shut. The navigator started

arguing that we would have to carry the bombs home because he couldn't get the door open. I turned the ship over to Jnr, the co-pilot, drew my .45 pistol and cocked it. I aimed it down towards the navigator and, over the intercom said, 'You son of a bitch, I'll give you a slow count of three to drop those bombs through the doors, or I'll shoot you and throw you out with them!'

Pause. Utter quiet on the intercom. 'ONE!' Pause. 'TWO!' Pause.

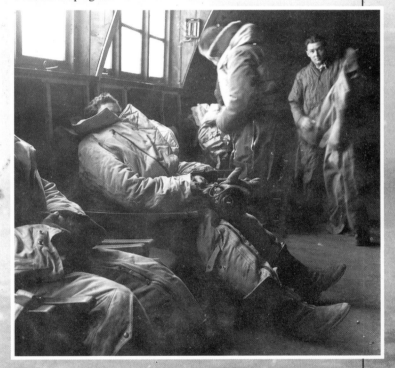

▲ RAF bomber crew prepares for a night mission over Europe. The flight suits, lined with sheepskin, were vital protection against temperatures of 40° below zero at 25,000 feet.

BARROOM! – and the bombs went right out through the doors and, of course, tore the doors loose in the process. I put the safety back on my pistol and reholstered it, then took over the ship again.

A little while later, the lead called us and asked, 'G George, what happened to your bomb-bay doors?' Before I could think of a suitable reply, my co-pilot smashed the button and blurted out, 'The skipper pissed on the bomb-bay doors and froze them shut!' Needless to say, when we got back, there was hell to pay. I was called up before the squadron CO and the engineering officer, and really blistered.

I said, 'I'm sorry I've caused additional work. My crew and I will work with you and your men all night if necessary to make repairs, but I am not going to get over the target, after all the efforts and sacrifices of all those people that made it possible, just to haul the bombs back – that might cause a little more work!' That was the end of that – except I went to Squadron Ops and said, 'Don't you ever post that man to fly with me again!' They never did.

Now, long years later, I think back to this and realise the extreme danger in which I placed my crew, ship and myself – but that was long ago and I was tough enough to do my duty as I saw it – and I didn't tolerate reluctance on the part of my crew. When I said 'GO', they better be moving.

I am certainly thankful that the navigator carried out his orders. He would have been dead and I court-martialled in less than three seconds more.

9 November 1944 – Fort L'Aisne, 6.00 hrs. This was the worst mission out of 36! What happened was, when the Lead opened his bomb-bay doors, he had a faulty release. That means something electrical failed and his bombs went out before they should have. When the Lead drops his bombs, you drop yours. No maybes about it. So we did. Right on a regiment of US troops sitting in trucks waiting to go in when we had bombed the fort.

You never saw a more miserable group of airmen than we were that night when we learned what had happened. It really hurt. Long years afterwards, I happened to be shooting the breeze somewhere with someone, and mentioned this incident. It turned out that he had been in one of those trucks. He said they'd have killed us that night if they could, but later realised – or were told – what had happened. But it brought back that terrible feeling again. The worst mission in memory.

Flight Sergeant Frederick Fish was a navigator with 153 Squadron of Lancasters, based at Scampton as the RAF's massive bombing campaign against German cities reached a crescendo. As he recalls, he spent his 22nd birthday on a gigantic 1,000-bomber raid to the industrial city of Essen in the Ruhr district in October 1944.

"The German flak was amazingly accurate, and we all had a very healthy respect for it. Apart from this and searchlights and fighters, there was bad weather, with possible icing, intense cold, with an outside temperature of minus 20° C or less at 20,000 feet (and the internal heating never seemed to work properly!), with gunners often coming back with iced-up eyes or ice on their faces. Also, when the flying bombs were crossing the Channel, navigators had to be sure not to stray into a restricted corridor, otherwise we would be shot down on sight by our own patrolling fighters. There was also a great risk of collision, of being bombed from above, from the vast concentration over the target.

Often, tired crews, within sight of the airfields in Lincolnshire (the heart of Bomber Command country) which were so close they almost overlapped on their circuits, would collide with other returning aircraft. So one had to keep utmost efficiency and vigilance in order to survive.

Fortunately we were given 'wakey-wakey' pills – benzedrine, I think – that kept one razor sharp mentally for many hours, but it meant you couldn't sleep if you had taken it and the operation was cancelled!

What with six tons of bombs, up to 2,000 gallons of petrol, plus flares, ammunition, oxygen hydraulics, coolants, equipment etc, we were literally flying bombs – so easy to realise why aircraft exploded when hit by flak.

It was not always appreciated that with so many aircraft (at times up to 1,000) over the target, there was a real risk of collision or being hit by bombs coming down from other aircraft at higher altitude. On 31st October 1944, 493 aircraft bombed Cologne.

As we approached the target, the Lancaster suddenly heeled over to starboard – we thought it was a near burst of flak under the port wing, so recovered and completed our bombing run. On the way home, the flight engineer saw a large hole, about the size of a kitchen table, in the starboard wing.

After a hectic exchange of four-letter words, it transpired that the wireless operator, keeping look-out

▶ 17 June, 1944: the havoc wrought on Clapham by one of the first flying bombs to hit London.

GERMAN JETS

The world's first jet-powered flight took place in Germany on 27 August 1939, almost two years before a similar event in Britain. Fortunately for the Allies, this lead was wasted – it took until April 1944 for the Luftwaffe to form its first jet-fighter unit, Ekdo 262.

Ekdo 262 was equipped with the Messerschmitt Be-262 *Schwalbe* (Swallow), a twin-engined machine capable of 540 mph. By comparison, the fastest Allied piston-engined fighter then in service, the P-51D Mustang, could only manage 437 mph. Beginning operations in October 1944, Ekdo 262 inflicted significant casualties on USAAF B-17 and B-24 daylight formations: in April 1945 alone, Me-262s of the élite *Jagdverband* 44 downed 50 bombers. At the same time *Jagdgeschwader* 400 was operating the Me-163 *Komet* rocket fighters, capable of 580 mph. If such aircraft had appeared earlier in the war, the Allies would have faced a major crisis.

◀ Short-lived scourge of Allied aircraft: an Me-262 on an airfield deep in Germany.

▲ Fred Fish and the crew of Lancaster 'A' for 'Able', 153 Squadron, Scampton. Left to right: F/O Ted Durman, Sgt Vic Morandi, F/L Whizz Wheeler, Sgt Scott, P/O Fred Fish, and W/O Bill Turner.

in the astrodome, had seen a 1,000-lb bomb hurtling towards us, but said he was 'too paralysed to speak'. By a million-to-one chance, it had missed vital parts, and a petrol tank by inches (the red tank could be seen about three inches from the jagged edge). A few feet either way would have meant certain destruction.

Luckily, the bomb had not completed its timing cycle, so did not explode on impact. On other raids, some were, in fact, hit, and exploded from our own bombs, or were severely damaged. In one case, I think, the entire nose section of a Halifax was sheared off, taking the bomb-aimer, navigator and wireless operator.

On another occasion, bombing the Leuna oil plant near Leipzig on 6th December 1944 (reputedly the second most heavily defended target in Germany after Berlin), we were up to 250 miles from the German frontier and 500 miles from our bases in England. The bomber stream was attacked by 487 aircraft and, as our navigation aid was jammed, we went 350 miles without getting a fix on our position.

First Lieutenant George Vanden Heuvel of 370 Fighter Squadron, USAAF was based across the Channel in France, flying escort for the bombers in P-51 Mustangs. On 26 December 1944, he was to escort the Ninth Air Force on a strafing mission which would return over Luxembourg.

"We were flying as squadrons, not as a group. There were four flights of four planes – 16 aircraft. We were at about 16,000 feet and 12 or 13 planes came down in front of us, into the sun. I was tail-end Charlie, and I saw them. I said, 'Bogies 12 o'clock ahead, high,' and somebody said, 'No, they're P-47s.' So the bogies turned – obviously they'd seen us and came down, and were coming in behind us.

I said these were FW-190s, and someone else again, said, 'They're P-47s.' Then, suddenly, the lead pilot called for a break. Four of them were coming around behind us. I was

▲ **Dressed to kill: Lt Vanden Heuval in flight gear and tie.**

on the wing of my leader and switched around and got on the tail of one. I was on my leader's tail – his guns didn't fire. I pulled up and shot at the enemy plane, got some hits and split on down, finally getting a good burst at him. He crashed into the trees on the ground.

When I pulled up, there was no-one about, so I went up to about 12,000 feet and saw another Mustang chasing another 190 across the ground below me. I went down and asked him if he needed any help. Yes, he said, he was out of ammunition. I pulled up alongside and moved dead ahead, then shot at the 190 three times. He pulled up and bailed out.

Years later, and through the records and friends of the Eighth, we met, and tracked down who shot whom. Only two German pilots had been shot down that day and survived.

Another time I got into compressability, when the plane's going too fast for the controls to work. It was very frightening. I was at 38,000 feet, and the air is thin up there. I was going at 600 mph in a dive, and the plane went out of control. Things were dampened, the stick was going all over the place, I finally got it controlled at 6,000 feet and saw 14 planes. Thinking they were Mustangs, I flew towards them, but they were Fw-190s. I got on the tail of one of them and started shooting at him. I got some hits, but about the same time, two of them made a head-on pass at me. I looked at my guns, and three weren't firing on one side and one wasn't on the other.

I split west – two were shooting at me from the back, two others from the side, then two of them ran together and crashed. I dived way down.

My squadron CO was about four miles away and he saw this and came over – but they had left by the time he got to me. He called to me to come back up – I was at 5,000 feet again. I went up but couldn't find him, so I went back for the bombers which were still coming in. I saw a box of B-17s with about ten 190s shooting at them, and I got on the tail of one. I tried to hit him with one gun, but it didn't pay off, and they started looking at me, so I left and went home.

▲ Back after the débâcle of Dunkirk. This time, prepared and trained, British troops go ashore on the French Channel coast. Bicycles are still the order of the day for transport once on shore.

War Stories

There were several ways to get the troops out of bed in the mornings. A former RAF corporal recalls an original method: 'We were under canvas in France, sleeping in bell tents, feet to the centre pole. At night the cockroaches would gather in their hundreds on the inside roofs of the tents. Our flight sergeant would walk around the camp just before Reveille, slapping all the tents with his cane. The sleepers would be covered in a thick black shower of cockroaches – that was guaranteed to get us up alright!'

Trooper Jack Border with the 22nd Dragons was part of 79th Armoured Division, and was a wireless operator/loader in a flail tank. These were among General Hobart's 'Funnies', and were adapted to clear mine-fields by rotating chains which flailed before them. Life expectancy of crews was low.

" By the time that I reached my squadron near Caen, the tanks were taking a terrible mauling. We could only do one-and-a-half mph in action, so you didn't have much of a chance of getting out of the way.

Eventually my troop, the 5th, was taken out. The losses had been so great that the troops were shared amongst 1, 2, 3, and 4 squadrons because, thankfully, crews had survived and some were to be redeployed. I was put into scout cars where my job was to liaise with the other squadrons. I was now always behind them tanks and saw a lot of what was going on. I was lucky because I had escaped from the flail tanks which were always at the mercy of the enemy.

I had watched flail tanks that had missed a mine in their sweep get damaged and lose a sprocket. They would then stop and become a sitting target – clearly seen. We lost a lot of people and tanks that way.

It was at Le Havre, I had left my scout car and stood on top of a tank and watched the town being destroyed by the bombers. I was thinking about what I was going to see when I eventually got to the town. When the air attacks ceased, the tanks began to move off. I remember seeing 26 tanks going in to clear the minefields and 19 didn't come back – a lot of crews were shell-shocked and had lost limbs. I became a bit worried as we couldn't attack from the sea and the land around Le Havre was hilly. We were going down into it. There were a lot of casualties and eventually it also filtered back that there had been a lot of civilian casualties too.

The civilians had refused to leave even though they had been given a warning by the Allies that the town was going to be attacked. This was because when they were overrun by the Germans, they had left their homes, only to return and find that they had all been looted, and when they went back they found that they had to start all over again, from scratch. So, of course, when they were told by the British to evacuate because we were going to attack, they said no.

So they stayed on, and there was a

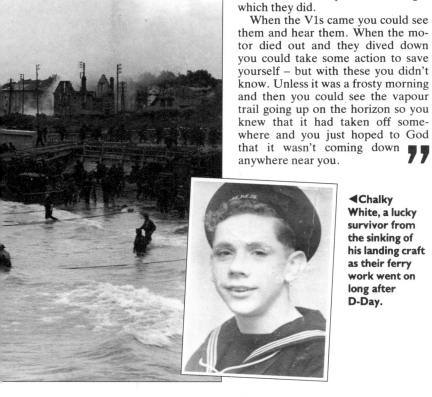

down. The V2s just came down. I felt that when they pushed the V2 up they didn't care where they went – to Britain – or anywhere – just somewhere where they would be certain to do the most possible damage, which they did.

When the V1s came you could see them and hear them. When the motor died out and they dived down you could take some action to save yourself – but with these you didn't know. Unless it was a frosty morning and then you could see the vapour trail going up on the horizon so you knew that it had taken off somewhere and you just hoped to God that it wasn't coming down anywhere near you. ”

◄ **Chalky White, a lucky survivor from the sinking of his landing craft as their ferry work went on long after D-Day.**

tremendous loss of life. Then we went in and it was all a jumble – but it was over quickly and we were pulled out as the flails were needed somewhere else.

We were moved on to Antwerp. The advance was so fast then – it was September and it took us just three days to get there. We weren't doing much until suddenly the Germans started dropping V2 rockets on Antwerp. We had heard that you couldn't hear them coming and this was right. The casualties were high, unlike those from a conventional bomb that you could hear whistling

Bill (Chalky) White was a stoker, first class, on Landing Ship LST 420. The task of landing ships was to carry in troops and machinery to the occupied beaches and then, as the men were brought back to the shore, to take out the wounded. He sailed from Portsmouth during the night of 5 June 1944 as part of the D-Day fleet.

“ We landed on Sword beach about 9 o'clock in the morning.

I had the middle watch – from midnight to four o'clock. At half past three in the morning I poked my head out through the hatch and I've never, ever seen anything like it. It was a sight or a moment I shall carry with me for the rest of my life. I could not believe what I was seeing. The sea, as far as you could see was ships, nothing but ships and the sky was full of planes, some towing gliders – it was unbelievable, a fantastic sight.

The troops were landed on the beach then we had to wait four or five hours until the tide took us off. For virtually everyone we put ashore, in numbers, we had back as many wounded and prisoners. It was a heart-breaking sight. Each one would have a label on saying what had happened. One would say, 'paratrooper – two legs and one arm blown off.' They were so courageous, there was no sobbing or feeling sorry for themselves. We took them back to Southampton, loaded up and went back again. Later we went back into Juno and Gold beaches as the others were filled up – we did that for three months because the troops had been held up.

In September that year we were ordered up to Tilbury and going up the Channel I saw doodle bugs for the first time. They were so low you could have shot them down – but we couldn't because we would have given away our position so we had to more or less ignore them – at the time we didn't know what they were even.

At Tilbury we loaded up with troops – a radar unit for the RAF – the first mobile unit they had. We were to take them to Ostend. We were going across and a force 8 or 9 blew up as we were approaching Ostend and there was a lot of debris in the sea. So, in the storm, we were ordered to go back to the east coast of Britain to shelter. We were the third in the line and were about five

▶ **Tanks and vehicles of the 2nd Gordon Highlanders with, on the right, a flail tank. An improvised 'Funny' with a suicidally dangerous job, the flail tank crew would undoubtedly think this a ghastly misnomer.**

miles off the coast when there was a bang.

A mine had gone off midships and 420 broke completely in two. At the time I was in my bunk and was catapulted across the room – a rude awakening. When I picked myself up I was in complete darkness and I could feel the ship listing. I made my way on to the upper deck. Most of the chaps were going aft. Fire was coming from the bridge and a lot of the chaps were going over the side, she had broken where the bridge ended. I saw a couple of friends, one had a smashed ankle where he had caught it on a bulkhead door. It was a nasty day, the tide was running fast and I stood there, knowing that

▶ **William Loveless – after his squadron's attack on 24 June, he was among the first wounded and had to be taken back for treatment.**

when I jumped I had to swim into the tide away from the burning oil. It wasn't a case of being brave, I had worked out I was going to be alright. I don't know why. I just felt that. The last to leave was the first lieutenant – who had just been made a skipper. He said, 'Well we had better go, stokes,' and I jumped. I remember plunging down into the water and looking up at the light, the swimming into the tide, it was just a matter of swimming and swimming. Somebody called out, 'Chalky I can't swim! I can't swim!' It's a thing that has remained with me ever since. There was nothing I could do about it.

Then someone else called from a float. There were a few chaps on board. Someone pulled me on board. I saw a steward who had climbed over the rail of the ship and was sitting on the propeller guards, crying – so obviously he couldn't swim. What could you do?

Then someone threw a line to the float from an LST as we got near to it one of us jumped off the float and swam towards it – it was very courageous – and brought it back. We could see our ship still burning. We held on to the line and they started to pull us in but the line parted. The sea was very strong, it was getting dark now and then suddenly out of the gloom appeared this trawler, HMS *Greenfly*. She put on her lights and after that I can't remember anything until I came to on board. **"**

Canon William Loveless, at the time a subaltern with the Reconnaissance Regiment, was sprawled in a Normandy field with six others on Saturday 24 June 1944. The Allied invasion of France was 18 days old as his squadron leader ordered the men to clear the enemy from weapon pits across a cornfield.

" I tell the men to get some rest, but my sergeant and I decide that, while there's light, we will venture on foot to the end of no man's land at Point 102, so we know exactly where to lead the advance.

Point 102 is a small wood. Peering into it, my sergeant and I wish we had not come. Dead bodies from a near-destroyed Duke of Wellington's battalion lie everywhere, bent into grotesque right-angle shapes as the blast of mortars caught them in their too-shallow trenches. White teeth glisten against blackened faces. Both my sergeant and I stumble for words in our shock.

Back with the troop, we try to get what sleep we can, but at 0330 I am up, pouring brandy for my car crew from a silver flask my father brought me on my last leave. My driver and gunner and I feel better. Edwards, never at a loss, toasts, 'Here's to your father!'

At 0400 precisely, we start moving up a track to Point 102. Suddenly the ground almost shakes to the noise of artillery barrage, which eases as we reach Point 102, and the cars edge along the rack beside the wood. Although the barrage has eased, bullets are clipping the trees above.

Now into the open cornfields. This

is the tricky bit, as we turn at right angles from Point 102. I am trying to follow a very small track between the cornfields, but in places we just plough on through the green corn. It is difficult to see. There is a lot of smoke, but we keep going.

Then, damn them, why has the LRC in front stopped? I try to get them on the wireless B set. No reply. Nothing for it but to jump out of the turret of my HAC and see what has happened. I shout and bang on the side of the LRC before they open the door. Someone mutters about not knowing the way, but I see they are just frightened. And so am I. I snap, 'Follow my car. I'll take the lead.'

Back in my car, I reflect grimly not only that the troop officer should never be in the first car – but also why. Every Sandhurst exercise I ever did began, 'The leading armoured car is knocked out. What will you do?'

But we carry on. It is nothing but green corn, high and straight, all around us, broken only at times by the sick-making crack of mortars and shells throwing up both earth and corn in their explosions. All of a sudden, there is an enormous bright flash, hardly 20 yards in front.

'God!' I scream. 'It's a projector! Driver, reverse! Driver, reverse . . . FAST!' In a panic, I pull every smoke canister discharge in the turret. To the gunner I shout, 'Co-ax . . . traverse front . . . FIRE!' and streams of 7.92 Besa bullets pour from our machine gun. But nothing happens. What now?

Next moment, I am on the edge of a slit trench, and a German soldier rears right up before me within inches. Without stopping to think of anything, I put my pistol in his face and fire it. He disappears and I jump

▶ **Sergeants Lewis and Walker, two cameramen who landed with the first troops at Arnhem, share a snack meal off their jeep with a local Dutch girl.**

▼ **In the *bocage* countryside around Caen, men of the 185th Brigade, 3rd Division, use felled trees as scant cover as the invasion continues in July 1944.**

the slit trench and run on. Then, hearing voices, I crouch in the tall corn. The Germans do not know I am there, and I remember how, when hunting animals as a boy, you had to keep completely still to surprise them. I take out one of the four-second fuse grenades, pull out the pin and lob it very carefully to where the voice are. An age seems to pass, waiting the four seconds – but then off it goes. There is a chorus of alarmed German shouting. I stand up as two Germans start to run away. I fire my pistol twice but they keep going.

I decide I must get back to the cars. There I find a cluster of B Squadron's assault troop sheltering behind the cars. Together we all make a concerted rush on the slit trenches, leaving Edwards and the rest of my own troop as somewhat baffled spectators inside the cars.

This time, several Germans run away, and we take two prisoners –

but in my moment of triumph, just when I am thinking 'OK and OK so far', it happens. The ground, corn and all, seems to open up by my left foot. I have time to say to myself, 'Did I think those others were close? They were nothing to this!' Then I am pitched on the ground. No pain. Only surprise. 'I've been hit,' I gasp, and all down my left side and leg is warm and wet with **"** blood.

Konrad Mikulla was an officer in the 9th Company of the 3rd Battalion of SS Division Der Führer. *He had been fighting on the Eastern Front since 1941 and been wounded out of battle three times. When the invasion of France was announced in 1944, he was anxious to be transferred to Normandy to join the fight.*

" In Normandy, it was a different fight to the one on the Eastern front. There we had as our opposition only masses of Russian soldiers, sometimes being outnumbered ten to one. But in France, it was a fight against masses of material the Americans could supply to the Allies in the fight against us. Single soldiers were sometimes pitted against fighter planes – soldiers, as I experienced, were being bombed by planes in the open field. Still, the dice fell in my favour. I was in the Falaise Gap and we fought our way out, counterattacked and kept the gap open on the 19th, 20th and 21st of August. In the afternoon, we had to cover the retreat again.

We had with us two British soldiers we had captured, whom we let go. In the POW hostel on a building site in Newtown, Montgomeryshire, next to the barracks of the Royal Welsh Regiment, I met a sergeant who was acting as a guard, who turned out to be one of the very men we had let go – so he got through.

On 23 August, I was near El Boeuf on a reconnaissance patrol. The patrol took about ten hours, and as we came back to the position to find our commanding officer, there were Sherman tanks there. So we ran for cover and waited until nightfall to try to rejoin our company. But it was in vain. After being behind the Allied lines for about three or four days, we were eventually taken POW. I can still see it today, just as it happened. My comrade, an *Unterscharführer*, was walking about 20 paces in front of me, when suddenly he stumbled upon a British jeep with two British medical orderlies on board. They had Red Cross flags on the jeep, and he could see that they were medics, so he lifted his hands in the air. I took cover and didn't know what to do. I didn't want to fight with the Red Cross, but I didn't want to leave him on his own. So, I stood up, took my MP and hid it behind a tree and walked up to the jeep as well. We were put on board and taken to a Brigade HQ. There, they gave us a cup of tea, and later on we were taken to a POW collection point. There were a number of trucks there carrying German soldiers from various army units, who had been taken prisoner. We had to hand over our pay books to the officers in charge. I was told straight away to join the other soldiers on a truck, but my comrade was given terrible hassle. He was handed a spade and two guys with a Sten gun told him to get off the truck – this was the end of the line for him. I tried later when I was in different camps in England to find him again, but never did.

It must have been the end of him. **"**

▼ A second arm to the Allied liberation of France stretches into the south where, on the road to Toulon near Ste Anne, a Frenchman in an armoured vehicle watches an Allied bombardment.

Ted Wood, a second glider-tug pilot with 570 Squadron, had flown on the D-Day mission in an Albemarle. Now converted to the more capacious Stirling, his squadron was briefed for Arnhem a month before the operation. They were to drop the 1st Airborne Division, divided into three lifts, to take the three bridges.

" Apparently the Germans had attacked the Guards Armoured Division soft transport and put them out of action somewhere in Belgium, so they had had to withdraw – it then took them some time to recover. So we took off from Harwell on the mission, on the 17th of September. We went in Vics of three until we reached the Dutch coast, where we met two other streams of Vics of three. We were then nine abreast as we went in, and it was estimated that there were 2,500 aircraft in the sky at that moment, at 2,000 feet. So what it sounded like on the ground, God alone knows.

Amongst that lot were 25 squadrons of fighter escort, and any fool who opened up on the ground, you would see the Tiffies go down – and they never missed. They just aimed the aircraft at the target and let the rockets go.

That went well and we reached Arnhem and dropped our gliders in the fields outside Arnhem town. I don't think we lost an aircraft at all.

Then the next day we went with resupply – the usual 20 containers and two panniers. We dropped them on the same place that we had dropped the gliders – it seemed alright again. We got a bit of flak, mainly after we'd dropped the sup-

plies, because we were flying at 500 feet with bomb doors open and flap down throttle back at 140 mph.

The fourth day we went, and we led 40 aircraft over France, this time, not over the North Sea. Over the battle zone you had to fly above 3,500 feet, because of your own troops, and we met cloud. We stayed above the cloud and got higher up at the rendezvous for the start of the run-in, at about 6,500 feet above 10/10 cloud. We'd got to get down to 500 feet, and make fairly quick decisions. I said to the old man that we'd better go underneath it – Holland is pretty flat and there are no large lumps sticking up – so we waggled our wings at the rest of the 40 and stuck our nose down. We broke cloud at about 1,000 feet and I said to the old man that I didn't like flying at 1,000 under that lot – you were a sitting duck. I suggested we got down on the deck.

The Dutch maps were very good, with every duck-pond and tree marked, so we went down to nought feet for this run-in. We climbed up to 500 feet as we crossed the Rhine. We were obviously the first in, and when we arrived at the new dropping zone, it turned out to be a field the size of a football pitch, completely surrounded by woods. I could see all this, lying in the nose, ready to drop the containers. Now, because the blokes the day before had had some casualties over the dropping zone, we had agreed it would be suicide to pull up after you had dropped, because you had no speed, and you were offering the whole of this damn great aircraft to a gunner. So we arranged that, as soon as the last container was away, we were going to go down. We'd slam open all four motors and go down on the treetops – you'd offer no target then.

▲ Ted Wood of 570 Squadron (inset) with his Horsa-tug Stirling on the first day of the Arnhem operation.

I was having a good look round as we were dropping the containers, and I could see our blokes in one corner of this dropping zone, burning smoke flares for us. I could see a couple of jeeps with a red cross on them – but it was obvious by the flashes, that Jerry had got the other three sides. It was like someone kicking the side of the aircraft in with hob-nailed boots, they were so close.

The old man was a lunatic pilot at the best of times – he was doing rate-four turns over the treetops in this damn great thing, and I could have picked leaves.

We were due to go again on the Friday, with a brand new aircraft because one of the flight commanders had borrowed our aircraft and pranged it. We were literally waiting to go when they cancelled it and said they were going to pull out what was left. Totting it up, from memory, we started the week with 34 aircraft and crews on the squadron, and I had 12 new aircraft delivered. By Friday I hadn't 12 fit to fly. "

HÜRTGEN FOREST

The Hürtgen Forest – 50 square miles of wood-covered hills to the south-east of Aachen on the Belgian-German border – was the scene of one of the bitterest battles fought by US troops in North West Europe. First attacked in September 1944 by the 9th and 28th Infantry Divisions, it was seen as vital to secure the flank of a future assault.

In reality, it was an attritional bloodbath. By November the two divisions had suffered over 10,000 casualties and their progress against dug-in German defenders could be measured in yards. The attack was resumed in December, by the 4th and 8th Infantry Divisions. Over 8,000 men were killed or wounded, with a further 4,000 evacuated with 'combat exhaustion'. The forest was taken, but at enormous cost.

▶ Americans fire 4.5in, eight-tube multiple rocket-launchers in the Hürtgen Forest battle.

Steve Weiss, an NCO with the 36th Texas Division, was in the Valence area in southern France when he and seven others found themselves cornered and took refuge in a farmhouse. With local police assistance, they were smuggled from under the Germans' noses and taken to meet the Resistance.

▲ Cavalaire Bay, now a popular resort, is host to anti-aircraft halftracks on Alpha Red Beach.

"In St Perez in a café, the Hotel du Nord, we were interviewed by the local French Resistance. They really grilled us. They wanted to know where we came from, what we were doing, what was the plan? etc. This went on for about an hour, and I felt for quite some time that they really didn't trust us. In those days, you could be taken out and shot, just like that. Finally they believed us and started serving drinks.

While we were there, someone said parts of the German Army were coming up by that side of the river, so we had to move on. We went up into the mountains about 20 km away, to this small village. There I met the man in charge of the whole department's plans. His name was Commodore François Binoche, and he had taken this small country hotel as his HQ. We got some rest, had some food, and then joined him and his Resistance people to harass the Germans. Binoche, who was a former Foreign Legion Officer, and I got along very well.

One day, he asked me if I would like to go out hunting rabbits. I said, 'Well, I come from New York city, and I never hunted anything – but why not?' He said that tomorrow, at a certain time, we would go together. I showed up and there was a major of the gendarmerie, Mathey, who was in charge of this 'hunting' operation. I said to him, 'I hear we are going to hunt rabbits.' He laughed and laughed and said, 'Rabbits? We are going to hunt Germans.'

We went out and attacked this house, because we suspected Germans were in there, but French fellows came out and said that the Germans who had been there had just left. From that point, the major, myself and one other fellow had this small French car and we spent hours looking for Germans. We would go to a building and ask, 'Have you seen any Germans?' Late in the af-ternoon, we got to one village, Soyons. One of the tyres of the car was low, so the major asked me to put some air into it while they walked into the village to see what was going on.

As I was pumping air into the tyre, I felt a force bang me up against the car fender, then I heard people yelling and screaming. I ran about 50 yards and saw that there had been an explosion. A tree had been used as a road block and the French in this village had some German prisoners who they wanted to move the tree. As they moved the tree, they didn't know that it had been mined by the Germans. It blew up and when I got blown against the car, eight German prisoners had been killed. I don't know how many French people got killed – Mathey, the major, got wounded and the other fellow I never saw again.

Now it became a big rescue operation. We tried to get the wounded to this small cottage hospital in the area. My job was to guard this German prisoner who was wounded in the hospital. He and I started to talk as he waited his turn to be looked at. We both spoke a little French, and we looked at each other's pictures and tried to make some kind of sense of the madness that was the war.

When I got back to the village where we had our HQ, some captain of the American OSS (Office of Strategic Services) had come from an area of some 60 km west of us, asking if we would join his unit – paratroopers, operational groups and things like that. I was uneager to do it. I really don't know why, to this day. I preferred to stay with the French, even though their fighting tactics were rather poor.

That was surely one of the most significant experiences of my life, in the process of which I made some life-long friends. In St Agrève there are still people who remember me, and we often get together. I saw General Binoche only last October."

► By the end of the year, the Germans are bogged down in the Ardennes in fierce winter weather.

Acting Corporal James Palmer of the Royal Tank Regiment had spent most of 1943 in Palestine. Then, not needed for the Normandy invasion, his regiment was sent to Italy. Here, after fierce fighting at Cassino, they moved north to continue the battle in the Apennines, just as winter was approaching.

" Our next operation was deep in the Apennines in the area of Spoleto and Perugia. It was wicked country, totally unsuited to tank warfare. In normal tactics, an attacking force would either make a frontal attack on the defence line, or would sweep round the enemy defence points, then cutting off that defensive point from its supplies. This could not be done in Italy because of

like confetti.

I must mention the dilemma of our infantry and the engineers who, having overrun the defences, would be pushing on in the hope of catching the Germans before they could settle in their new defence area. The Germans were using a new type of mine with a wooden case, and being of wood, they were difficult to detect with the normal mine-detectors we had. These mines were mainly antipersonnel and exploded about a foot from the ground when detonated by trip-wires or pressure. The certain casualty of these charming devices was both legs blown off below the knee.

German artillery was sophisticated in the extreme. Their 88 mm gun was far superior to our artillery and they had a fiendish multi-barrelled mortar gun which could fire up to six shells at a time. The one feature of the Italian campaign that was a constant

the difficult terrain.

A few German 88 mm guns on the top of a mountain with a good observation post giving firing instructions, could hold up a whole division of infantry for days, and our tanks had only to move to invite a thunderous barrage of shells. Our infantry had to fight for every inch of the way up the mountain trails, and when they did storm the defensive points, invariably they found the enemy had withdrawn and established a new line of defence on the next ridge.

It was always the same – capture the heights then look north, and there was another hill to fight for. A small group of infantry would delay our infantry climbing in the top of the mountain stronghold, while the main German force would be withdrawing and preparing the next stand. They would, of course, leave a trail of blown bridges over the rushing mountain streams and scatter mines along all possible trails,

worry was that we were for ever under shell fire. Often we could look across a valley and see a flash of light, then we would hear the horrible whistle of air as the shell soared through the air – then we would see a plume of smoke as it landed, and a few seconds later we would hear the clump and thump. This time-lag always fascinated me.

The most awful times were when the shell landed close and the air was full of hissing and whining white-hot shrapnel pieces that peppered around like metal rain. Our actions were so close that we were always within range. On our previous campaigns we had always been able to get out of firing range to re-equip and prepare for pitched battles. Here there were no pitched battles as such – but a continuous probing forward with quick, sharp actions lasting a couple of hours, when concentrated attacks were resisted by fanatical German youths who thought

▲▲British machine gunners and a range-finder take aim from a position blown out of the rocks on Monastery Hill, Cassino.

▲7 February 1944 – long-range US artillery reaches across the valley to pound German positions on the hillside at Cassino.

▶As rains set in and the dry ground turns to a quagmire, the Allies struggle to keep up the necessary rate of advance.

that to die firing a machine gun was the only way to Valhalla.

One such action was near to Perugia on the eastern slopes of the Apennines. We had been moving very slowly northwards, a few miles a day, with the rain pouring down and the mountain streams turning into torrents. The infantry had been moving from one hole in the ground to the next, and we had been giving mobile gun support when they were held up.

On two occasions we had been requested to advance in front of the infantry to knock out some troublesome machine-gun nests. As soon as we got forward of the infantry, there was a terrific barrage of artillery fire and mortar fire rained on our tanks. Although this did little harm to us, it fell mainly on the infantry in their fox-holes. They screamed for us to get the hell out of it, as our help was only making it worse for them. That was how things went – infantry needed our support, but when we gave it, the poor lads were pulverised as the tanks became enemy targets.

One day we were attacking a small mountain village, held by the Germans near to Urbino. Finally the village was stormed by the infantry, but the Germans had withdrawn to the cemetery on the northern slope from the village. The German infantry had set up numerous machine guns behind the solid granite tombstones

Private William Ernest Wright of the Royal Irish Fusiliers had been in action in North Africa, Sicily, Cassino and through Italy – and by the time he and his company reached the Po, he felt that they had all become dehumanised by exposure to battle. The weather had deteriorated as they entered the mountains.

"After Rome, we were ducking from one side of Italy to the other. We were a crack force because, by then, we had been in the business for four years – we had to be good.

Just north of Rome, we took a castle which overlooked a lake. The whole of the wine cellar was completely intact. Why it hadn't been shipped back to Germany, I'll never know. We found the most beautiful wines and brandies, and for about four days we were as drunk as lords!

There was one bloke – a stretcher-bearer – who was an alcoholic. He was covered in decorations for his bravery in battle, but they found out later that he had been taking morphine.

We were told that we would be going into battle, so we laid off the booze. The next morning, we were all on parade – all except the stretcher-bearer, and we needed him for the other end of the stretcher. We searched and searched the castle, then someone suggested we look in the wine cellar which had, by then, been locked for two days. Just as he said this, there was a banging from inside the cellar door. When he was let out, the man marched out very straight – then fell flat on his face. He had been in there for a week. That man stayed with us right until the end, and saved many lives.

We were pretty well bogged down at the Po because of the weather. The Germans knew that it was only a matter of months before the war would be over, and we knew that it was nearing the end too – but then again, you can still get killed during the last minute of a war.

What stood out most in my mind were the patrols. We would go out and shout things at them which we had learned in German – 'Put down your arms', and, 'Come on, don't be silly. Surrender. It's all over'. Their answer used to be a bloody great burst of machine-gun fire. It was a bit stupid, shouting at them, but we were young. Sometimes we had a pint of vino in us too, which made us more daring. A lot of Germans did surrender – usually shell-shocked.

There was a wine tank near us, in the Po Valley. It was about 15 feet high, and it stood out in the yard of a deserted farmhouse. By this time we were virtually alcoholics – every time we went out, a sniper would have a go at the barrel and we would go and get the wine under cover of darkness. It was rough, but good.

One night, the blinking wine stopped – just like that. By this time, I had a stripe – I was a lance corporal, so I could give orders. I said to this bloke 'Nip up and find out what's happened'. He came back and said, 'You're not going to like this. There's an old woman's body in there.'"

and gravestones. Some of these tombstones were built above ground like boxes, and it was behind these shelters that the machine guns were sited.

It was a macabre scene – both infantry were firing from the shelter of grave headstones and were only about 25 yards apart. Mortar shells from each side were plonking and thumping and we were on the side lines, unable to fire for fear of hitting our own lads. It was like watching a film and didn't seem real. The crash of mortar shells and crackle of machine-gun fire – the whine of zinging bullets and the whiffs of cordite were all there. Tombs were bursting open when hit, and human bones and skeletons were flying through the air. Men were wounded and lying among long-dead human skeletons, and we were watching it all taking place before us, frozen and unbelieving.

I remember my thoughts at the time – I thought I was going mad. Where was it all going to end? For over four years I had been part of the destruction of mankind, but each day had shown me deeper depths of human madness. Would it never end – or would it end with me being a victim of this frenzied desire for the extinction of the human race? I felt sick of it all, and despaired of the madness of the world. I lost all belief in the sanctity of human life."

Signalman Gus Britton, aboard HM Submarine Uproar, was sent out on a patrol in the Mediterranean on 2 March 1944 from moorings at Maddalena, just north east off Sardinia. The destination was the Gulf of Genoa – the aim was to keep the seas safe from the threat of U-boats – one of which they nearly bagged.

" South of Ajaccio our hand-cranked radar gave warning of something in the darkness, closing on us. The impeccable, imperturbable voice of the radar operator floated up the voice-pipe. A public schoolboy, he wore his only blazer and shorts and boots on patrol, all of which took on a greasy sheen after two weeks at sea, as did his close-cropped hair. He also doubled as the wardroom flunkey, and he once removed a swimming cockroach from the captain's soup with a grimy thumb and forefinger with a dignity that reflected great credit on the teachings of his *alma mater*.

The intruder, a French destroyer, was satisfied with my reply to his challenge, given on a shaded Aldiss lamp, and disappeared off our radar screen.

The Gulf of Genoa was empty of targets, so we moved west to Toulon, stopping on the way to shell a ship in Oneglia harbour, but retiring when the shore batteries expressed their disapproval. For three boring days we were dived in the area, listening to the local anti-submarine group, known to us as 'The Posse', sweeping the sea. They were often in contact with us and unaware that just a few feet under their keels, 33 people were holding their breaths as the ships went noisily overhead.

At 0800 on March 30 I took over the helmsman's duties for another boring watch. The weather was good and the periscope could only be used sparingly, the listener being relied upon to tell us what was happening overhead. The coxswain, berating the forward hydroplane operator for not keeping the correct depth, made

▼ Signalman Gus Britton on the bridge of the submarine *Uproar*. The bracket below the name was used for attaching aircraft recognition flares.

▼◀ U-boat U-466 with, inset, her ship's crest. Despite her escape from *Uproar's* attack, she never put to sea again and her crew was dispersed.

me look round.

I caught sight of the listener's eyes and mouth suddenly opening and his hands clamping his headphones tight to his ears. Recognition came to him. 'Hydrophone effect bearing green four five. Diesel. U-boat, sir!'

In seconds the boat was at diving station. Lieutenant L E Herrick, our New Zealand captain, always soft-voiced, calm and courteous, even when trying to sink a U-boat, had a quick look at the target and ordered, '80 feet. Full ahead together.'

A succession of orders followed which made the boat ready to fire its torpedoes. While we were deep, he announced that we were attacking an Italian-built boat. He then went to the 'fruit machine' – an early form of

computer, and cranked in all the information he had been able to glean from his one look and from what the listener was telling him – which would give the angle of deflection on firing and ensure target and torpedoes arriving at the same time.

We came slowly back to periscope depth and, because we were badly placed for an attack, and it was now or never, four torpedoes were sent on their way. Stop-watches were carefully scrutinised but the seconds and minutes passed without the expected bang.

We had meanwhile gone deep and speeded up to get away from the firing position, but as the Posse continued trolling unconcernedly around, it was obvious that they were unaware that four Mark 8 tin fish had passed through their midst.

It took some time before the Germans realised that the four explosions on the beach had come from a submarine – but we had fled. On falling out from diving stations, I found the atmosphere in the fore-ends quite cheerful.

It was not until 1985 that I discovered the U-boat which we attacked was the U-466. On writing to her captain, I received a cordial invitation to the boat's reunion. Her captain, Gerd Thater, was a well-built, cheerful man, and welcomed me to the weekend get-together of the crews of the two boats he commanded. It was good to be with the men that we had so narrowly missed killing. 🙶

▲ *Leutnant* Gerd Thater, right, of U-466 after a patrol and, pictured right, submariner Joe Eckert.

Joe Eckert, at the age of 18, threw in his job repairing Ju-88 aircraft at a VW works and joined the Kriegsmarine to become a submariner. After six weeks' training, then U-boat instruction, he was on his way to join U-616, his new home until her last voyage on a patrol in the Mediterranean in May 1944.

🙶Our captain, Siegfried Koitschka, drove us to a state of efficiency that must have been hard to match by another boat. He had previously served as a watch officer with the famous Erich Topp, who commanded the U-552 – the Red Devil boat, so called because of the emblem painted on the front of the conning tower. We adopted the crest of a red devil with a pistol in each hand.

After setting off on operations in February 1943, U-616 patrolled the waters off Norway, the Atlantic and Mediterranean. Fighting the French *gendarmes* in Toulon or fighting the British and Americans at sea was all the same to us, and made for great *esprit de corps*. With Koitschka a holder of the Knight's Cross, we were perhaps a little unbearable when ashore, full of our own import-

ance, and if our 'chummy' boat was in – the U-410 under her skipper, Fenski (another Knight's Cross holder) – we were even more boisterous in the bars of Toulon. But perhaps we could be excused our high spirits. Kipling, in once of his poems about British submarines in the first war wrote, 'We arrive, we lie down, and we move in the belly of death.' We knew what he meant, and that our time would surely come.

U-616 sailed on her final patrol, from Toulon, on the 3rd May 1944, bound for the North African coast. On the 14th we attacked a convoy and torpedoed two ships, which managed to make port safely. All we received in exchange were several depth-charges from an American escort, but we just went deep and carried on with reloading torpedoes, then playing cards. When we surfaced to charge our batteries that night, an aircraft attacked and bombed us, and down we went. Any attempt to surface found an unwelcome visitor in the shape of a Wellington aircraft from 36 Squadron. We stayed down and later surfaced to find an aircraft coming at us

through the darkness. An exchange of gunfire took place and down we went again. Unknown to us, we were the star of an 'Operation Swamp', which was an operation devised to swamp the area where a U-boat was hiding with ships and aircraft, waiting for him to surface with exhausted batteries. Coming out from the nearby ports were eight American destroyers, all intent on cooking this particular German goose.

Koitschka was not unduly concerned and ordered all unnecessary electrical gear to be switched off to conserve power and conferred with the navigator on which was the best way of eluding any pursuit.

Probably early on May 15th, the USS *Ellyson* opened the ball with a pattern of depth-charges and, as the hours passed, it seemed that the whole of the US Navy were above

into the water, accompanied by a muffled explosion as our U-boat headed for the bottom of the Mediterranean.

The Americans were most kind to us after the initial display of weapons, as we crawled over the side and flopped down exhausted on the deck. Regular reunions between the crew of the U-616 and the *Ellyson* crew are held in Germany or the USA. Our adventure was not quite over, because, as the *Ellyson*, with her prisoners, was heading for Oran,

◄◄U-616 at La Spezia after a patrol. In the background, hand up to his chest, is 'German Joe', a British resident since being a POW.

U 616

◄The insignia of U-616, the red devil, adopted from the captain's former ship's emblem.

us, intent on our destruction. At first Koitschka ordered bursts of high speed and alterations of course, but with the battery getting lower, we went deep and prayed. I cannot be sure how deep we were, but I would think possibly deeper than 800 feet, which made the good old U-616 creak a bit.

Everything but the kitchen sink was being dropped on us and all sorts of tactics were being tried, including creeping attacks, in which the ship did not appear to alter speed to deliver its attack, and our listener had no way of knowing that it was an attack developing. Fortunately for us, a new engineer had joined the boat, his own being sunk by a bombing raid on Toulon harbour, and to Lt Karl Friederick Kieke we owed our lives. At 800 feet, possibly deeper, the submarine is subjected to considerable pressure and any mistake in handling would cause the boat to cave in. Twelve destroyers

carried a lot of depth-charges and they were quite free with the favours – 18 charges coming down in one pattern was common.

Eventually, the battery power, without which we could not operate, began to fail, and Koitschka ordered everybody to don life-jackets and to be ready to jump overboard the moment we surfaced. With the last dregs of the battery power, and with high-pressure air screaming into her ballast tanks, U-616 made her last dramatic surface. The longest hunt of the war was over, lasting over three days.

The crew got out of the boat in record time and jumped over the side, not even pausing to look at the ships that surrounded us. Shellfire and machine-gun fire were whistling past our heads and it was surprising that only one man was slightly wounded. The U-616 careered on her way, pursued by gunfire, the last two people diving off the bandstand

▼Second from right, Dr Neumann, awarded the Iron Cross for his skill in performing an operation in submarine conditions. Inset, Leading Artificer Karl Wahnig of U-802, who witnessed Neumann's work off Halifax, Nova Scotia.

three torpedoes from the U-960 missed her! U-960, new to the Mediterranean, became the subject of another swamp operation, and was sunk with the loss of 32 of her 52 crew. U-616 did not lose a man.

After many trials and tribulations, including picking cotton in Mississippi, I eventually arrived in England as a POW in Moberley Camp, which is a very short distance from where I have lived since the war, married and made a good living at distributing lime to farmers – every farmer for miles around knows 'German Joe'. **"**

KARL WAHNIG – U-802

'On April 11 we had had a lot of air attacks and were very badly damaged. The depth-sounder had broken down, but we had a gadget called echo load, which you throw overboard - you measure the depth by the time it takes for the sound to come back as it explodes on hitting the sea bed. A seaman petty officer on board was in charge of the echo load, and while he was handling it, the cannister with all the charges exploded, injuring his face and left hand. We had to dive down and settle on the sea bed, so that our doctor could operate. First he had to amputate his finger, as he was losing a lot of blood. Then, five days later, complications arose with the PO's eyes. Although a doctor carries surgical instruments, he didn't have an implement to take an eye out. So we had to make one ourselves, in the engine-room, from a brass rod. It was the shape of a pair of scissors with two bars across each end, so he could get right behind the eye and take the left one out to check if there were any complications there. History has proved that this operation in a U-boat is one of the most outstanding achievements of medicine at war.'

1945
V FOR VICTORY

Fighting men remember sweet success – and bitter defeat

There were no guarantees of swift Allied victory in January 1945. No-one could doubt that the remaining Axis powers – Germany and Japan – were close to defeat, but with the Western Allies recovering from the Ardennes counterattack and bogged down in northern Italy, with the Soviets still on the Vistula and the Americans fighting hard in the Philippines, it was obvious that tough battles lay ahead. The fact that, by May, Germany had collapsed and by August Japan had surrendered, was therefore quite remarkable.

The reasons are not difficult to see, in hindsight. In western Europe, Hitler had committed too much military power to the Ardennes and, with the cities of Germany under constant attack from the air, the industrial and human capacity to wage war was fast disappearing. On the Eastern Front, the Soviet build-up was overwhelming and, with two other fronts to cover, the Germans could not stop the juggernaut once it started moving towards Berlin.

The situation was slightly different in the Pacific and Far East, where Japanese fighting spirit remained strong – but a combination of military defeats, economic blockade and city bombing by the USAAF from bases in the Pacific was doing irreparable damage. When the Soviets declared war and the Americans dropped atomic bombs on Hiroshima and Nagasaki in August, Japan had nothing left.

THE REICH IN RUINS

Allied forces make the final push to cross the Rhine – and arrive in a shattered landscape. A seemingly huge task opens up for the Allies to bring order to a stricken and hopeless nation.

I t took until mid-January 1945 for the Allies to recover all the territory lost in the Ardennes, but by this time, German reserves had been drained. The Allies reached the west bank of the Rhine all along its length in February and March, with the aim of making assault crossings in north and south before driving deep into Germany. On 7 March, US troops seized a bridge at Remagen in the centre, but then on 22/23 March, Patton's US Third Army crossed in the south and, 24 hours later, Montgomery's 21st Army Group did the same in the north.

Eisenhower left Berlin to the Soviets and shifted the advance to central and southern Germany. As Montgomery squeezed out the Ruhr, US armour raced ahead. By early May, the Allies had linked with the Soviets on the Elbe, Patton had entered western Czechoslovakia and other US forces had met up with the Allies advancing through the Alps. Germany was finished.

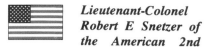

Lieutenant-Colonel Robert E Snetzer of the American 2nd Engineer Battalion had landed in Normandy on D plus 3 with the Second Division, soon to become part of George Patton's Third Army. After fighting a way through to the Ardennes, often under heavy shelling, they were poised to enter Germany.

" On D plus 163 we were in Germany, on the Siegfried Line, and now our job was road maintenance and other support of the 23rd Infantry. One day we blew up 49 German pillboxes. We followed the infantry through snow-covered forests, wild and desolate, clearing the main supply routes, often suffering vicious shelling.

The fighting went on and, by the 23rd December, the engineers had endured three solid days of artillery

grouping, getting ready to go back on the offensive. I assumed command of the Second Engineer Battalion, and we were still using tank bulldozers, truck ploughs and every possible means to keep the roads open.

In February we moved on, town after town, busy with mine-detectors, opening up the roads, sometimes behind, sometimes in front of the front line in the push to the Rhine.

On February 29 the 110th Infantry crossed the Rhine at Hünningen, and by March the Third Army had crossed south of Koblenz.

By March 7th we were really rolling through Germany. We were moving in as conquerors. The people were all bewildered and scared. We'd pick out the best house for our command-post and billets and kick the people out, spend the night then move on the next day.

The rain continued incessantly, with zero visibility. The weather was

ending columns of vehicles and tanks rolled steadily along. Most all of the 78th and 9th Infantry and 9th Armoured Divisions were across now. The Rhine had finally been crossed in force. "

Quintin R Wedgeworth was navigator in B-24 bomber, Sweet Eloise, *as the US Eighth Army Air Force continued their pounding of the German homeland. On 6 February, the pilots were called for a briefing for a mission to Berlin – 'The Big B', as it was known – a target which, historically, was nobody's favourite.*

" There were groans aplenty this morning when the briefing officer rolled down the map and announced the target – Berlin. The B-17s had gone there three weeks ago and although the weather had been very good, the Luftwaffe did not contest the attack. However, the flak was something else again. Nearly every formation had been hit, with 21 Forts going down over the city and six more subsequently crash-landing behind the Russian lines. Of the returning aircraft, 93 suffered major battle damage. It looked like a long, hard day ahead.

Group take-off was scheduled for 0910 hours. Our ship was 15 minutes back in the line-up. We formed up at 13,000 feet as planned, but that was the last thing that went by the name 'plan'. I have no idea who the lead navigator was. All I can tell you is that we started off by missing check-points X, Y, Z1 and A.

Somehow we managed to stagger across the Channel, entering the Netherlands about three miles south of check-point two. However, although back on course, we had fallen ten minutes behind schedule, and by the time we reached the fighter rendezvous point (FRP) near the German frontier, we had peaked out at 22,000 feet.

We also missed check-point three, making it six out of eight. Instead of following the normal route, which squeezed through the corridor in the flak defences at Osnabrück and Dummer Lake, we continued almost due east over Vechta before making our turn. We picked up the planned route (finally) between Steinhunder Lake and the Weser at 1216 hours.

By 1230 hours I began to get a little overanxious – I guess the poorly executed navigation was making me nervous. Although I was reasonably sure that we still had some 60 miles between us and the IP, we were scheduled to start the bomb-run at 1236 hours! At any

▲ Crewmen of the 9th US Air Army Air Force brush snow from their B-26 Marauders prior to a mission.

◄ US paras wait for take-off on the greatest airborne operation of the war – the Rhine crossing, Operation Varsity.

fire.

My God, it's an awesome sight and sound to live with - this constant wrath of the gods of war. It was cold and crisp, and I could see high-altitude aerial battles going on, with the planes criss-crossing and leaving vapour-trails.

By the middle of January 1945, the Americans and British were re-

cold and damp - mud, mud, mud. However, we are over the roads before the surfaces begin to break down completely.

March 8: V Corps and Division surged forward. The Infantry pushed east to the Rhine.

March 9: the motorised 23rd Infantry pushed east to the Rhine, which it reached that evening. There was virtually nothing for the engineers to do. The movement through Germany was quick and seemed almost effortless.

The next day, we crossed the Rhine over the great Remagen Bridge, which had been captured intact. Doughfeet of the 9th Division were streaming across on foot; un-rate, I commenced to set up the bomb control panel – and wound up with burnt fingers, so to speak! My eagerness, however, had disclosed an inherent malfunction in the system that would have surfaced later anyway. A short in the electrical circuit triggered the release of four of the 500-pounders!

In turn, their weight peeled the doors right off the belly of the ship without so much as an excuse me! The ensuing drag didn't help the already difficult job of formation jockeying, and the on-rush of arctic air into the waist and tail positions didn't tend to help matters back there either. I had instantly made everyone's s--- list, except maybe Timmons'. Even so, I had learned something. Never again did I touch that panel with the doors closed! According to my calculated position, the bombs fell at 5243 N-1040 E, somewhere near the village of Wittingen. As I had suspected, we were still some distance from the IP – 20 minutes to be exact. The point lay just to the north east of the confluence of the Haval and Elbe rivers.

Ironically enough, the 63-mile bomb-run was one of the better legs of this entire mission. It went without a hitch, although the flak was moderate to intense and accurate enough to damage three of the ships. Our specific target was the Stettiner marshalling yards in the north-east part of the city. The drop had to be made by H2X radar, and went unobserved. The withdrawal and regrouping matched the execution of this

morning's proceedings. From what should have been two short legs, totalling 15 minutes, we circled eastward and north for 45 minutes! With a TAS in the vicinity of 240 mph, to what amounts to 172 miles! We must have crossed the Oder River and on into Poland! It wasn't until 1344 hours that we finally straightened out and set course – 274 degrees. After a lot of extrapolation, crystal balling and just plain wild-ass guessing, I picked a spot near Ebeerswalde as a starting point for my dead reckoning.

It was late (1722 hours) that evening when we finally got back to Wendling – 46 minutes after the ETR! As we peeled off into the landing pattern, I went aft as usual to wait. Mac was alarmed over the fuel gauges. They were reading empty. Boyd did not want to break into the landing order, reasoning that everyone else was also low.

Mike and I both sensed the urgency in his unusual behaviour and conveyed our concern as well. Fortunately, Boyd got the message and proceeded to crowd into the pattern, touching down at 1725 hours. Before we reached the end of the runway, one engine sputtered and ran out of gas – another quit as we taxied to the hard stand! Now that's close!

It had been our longest mission to date. But it was not the duration of the journey that plagued our thoughts that night! We had gone to Berlin (one of the most heavily defended cities in the world) and it had been a milk-run!

Sergeant Derek Glaister with the 7th Parachute Battalion was dropped into the Wesel area on 24 March as part of the force intended to strengthen 21st Army Group's bridgehead to the east of the Rhine. The overall operation was a success – but individuals often paid dearly with their lives or their futures.

" When we got to the Rhine it was murder, because Jerry knew we were coming. Every farmhouse was occupied by Germans. They put a lot of smoke down, so instead of coming down to 400 feet, which is the lowest height you can drop from, we had to go up to 1,000 feet.

We were also travelling quite fast. I was No 20 – last man out – so you can imagine how far off target I was. Miles out. I and ten others came down near a farmhouse which had an 88 mm gun just outside it. Just before my feet touched the ground, a bullet smashed through my left elbow, so I lay on my stomach and pretended to be dead. I saw nine of the others come down, some into trees. The Germans shot them as they hung there helpless – it was a sickening sight.

I was in big trouble – I am left-handed and my left arm was useless. But when five Germans came towards me, I got hold of my Sten gun in my right hand and, as they got **"**

▼ A woman walks with her family in Berlin – the shoes she wears are shared with a neighbour, with whom she makes arrangements as to who has the use of them on which days.

▼▼ A Berlin woman refuses to part with her bicycle to a Russian soldier who wants to buy it – even the tyres are priceless.

FIRESTORM

Firestorms occur when incendiary bombs are dropped on to a city in sufficient concentrations to swamp the firefighting services and create a strong central conflagration. As the hot air rises, cooler air rushes in to take its place, acting like a gigantic pair of bellows. Buildings – and people – melt. But the creation of such a phenomenon cannot be guaranteed using non-atomic weapons. A firestorm had devastated Hamburg in late July 1943 – only two more were to occur using conventional bombs, both in 1945.

The first was Dresden, hit by nearly 800 RAF Lancasters on the night of 13/14 February. The city was burnt out and up to 50,000 people died. Less than a month later, on 9/10 March, 279 B-29 bombers from the Marianas devastated Tokyo.

▶Dresden after the firestorm. Much controversy surrounds the destruction of this cultural city.

close, I fired and I think, killed them all. Then I made for the farmhouse, hoping to get some help, but I saw German rifles poking out of every window.

I tried to give myself some cover by throwing a smoke bomb, but just as I was making for the nearest ditch, a German SS officer came up and shot me in the back from ten yards away with a Luger pistol. (I shall never forget him – he was about six foot four and covered in boils.) Of course, I spun round and fell down, and this officer grabbed my left arm and shoved it through the straps of my webbing. Then he took my water bottle, flung it in a ditch and looted whatever he could. I was worried that he'd finish me off with my knife, but I had the presence of mind to lie on it, and when he had gone, I got hold of it and threw it into the ditch.

I lay there feeling pretty rough –

my left arm was like a great black pudding by then, all swollen up – and watched those poor fellows swinging in the trees. Then one of our gliders came over, but the 88 mm cracked it open like an egg and the jeep, gun, blokes – all fell out. Point-blank range – they couldn't possibly miss at 50 feet.

Towards evening I was still lying there, in one hell of a bloody mess. I was finding it difficult to breathe because the second bullet had touched my lungs. Then a couple of captured airborne soldiers came by – a glider pilot and Lance Corporal Butler from my own battalion. They asked their German escort if they could pick me up. So they gave me a shot of morphine, which helped, and put me in this wheelbarrow. They carted me along in this farm wheelbarrow, along a bumpy old road until the Germans took them away for interrogation and I was wheeled on to a big mansion near the town of Hamminkeln.

At dusk a German lorry came along and two Jerries picked me up like a sack of spuds and dumped me in the back of the truck on top of some dead blokes sewn up in sacks. They must have thought I was dead.

That was the first time I fainted – my wounds had opened up and were bleeding again.

I came to in a German toilet with my head near the pan. That was where all my troubles started. Two orderlies took me into an operating theatre and pulled my clothes off – which was very painful. They must have been operating on some chap and they slithered me straight on to the aluminium table which was still covered in his blood. Then they put an ether mask over my face and out I went.

I woke up five days later, my arm in a Nazi salute in plaster and paper bandages all around my back. No medicines or antibiotics. My back had opened up again as the stitches had come apart, so I was carried off to be restitched. When we got to the top of some massive stairs, I was tipped off – deliberately, I'm sure. I landed on my head, breaking my nose and smashing the plaster.

There was a hell of a row about it and those orderlies didn't appear again. They stitched me all up again and put another plaster on, still in a Nazi salute. Then they had a go at my nose with no anaesthetic. They probed about, pulling bits of bone out, but they went too close to my eye and damaged it, so I've still got permanent pain and double vision from that.

I lay in that hospital until the British arrived. They flew me over to the RAF hospital at Wroughton and sent for my wife and parents as they didn't expect me to live. My father was also in hospital at the time, having his leg amputated as a result of World War I. When my mother and

◀Derek Glaister – one of many young men who grew up quickly on the Rhine crossing operation.

BERCHTESGADEN

Berchtesgaden lies in the south-east corner of Germany, close to the Austrian border. Renowned for its Alpine scenery, it was where Hitler built his retreat – the Berghof – on the Obersalzberg mountain. Convinced that it would be used as a base by diehard Nazis, the Western Allies gave its capture high priority. In early May 1945, the US 101st Airborne Division was given the task. At the same time, General de Gaulle ordered Leclerc's 2nd Free French Armoured Division to beat the Americans to it.

In the event, the US 3rd Infantry Division, in Salzburg to the north, realised that they were closest and, against all existing orders, the 7th Infantry Regiment arrived late on 4 May, only to find that the Nazis had gone.

▶ Hitler's mountain retreat, where he would entertain and relax, after the Allied takeover.

wife came into the ward, they went straight past my bed – they didn't recognise me.

I had pneumonia by then, so they put in a tube to drain off the fluid and sent me by ambulance to an orthopaedic unit. The tube got dislodged and came out in the ambulance, so they pushed it back in again, nearly choking me when it reached my lungs.

When at last they got around to getting the German plaster off, one of the nurses fainted. The stench was bad enough, but the plaster was full of maggots, put in by the German doctor to eat the dead flesh. No wonder it itched. A surgeon took one look at my arm and said 'Off,' just like that. But there was a lady doctor, Miss Wagstaff, who said she'd like to have a go at saving it, since I was left handed. The surgeon said it would take years and still might not work, but they tried it. It took three years in hospital and 55 operations to get me where I am now, which is 80 per cent disabled. **"**

John Leopard was serving with the 10th (City of Glasgow) Field Regiment, RA, 52nd Lowland Division, during the rapid advance by the Allies in early 1945. His troop had been tasked with covering the attacking infantry as they forced a passage over the Dortmund-Ems Canal.

" I selected a somewhat exposed gun-position to take advantage of a clear view of the canal at the crossing point. There seemed little danger to the troop, since we had been told that the only immediate opposition was likely to be from the local training camp.

I established my command post in a small shed in our field, and there set up my artillery board. Imagine my surprise when a volley of shell fire fell in the area of our gun-position. I ordered my assistants to dig a slit trench in the earthen floor. Hardly had the lads started to dig,

when the stench from disturbed dung made the shed untenable. We left the shed and I had to set up my board in the back of the scout car.

A second volley of shots arrived, one of which demolished the shed in which we had so recently been working. One of the gunners had been wounded, and as I ran across the field to make sure he was being properly treated, Jerry threw a few air-burst shells at us.

This was getting a little too much. We bundled the wounded man into one of our light trucks and I told the driver to ask permission for us to move into another gun position which was less exposed.

When I returned to the scout car, found that one of the shells had burst over the vehicle, and scores of shell fragments had torn through he canvas top and peppered the artillery board where I had been working. I then found a vantage point from which I could see much of the enemy-occupied territory beyond the canal. If they fired again, I

▼ The preliminary bombardment over, US troops cross the Rhine in assault boats, ready to link up with the airborne forces already on the eastern side. Together they would *Blitzkrieg* through a broken Germany.

hoped, somewhat vainly, to catch a glimpse of the gunsmoke, so that we could send something back. Hardly had I taken up my position, when a further salvo reached us. I swung my binoculars up, just as I felt somebody grab at my shoulder, I turned to find nobody there – but noticed that one of my cloth officer's pips, worn on the shoulders, had been ripped off leaving just a few threads. The work of a shell splinter, no less.

My driver had returned by this time with an officer who brought permission to withdraw. Never before had I witnessed so speedy a limbering up of guns. We attended to some more wounded and **"** left with relief.

Ted Wood, having seen his squadron, 570, badly mauled in the Arnhem operation with the loss of many Stirling aircraft, was briefed to take part in the Rhine crossing. Leading the flight, his aircraft was towing the general commanding the operation, General Bols, into the fray.

" We actually saw a V2 take off – the white corkscrew went straight up into the sky from the other side of the Rhine somewhere. Now as we were coming up to the area – and I'd studied the map pretty carefully and listened to the briefing – I remembered that the chap had said that there was a bit of Jerry resistance on the port side, so we

▼John Leopard, second from right, front row – a few narrow escapes within the space of a few hours on the advance through Germany made him feel lucky to be alive.

were to keep well in tight and not allow ourselves to drift off course at all.

Of course, the troops had already crossed the river overnight, and we were dropping this lot on top of our own troops as an immediate reinforcement.

My pilot, an awkward type, said, 'Are you sure you've got it right, Ted? The bloke over there, leading the others, seems to have a different idea from you.' I said, 'I don't care what he's doing, but you do what we're supposed to do. We're aiming for that clump of trees.'

I'd hardly said that, when that bloke came out of the sky. You never saw anything like it – the whole stream then moved over. Needless to say, my pilot agreed not to argue any more.

Anyway, we dropped that lot – and it was then we saw the devastation on the ground. I've never seen ruins like it – I'd seen bombing in London, but there were absolute ruins all the way along the **"** built-up areas here.

Acting Corporal James Palmer had returned to Britain from Italy, only to be posted to Germany in April, just as the Allies were drawing their conquering rampage through the stricken Reich to a close. The scenes which greeted him in the cities – and especially the camps – defied description and belief, and would haunt him for ever.

walls and watch towers. Over the entrance was the name, 'Belsen'. We had heard tales of concentration camps, but had been a little sceptical that anything so horrible could be true – but there we were, at the gates of Hell itself.

There was a large notice saying 'Typhus. Report here'. We were given overalls and overshoes and then sprayed with a powder and given face masks. There was a horrible smell, and we were told that

▼ **The Allies have liberated Belsen, and women, some still wearing their striped uniforms, prepare to leave. They were the lucky ones – over a million had perished in this infamous camp during the course of the war.**

were pushing earth into these mass graves after pouring drums of lime on top of the stinking carcasses.

In wooden huts there were rows of wooden bunks along each side, almost up to the ceiling. Bodies lay on these bunks, naked and filthy. They were moaning and feebly moving in spasmodic jerks, too weak to crawl out of the piles of rubbish in which they lay. The smell was sweet and nauseating.

Rats as big as rabbits were scuttling around, and some were gnawing at the corpses lying beside the roads. A few people were stumbling about, dazed and demented, and one women was giggling to herself and nursing a dead rat.

The camp commandant, Kramer, was shackled in chains and was daily paraded round the camp under heavy escort. There was a gas chamber and an incinerator that was choked with burnt human bones. Thousands of prisoners had been held in this camp – mostly Jews and slave labour from every European country – and they had all been systematically starved and allowed to die – but not with dignity.

Local *Burgomeisters* were made to assist with the burials in the mass graves and to dig latrines. They pleaded that they did not know what

Hamburg zoo had been bombed, and wild animals could be glimpsed through the ruins. A giraffe was popping its head over a wall and an ostrich was strutting along, quite unconcerned, near the lake. An elephant had been taken on the strength of the engineers and was helping to pull down unsafe buildings. The whole scene was macabre and unreal.

Whole villages had been burnt to the ground, crops flattened, roads blocked with rubble, and civilians sat at the sides of the roads with their few remaining belongings on carts and wheelbarrows. Thousands of German soldiers sat waiting to be collected as prisoners.

We arrived at a small village called Fallinbostel on the River Aller, and this was our final destination. We moved into the old cavalry barracks just outside the village and the day that we settled in, the bomb burst. There had been found an unbelievable atrocity of a concentration camp, and it had to be sorted out. The next morning we were loaded on to trucks and wended our way along narrow tracks between the pine trees.

Then we were at the gate of a huge prison camp, bounded by high wire

once we got through the gates, we were going to get a shock, but the place had to be cleaned up.

We walked slowly through the gates and on our left was a hay cart with high trestle sides. It was full of dead, naked bodies, who all looked like children and babies. It was horrific, and the stench was wicked. Some of us vomited. The bodies were like skeletons with the bones showing clearly, the stomachs bulging and their heads shaven and swollen like eggs. The eyes had sunk into their sockets and their jaws were hanging loose. Bodies were lying around alongside the huts and we didn't know if they were men or women, dead or alive. All were motionless and looked like bundles of rubbish.

A bulldozer was digging a huge trench about eight feet wide and 50 feet long. Further along, a similar trench was being filled with bodies by a group of SS prisoners. The bodies were being laid in rows crosswise, but rigor mortis had set in and some bodies could not be laid flat. The German prisoners were breaking the arms and legs of the corpses so they could be straightened out. The trenches were filled with layers of bodies, then the bulldozers

▲ **The American liberators of Buchenwald concentration camp confront the unspeakable – truckloads of dead victims of the Nazi pogrom.**

► **Prisoners of Unterbreizbach POW camp with Leo Keys, second from left, front row, in front of a 'White Cliffs of Dover' backdrop, painted for a camp show.**

had been going on. Commandant Kramer himself admitted that he could not cope and the camp should only have held 3,000 prisoners, but eventually there were over ten times that number, and food stopped coming in. This was his excuse, but it did not explain the medical experimental unit or the gas chamber, or the charnal house – or the lampshade in his office made of human skin.

Eventually further troops were drafted into the camp, and we had to return to the reinforcement unit at Fallinbostel. I said farewell to the charnel houses and returned to a world of relative sanity, but the memories will remain with me for ever.

Leo Keys had been a POW since his capture at St Valéry en Caux in May 1940. His war was spent at the Unterbreizbach POW camp, working in the local salt mine, then a sugar factory. He was recovering from a working injury when the Allies arrived in Germany and began to liberate the towns and camps in his area.

" Suddenly in Meiningen there was a large influx of POWs who had marched through the winter away from the Russian advance. Those that survived – for many died – had pneumonia and were very weak and ill. Those who were fitter were asked to form parties to dig mass graves in cemeteries, where the bones of the long-dead were dug out to make room for those of our comrades who had sadly not made it in the last lap of war.

It was during this time, with Allied aircraft flying around us both day and night, strafing the railway lines, that I got jaundice and was taken back to Obermasfeld. This was about the 20th March, and I was put into one of the wooden huts outside the main hospital building. We could hear the battle noise coming nearer and nearer, and German tanks and armoured cars speeding in both directions around us. On my way I watched Germans building barriers on the roads. How they were supposed to stop the tanks, I could not imagine.

On the 31st March 1945, the German doctors and guards at Obermasfeld marched away and left us on our own. We posted guards and kept out of sight as Germans sped by, now only in one direction. Early in the morning of the 1st April, I heard the German Land Army girls march out of a nearby dairy singing. Two hours later tanks suddenly drove up to the main hospital gates. A large red cross had been made on sheets and an officer jumped out of the first tank and said in a broad American accent, 'Does anyone here speak English?' Imagine his surprise to find us there – for he didn't know. In no time, to our horror we were surrounded on all sides by tanks and the Germans were firing mortars over the hills at us and the American Patton spearhead. I hid under my bed in my pyjamas until we took cover in the main hospital building, but not before the Americans had supplied us with cigarettes and loads of eggs from the nearby dairy. I had the omelette of all omelettes to celebrate our liberation.

The German medics and guards from the hospital marched out of the surrounding woods and gave themselves up.

After we had been in the cellars of the hospital building for a few hours, a number of heavy lorries drove up at about four or five o'clock in the afternoon, and all walking patients were loaded as they were. I was in my pyjamas and a blanket, which my mother-in-law-to-be had sent me from England.

It was a fantastic, unimaginable sight we saw as we drove through the countryside and saw the size and extent of this spearhead. Hundreds and hundreds of items of armour. What a difference to what we had to put up with when we landed in France in 1940! We were taken to a village that had only been captured that morning. People were put out of their homes and we were put in and slept in feather beds. The American Army in this situation were quite unbelievable. Imagine a village just captured. POWs just liberated. They had a hall with a band playing. White bread! Food and drink! It was all too much to imagine after our past experience. I got some clothing from the house and a large pair of ladies' stockings, which I brought home to Ilse. Needless to say, they were too big.

The pockets of Germans were still around us and, except for our American hosts, we were not armed. While driving here, tracer bullets were fired at us through the night. I sat in the middle of the lorry, which I thought the safest. For food we got iron rations from the American spearhead who were moving forward all the time. It was eight days ahead of the infantry. To supplement our ration, we got a German to slaughter a piglet, which was scalded in the kitchen of the house we occupied, and jaundice or not, I had pork chops for breakfast. "

▶ The salt mines at Unterbreizbach where local POWs worked seven days a week and were rewarded with POW money to spend on small luxuries.

FEBRUARY

14 Most destructive raid of the war in Europe on Dresden, by RAF and USAAF Canadians and British reach Rhine 40 miles NW of Duisburg

15 Russians now covering approaches to Danzig; Breslau surrounded

16 US paratroops land on Corregidor Island

17 US troops capture whole of Bataan Peninsula

18 US Third Army have pierced Siegfried Line

19 US Marines land on Iwo Jima

20 First of 36 consecutive night raids on Berlin by RAF

21 Allies cross the Irrawaddy

22 Allies launch Operation Clarion: 9,000 aircraft attack Central German communications

23 US Marines raise flag on Mount Suribachi
Russians capture Poznan after month-long siege
US attack towards Rhine begins

24 Germans wipe out Russian Hron bridgehead NW of Budapest

28 Rokossovsky takes Neustettin
British-Indian IV Corps take Meiktila airfield

MARCH

2 US Third Army takes Trier on Moselle

3 IV Corps takes Meiktila Manila liberated

5 German Second Army cut off in Pomerania as Soviets reach Baltic

⊙ *Marc Sawicki, a Pole, had served with the Polish Carpathian Brigade in the desert but found himself away from the action. Having joined the RAF and qualified as a pilot, he flew reconnaissance missions in northern Italy, in advance of the line in which the ground troops were advancing.*

❝ On one occasion I had completed my task of reconnaissance when I noticed a staff car on the other side of the River Po, which was accelerating instead of stopping and hiding. Normally when one was flying, when the Germans saw the plane they would usually stop and hide. But this one was in a hurry, so I thought it must be someone important from the German headquarters. So I said to my number two to go back to base, because we hadn't got much petrol left. He went and I went into a vertical dive and started firing. I had some ammunition left still. When I got him on target, he suddenly swerved from the road into the trees and stopped and from four places there were sparks coming up at me – it was a battery of anti-aircraft guns, with which he had obviously wanted me to get involved. This was a very uneven fight, because I had only my guns and there were four of them. So they hit me and one of the first shells cut off the mirror above my head and then I felt

hits on my body. One of the propeller blades was cut off, so it started vibrating. I had to switch off or reduce revs. But I was on a very high speed – about 360 or 380 mph. When I pulled out they were still firing, and I knew I had to bale out because there was oil coming from the engine. I had to pull out the hood ready for baling out, but when I was pulling it out, I was hit underneath, and one of the shells exploded in my parachute on which I was sitting. So there was no chance for me to use the parachute – I had to crash.

Then I had a shell come up under my arm and explode in the dashboard. This opened up the petrol tank in front of me and the fumes and oil started coming up. I knew that if there was any spark now, my uniform was covered with oil – I had to crash land and get out quickly.

This was in country where there were lots of canals – a very flat area. There were a lot of trees for silk worms and in between there were wires for wine-growing. These wires were a terrific obstacle to crash landing. I knew someone who was decapitated by one of these wires. Knowing this, I decided to land in the canal – these were usually shallow, so I knew there would be no trouble once I crashed. There was not much choice – there were seconds only to descend, and they were still firing on me. There were seconds only. Suddenly, as I was turning, with the engine out of action and gliding down at a very steep angle, I

▼ Marc Sawicki of 318 Polish Squadron in the cockpit of his Spitfire which was shot down with a total of 54 hits while on a low-level reconnaissance flight in northern Italy.

▼▼ British infantry use assault boats to cross a canal near the River Po in Italy. Their victorious push to the north would eventually link them up with the other Allies who had liberated Germany on the other side of the Alps.

saw a very narrow crescent of meadow between the canal and the embankment, which was along the Po river. This was against the Po flooding. I pressed harder, although I had excessive speed. I crash landed and because so many shells hit my plane, when I hit the ground at an angle, I was catapulted out in just a small space, to about 11 yards away. I knew this afterwards because I visited the area after several days, when it was occupied by our forces. I was able to see where I landed and where the plane was. I lost consciousness and when I recovered I could see within about 100 yards German soldiers walking along. I couldn't make out why they did not come and get me – then I worked out that they were on the other side of the canal, and they couldn't cross without boats, and we had smashed all their boats on previous occasions. I learned after that they had to dismantle doors from a barn and use them as a raft. Then they got across to find me. On the other side of this

embankment, I could see the chimney of a dwelling house. I crawled there and after a while I found an old man. He started interrogating me, asking who I was. I told him I was an airman, and he said, 'I can see that. Are you German or Allied?' I said I was English. He said 'Are you sure?' I said yes, and that I was Polish. He asked in Italian, '*Polacco tedeschi*? *Polacco Inglese*?' I said I was '*Polacco Inglese*'. He explained that there were already two Germans patrols looking for an airman, and that if they found me hiding there, they would shoot the family. They never realised though, that anyone could land there, and so they were on the other side of this embankment and couldn't find me.

He gave me a drink of very strong Italian stuff, and pushed me out of the house. His family came out of the shelter and urged me to leave because they were afraid of being shot. ❞

THE CURTAIN FALLS

No two enemies could hate each other as do the Fascists and Communists, so bitter fighting marks the collapse of German resistance.

The massive Soviet invasion of eastern Germany began on 12 January 1945, when 1.5 million troops, with massive artillery, armour and air support, fell on German positions from East Prussia down to southern Poland. The Germans stood little chance. By 17 January, Warsaw had fallen, while Soviet units encircled Army Group Centre and pushed west through Army Group A.

Meanwhile, in Hungary, Budapest had been taken. A disastrous counterattack at Lake Balaton left Hitler no reserves. Thus, on 4 April, the Soviets quickly seized Vienna, followed two days later by the main assault on Berlin. German defenders, aware that the end was in sight, clung tenaciously to their positions, but as Rokossovsky pushed north west, Zhukov and Koniev fought through to the capital. By 26 April they were on the outskirts – by 2 May they had split the city. By then, Hitler had committed suicide. The '1,000-Year *Reich*' was over.

Hendrick Verton, a Dutchman, was one of the thousands of Western European volunteers to the German Waffen SS. In February 1945, he was with the 11th Company of the 1st Regiment of the SS Infantry Battalion A and E, fighting last-ditch battles against the Red Army on the outskirts of the fortress Breslau.

❝ With only a handful of men we set up a sort of human barrier on the long road between Frobelwitz and Leuthen. The terrain was flat, only a few thin little trees stood at the edge of the road. We placed a man at about every 100 metres along this road, alone, forsaken and unprotected in the icy snow storm,

▲ The Red Flag is hoisted above the shattered roof of the *Reichstag* as chaos still reigns in the streets of Berlin below. What seemed the most momentous event in Berlin's history would, in fact, be only the beginning.

▲Suffering a fourth Soviet winter, German troops put off the inevitable moment of defeat or withdrawal.

▼A King Tiger tank rolls into a Budapest square, where the German Army is eking out its last days of occupation.

armed only with a rifle, a machine pistol or a *Panzerfaust*, waiting for the enemy. Stiff from the cold, the snow rendering the next man in line practically invisible, we felt totally wretched and abandoned. We stood along this god-forsaken road for one long afternoon and night without replacement. It was only by shouting out to one another now and then that we could make sure that we weren't the last men guarding Europe.

In the early morning our sparsely-manned front-line was suddenly withdrawn to the village of Leuthen. The inhabitants who still remained in the village crept out of their cellars astonished, when they saw us. They were expecting the Russians to march in at any moment.

In the afternoon Russian tanks appeared. Further away, three enemy tanks fired on the village without causing much damage. They were probably scared that we had hidden anti-tank guns and so in the daylight they kept at a safe distance. The remaining inhabitants of Leuthen begged us to abandon the village, so that they could hand it over to the Russians without a fight. We then asked the women of the village whether they were not afraid of the Russians. This animated debate was broken off by the order to withdraw.

At the edge of a wood, east of Leuthen, we waited for evening to come. The enemy noticed our withdrawal and soon took over the village. From Leuthen enemy shell-launchers and tanks fired upon us in the wood. Russian infantry tried to break through our lines from all directions, but we managed to hold off all attacks. As we chased a raiding party back to Leuthen, we heard the desperate cries for help from the women in the village.

The next night we were dug in along the road to Saara. The enemy attack was only expected towards morning and we were given the order to defend the road right down to the last man. Faced with this 'rosy' prospect we hung around for hour after hour in our wet foxholes and tried to scoop the water out with cooking pots.

In the first light of dawn the Russians sent us an ice-cold morning greeting. We were suddenly fully awake: they were now firing at us. Initially, the heavy shells landed one by one behind us in the woods, but these were soon followed by more, landing in front of us in the field or on the road. Heavy Russian artillery and anti-tank guns ploughed up the terrain. The shells came wailing over our foxholes and splinters whistled in all directions. The earth rumbled, clumps of sand and stones clattered on to our steel helmets. There were no wounded, if you were hit that was the end of you.

The man in the next foxhole to me was dead. I shouted to my neighbour on the other side, and thank God, he was still alive. With eyes wide open, we watched as the vastly superior enemy pushed closer. We saw our left flank pushed back in a merciless hand-to-hand combat, which meant that the link to my group had been cut off. We were now alone in our holes beside the road. The Red Army soldiers edged forward in groups towards us. The platoon commanders moved forward and fired

Very pistols into the places where they thought the enemy fire was concentrated. An anti-tank gun, pulled by a horse, moved forward with the attacking infantrymen, and joined straight into the attack with a few rounds, before advancing further. We were left with no other choice but to sell our lives as expensively as possible. Our situation was now hopeless. Death was now so near. I had no hope left. We looked behind us helplessly. At the edge of the wood the Company Commander was shouting, but we couldn't understand him. Next to him stood our platoon commander, Habr, pointing excitedly towards the stream, which ran out from the road across the open field to the wood. We now understood what he meant and with our last drop of energy and a quick leap, we reached the water, one after another. Machine-gun rounds whistled over our heads. But every man, who had managed to crawl out of his hole, reached the wood. **"**

SS *Martin Vajen was just 18 when the war ended, having been conscripted into the Leibstandarte Adolf Hitler Division of the SS when he was 16. After recovering from wounds received in the Ardennes, he was directed east where, after a journey under bombardment, his unit was pitched into a battle in part of Prague.*

BALTIC EVACUATION

When Soviet troops entered East Prussia in early 1945, they were thirsting for revenge, having witnessed the results of Nazi rule in their homeland. As stories of rape, pillage and murder spread among the German population, many tried to flee.

Those who had not done so by late January found the overland route to central Germany blocked. They turned instead to the sea, hoping to be picked up by German ships from ports in the Gulf of Danzig. Despite mining by the RAF, Soviet submarine activity and shortages of oil and shipping, over two million soldiers and civilians were evacuated.

But it was a costly business. Between October 1944 and May 1945, 24 German merchant ships were lost to Soviet submarines, including the liners *Wilhelm Gustloff* and *Steuben*. The former left Gdynia on 30 January 1945, overloaded with more than 8,000 passengers. Torpedoed that night in atrocious weather, the liner sank and only 964 people survived.

◄ In face of overwhelming Soviet air supremacy, the anti-aircraft gun, mounted on the bow of this German boat transporting troops from eastern Prussia, would be of little avail.

❝ We only had our rifles, no *Panzerfaust* and no heavy weapons. The Russians had heavy artillery, tanks and fighter planes. What chance did one have with a carbine against this onslaught? Suffice it to say, we were overrun. Then, three of us spent 14 days behind the Russian lines. We got a clear picture of the brutalities committed by the Russians. We were captured twice – we escaped the first time in darkness. The second time, we were taken off by a Russian officer. He spoke good German and took us to a camp in a small village which had been set up by the Germans for French POWs whom they sent out to work on the land. There were about 25 Germans there, who told us they felt safer here than outside, where they'd be bumped off by the Czechs.

Not choosing to wait around, we made a break for it across the open fields into the woods, and we made it. I'm convinced that those who stayed there were carted off to Siberia.

I remember seeing on one street 10 horse-driven carts, behind which

groups of women walked with their hands tied. They were either Wehrmacht helpers or nurses, and behind each group were two Russians with whips.

We arrived in a village, which seemed to be empty. Then we spotted about 50 German soldiers hanging from trees or lampposts. Who had strung them up? On the outskirts of another village we took a little break, and down below in the village we could hear constant shooting. We asked some people what was going on, and they told us that all soldiers down there had to strip off, and the ones who had their blood-group tattoed under the left arm would be shot straight away. We had these tattoes, and so we got out quick through the garden into the bushes. The hunt for Germans got more frantic after 8 May. We only dared to make our way westwards during the night.

On another occasion, we came across some open ground in the woods and found ten German soldiers who had been shot dead. They were still warm, and while we were there, an old man suddenly appeared out of the woods; he must have been about 70 or 80 years old, and he told us that if we were Germans, we'd better scarper quick, because the Czechs would soon be back.

We skirted around towns and villages, and I remember, in one town we could hear a lot of shouting in the woods. We met some German refugees and asked them what was going on. They told us that the Czechs had rounded up all the Germans in the market place and were about to finish them off.

Eventually, we reached the frontier between the Russians and the Americans. It was a stream about 6 metres wide. On the bank a pair of

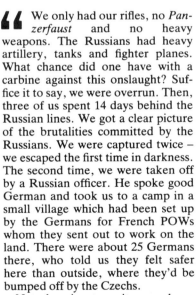

Russian sentries walked up and down. We took our chance to scramble over to the other bank. They only saw us when it was too late. We had made it into Bavaria, and from there we headed north.

I remember, it must have been about 20 May 1945 and we were going through Thüringia towards Erfurt. The town was occupied by the Americans at this time and we got a bit cheekier. We stepped on to the road and stopped a car, which was heading in the direction of north Germany. It was an English car, pulling a trailer full of flowers. Perhaps the driver was German? There were two English-speaking women in the car and one of them got in the front, while my comrade and I sat in the back with the other woman. We got checked a lot, but the women showed their papers and we were allowed to pass.

Then, at a railway crossing, we had to stop and the guard wanted to see our passports. As we had none we were taken off to a prison.

Eventually we were taken to a camp near Le Mans. When we got there, we were told there were 40,000 prisoners there, of which 1,500 were SS. Many of the men were starving to death. In the evening men came round trying to recruit for the Foreign Legion and offering bread. If you volunteered, you could leave the camp straight away. I remember a teacher from Schleswig-Holstein persuading me not to sign up, because I'd soon end up in Indochina.

Major-General Vladimir Antonov was advancing on Berlin as the battle for the German capital developed. With the 301st Rifle Division he entered the outer suburbs of Berlin, accompanied by General Fomichenko's division. On 23 April he received orders to take Karlshorst and force the crossing of the River Spree.

" The advance to the centre of Berlin was beginning. The Germans concentrated between Treptow Park and the Landswehr Canal. They turned every block of flats, every building, into strongpoints. They had blown all the bridges and given the orders to resist to the last man. I have a photo of a large barricade on the Wilhelmstrasse which we had to destroy with heavy artillery.

April 7, we turned towards the Ministry of Aviation, the *Gestapo* building – Hitler's headquarters. This was the Imperial Chancellery and the houses along the Wilhelm and Saarland *Strassen*. All these objectives were on the line of our advance. Our division conducted itself extremely bravely during the fierce fighting which took place, not only for houses, but for individual storeys in these houses.

On the 29th we occupied the *Gestapo* headquarters building, and on the 30th, during the storming of the Aviation Ministry, the commander

▶ Confident and in strength, Russian soldiers arriving in Berlin pause for a welcome wash and brush up before the final push to take the city. From here, they would have to fight fiercely for every street and house.

of a self-propelled gun crew, Lieutenant Alexei Denichuk, particularly distinguished himself. He broke through the northern fence of the ministry gardens and saw, through the foliage, the huge grey expanse of the buildings, topped by an enormous eagle. He gave the crew the orders to open fire on the scavenging buzzard. The crew fired twice, the walls rang out to the sounds of the shells, but at the same time, a burst of machine-gun fire came from the

rear, somewhere on the top floor. Our guns silenced the machine gun, but Alexei was gravely wounded.

On instruction of our HQ, we first sent back the parliamentary deputies who came to the regiment, and then we received instructions to dispatch them to where negotiations were taking place, including those between General Krebs and our acting commander, General Sokolovsky.

We found that these negotiations had not led anywhere and at 1830 hours, our divisions, amongst them the regiments of the 1050th and 1054th, went straight out to storm Hitler's headquarters.

Our Soviet officers and men broke into the grounds from the direction of Hermann Göring Strasse and engaged the SS regiment of General Mönke in fierce combat. They were covering the building. Their instruc-

◀▲ Russian mortars (left) and heavy artillery (above) turn the streets of the German capital into a raging battleground.

tions to burn Goebbels' body, which had been brought out on to the ground, weren't fulfilled, as our troops had already broken into the grounds.

There then developed a heavy night battle, so the troops of Captain Shepovalov and Platoon Commander Khramov beat off the SS guards. Amongst the front-line troops was a political worker, Major Anna Nikulina. She, together with other soldiers, broke through on to the roof of the Chancellery and planted a banner there. I went into Hitler's reception hall myself. There the fascist coat of arms was hanging, and I gave instructions to have it taken down. I was then brought his – Hitler's – personal standard.

On the evening of May 3rd, troops near the bunker unearthed two corpses. I instructed them to cover them up again, as it was still dark. The next morning, representatives of the High Command Commission, including an interpreter, Yelena Rezhevskaya, came and collected Hitler's corpse, although it wasn't known at this stage that it was his. They took the two bodies away for autopsy. Two weeks later they ascertained it was Hitler's body, together with that of Eva Braun. So, for us, the war in Berlin was at an end. We felt a sense of insult and slight for the German people – we saw the destruction of towns, the smashed houses and flattened squares, the white flags hanging in front-room windows. We saw this and thought what a scandal and what a tragedy it was that the German people had been led to by the fascist authorities.

SS Untersturmführer Heinz Landau had fought furiously through the Battle of Berlin, but as Soviet tanks closed in, he was trapped in a cellar. Felled by a blow to the head, he finally came to, a POW of the Russians. His feelings were of being upside-down and moving along – and of not knowing where he was.

"My memory started flooding back. I got knocked out and, but for my helmet, I would be dead. I opened my eyes and, to my horror, took in what I already suspected, but would not admit to myself. Two Ivans were dragging me along, each hanging on to one of my feet, my shoulders and head bouncing all over the cobblestones.

When they noticed I had come round, I was turned right way up, tottering to my feet. I had obviously been beaten and kicked while unconscious. I was covered in blood from head to toe and felt as though every bone, every muscle, in my body was damaged. Several teeth were broken – one, at least, missing. Someone turned up with a bucket of cold water, which was unceremoniously emptied over my head. I was now standing, frightened to death, but would not let them know it. I was completely surrounded by 50 or 60 of them.

Why had they not killed me? What had they got in store for me? One of them approached me, as cautiously as though I were still armed, put a hand out and flicked open one of my

pockets, at the same time jumping back. This made me smile. These chaps were afraid of me, even under these circumstances. He came back shamefacedly and went through my pockets.

I figured out what was puzzling these chaps. It was my uniform. One of my captors must have ripped my silver-grey epaulettes off, and without these, my uniform was simply that of a private in the tank corps. Furthermore, my flashes did not display any SS insignia.

The crowd was getting hostile again and the first punches and kicks were beginning to find their mark. A grim-looking, heavily armed party was making its way towards me, led by a poisonously green-peaked-capped NKVD officer. I was beginning to feel quite sick again.

I was kicked, pushed and shoved into whatever direction I was supposed to take, and so my nightmare walk through Berlin started. Fortunately, they were never quite sure what exactly I was supposed to be.

Every Russian man or woman who felt so inclined was welcome to have a go at this German who no longer had the ability to defend himself. Thus I was slapped, kicked, rolled about on the ground, used as a football, then spat on, and even urinated on. The highlight of this introduction to 'civilisation' in 'barbarian Germany' was getting straddled by a Russian woman in uniform, minus underwear, who then proceeded to empty her bladder all over me to the delighted howls of the mob.

Eventually 'Nutcracker NKVD' got bored with the show and I was once more dragged away for another

were 18 to 20 and came back when we were 20 to 25. At first we rejoiced – then we got frightened. What would we be able to do in civilian life? Our former schoolmates had already graduated from colleges and universities. But what were we? We weren't fit for anything – we had no profession or trade. All we knew was war, and all we could do was fight. We were eager to forget all about the war. I quickly made myself a coat out of my greatcoat, and replaced the buttons. I sold my tarpaulin boots at the market and bought myself a pair of shoes. When I put on a dress for the first time, I burst out crying. I didn't recognise myself in the mirror. **"**

▲▲ **Russian IS-2 tanks smash into Berlin, the buildings already in ruins from RAF bombardment and their own artillery fire.**

▲ **For Russian and US soldiers, an Allied victory in Berlin is to be celebrated – among the generals, however, Berlin was still to be contested.**

▶ **Jubilant Russians fire a victory salute from high above Berlin.**

walkabout. The next couple of miles were a bit better, as I had to be literally dragged along and no-one could get near enough to do any further damage. It was about this time that I first noticed German women being dragged into the streets, knocked into the gutter and raped, sometimes to death.

A black-leather-clad Red Air Force pilot came up to me. His head was heavily bandaged and he made a beeline for me, put his left arm out, pushing his fist into my chest. Then he pulled his service pistol from its holster and pushed the barrel against my forehead.

'Kneel down and beg for your life, German dog!' I looked him in the eye and did nothing at all. His knee came up unexpectedly and caught me in the groin. Down I went on my knees. 'That's better, Nazi swine.' I got to my feet and looked him in the eye. He lifted his pistol high and hit me on the side of my neck. I fell to the ground but immediately scrambled to my feet. There followed a furious exchange of gems of the Russian language quite beyond my powers of description. NKVD convinced the man that he was responsible for me. I gathered I was to be taken to Divisional HQ for interrogation.

After further battering, I reach Div HQ late in the afternoon. I was led into the yard where there were a few other POWs, but I kept away from them. I sat for a couple of hours in the company of my guards, to whom time did not seem to matter. Another NKVD officer asked what had happened to my papers. I told him they were lost when I was captured.

Night fell and we still sat in the yard. I lay down and slept the sleep of exhaustion. **"**

★ *Valentina Pavlovna became a gun-crew commander in the Red Army's Anti-Aircraft Regiment 1357. After suffering a crippling wound and gangrenous frostbite, she made a slow and painful recovery without amputation. She was back with her crew when news came of the end to hostilities.*

" I celebrated Victory Day in Eastern Prussia. There had already been a lull in the fighting for a couple of days – nobody was shooting. Suddenly, in the middle of the night, there was an air alarm. We all jumped up. Then we heard, 'It's victory! They've surrendered!' That they had surrendered was very good, but the main thing which we grasped at once was that it was victory.

Everyone started firing whatever was to hand – a sub-machine gun, a pistol. Some men were wiping away tears, others were dancing. 'We're alive! We're alive!' Afterwards our commander said, 'Well, you won't be demobbed before you've paid for the shells. What have you done? How many shells have you fired?' It seemed to us that peace would reign in the world for ever. No-one ould ever want another war, and that all the shells must be destroyed . . .

How I longed for home – even though I had neither mother nor father. But I bow low to my step-mother. She gave me a motherly welcome. I called her mother afterwards. She had been waiting for me eagerly, although the hospital head had written to her so that she should be prepared, that they had amputated my leg.

We went to the front when we

SS *Hans Dieckmann was with the 12th SS Panzer division 'Hitler Youth', and had fought at Normandy, in the Ardennes and in Hungary. His final taste of action was against the Russians in northern Austria. Here his unit heard of the German surrender in May 1945 and promptly delivered themselves into American captivity.*

" It was 7 May 1945. We were with the remainder of the 7th Battery in Asten, Austria, at the Eastern exit to the town, the barrels of our guns pointing towards the Russians, who were about 6 km behind us. The news of the capitulation over the radio shocked us and we fired off our last 40 shells in the direction of the Ivans. We then blew up our guns and ammunition, climbed on to our remaining trucks and headed off in the direction of Enns, where the Americans were supposed to be. Food was dished out, the famous Meyers tins, bread, boxes of canned food, cigarettes and tobacco. We then had to destroy our pistols, rifles and other weapons.

With mixed feelings we were heading towards an uncertain future. It was 1 pm and we were approaching the railway bridge at Enns, fighter planes overhead, as American Jeeps came towards us.

We then drove in the direction of Linz and arrived at a huge clover-covered field, in which about 22,000 men were gathered. We were allowed to keep our vehicles, which meant that at least I had a roof over my head. The same evening, the first Americans came over to us at the camp: front soldiers, just like us. We understood one another. Chewing-gum and Camel cigarettes were handed around.

The men in the camp were sorted out into Navy, Airforce and Army personnel. Secondly, our comrades from the *Totenkopf* Division were weeded out and taken away – they were to be handed over to the Russians. The Americans were in no position to be able to feed this mass of prisoners. After 14 days of internment, many of us began to starve. We then saw the first concentration camp inmates coming from Mauthausen – they threatened us, with their fists raised, but the American guards ensured that there was no trouble.

We were then split up into groups of about a hundred, and officers from the regular army were assigned to take charge of us. This caused immediate anger, as they soon made it plain to us that they were going to apply the thumbscrews.

With 14 other men I was taken to a motor pool in Linz. Our American Master-Sergeant, Peter, who was from Texas, was very pleased with us. So, one day he ventured to ask us

whether we couldn't get hold of some wine and some girls. Now, girls you could forget, but we told him we might be able to come up with the wine. One of our comrades came from St Florian, and the wood-chopping party went there every day. Peter cleared it with the camp guard for our comrade to go to the town, where he spent the day with his family, returning with 15 boxes of wine.

I then explained to Peter what we would like in return. In the village, not far away, there was a dance on Saturdays, and the 15 of us wanted to go. Peter managed to bribe the guards with wine and we managed to stay out there from 8pm until 1am. But, when we got back again – the guards didn't want to let us in to the camp.

What had happened was this: the guards had feasted on the wine, were all drunk and had been replaced, and so we had to convince the new ones that we were actually from this camp. **"**

VICTORY ROLL

In Burma the days tick by to Allied victory, but in the Pacific there is a hitch. However, with the dropping of the atom bombs, Japan concedes defeat – but what can be done with their newly acquired empire?

Having secured the island of Leyte in December 1944, the Americans moved on to Luzon. In January 1945, amphibious landings were made in Lingayen Gulf and Manila Bay. But it was to take until August to liberate the Philippines completely.

By then, the 'island-hopping' campaign through the Pacific was closing in on Japan. In February, US Marines assaulted Iwo Jima, and in April, Okinawa. Both campaigns were costly, auguring ill for the invasion of Japan itself, scheduled for 1946.

But by early 1945, Japan was under pressure from all sides. In Burma, the British fought south to Mandalay in March, then to Rangoon two months later. In China, the Japanese lost ground to national troops; in Manchuria, to the invading Soviets. The atomic attacks on Hiroshima and Nagasaki ended all resistance in Japan, and with that, World War II was finally over.

Major Dick Rubinstein, working with Force 136, SOE, had been drafted to Burma to work with local resistance groups to carry out raids on the Japanese as they advanced towards Rangoon in an attempt to stop the Allied progress before the monsoon season began. His diary recalls the following.

▲ The carrier USS *Franklin* tilts crazily after being hit by Japanese bombs in March 1945. 724 men died in the attack, but the ship was repaired.

▶ Dick Rubinstein of Force 136, Burma, takes a well-earned break between nerve-wracking special missions.

❝ 25 January 1945 – written 22 February. Felt really rotten all the afternoon – and very frightened. Thought I could never face another op after this and was very annoyed at

the lights yet.'

Away in the end, and felt most relieved when I heard the engine note change and I went.

Put my hands up to protect my face on the slide and the chute seemed to be open before I got them down. A rough opening and I thought I had twists, but all OK. Seemed very high and was drifting away from lights. All very quiet and still. Watched the wind blow in the edges of the canopy and then a slight wind started a slight oscillation, which soon died. The moon was very bright and even colours showed up. I was over paddy with a large stream below, and seemed to be going on to a barn, so I pulled on the left lines and seemed to swing away. Saw then I was going for the stream and very relieved to see I was over it, when the ground started coming up. It seemed to be coming pretty fast and I went into some long, green stuff on a slope at about 40 degrees. Luckily I had made up my mind to roll into the slope, otherwise I would have rolled to the bottom into water, for I was near a tributary of the stream.

Took a bit of time to get the harness off because I had a haversack tied over the top. Saw people with torches running towards Hugo. I had seen the other lads on the way down. I shouted to him if things were OK – they were.

Some levies ran over to me, took my chute and took me over to Bill Howe.

They said they had shouted up to us 'It's all OK.' I had shouted down 'Hullo down there,' but neither had heard the other.

Walked up to Man Kau Kaw village and was given more coffee and a bed with three blankets in their hut – a grand reception, all fear gone and glad to have arrived. **"**

the off-hand manner of some of the non-op types there, who kept saying, 'Don't worry, old boy, the chute won't open anyway.' All very funny, but not appreciated.

When the take-off came, I felt much better and took quite a lively interest in what was going on. The RAF crew were very good and during the three-and-a-half-hour trip gave us blankets, oranges, tea and gum. Was quite easy during the run and didn't feel so bad on the slide.

Sat there for 20 minutes, knees knocking a bit, and was given more tea. My mouth was so dry the gum fell apart. The only thing that annoyed me was that the dispatcher would keep saying, 'He's not seen

Captain John B Scollen, of 656 Squadron RAF had served with the Royal Artillery in a survey regiment in North Africa and Italy. After qualifying as a pilot, he was sent to Burma to perform observation post duties, and in this capacity he witnessed the battle for Meiktila in the jungles of Burma, and its aftermath.

" Shortly after we entered Meiktila I visited a number of Jap gunsites with an expert on their artillery who told me a good deal about the different types of guns we found. It was a grim experience to visit these gunsites, many with their crews still lying dead around them – but it was worthwhile because I knew little of the types of guns that Japs used and learned more from inspecting the guns themselves than from studying the official literature on enemy equipment.

These gunsites, like the rest of the town, were scenes of the most terrible destruction. Almost every building in Meiktila was gutted by fire or shattered by blast and to drive through it when we first took it was a sickening experience. Jap dead lay by the roadsides and in the ruined houses and there hung about the place the dreadful stench of death that overcomes one with horror at the time and remains in the memory afterwards like a nightmare.

To locate the Jap guns that were firing into Meiktila was by no means easy. It required vast amounts of patience and not a little luck because their guns were almost always dug deep down under cover where they could not be seen from the air, and even their flashes were difficult to

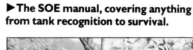

▶ **The SOE manual, covering anything from tank recognition to survival.**

24 Red Armies from north and south link up in Berlin
British Second Army enters Bremen
Eighth Army captures Ferrara; US Fifth Army takes Spezia and Modena
Fourteenth Army takes Pyinmana, Burma

25 Russian and US troops meet 60 miles from Berlin; eight Russian armies encircle Berlin; RAF attack Berchtesgaden
US Marines seize islands off coast of Okinawa

26 Germans at Bremen surrender; Russians capture Stettin; US Third Army takes Regensburg
Second Ukrainian Front capture Brno
Italian Partisans take Genoa and stage revolt in Milan: American Fifth Army captures Verona

27 French capture Ventimiglia
Russians 80 miles NW of Berlin

28 US Seventh Army takes Augsburg and reaches Austrian border to the south
US Fifth Army take Brescia
Mussolini and mistress shot while trying to escape

29 British Second Army near Hamburg; Russian forces in Mecklenburg; US Seventh Army reaches Munich; US First Army liberates Dachau
German armies in Italy sign surrender terms: British Eighth Army secures Venice and advances towards Trieste; US Fifth Army enters Milan and contacts Eighth Army at Padua

30 Hitler commits suicide with Eva Braun
US Seventh Army clears Munich; French take Friedrichshaven and cross into Austria; US First Army at Ellenburg

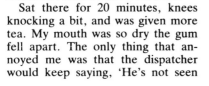

◄February 1945: US Sherman tanks move through the ruins of Manila. On 3 March the city was declared totally secure. Over 4,000 American prisoners were released from prisons here. The clearing of the Philippines was to cost the US Army dear, with a loss of near 146,000 casualties.

spot. On the 25th March I was cruising about north of Meiktila, looking for a single Jap gun that had been giving us a great deal of trouble by firing rounds into the town at irregular intervals. We had all tried to spot him, but without success, and he was such a nuisance that we were pressed to keep on trying so that he could be put out of action.

I searched for well over an hour in all the suspected areas, but could not find a trace of him, though I kept getting reports over the radio that he had fired again.

He always seemed to fire just when, for some reason or other, I could not observe him, but more than once I felt a thump in my seat from his blast as he fired. And then, just as I was about to give it up and go back, I spotted him.

I had been airborne for nearly two hours and therefore had little petrol left. The light was beginning to fail and I had already told the guns that I was going back. As I turned south to leave the area where I had been searching, I turned round in my seat to keep my eye on the area through the back of the perspex roof of the cockpit as I flew away. And that was how I saw him. There was the unmistakable red muzzle flash of a field gun – a sight that was familiar from flash-spotting days – and I shouted over the radio that I had got him and gave orders for the guns to get into action again. I kept my eye on the spot where I had seen the flash and the gunsmoke as I swung the plane round to fly back to give fire orders and observe the fall of shot. The gun was deep in some bushes and even when I was right overhead, I could see neither the gun nor its crew.

I had very little time to spare and

▲Under heavy fire, US Marines crawl up one of Iwo Jima's ash hills, February 1945. The capture of the island gave the US an 'unsinkable carrier' from which to launch its final deadly attacks on Japan.

had to engage the target with all speed. I was firing medium guns and I put down about twenty 100-lb shells all around the target. Two of them fell into the actual clump of bushes in which the gun was hidden. I could not see what effect they had, but their explosions covered the target area and the gun did not fire into Meiktila again. This was the first time that anyone on the flight had spotted and engaged a gun in this

way, and as an ex-flash-spotter, I felt rather glad that I had got him.

The light was going so rapidly and my petrol gauge was so low that I did not sign off as I usually did, by beating up the guns I had been firing, but flew back to our strip. We never approached the strip directly, in order to conceal from the enemy, if possible, its exact location. We used to come down low some distance away and then fly round the lake just above water level on the final approach to the strip.

That night the light was so far gone as I came in across the water that it was unusually difficult to assess my height. Several colleagues in the flight, concerned for my safety, posted themselves along the strip, waving electric torches to help me touch down and as I flew across the darkening lake, the little pinpoints of light ahead were a great encouragement. I landed safely – to their relief as much as my own.

In the next week or two, we all located and engaged a number of guns, and our services were much in demand. Once I was called to deal with an anti-tank gun which was giving our tanks a lot of trouble just north of Meiktila. They told me exactly where he was – but he was so well sited that they could not deal with him. I looked and, although I could not see the gun, I could see some of the crew. Perhaps they were too concerned about our approaching tanks to remember to keep under cover. Jap uniform was dark green – not unlike our own when seen at a distance, except that they usually wore leggings or high boots, but they wore caps of a lighter colour. I engaged the gun and two of the 20 shells I fired must have hit the target. **"**

► **A US Marine pauses for 'chow' on Okinawa, April 1945. With Japan now under direct threat of invasion, the defence of the island was often fanatical, and did not collapse until late June.**

▼ **A Grumman Avenger pilot 'mounts up' on board the carrier USS *Bunker Hill*, in preparation for a sortie over Iwo Jima. The US fully exploited their air superiority, constantly bombing the entrenched Japanese positions.**

Masatake Obata, a resident of Tokyo, was a retired soldier with a manufacturing business making component parts for aircraft. On 9 March eight people were living in the Obata household. This was the night that American General Curtis LeMay decided that his bombers would 'burn up' Tokyo.

" In the house were my wife, four children, two sisters and myself. My sisters actually lived up by Ueno Park but they had stayed for dinner and were gossiping with my wife. At about 8 o'clock that night of 9 March, Radio Tokyo broadcast a preliminary warning about an air raid. They decided to stay overnight.

The air raid began at about mid-night. When I saw that it was serious I changed into my air raid warden's uniform and prepared to go on duty. I told my wife and children to get dressed and go out of the house. I took them all to Fuji Park and then went to a meeting of my neighbourhood association. There we decided all the families should go to Sumida Park, one of the big open spaces, where they would be comparatively safe.

After that I put on my helmet and began my patrol, moving from door to door, checking to see that no one in our neighbourhood had made the mistake of trying to wait out the air raid at home. I found some people, mostly young women with children and old women, and told them they had to go to Sumida Park.

Then I started back for Sumida Park myself to meet my family. The bombing had started, and many houses were burning from the incendiary bombs the B-29s were dropping. The smoke was very heavy and it was hard to breathe. I also noticed that a strong wind had sprung up and the fire was being carried by the wind from house to house. Everyone was wearing his air raid hood, but I saw some people whose hoods were burning, and if they took off their hoods their hair began to burn.

Suddenly a whole cluster of six-pound bombs dropped not ten feet away from me. Before I could do anything, the cluster exploded and one bomb blew up directly in my face. I was wearing one of the conical Japanese army helmets, but it did not help because the bomb came up from underneath. The impact knocked me down. The steel helmet

fell off and that is the last I knew. I became unconscious.

Maybe I was unconscious for an hour. I don't know. When I woke up I found that my shoes had burned off, and my toes had melted. My hands and arms were so badly burned that they were black. I had burns all over my body.

I could not use my hands. I rolled on the ground, trying to put out the fires in my clothing. I got up somehow and walked toward a trench alongside the road. The bombers were still coming over, and the firestorm had begun. A fierce wind was blowing flames everywhere.

I walked into the trench. I felt as if I was walking on tennis balls – my feet had swelled to three times their normal size. I went to an air raid shelter and found several other people there, all badly burned.

When day came and the last American plane had gone I knew I had to find help so I headed for Sensoji Hospital behind the Akasaka Shrine. When I got there a doctor looked me over. A nurse took off my burned clothes and treated my burns with salve and bandaged them. When they were finished I was a mummy. I heard a nurse ask the doctor which ward she should send me to. The doctor said, 'No ward, take him down the basement to the morgue. He is as good as dead.'

So they took me to the morgue and I lay there for five days without food and water, until my sister finally found me and saved me. My wife, children and other sister had all been killed when the firestorm raged through Sumida Park. Thousands and thousands of people died that night, almost all women, children and old people. There are no records, but perhaps 200,000 people died that night in the firestorm over Tokyo. The bodies clogged the banks of the Sumida River like charred logs. **"**

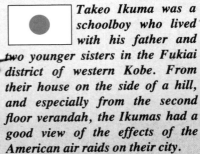

▼ **Gurkha troops make their way to Mandalay, Burma. The strategically vital town fell to Allied forces in late March, after weeks of fierce fighting.**

Takeo Ikuma was a schoolboy who lived with his father and two younger sisters in the Fukiai district of western Kobe. From their house on the side of a hill, and especially from the second floor verandah, the Ikumas had a good view of the effects of the American air raids on their city.

" I remember the big raid of 5 June particularly. The bombers came over in broad daylight, big silver aircraft floating through the sky. It was a hot summer day and first the smoke from the bombings hung in the air, rising slowly. But then the wind came up and the fires began to spread.

I saw one brave Japanese fighter plane crash into a B-29 and then I saw the parachutes stringing out in the sky behind the plane as it went down.

After half an hour my father and the girls said they were going to the refuge behind the hill. I wanted to stay and watch, and anyhow it was my duty to stay and fight the fire if our house was bombed. Somehow I knew that this was the day we would be bombed. We had always escaped before but this time I watched as the bombers came nearer and nearer to our neighbourhood, as if they were looking for us.

After one hour of raiding, the black smoke was moving swiftly toward our district of Fukiai. Yes the bombers were coming our way.

Most of the people had already left the area even though it was illegal to do so. Every house was supposed to have its *rusuban* (caretaker). But in the past two months there had been so many raids that the Home Ministry's orders were being disobeyed every day. As

◄RAF Thunderbolts maintain the Allied air monopoly over Burma – crucial for the rapid ground advances of 1945.

►A Royal Navy convoy heads for Rangoon, secured by both airborne attacks and amphibious landings on 3 May.

▼The wreckage of a Japanese Nakajima 'Oscar' on Akyab airfield, NW Burma. The Japanese abandoned the field in February 1945.

everyone knew, once the firebombers came and hit your house, there was nothing that could be done to save it. The material in the bombs burned everything. As the bombers came closer I could see the tiny bombs dropping from the big silver birds. They were the little incendiaries – the worst kind.

Soon the bombs were falling ever closer and then several bombs struck our roof. Dozens of four-pound bombs hit us and immediately began to burn. I tried a bucket of water, but it just seemed to make the fire burn brighter, and there were twenty places on fire now. There was nothing to do but try and escape. I had waited a long time. Fires were burning all round the house. I decided the best way to go was to follow the electric rail line because the embankment was free of houses. But to get to the line I had to walk through the neighbourhood and all the houses were burning. I met many people moving toward the mountains, carrying their belongings or their children on their backs – suitcases, boxes, bags, and even futons. As I went along I saw all sorts of things abandoned. Down in the valley the sky was no longer visible, the air was full of smoke and I could hear people crying out all around me.

I looked at my left hand. It had turned a strange white colour, and it began to throb. I had been burned somehow by a fire-bomb. I came to a large barrel of water put on the side of the road for the firefighters, and wanted a drink. But the surface was covered with black scum. So I kicked the barrel and then went on.

I reached the edge of the hills at Noda Michinaga. The whole area was abandoned. I walked down the hill to the plain and all around me I saw people walking, stumbling, and many of them were now abandoning their goods and luggage. The place to go was the upland ahead, where the houses were so few the bombers would not bother with them.

Finally I reached the hills. Below I could see Katano Kijo landing, once a beautiful green grassy area, but now scorched and seared. It had been a shelter area, and it had burned like an inferno, trapping thousands of the people who came into the boxlike place seeking shelter. From the hill I could see the Kobe had burned, from Fukiai to Kuta. Everything was burned up.

Then I suddenly remembered my father and sisters. Where had they gone? I walked down into the shelter area and began to search for them. I became very tired and sat down with my back against a concrete wall. I fell asleep. When I awakened I saw more people streaming out of the city toward the hills. I went to look for an aid station to have my burns treated, and finally came to a school that had been turned into a hospital. A doctor looked at my face and immediately gave me some sugar. He looked at my back and told me to lie down. I had a deep wound in my back. A firebomb had exploded right next to me, and I had been burned and wounded by shrapnel at the same time. The doctor had seen scores of such wounds that day.

I rested a while and then began to search again for my family. I found them finally. We went back to the house. There was nothing left but ashes and junk. The authorities gave us food, as well as futons and a canvas tarpaulin to keep the rain off. We stayed near our house for five days, then we knew we must do something.

We decided we would have to leave Kobe and go to stay with my father's family. So on the fifth day after the great air raid, we went down to Kobe central railroad station and bought tickets that would take us to a new life. Then we got on the train – and headed for Hiroshima. ❞

◎ *Sidney Lawrence, a leading-aircraftsman, had been in the RAFVR in 1938, then was sent to Singapore in 1940 with 36 Torpedo Bomber Squadron. He was finally taken POW by the Japanese in Java in March 1942. 'Officially' dead, he eked out the war in POW camps, finally arriving at a camp in Nagasaki, where he was in August 1945.*

❝ It was a camp called Seisumashi, and there were quite a few other mixed POWs – Japanese, Aussies, a few Americans, and some British.

At that camp we did all sorts of jobs – I've been in coal mines, I've been stevedoring, road-making – all sorts of things – we were slave labour.

When it came to the very last, to Nagasaki, the Japanese said quite definitely, that if they were invaded, under no circumstances would they do other than kill every prisoner. They made that quite plain. In Nagasaki itself, they were going to put us into caves, which we dug out ourselves, and they were just going to blow it in. But we were all to be killed. No prisoner was to be left alive once they were invaded. Everybody knows that the Japanese treatment of us was vile. They hadn't the same standards as us at all. They were quite a different culture. Of course you were just beaten up and knocked about – in certain cases you were tortured. They had all sorts of forms of cruelty, which they didn't consider cruelty, actually. In actuality, I've seen them knock about

their own soldiers the same as they knocked us about.

On 9 August, I was working at the camp, near the Mitsubishi Works – it was about 11 o'clock in the morning when they dropped the bomb, and I actually saw it coming down. It came down on a parachute.

I was working in the open, and I was fortunate enough to get away with not being rubbed out with the bomb or being very badly burned. The amazing thing is the effects on me afterwards. I came out in all sorts of strange boils with green pus. I had various different skin complaints. I still suffer from some problems. I still have my hands splitting between the fingers. All my extremities were affected, and it used to look as if my fingers were dropping off. Fortunately that has gradually gone, but only in the last few years. My feet are still the same – every now and again, my skin splits between the toes and it looks as if my toes will drop off. I have to use a certain ointment and deal with it myself. Right from the beginning here, all the doctors said they didn't know what to do with me – they knew nothing about how to treat the effects of nuclear bombs. They suggested I go back to Japan to get them to treat me. This was how we were treated – appalling really. Some of the fellows went into mental asylums, purely because of their bad treatment when they came home. Nobody cared.

They thought at one time that I had radiation sickness, but I didn't, fortunately.

I saw the plane fly over, then the bomb dropping. Then a blinding flash. There were other people around me who were burned to a cinder – and I was saved by a pile of rubble. Prior to their dropping the bomb, the Americans came over and just bombed us and there was a lot of devastation caused. Of course we were the ones who had to clear it up. We used to hope they wouldn't come over as we were still trying to clear the place up.

The horrifying thing was to see that people were just shadows. You didn't find the body, but you found their shadow, emblazoned in the concrete. The person wasn't there – they had gone up in smoke. That was alright. They were dead, gone. The horrible part was to see the torn limbs and flesh hanging on so many of the Japanese. I ended up helping the Japanese, and trying to do everything we could, those of us who were still alive and able to. They couldn't understand that we were trying to treat them. The Americans came over and dropped food to us on parachutes – and it was food galore, like we hadn't seen in years. It was K rations, and we shared them with the

▶ Sidney Lawrence, miraculous survivor of the Nagasaki atomic bombing. He recalls that afterwards he heard American radio talking of 'the TONIC bomb', because 'ATOMIC meant nothing to us. What on earth was a tonic bomb?'

▲ Hiroshima, 6 August 1945: the first atomic bomb is dropped on Japan, killing at least 80,000 people.

◀ Repairing one of the engines of a B-29 Superfortress. Massive size and bomb capacity made it the natural vehicle for the atomic weapons.

Japanese. They couldn't understand why the few of us that were left didn't turn on the Japanese and kill them. We were British. We couldn't. We helped them and they were grateful – but it was a horrifying sight to see the horrible burns and the way the flesh hung off them.

Buildings were actually destroyed altogether. Things were on fire and just went up in flames. There was one building with its steel girders all twisted, and it looked as if it was still intact. You hit a girder with a stick, and the stick went right through it. It was like brick dust. The girder just looked twisted. It was frightening.

It was quite a little while before I

came to my senses after the blast. I was with one particular guard, who also escaped being killed. He was in such a state that he just put his rifle down and ran for it.

The biggest horror in the after-effects was the utter silence. I had been used to bombing of all kinds and after it you heard cries for help and noise – things happening. The eerie thing was the silence.

The movement of the Japanese around, who could move – well, they were just scurrying about like mice. We were all in a particular kind of daze. Around me there were 35,000

iest bomb which has ever been dropped. The one at Hiroshima was a neutron bomb, but this plutonium bomb was filthy – and the authorities like to keep it quiet. The two are set off in a completely different way. Plutonium effects on human beings are disgusting. You've seen raw meat hanging up in a butcher's – Japanese doctors had no idea what to do with the wounds.

We had to heap up bodies and set fire to them – the horror of that. We had to do it, or there would have been plague.

When the Americans came to

They used to bow to us. They were grateful for what we were doing. I used to help with the surgeons and doctors, and I would ask if they had anything I could use to help the wounded. They had some odd stuff but we didn't really know what to do. The doctors had never treated anything like it at all.

We had gauze and a dark brown sort of ointment with a ghastly smell, just to soothe. I was cradling dying people or trying to put this stuff on their wounds. Some of these were the very Japanese who, a few days before, had been treating us most cruelly. But that was us, not just me.

Some of the fellows from the camp left and tried to get to Tokyo, but I knew it was too far. I don't know what happened to them to this day, but I don't see how, in the condition they were in, they could have ever reached Tokyo.

The hills around Nagasaki saved a lot of damage. If you looked at certain hills, it was as if someone had taken a whitewash brush and run a

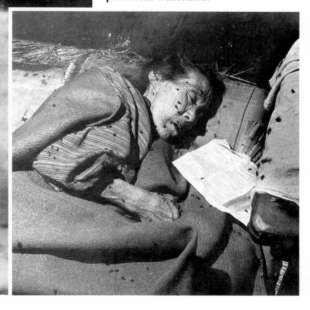

▼ **A survivor of the Hiroshima blast. In seconds her thriving city had become a poisonous wasteland.**

dead – and I was still alive. That's the time when something horrifying happens to you. You ask yourself, 'Why me?' You feel terribly guilty – guilty for being alive when thousands around you are dead. I feel guilty today.

From the moment that all this happened, I felt at one with the Japanese, and all the misery and starvation, all the three and a half years of what I had been through seemed to vanish. I felt they were the same as me and I was the same as them. That's why I've never had any hatred. I cannot hate them in any way, for all that they did.

The bomb at Nagasaki is the filth-

fetch us out, I was in a pretty bad state. When they landed, one of them came over and looked me up and down. He went for his revolver in its holster, and said, 'Who do want me to shoot?' He was a big, tall fellow with a shaven head, real American style. I said, 'You put that revolver away. You don't shoot anybody. If you shoot one of these Japanese, I'll kill you myself. All I want you to do is GET US OUT OF HERE! But don't you shoot any Japanese in front of us.' He couldn't understand how deeply these few of us felt about the horror. After the bomb, we were free to come and go – they didn't look on us as prisoners.

line straight down the side. One side was burned and scorched white – on the other the grass was growing, untouched. Trees – if you looked, one side of the tree was burned to a cinder, and the other side still had leaves on.

The mushroom cloud was there for quite a time. We were very fortunate inasmuch as two days later, we had a typhoon, and there were terrific winds and torrential rains. I think that was a godsend, because this terrific wind was blowing the dust away to sea, and the rain was washing down the ground. It was awful at the time, but I really do **"** think it saved us.

WINNERS AND LOSERS

Although, if given the choice, anyone would choose victory, the end of World War II leaves many wondering if, at the end of the day, it is not as hard to win as it is to lose.

The first large-scale surrender of German forces occurred in northern Italy on 2 May 1945. Twenty-four hours later, at Montgomery's headquarters on Lüneburg Heath, a document was signed, covering northern Germany, Denmark and Holland, to come into effect on 5 May. Two days later, a similar document covering all fronts was signed at Eisenhower's headquarters in Rheims, effective from early on 9 May. The Western Allies celebrated 'VE (Victory in Europe) Day' prematurely on 8 May. Although some German units continued to fight in Czechoslovakia for a further 48 hours, the war in Europe was effectively over.

Three months later in the Pacific and Far East, however, many Japanese soldiers refused to believe their Emperor's surrender, broadcast on 15 August. Thus, it was not until 2 September that formal documents were signed aboard USS *Missouri* in Tokyo Bay.

 Admiral Karl Dönitz had been Commander-in-Chief of the Kriegsmarine since 1943, when he succeeded Raeder. It was he who had masterminded the U-boat campaigns against Allied shipping and so nearly cut Britain's supply lines, but now, after Hitler's suicide, it fell to Dönitz to supervise the German surrender.

▲ Still very much in the war, front-line troops in Burma gather round a radio to hear the news of Germany's last hours.

▲▶ Admiral Karl Dönitz – a well respected strategist and C-in-C of the German Navy – now Hitler's chosen successor.

"When I got the telegram from the headquarters of Hitler on the evening of 30th April, I knew that now I was the chief of the German State. But I knew too, that Himmler had the opinion that he had the biggest chance to be the successor of Hitler. And that's why I thought it to be necessary that I spoke to Himmler at once because this man was still a powerful man in the country. When he got my demands he should have come to me at once – but he answered by telephone that it was not possible for him to come. And then I let him see that it was necessary that he had to come – and then he came.

I didn't know what would be the end of this discussion, it was for me a

big question and that's why I put, under a piece of paper, my revolver on the table. And he was sitting down and I gave him the telegram which I had got, and in which it was said that I am the Chief of State.

When he had read the telegram, he got pale and he stood up and bowed and told me, 'Please let me be the second man in your state.' Then I told him that I have no position at all for him in my state – not one, no . . . and then he was not content and he spoke against that – but he had no success. I didn't change my opinion and after, from that time of discussion, I stood up and he had to go. He went home and I was very glad that the end of the discussion with Himmler was like that, because I had the feeling that he wouldn't do anything against me. **"**

Doctor David Bradford was a clinical student in his third year of studies at Bart's Hospital in London when his year was asked if they would sacrifice a month of their training to go abroad to do relief work. Expecting to go to Holland to work with the starving children, he learnt his destination was Belsen.

"We were taken down in army lorries to Belsen camp itself. We didn't know what we'd find at all. As we went in, we went in through the gates – which were actually open, although there were sentries on the gates to prevent the inmates from leaving, and we went to a room where we had DDT powder sprayed over our hair, into our clothes and so on, because there was a danger of typhus, which is carried by insects and bugs.

When we got there we found a number of huts, like any hutted camp. Here there were about 120 huts and this awful pall of smoke and the smell hanging over the camp. There were terrible skeletal people walking about.

I was allotted a hut with a fellow called Eddy Boyd, who was at UCH. We just had to go in and start clearing it up. The hut was about the size of a tennis court, but some six to eight feet narrower. There were supposed to be about 450 people in this hut. One end was partitioned off and there were three-tier bunks, about 24, and a table and chairs. The rest of it, the inmates were lying on the floor, their heads to the walls, all down the sides. Down the centre they were lying head-to-head. You had four rows of people, just lying there in rags. There were no blankets, and they had old clothes and overcoats covering them.

Our first job was simply to go round and see who was alive and who wasn't. You couldn't do anything else. There was no question of treating them at this stage.

There was Eddy Boyd and I, and each hut was allotted two Hungarian military personnel who had been left behind by the Germans. I think the Hungarians were not combatants, and they had been orderlies around the place.

We were told these men were to do the heavy work – which simply consisted of moving the dead from the hut. Eddy Boyd and I went

round and we found, on the first day, about 20 people just lying there dead. As we carried them out, their clothes were immediately taken by the other inmates, and they just used them to cover themselves to keep warm. They were all so close together – they were lying touching each other all around the hut. Just as you have seen on television, the bodies were just carried out in the most undignified manner – they got a couple of arms, a couple of feet, and they were just dragged out and put in a pile near the door.

Twice a day, a tractor came round with a flat truck, and the bodies were unceremoniously laden on these trucks and taken round to an open pit, which would be about 50-60 yards long and 30 yards wide, and just chucked in unceremoniously. They would then be covered with lime and twice a day this wagon would come round. We used to get up about half past seven, have breakfast. Half past eight we would be taken down to the camp each day, and each day, two or three people were found to be lying dead there.

Our job was mainly to clear out the dead and to try to decide who was likely to go on living and who wasn't, and also to see that whatever food there was was evenly distributed. What one found, of course, was that, although there were 450 in the hut, some were up and about, and there were probably about 600 people who slept there. There were some ambulant people, and it was natural that they were the ones who got the food. Our job was to see that the food went to those who really needed it. The food we had to give to them was pretty pitiful in a way. Of course they couldn't have a proper meal. We used to give them something called Bengal Famine Mixture, which was a high-protein diet with

▼ **In Italy, British Coastal Force Ratings show off the spoils of a captured German E-boat.**

FALL OF KÖNIGSBERG

As Soviet forces attacked the *Reich* in early 1945, Hitler demanded that key cities be transformed into 'fortresses' to stem the tide. One such was Königsberg, capital of East Prussia. In fact, those in the city had little choice. By the end of January 1945, they were trapped, their backs to the Baltic, with Hitler refusing any form of evacuation. Soon afterwards, Soviet advances split the defenders of East Prussia into three groups – around Heilsberg, inside Königsberg and in the Samland peninsula. On 6 April, Vasilevsky's 3rd Belorussian Front assaulted Königsberg fighting for the city, street by street against desperate defenders. Three days later the battle was over, allowing the Soviets to sack the city. Up to a third of the population died.

Chaos reigns in the streets of Königsberg as Soviet forces overrun one of Hitler's 'fortresses'.

glucose in it and added vitamins. It would come round in great cans, and we would dole it out, trying to see that those who really needed it, had it. Sometimes we were lucky enough to get some biscuits or potatoes in their jackets, which were cooked in a great cauldron in the cookhouse.

As time went by, the hut got gradually emptier and with my hut, hut 14, we had managed, with some of the other students, to clear out huts 16, 18 and 20 – there were odd and even numbers on either side of a track. So these were next door, and as time went by we got these three huts which had been done up into some sort of primitive hospital.

The only medication we had was aspirin tablets, a very primitive M and B type compound, a sulphonamide which was an early antibiotic, called Prontosil, and opium tablets, which were presumably some sort of laudanum. And we just handed these out like that. There were people in pain – they had sores and they were just lying there in pain. We would dispense these tablets simply to give relief. The main thing was to get fluid and vitamins into them.

The first fortnight we were cleaning out Belsen itself, actually in the huts. The first week we didn't have any time off at all – we worked seven days flat-out. After that we were given a morning off a week, and an afternoon on another day. It was insisted that we do this because it was fairly hard work. It was a bit of an ordeal and we were young.

Being as young as we were – I was about 23 years old at the time – one could stand it more. If one had been more mature, if one had to face it now and realise that the people who were in this terrible state, were human beings – somebody's mother, father, son and so on – I don't think one could have borne it. As it was, they were almost unrecognisable as human beings, and of course we were young medical students, and they were all foreign – couldn't speak English, so I had a young Pole as an interpreter.

An area was kept separate for typhus cases, obviously. There was a lot of tuberculosis, and we were able to get their chests X-rayed. It was quite an efficient service. You'd fill in a form and they would be taken down to the X-ray department by orderlies. The next day you would get an X-ray report.

We had to treat a lot of abcesses, bed-sores – and their general condi-

◄ A Buchenwald survivor, stripped of individuality and self respect, meets his American liberators.

tion was poor. There were people who had poor nourishment – they were likely to get secondary infections and pneumonia.

People have asked how I could possibly stand it, but I think it was because we were young. One didn't think of catching anything oneself. Some of us were afflicted with diarrhoea – and in fact, two of the Barts men got typhus and had to be flown home. We were fit people – the worst thing we could get was probably a sort of dysentery.

There was a crematorium there, and at nearby Bergen there was a room full of watches, one full of human hair, because the people were shaved before they were incinerated. There was another room full of trinkets and things which had been taken from the inmates. **"**

Acting Sergeant Jack Durey, with the 2nd Battalion, Hampshire Regiment, had been taken POW at a canal near the Belgian border, and was subsequently held in **Stalag XXB at Willenberg** *which stood near a tributary of the Vistula. It was in mid-January that a rumbling noise began and a glow appeared on the horizon.*

" A German officer came along the column asking if there was a padre who would volunteer to stay in Marienberg with the POW hospital there. I had been in the *Stalag* some time, as I had been put forward for the next repatriation board with a duodenal ulcer and bronchitis problems. Although, at the time, feeling well, it was the depth of winter and I

▼ The 13,000 unburied bodies at Belsen have been interred. Now the clothes they had on arrival at the camp must be sorted – and used.

did not consider my prospects very highly on a forced march across Germany.

It seemed to me that, if I could get to the hospital in Marienberg, I might fare better than with the column. The idea to those around me was ridiculous. Take a chance with the Russians? No way. However, two elected to try with me, and so, as the column moved off, we slipped through the hedgerow out of sight. When all were gone, we emerged and set off for Marienberg.

The hospital was a large old house in its own grounds, with gates at the entrance and a tree either side. Between the trees was stretched a banner made of three sheets pinned together, showing a red cross either side of some Russian wording in between.

There were several doctors – one British, one French, one Belgian and a South African dentist. The medics were carrying the bed patients down to the basement and had barely finished when shells started coming over – but not close. The walking sick, several medics and ourselves had to settle for the two air-raid shelters that ran either side of several huts in the grounds. The shelters,

allowing room to only stand side-by-side, had an air vent half way along, and a deep hole dug into the side and down as a latrine, with chlorine disinfectant, that was choking. We supposed that within 12-24 hours we would know if we had a future of not.

The fact was that Marienberg was the last town before Danzig, and so the battle raged above us for seven days. We were trapped there without food, water or exercise. It was an awful experience that I cannot write about, but only one got wounded and one other killed. Eventually, tanks could be heard and firing died down. After a brief deathly silence, we were called out. It was painful to move, but outside the gate stood an enormous tank, a Russian officer conferred with the doctors and sheepskin-clad infantry peered about with sub-machine guns – but the atmosphere was victorious. The Russians had nothing to offer us, but allowed the medics from the basement to form a foraging party with an escort who eventually returned with a sack of flour, with which we made pancakes of a sort, and with water and our Red Cross food which had been isolated in one of the huts. We made a meal and went to sleep until the following morning, when we cleaned ourselves up as best we could.

With my companions, wandering about the grounds, I found a German heavy machine gun on its side, and three dead Germans immediately above where we had been in

▲ French 'slave labourers' welcome American liberation forces as they arrive in the town of Herforst.

the shelter – a matter of a mere two metres, apparently knocked out by mortar fire. A Russian mortar platoon arrived and set up the largest mortar I had seen right next to the hospital. We thought it was a token of protection, but as soon as they were ready, started firing off at some target across the town. We lent a hand, carrying boxes up from the road, but soon came on the receiving end of heavy artillery fire (I am deaf as a result). The platoon smartly packed up and left. The Germans were mounting a counterattack and we had to round up carts from the locality, load the bed cases and move out, pushing and pulling them.

The journey took several days, during which at least one died from exposure each day, and through this stage of our travels, we were too occupied to notice anything but our efforts. Arriving at a large hospital in Rosenburg, all were taken in except we three – the padre who had volunteered (a Captain King), and the two medics. We were told that no help

was available – we were to go home, but stay on the roads, or be shot. The padre was given a piece of paper with one Russian word written in pencil, to show at check points. After one night in a warehouse, we decided we would fare better if we split up, so, taking a copy of the paper, we three were alone again.

From there we walked to Deutsch Eylau, where we found a group of French POWs. Together we rounded up a stray cow, killed it, cooked some – but were unable to eat it. We saw large numbers of civilian bodies lying spread out across the fields on either side, and some bodies crushed to mere imprints on the roads. At junctions there would be groups of civilians, mostly elderly, as many as 20, sitting or squatting, huddled together. They were dead too, but not shot. Apparently they had frozen to death, waiting for they knew not what. One still had his pipe in his mouth.

From Deutsch Eylau, the next part of the journey took us into Poland. Here there were no bodies and villages were occupied. We were told that leaflets had been dropped telling them to get out for 24 hours, then to come back.

On return, each house had to display a little red flag and a central house had a large one. They were now communists.

One day we caught up with a column of slow-moving German POWs who were a pitiful sight. We had no wish to get involved and perhaps included with them, although by now we knew how to shout *'Ingliski Soyusniki!'* at any approach, while offering our bit of paper. Our caution was soon further justified when one German fell on the wayside. Without any compunction, one of the two Russians following behind, pulled a pistol and shot him through the head when his companion took the dead man's disc and wrote down his details in a notebook. We followed the column for several hours and counted 14 shot in the same way. We decided that some fell out, not from exhaustion, but as a deliberate act of suicide. Eventually we arrived at Thorne and stayed the night in the main railway station. We moved on again until we came to Warsaw. Through all this, we had no idea of direction, but continued as directed at the various checkpoints on presentation of our piece of paper. At Warsaw we were again billeted with civilians and stayed for three days in a suburb.

Unfortunately, one of my companions was unable to continue. His boots were completely worn out, and his feet were in a bad way, so we left him there in the good hands of our hosts and did the next part to Lublin.

Here we were taken to a railway goods siding where we were taken over by three American civilians who gave us a K ration and handed us a cigarette apiece. They apologised for the circumstances and we

bedded down for the night on straw. The next morning, with others assembled there of various nationalities, we boarded a troop train.

Each wagon had a small stove in the centre and there was a small amount of coal. A sack of dried bread pieces was also there. The train journey took nearly a week, with one stop at Tarnapol, where we received a large bowl of soup. We were also transferred to another wagon because the fierce blizzard we were travelling through had ripped the roof loose, and we had been holding it down by attaching scarves etc to the hooks. We arrived in Odessa, where we were given a delousing and a shower, then were taken to a British boat that had a Red Cross boat alongside, transferring new uniforms and clothing.

As an NCO, I was at the head of the group, having been called out by names and numbers taken earlier, when a brass band playing *Colonel*

◄ Jack Durey – one of a group of Willenberg POWs who survived the crossfire of Germany's last-ditch attacks to return to Britain from Odessa.

► The representative of the SS Supreme Commander, Karl Wolfe, surrenders German forces in Italy.

▼ Major Lisanori of the Japanese Twenty-eighth Army surrenders in the Sittang area of Burma – one of the last pockets of resistance.

Bogey arrived with a few more strays behind. At the head of these was Captain King, the padre. Naturally he took precedence and half way up the gangway he turned and put up two fingers in a victory sign, saying 'I beat you after all.' He was a fine man and an inspiration.

During our journey via Port Said, Naples to offload Italians, and Marseilles to offload French, we joined a convoy at Gibraltar, and docked at Liverpool. There was a platform with the mayor and dignitaries, a large band playing and a huge crowd on the quayside. I believe we were the first POWs to return. 🙶

Trooper Jack Border of the 22nd Dragoons had miraculously survived the D-Day assault, in which he had been a wireless operator/loader in a flail tank. Moving to scout cars, he followed the Allied advance up to Holland, where he spent the last part of the war, just south of Nijmegen.

🙶 In May I was stood down – we were resupplying, but on the 2nd May one of our sergeants was killed, the last one of ours to be killed during the war from our squadron.

Then the news came that it was all

over, and there was just a flood of relief. Nobody had wanted to go on, we had been through a miserable winter that year – it had been so cold. I had never felt so cold in all my life.

In the towns there was euphoria – flowers, people cheering – but all this really belonged to the men who had gone before – they had done the hard work.

Our tanks were handed over in June because the 22nd Dragoons were going to be disbanded. The first thing the officers did – because we were a cavalry regiment – was to swan off to get some horses. I'd opened my mouth and had told one of the officers that I used to ride, and another of my colleagues said that he was a blacksmith, so the next thing we know, we are looking after 21 horses, even though I was a driver. I still had my scout car and was billeted with a German family where the mother had lost her husband and the daughter's husband was a POW somewhere – and of course, we were in their home.

The first night, I don't think I shut my eyes. We had been forced on to

▼ **The now famous 'A-bomb Dome' stands as one of few recognizable landmarks in stricken Hiroshima.**

them, and I quite thought they would get at us because of all the tragedies they had probably faced because of the Allies.

But they were no different from us. We're all human beings, after all's said and done.

I stayed in Germany from June to the end of the year before being shipped home, and then on to Egypt and Palestine – but that's another story. 🙶

Stoker Bill (Chalky) White survived the sinking of his landing craft in the Channel late in 1944 and was then sent out to the Pacific, where he was when the Japanese surrendered in summer 1945. Following the bombing of Hiroshima, he and some other crewmen went to see the site of the first A-bomb.

🙶 I was on the mine-laying cruiser HMS *Manxman*, which was the fastest ship in the Royal Navy. I went up to Tokyo and went to look at Hiroshima about three months after the bomb had been dropped - and I couldn't believe the sight.

It was devastating. We didn't know anything about the bomb - we had no idea what an atomic weapon could do, and we had picked up photos from Hong Kong, taken more or less directly after the explosion had occurred.

When we went ashore in Japan, all the Japanese would bow to us. They had surrendered - the very thing the Emperor had always said they wouldn't do.

Hiroshima looked like a hurricane

had gone through, followed by a fire. I thought, 'How could one bomb do this - just one bomb?' We didn't discuss it because we were so glad the war was over, but when I saw Tokyo, it was just as bad - and that had only been fire-bombed and not touched by nuclear bombs.

You know, nobody had warned us or spoken about radiation. It was just an atomic bomb that had ended the war. People say it was a dreadful thing to do, but you can only die once - it doesn't matter how, and of course war is total war. Women and children are involved. This is what some people don't seem to recognise. The bomb saved many many lives. Can you imagine what would have happened if we had invaded Japan?

I wouldn't have missed the war for the world. It let me come to terms with myself and it taught me discipline - how to live. The Navy, the ship, was a home. We were always together. I had joined up at 17, prompted by my brother who had recently joined. I went to Lewisham where they asked me how old I was. I had said 18. They said not, but if I came with a birth certificate, I could then prove I was. So I went home and, with my young sister's help, I altered it and then went back. I spotted an old petty officer wearing thick glasses, so I pushed it under his nose, he took one look at it, and I was in. It was the best thing I ever did. **"**

Able Seaman Gunner Len O'Keefe was aboard the destroyer HMS Rotherham, which had been involved in the Fourteenth Army's taking of Rangoon, when news came of the liberation of Europe. While the ship was docked at Trincomalee, Ceylon, where the fleet was based, Lord Mountbatten came to address the men.

" Lord Louis Mountbatten, the C-in-C South East Asia Command, came aboard, stood on the fo'c'sle, said, 'Gather round, lads,' and thanked us for our past efforts. He said the next job was the invasion of Singapore.

Well, the dropping of the atom bombs altered everything, and turned the invasion planning into one big rescue operation, because of the plight of our people who were Japanese prisoners of war.

As we left Ceylon, the fleet made an impressive sight. It included merchant ships and two big white hospital ships with their distinctive red crosses. During the voyage we were despatched with two motor launches to take the surrender of Singapore Naval Base.

Our first lieutenant said, 'Let's show the Japs smart British tars,' and asked us to dress in our No 1s, which was our best tropical going-ashore rig.

▲ **Able Seaman Len O'Keefe, right, and a crewmate from HMS *Rotherham*, which had the honour of being the first RN ship into Singapore Naval Base.**

▼ **C-in-C of the Japanese 10th Zone Fleet, Admiral Fukudome, seated left, surrendered his command to the British at the same time as Lord Mountbatten took the surrender in Singapore town.**

As we steamed up the Jahore Straits, at that moment we never trusted the Japs, so the 4.7 in guns were loaded, but trained fore and aft. I can see the lads now, in line of the fo'c'sle – the water as flat as a pond with only our bow wave and those of the two MLs disturbing the water. It was so peaceful – but we were all thinking the same thing. Were those 15 in naval guns going to open up on us?

Thankfully nothing shattered the peace and as we came alongside, there were Japs with white armbands to take our lines and help us tie up.

Some of us went ashore as landing parties and met some of our POWs from Changi Jail. They were overwhelmed to see us.

One man hugged me and said he was a regular soldier who had finished his tour of duty and they were going back to the UK when war was declared, so his regiment had to stay. He was taken prisoner and had been away from home nearly 10 years. He hugged me again and said, 'It's OK now – the Navy is here.' And he started crying. We took them back to the ship and the lads gave them their rum tots and food.

In the warehouses were found crates of cutlery, plates, cups etc – all untouched by the Japs who had no use for them, so every mess deck was supplied with new cutlery and china. Some lads even brought back a piano and asked permission to bring it aboard – eventually we presented it to the fleet canteen in Trincomalee.

Our captain, Captain Beeks, DSO, RN, took over a large house nearby and I was detailed one morning to don my best uniform and stand outside the house. A big black car pulled up in the driveway and out stepped the Japanese Admiral, Fukudome, the C-in-C. He walked down to me and I saluted, which he returned, then I took him inside and handed him over to our chief petty gunnery officer, who took him to the captain and other officers to sign the surrender. **"**

1946
THE VERDICT OF HISTORY

First-hand memories from the early days of an uneasy peace

Once the euphoria of victory had disappeared, the Allied powers faced enormous problems. Vast areas of Europe and Asia had been devastated, economies disrupted and populations dispersed. What was needed was a period of settled peace, during which recovery could begin. In the event, despite the hopes expressed through the new United Nations, 'peace' was, for many, a misnomer.

In eastern Europe, for example, the Soviets imposed their own rule and created new national boundaries as Stalin formed a buffer between the USSR and the West. This inevitably alarmed Western governments, who interpreted the spread of Soviet influence as expansionism, with Western Europe as the ultimate objective. Instead of withdrawing to allow liberated and occupied territories to recover at their own pace, Britain and the USA found that they had to remain to confront the menace.

Nor was the spread of communism confined to Europe. In the Far East nationalist pressures for an end to pre-war empires seemed to be dependent on communist support. As revolts developed in Indochina, Malaya, Indonesia and the Philippines, it was easy to see them as part of an orchestrated campaign for world domination. This was a simplistic view, but out of it grew a new confrontation and new wars.

BRAVE NEW WORLD?

The men and women who won and lost the war are arriving home to pick up the threads of their lives – but the post-war world is not that simple.

In Post-war Europe, where the very fabric of society had been torn apart, the people faced new hardships which not even aid from the United Nations and the victorious powers could alleviate. The victorious Allies discussed peace treaties with their erstwhile enemies at Potsdam in July 1945, and the details of settlements with some states – Italy, Romania, Bulgaria, Finland and Hungary – were hammered out during 1946. But the important question of treaties with Germany and Austria was delayed by this, and by the time they came up for consideration, Europe had changed. The Soviets had pre-empted any settlement by altering the borders of Poland and engineering communist governments in eastern Europe, and this, coupled to intransigence over the future of Germany, made the Western Allies cautious. On 5 March 1946, Winston Churchill spoke at Fulton, Missouri, of an 'Iron curtain across Europe' – it was a powerful symbol of a new reality.

Margrit Harmsworth (neé Verbarg), was 13 years old in 1946, and was living in the village of Lavelsloh in Lower Saxony. Having lost her father, who died in a Russian POW camp during the war, and her mother through medical neglect in 1948, she married an English serviceman and settled in England.

" It took a long time for life in the village to get back to anything like normality. For many years afterwards I never really adjusted to the fact that my father was dead. Because he was in Russia, so far away, whenever I heard that someone was coming to see me, I would immediately think: 'It's him.'

To be honest, conditions had got really bad from 1944 onwards, and it was awful after the war. We had bread made from corn – it was yellow and fell to bits in your hand – in fact just about everything was made from corn. My mother could work on the farms, and for a day's work she would get perhaps a dozen eggs or a bit of streaky bacon.

When the British were there, after we went back to school, school-children got this American aid, I think – baked beans or chocolate drink, or something. So, you couldn't say we had nothing to eat. But I remember one particular morning, my mum had no butter, so she put black coffee and sugar on my bread, just to moisten it. Anyway, this particular day, a doctor came from the town to examine who was in need of aid. And I was quite bonny, in comparison to some of the others, so he put me down as not needing aid. But I explained to him that I was only given this bread with black coffee to take to school, so he changed his mind.

Now, before the war, my father worked as a butcher, and he had his own slaughter house in the back garden and he did his own sausage-making, etc. We had a big garden. I used to work in the slaughter house with him. I was only six years old. When he was slaughtering a cow I would hold its tail. I was the boy he didn't have then – my brother was only a baby then. My mother would work in the shop and do the house-work and I was just a little girl running around.

The slaughter house was sold along with the house during the war, and we had to move into a flat. To start with my father worked in Hanover as a butcher until he was called up for the army.

After the war, you couldn't buy anything. My mother carried on

◄ In the American sector of post-war Britain, a Soviet tank rusticates and settles into the landscape, used by local children to stage a puppet show. Children in the new Europe would need all the light relief they could get.

► A Frankfurt woman waits for the US truck drivers to dump the forces' unwanted food from the cold store to supplement a meagre diet. Inset, Margrit Verbarg (left) with post-war friends.

working on the farms for food. We stayed in the flat until she died, when my brother, my sister and I were sent off to different places. I went to my grandparents, to work for them in service. My mother had arranged for my sister to go and live with her sister and my brother went to her brother's.

I must mention the refugees. Now, there was a decree passed, I think it was done in wartime, that the authorities could commandeer one or two rooms in your house, in which they could place refugees. You had no choice. When the displaced persons came after the war from the Western territories, I remember the *Bürgermeister* just coming along and saying that we had to give up rooms to these people. I believe, actually, that this law still stands. A number of these people actually settled in the village and their families still live there. There was certainly some friction. Human nature being human nature, people would claim they had more than they really had, before they lost it. So, they would sometimes say, (particularly the children), 'Well, we were better off than you.' So, there was quite a bit of resentment against the refugees.

The biggest problem was that, though all the livestock was there,

and the people still had their farms, nothing was worth anything, and the transport system was not working. Money had completely lost its value. You could get things with butter or other foods.

After my mother died, we got orphan money – DM 30 a month; this was 'half-orphan' allowance. If it had been known that my father was dead, we would have got DM 60. This was the new money, of course. This was after currency reform, in 1948. As I remember, the currency reform worked like this. I had 1,000 Marks in the bank – that was 1,000 old Marks, Hitler's money. Now everybody was given a basic 60 new Marks in exchange for 60 old Marks plus, if you had savings, 600 Marks of that. So, that meant for 660 old Marks, I got only 60 Marks in return, and I got nothing for the other 400. My mother died a week after the reform, so we got her 60 Marks, but a week later, we had to pay for the funeral. My 60 Marks went straight away on a black dress. I remember going into a shop in Lavelsloh. It was a great feeling to suddenly have money, with which you could buy things, but I paid out 12 Marks for a headscarf and the dress material cost 21 Marks.

The Germans, particularly from that generation, have always been keen savers, but they've always had in the back of their mind the fear that the value of their money could suddenly be taken away. They saw it after the First World War, then after the Second, and recently, of course, the same thing happened to the East Germans. "

George Clare was a Royal Artillery Bombardier attached as an interpreter to the control Commission for Germany (British Element). He was a second-generation Viennese Jew who had travelled to Britain after the Anschluss. He eventually arrived back in Berlin with the Allies and formed these impressions.

▲ Gustav Rossler, the Nazi Werewolf leader, who tried to perpetuate the Nazi struggle in Czechoslovakia after the war, is made to reveal an arms cache.

▼ Returning German troops arrive in Willingen – exhausted and in many cases too weak to walk.

" I'd been in Berlin before the war and I spoke the language, so I was able to make some comparison when I returned in January 1946. I was first the deputy and then the British representative on a committee that was responsible for seeing that nobody who was a Nazi got back into culture or media life and so was in a position to watch as Germany and Germans emerged from their defeat. When I arrived, my first encounters with post-war Germans were with a heavily defeated people – a people that had lost whatever inner strength they had had – people who were starving and who only wanted to survive. They were quite prepared to lie, provided it would help them to survive.

My feelings towards them were made up neither of hate nor pity, because you cannot hate a whole nation or a city. They pitied themselves so much that no outside pity was actually required – they had brought their state upon themselves.

There wasn't a German left after the war who had ever been a Nazi although I once came across a Waf-

fen SS soldier who was honest and proud enough to admit it. He was a young man who had been conscripted into the SS late in the war and who only wanted to get back to a normal life. It was a rare moment of honesty. Most men would tell you about how they had been passionately in love with a young Jewish girl in the thirties but had had to break off the romance because of the situation. A rough count indicated to me that many times the complete Jewish population must had been in Berlin before the war and all in love with a nice German boy!

There were a few dyed-in-the-wool Nazis left, but these were people that had not committed a crime; they believed in the politics. They would appear before a denazification panel and if they were of no importance they were classified as 'fellow travellers' and given a low-value ration card which only lasted for a short time. It was the German authorities themselves who distributed the rations and the quantity varied. For instance, coal miners in the Ruhr got more than some old biddy in Berlin. Everyone used the black market and most girls knew how to use their bodies to obtain favours from the Western powers. Those who worked for the occupying powers were generally better off.

Berlin at this time was governed by the four powers – the British, Americans, French and the Soviets, and for a time we all got on well, although the Soviets came to Berlin with the most dismal reputation of any nation except, perhaps, the Germans themselves. They had raped and pillaged on the way in and carried on when the war was over.

But slowly they tried to make up for this by convincing the world that they were basically a highly cultured nation. They immediately demonstrated this by getting the cinemas and theatres working again. The Western powers were at first a bit slow on this because they were looking after organizing the ordinary services, from electricity to street-sweeping, but eventually they cottoned on that people who had nothing to eat would forget their hunger pains if they had some good entertainment. And so more and more theatres were opened in the Western sectors.

The early days of the cultural committee did not reflect the tension of the Cold War to come. The Soviet cultural officers were the most highly educated people in all the Control Commissions. They were all university professors who spoke perfect German and who knew the German culture inside out, while we just put in whoever seemed suitable. At first the Soviets selected highly efficient, educated people, who were then part of the so-called 'Leningrad mafia' from Leningrad University, many of whom had actually studied at German universities in their youth – but they were replaced by the Moscow mafia, which was a much stricter regime following the Stalin line. But life in Berlin was changing, people could and would disappear. Second-line anti-communist critics and journalists were kidnapped, never to be seen again.

But in the end, in my view, the Western Allies, particularly the Americans and the British, laid the foundations for the best Germany we have ever had. "

RETURN OF GERMAN POWS

When the European war ended in May 1945, the Allies had nearly seven million German prisoners of war on their hands. Some had been in captivity since 1940, but the vast majority had surrendered in the final battles that destroyed the Reich.

Those in Western hands were generally treated correctly, according to the rules laid down in the Geneva Conventions. Officers were not expected to work; the men were used to clear up war damage or to help on the land. Some, suspected of war crimes, were removed for trial, but the perceived need to return POWs to the Western sectors of Germany as a workforce caused most of this latent manpower to be released by 1947.

The same was not true of POWs in Soviet hands, most of whom were transported east to Siberia. There they were put to work in labour camps and, with little medical care available, many died of disease or exhaustion. The last of the survivors did not return to Germany until 1955.

▥ *Ilse Aschner, 28, an Austrian living in Vienna, had been categorised as 'Jewish' under the terms of the Nazi Nuremberg Laws. After spending the war in exile in Britain, she returned in 1946, and learned of her parents' deportation and extermination. Their flat remained, but a new family had been moved in.*

❝ In England, I began to try and sort out how I could get my family out of Nazi Germany. Although I could never have guessed what fate lay in store for the Jews, I knew that my family had been robbed of any opportunity to work – and with it their livelihood.

At the end of August 1939, my brother turned up completely out of the blue at the vicar's house, where I had found a job as a governess. He

had a briefcase with him, which contained some underclothes. My parents, he said, were only waiting for permission to take their luggage with them – the situation was coming to a head . . .

Shortly afterwards, a postcard arrived from father – from the Dutch border. They had set off, leaving their luggage behind, but the Dutch wouldn't allow them travel across the border because they had German passports. This was 3 September 1939 – the English had just declared war on Germany, and would probably not allow enemy nationals – with German passports – ashore. German passports? They were stamped with a 'J', for God's sake. They were on the run.

About three days later, we managed, with the help of the vicar and his wife, to send a telegram to the Dutch border, explaining that they had an immigration visa.

It arrived too late. Having escaped

▲▲ **A smiling Maj-Gen Diprova, commander of the Russian garrison in Berlin, rides through the city on a T34 tank after the suppression of anti-communist riots, 17 June.**

▲ **The trappings of a divided Berlin are complete – the weather is cold but not as cold as the impending 'Cold War'. The division of Berlin would be just the beginning.**

the German machine of destruction, they were turned back at the border. Jews, sent back to Germany – to certain death.

It was only when the war was over, after returning home from exile, that we were able to piece together what had happened. They had got desperate – no hope of escape, no way of contacting their children – so they returned to the safety of their flat. But a Nazi functionary named Hartl had taken a fancy to their flat and took it over. My parents were removed to one of those infamous mass lodgings for Jews in Vienna's II district, and had to leave all their belongings behind in the 'Aryanised' flat.

They were deported in 1942 to Riga. My father died in July 1942 and my mother was taken further down the line to Stutthof, near Danzig.

We heard nothing, until a few years after the war a huge mass grave was found near Stutthof: just as the Red Army were nearing the camp, the inmates were liquidated and buried in mass graves. Not one witness was allowed to survive.

I knew nothing of all this, when I returned home in 1946. The first thing I did was so seek out our flat. The doorplate read 'Hartl'. I tried to find the concierge, who turned out to be the same woman as before the war. She cried as she told me about the Aryanisation and my parents' disappearance.

Vienna was occupied and divided into four sectors. The flat was in the

Russian sector. I went to the *Kommandatur* and described my case. I lodged my claim with one of the officers and was given a letter to the accommodation office in Vienna. It read: '9 September 1946, USSR-*Kommandatur*, Vienna IV. Attn: Herr Rusa, Accommodation Office.

Until 1939, flat No. 9 in Seisgasse 18, Vienna IV, belonged to the Jew, Gustav Römer, who was evacuated. The flat was then taken over by the Nazi, Hartl. The former owners have the right, on the basis of the enclosed documents, which confirm the authenticity of their claim, to reclaim their flat, since the Nazi occupiers are compelled to leave.'

Herr Rusa at the accommodation office did not agree. 'The way I see it,' he said, 'one can't simply dump the present occupants on the street. Suitable alternative accommodation has to be found for them.' I was to be grateful that I'd found a place to stay with a girlfriend of mine, who had been bombed out – how many other Viennese were as fortunate as me to find a roof over the heads? I would have to be patient – it might take years until a suitable flat had been found for Herr Hartl.

It was not until 1953 that I could finally move out of the dreadful lodging room where I was living, and could move into my own flat with my husband and child, without any help from the state nor any public office. On my parents flat, however, the 'Hartl' doorplate remained until January 1988. ❞

▶4 April 1950: the people of Budapest celebrate the fifth anniversary of release from German occupation – presided over by portraits of Lenin, Stalin and party leader, Rakosi.

▼An uneasy co-existence reigns at the Allied *Kommandatura* Berlin, as US and Russian flags are lowered at dusk.

THE TRUMAN DOCTRINE

On 12 March 1947, US President Harry Truman pledged 'to support free peoples who are resisting attempted subjugation by armed minorities or by outside pressure'. Known as the 'Truman Doctrine', this was a far cry from the euphoria of 1945, when President Roosevelt had promised to pull US troops out of Europe 'within two years'.

What had changed was the Americans' view of the Soviet Union. In 1945, Stalin was a valued ally and the Americans had presumed that he would help establish a new 'world order', dedicated to peace. That perception soon changed. In Europe, the spread of communism in countries occupied by the Soviets persuaded the West that Stalin's aim was to dominate the entire continent. At the same time, in the Far East, the connection between communism and insurgency suggested that a more global threat existed. The Truman Doctrine was an indication that the US would stand firm – communism would be 'contained'.

◉ *Miroslav (Mirro) Mansfeld had escaped to Britain in 1940 and fought with the RAF as both a day and night-fighter – until his chance came to return to his native Czechoslovakia after the war. His first posting, after arriving to euphoric greetings, was to the Czech Air Ministry in a country now under Russian control.*

❝ In Czechoslovakia we had President Beneš back, and everything was going alright – but they noticed that there were a lot of communists about. They had stopped the American Army from taking over Prague, and they stopped at Pilzen. They couldn't go on to Prague because the Russian Army was to take over – they were to be celebrated as the liberators of Czechoslovakia.

So, in 1945, when we got back, everybody said, 'Don't worry about the communists – next year is the election and everything will be alright.' We said we would wait for it – and then a year later, in May, I believe it was, the election came. But prior to that, the Russian Army, with tanks, went from Austria to Eastern Germany and Poland, through Czechoslovakia, and that was enough for the people to recognise the communists.

The communists won about 40 votes in the new election and Gottwald, the ultra-communist, became Prime Minister, Beneš stayed as President and Jan Masaryk, the son of the first president, was Foreign Secretary, as he had been in exile.

Suddenly communism had started. We didn't have what you might call an 'education', but in a general way there was an officer on every station who looked after the welfare of all the officers. The welfare was to make sure of who was communist and not communist, and make sure that the station commander led it in a way the communists wanted.

I didn't become a communist – many of us didn't. When they asked us, we'd say, 'No thank you very much.' I was brought up without being political, because I joined up when I was not yet 18, and in Czechoslovakia the air force never voted – we were non-political. We said as much and that we were not going to become political here.

There were some chaps who didn't go and fight, and stayed at home. They knew they were a little bit disadvantaged here, so they joined the communist party and they started to go up and up. Because I was so open against the communists – I would say, 'I'm not a communist. I don't want to be' – my promotion was stopped for a year. I had come home as a first lieutenant, then my promotion to captaincy was stopped and I noticed other chaps who were younger suddenly becoming captain. This was because they had signed up with the communists. Even my very close friend became a communist. His mother had been in a concentration camp and became a communist over there. When my friend Frank came home, he naturally went to see his mother and he became a communist. Then, suddenly had had promotion. He came to me and said, 'Because I am in the party, I know you are not a communist – you are a socialist.' I said, 'There is no other party.' 'Yes, but you should have been a communist.' I said, 'Now look, you either shut up and we are friends – or if you start talking, you can get out.' That was that. He meant well. He wanted to let me know that there

▲Waste not, want not – Berliners dismantle the *Spandauer Stahlindustrie* factory following its use repairing freight cars for the railways.

▶In the new Czech communist regime under Gottwald, a column of the workers' army on the *Karlsbrucke* in Prague – their task, to police communist rule.

could be someone spying.

Before the war, when the Germans came in, you could speak openly in Czech against anything the Germans had done. My mother was born in the Austrian Empire, and I was too, but by the time I went to school, it was the Czechoslovakian Republic. The old people knew repression – and once more the Germans came and you couldn't speak again. But in 1946, after the election, you couldn't even speak to your friend about it. You just kept mum. The difference was also that in 1945, the same as before the war, people across the street would wave and greet you – and after 1946, everybody just walked, didn't see anybody else. People were very frightened –

it was the time to refurbish the squadron, make it operational on Mosquitoes and train the rest of the people. There I was, flight commander. We had the living quarters for the airmen there on the airfield. As I looked around, I came across a picture of Tomas Masaryk, the former president, and I put it in all three huts. Suddenly an officer comes to me and says 'Look, I am the Welfare Officer here, and you can't have that photo there.' I asked why not. 'Because he is dead – he was president before, but you can't have it there.' I said it made no difference, I hadn't got anything else to put up. 'No, there is the prime Minister – you can have his picture, but not this one.' As luck would have it,

in Prague, I saw a picture of President Beneš, and behind him was the picture of President Masaryk. I immediately took three of them, had them framed and put them in the barracks.

Come 1948, the communists were taking over more and more, and there was no escape from it. We had a Russian colonel on the station who was a very good pilot, and he kept an eye on us. Of course, he didn't come direct to us, but he said to the Welfare Officer that he didn't like this and that . . . as flight commander I could feel this.

Eventually they even took the pictures out of the living quarters – I didn't put any other pictures there – I didn't want Gottwald there.

I remember before the war, when I went to Russia to collect aeroplanes there, when you spoke to the people, you saw that they thought quite differently. I was on a train once, and this chap was trying to have a conversation with me, as to why I was not a communist. He said, 'This is all mine,' pointing to all the land. I said, 'Go on, then, burn this field.' He asked what I meant. 'Go on, if it is yours, go on and burn it.' 'Oh, I can't. The commissar would be angry.' 'There you are, it's communal – it's not yours.'

Another time when I was in Russia a girl invited me to meet her family there. I was trying to learn Russian as it is a little like Czech, and her sister asked me, 'What party are you?' I said I was not in any party at all. She said that I must be a very bad boy if I was not in a party at all. I said, 'We have a restaurant, and all people, all parties come there. As we make more money, we buy a house, and then we start again. Now half the street is ours, plus the restaurant.' The other girl – the one who

they didn't know who was on the other side. There was just one year after the war when people could say what they liked to their oppressors – then, a year later, it was 'Yes, master'.

We had a reunion of the ex-wartime flyers in Prague, and Jan Masaryk was there as a guest of honour. He gave us a speech – not a bolshi speech. He didn't like the regime, even though he was the Foreign Secretary. At the end he said, 'Brothers, if anything happens, you know where to go,' and he gestured with his thumbs up behind him. He meant Great Britain.

At the time of the election we had been in England, and on our return

1946

DECEMBER

2 Five British soldiers killed by bombs in Palestine

19 French garrisons in Vietnam under attack from Viet Minh

1947

FEBRUARY

10 Peace treaties signed in Italy, Romania, Bulgaria, Finland, Hungary

MARCH

4 Treaty of Dunkirk signed between Great Britain and France

12 Announcement of the 'Truman Doctrine' by USA

MAY

23 Mountbatten's proposal to partition India accepted

JUNE

5 George Marshall, US Secretary of State, outlines aid programme to Europe: the Marshall Plan

JULY

21 Dutch colonial troops attack Indonesian nationalists

AUGUST

15 Pakistan and India become independent

SEPTEMBER

1 Hungary votes in Communists

NOVEMBER

16 British troops start to leave Palestine

29 UN passes resolution to partition Palestine

had invited me – immediately asked, 'Could I come back with you – to Czechoslovakia?' Suddenly communism was out!

In 1947 they were stabilising the communist system. You could hardly speak. You could see the people who were communists started to speak differently. Eventually one of the colonels who had been in England, and who wanted to be a general (they had passed him over too) flew to Pilzen. Being the higher ranking officer, he always called me Mansfeld, but this time, because he was also a communist, he called me Mirro, my christian name. He landed at the station and called me to the aircraft and said, 'Mirro, here, I have it – you are a colonel. Just sign for the Communist Party. You will be Station Commander here.' I said, 'Look, Colonel, I will have to think about it. I have only just heard what you've told me.' I was a staff captain then, and this would be a jump of two ranks, to lieutenant-colonel to colonel. He said, 'Don't leave it long.' But just before that, in 1947, we had decided we were not staying. We started saying, 'That's not for us, here.' We knew where to go – Masaryk had told us. The station adjutant was a very good friend of mine, who was here. I flew with him in the Mosquito from England to Czechoslovakia. I went to him and asked him if he had seen it, that Colonel So-and-so was here. He said, 'That's it,' and he went to the safe,

opened it and took out the passports. He gave me mine and said, 'Now we have to leave.'

Unfortunately, before us was General Janaczec, who was the C-in-C Czechoslovak Air Force in England during the war – and they caught him trying to get out. So that route was finished. I went to Prague and contacted people I knew were going out. One of them lived in a block of flats with a concierge – an old lady. I used to go there, and she would greet me and say it was alright to go up. One day, I had lost contact with the people who were going to take us out, and I went to see this chappie to see if he had any better contact there. I went to open the gate, and there was the old woman. 'Where are you going?' I was amazed, what was happening? 'I am going to see Major So-and-so.' 'He's not at home.' Good Lord! Still, I said. 'It's alright. His wife is in, and I'll go and speak to her.' Suddenly, she grabbed me by the hand and said, 'Don't go there!' I said thank you, and I left. There were two men from the secret police waiting with their pistols for anyone to come in. The major had already been taken to jail. You see, the people speak like that because they are afraid, but when it comes to the heart, they will give. Several times in my life I have been near to death, but that was the nearest, even though I've had a crash in an aeroplane. Suddenly my heart stopped when she told me not to go. As soon as we crossed in, we went to the police in Germany and they took the passports and pistols and reported us to the Americans because we were in the American zone. The Americans interrogated us and when we explained that we were all ex-RAF, they sent us to a house with all these refugees.

During the war I had been in Max Aitken's squadron – the *Daily Express* chappie. I wrote him a postcard – he was an MP then, which said, 'I just want you to know that I'm not a communist. I'm sure you are not surprised.' Well, the RAF didn't know about our going into Germany and Max Aitken informed the RAF here and they sent to all the camps to find out who the ex-RAF chaps were. They took us out of the camps and flew us free of charge to England. I was one of those who wanted to stay in. Max Aitken said I should come to the Daily Express, because he thought with it going on sale on the continent, I may be useful to him there, but I said, 'No, not yet. There may be a fight, and I want to be right in there from the start.' I was then ten years in the Air Force. I never thought I would be 52 years 'in exile' here!

" Stalin, at the Yalta Conference, which was attended by

WarStories

As the British took over the now 'liberated' towns of Germany, they commandeered accommodation as necessary. One German woman remembers a group of Brits taking over her apartment on the fourth floor of a block. Her mother was deferential to their commanding officer so, although other flats were a shambles, hers was immaculate, except for one small problem – the result of the only communal toilet facilities being in the basement. The preserving jars in which her mother kept conserves for her father, had been put to quite a different use.

President Roosevelt and Churchill, said that he thought that 50,000 of the general staff and officers should be gathered together and summarily executed. He wasn't joking. President Roosevelt said, 'Oh well, perhaps 49,000.' But Churchill said that he'd rather be taken out into the garden and shot at once than be party to such an iniquity. But the Russians persisted, almost until the end, saying that there should be no trial – these men were criminals, and they should be executed the moment they were caught.

I think that the trials fulfilled their purpose. No doubt, when we first initiated the idea of these trials and of laying down the rules of international law in this way, we were a bit starry-eyed, and we hoped that all the great powers would cooperate together in enforcing international law in the future. But you know, it often happens that parliament passes a law, and it isn't universally obeyed.

The Nuremberg Tribunal was specifically called a military tribunal. It's true that the Russians were the only people who wore uniform on it. None of the other judges were soldiers – they were all professional

◀▼ Although fraternising is banned, the laws of supply and demand prevail and many former BDM devotees gladly keep company with the conquerors.

▼ The Nuremberg Trials: what is left of the Nazi top brass sit in the dock as their war crimes are recounted and assessed.

judges in their own country. But the Russians were very largely guided by the British and the Americans in regard to the procedures and the actual part they played. They were decent and honourable men, and worked in close co-operation with them, except in regard to one matter – the murders in the Katyn Forest.

They insisted on alleging that the Germans were responsible for the murder of these Polish officers in the Katyn Forest. It had already become a matter of grave doubt whether this was the case. There were those who said that it was the Russians who'd murdered them, because they were members of the old Polish officer class, and hostile to communism.

I asked Maxwell Fyfe, who was my deputy, to look into this. He thought the evidence left the whole thing in doubt, and that we should not include it in the indictment. Both the American chief prosecutor and I saw the Russian chief prosecutor and said we must stop this – but the Russians insisted on putting it in, and in order to avoid a complete breakdown between us, which would have had repercussions far beyond the trial, we had to accept.

I was rather surprised at the appearance of the defendants. I thought, 'Well, if I'd seen these people on the Clapham omnibus, I wouldn't have looked at them twice.' I think this was true of all of them, except perhaps Hess and Ribbentrop, who both looked pretty miserable creatures – and Göring, who looked a very remarkable personality (not as he looked during the war in earlier days, because he'd lost a great deal of weight – he'd been kept off drugs). Nonetheless, he was a dominating personality, and in a sense, all through the proceedings, although he only took an active part in them when he was giving his evidence, he did dominate the court. He was the outstanding personality in the court, and you know, sometimes in the course of a long trial like that, lasting over 200 days as it did, something would go wrong. You would ask a witness a question, and the answer you expected to get was 'yes' – and the witness would answer 'no'. And at that point, you had to be very careful not to catch Göring's eye. He was sitting at the corner of the front row, and if you glanced across at him, or caught his eye when there was an incident like that, he would raise an eyebrow and shake his head in a rather smiling way, and it would be difficult not to smile back. He was a very remarkable personality, and in some ways a blackguard – but certainly an engaging blackguard.

▲ German citizens are made to attend showings of filmed Nazi atrocities – in this case, only seeing can be believing in the process of denazification.

◄ Tom McCarthy – a fascinated bystander at the Nuremberg war crimes trials.

Grenadier Tom (Boysie) McCarthy volunteered for special duties in 1945 and joined the British War Crimes Executive for duty at the Nuremberg war trials. It was a posting that offered him the perfect platform for his undesirable skills for blackmarketeering and procurement!

❝ For us squaddies there were many females because they had lost so many of their men – their husbands and lovers. Although we were mixed in age we all needed women. But where were we going to find them? One day I was at the railway station which was about six miles from our camp outside Nuremberg and I saw all these girls waiting for trains that would never arrive.

I couldn't believe my eyes – all these girls, just standing around. I went back to Zirndorf, where we were based, and was talking to a driver about girls, so I suggested to him that we take a lorry and drive down to the station because there was a load of girls there. 'If we take fags and chocolate and stuff they'll

and into the kitchen, I asked the cook what it was. She told me it was a camp for the Jews. It was odd, I suppose. I didn't expect to see anything now the war was over, but then she pointed to a lamp shade and to the soap and pointed to the camp. I couldn't believe it. The shade was made of skin and the soap from bodies and bones. I thought, 'She's got to be kidding . . . God, I've been washing my hands in this.' She had put a meal on the table but I couldn't take it. I went outside and spewed. Nothing like this had been mentioned to us, not even at the trials. How could people do such a thing? It taught me a lesson. It was the only time I thought, right, I should be in uniform because, after the war, I had thought it had all been so futile. **"**

do anything for a night's sleep.' It was so very cold down there.

We took a three-tonner down with a couple of mates. At the station, I took one platform and my mate another; he didn't have much luck but I'd picked up a bit of German and got three or four girls. At first they looked a bit dubious, but it was always better to get two together as they were friends and were easier to talk to. We took them back to the gymnasium and had a party! We gave them fags and things and they had a good breakfast in the morning and we took them back to the station. It soon built up – we were going there three or four times a week. The older guys had to pay more because they had no chance of getting a nice looking girl. It was all done with cigarettes – cigarettes were money, it was the currency.

I was interested in the trials and when I got the time I would go and watch the proceedings from the balcony. The Germans would be in two long pews, like in church. I'd watch them – they looked pale and yellow. You could listen in English. All our fellows were there: Neave, Birkett, Shawcross, Maxwell Fyfe and Elwyn Jones. Looked after by the Snowdrops – the Americans – about 21 Nazis were on trial, Göring, Hess, Ribbentrop, Dönitz – all on trial for their lives. I thought at the time that they really had no chance. But one day, Göring was wiping the floor with them, especially the American prosecutor, Jackson. He didn't know what day it was! It was Shawcross who jumped to the defence of the American and started having a go.

Overall like, it was quite strange

because I thought the Germans were really geared up to fight – good fighters, almost the equals of us, because I thought we were the best but then, they had lost. But what had we done? We sort of stuck an atom bomb on Japan, burnt Leipzig to pieces, all sorts of atrocities. Stalin was committing genocide – all these crimes against humanity that we were trying **them** for and we were doing the same sort of thing ourselves. The only time I ever saw the Germans get scared was when they were shown the films of Belsen and that. They would show it on a screen in the court and they would force the Germans to watch the terrible scenes. The Germans would try to avert their eyes. I think this really got home to them. It was right there in front of their eyes and they realised that their number was up. That finished them.

When it was over, one weekend I was sent for by the colonel, who I didn't get on with, and was told that I was going down to Bohemia to beat at a shooting party. I didn't know what he was talking about. It turned out to be a wild boar shoot with a baron who was now great friends with the Allies. The house was like a Scottish baronial house and everybody was wearing God-knows-what – it must have been traditional dress. So off we went to do our beating. It was awful but at the end of the day we went up to the castle for something to eat.

First of all I went for a short walk over a small hill. I could see a camp with towers and barbed wire and that. I didn't think it was too strange, but when I went back to the castle

▲▲ Gatow Airport, Berlin: a British four-engine Avro York aircraft is prepared to fly out from another airlift mission.

▲ Back home – to a strange new life – ex-POWs from the Far East disembark at Southampton docks.

▶ Sign here. With back pay settled and discharge papers, a new civilian is about to be born.

James Palmer, having done his share of work in the clearing of Belsen and general 'peace-keeping' in post-war Germany, finally learned the day of his release from the army. He had served in the Royal Tank Regiment in France, North Africa, Burma, Italy and Germany – at last he was to come home for good.

" At last the date of my release was determined. I was due for demobilisation on 23 January 1946.

The major sent for me and asked me to stay for a while, but I had had enough and couldn't get home fast enough. The night before I was to leave, the lads in the unit threw a big party. We were sleeping in a stable and had organised the horse stalls as individual sleeping rooms. It was all cosy and warm, and there was plenty of room. In the centre of the stable we had placed long wooden tables and had scrounged some pot-bellied iron stoves which we had roaring all day long. The German prisoners had been made barrack orderlies and had to see that there was plenty of fuel.

The night of the party was well organised and the cooks had done a good job. There were cakes, tins of fruit, sausages, ham, roast chicken and barrels of wine and lager. Everyone got stoned and finished up dressed as jungle natives wearing the straw from around the wine bottles as skirts and completely covered with cocoa and boot blacking. The major came in about midnight and when he saw most of us playing Tarzan on the stable rafters, he had one drink and left us to it.

The next morning I left with about ten other lads who had arrived from other units, and our lorry was decked with flags and a huge banner saying, 'England next stop!'

The white cliffs of Dover got nearer and nearer, and in no time we were walking down the gang-plank and boarding a train going north. Across the border into Scotland we went. All through the night we travelled and in the early hours of the morning we pulled into Glasgow.

What the hell were we doing here?

When we got out at the station, we were given some breakfast and then had to march through a warehouse and hand in our webbing equipment, our side arms and the greater part of our gear. We were left with our small valise and our personal possessions and our kit packs, and were back on the train by mid-afternoon. We started off the way we had come.

What a bloody organisation. We had been taken all the way to Scotland to hand in our equipment, and now we were going all the way back to Ashton Barracks to be demobbed.

It was nearly midnight when we arrived at London Road Station, Manchester, and a convoy of lorries was lined up to take us to Ashton Barracks. We arrived at about one o'clock in the morning, and were told that we would be demobbed the following morning. We were blazing!

Here we were in Manchester, and only a bus ride away from home, and they were keeping us another night because the staff had gone to bed! We played hell, and eventually the staff were routed out of their beds and, with a lot of moaning and groaning, agreed to get us demobbed. It was a bloody shame for them, to work at night – stuff them!

In spite of the bad start, I must admit that once they got going, the system worked beautifully. By the time we had finished, we had a cardboard box full of civvy clothes and

we stood there in our battledress while the box was tied up with string.

Those of us who lived in the Manchester area got a lift, then we drifted off in twos and threes. I was with another lad from Wythenshawe and Piccadilly was deserted at three o'clock in the morning. The warehouses in Portland Street were gaunt shells after the terrific bombing and the area of Piccadilly was an open space. A taxi was prowling around and we flagged him down. We piled in, but the driver kept muttering that Wythenshawe was a long way and he was tired. When he pulled up at Benchill, he said that that was as far as he was going. He demanded £5 fare, which we thought was a bit thick, and while Joe was arguing the toss, I let his back tyres down and I gave him £3, which I thought was fair. We scuttled off, leaving him cursing and swearing about 'bloody soldiers' being of doubtful parentage.

I trudged up Brownley Road and was at home at last. My journey had ended. A new life was before me, and with hope in my heart, but with a nagging fear of the future, I dreamed of a better life in front of me. Would this world of peace be a better place for us all, and would the last six years have taught us a lesson? Time only would tell, and in the meanwhile, I had my memories to cheer – and at times to torment – me for the rest of my life. **"**

🎯 *John Idwal Roberts had been a POW with the Japanese since his capture in early 1942. Weighing only six stone and suffering from beri-beri and malnutrition, liberation came not a moment too soon. Only after treatment and convalescence was he deemed fit enough to undertake the journey home to his family in Bangor, North Wales.*

❝ I could have come home. They said I was well enough to go to the Princess Mary Hospital, Hulton. I said if I was going home, I wanted to go home to Bangor, and get off the train and have a pint on the way home. The doctor said he was going to India and I said I'd go with him.

Christmas 1945 we went to Jalahalli in Bangalore, and by this time I was able to walk around. I was a half-day patient. They kicked me out New Year's Eve 1945/6.

We came home from Bombay on the *Capetown Castle*. I was the only POW on board – the rest were all medical repats or time-expired men. We arrived at Southampton, February 5, 1946. First thing I thought was 'Don't they all look ill?' All the people on the quayside looked so pale, and we were brown and, by this time, I was 13 stone – fatter than I am now. Poor devils had been on rations in Britain.

I fell in with the Rs when they were called to go to Princess Mary Hospital. I said I wasn't having that. I went up to the sergeant and asked where the ex-POWs go. He said,

'We haven't got any here. They go to Cosford.' I said, 'I've got news for you. You've got one.' What – my feet never touched the deck. I was in front of the CO who was OC troops. He wanted to know where I had been. He apologised to me – where had I been sleeping? C Deck. 'No wonder we had a spare cabin.' There was a cabin reserved for me but they never found me to put me in it. There was a second-class cabin, I would have eaten in the warrant officers' lounge – but I was happy where I was. An air commodore apologised to me and promised me I would be the first man off the ship the next morning. Next day, at the bottom of the gangway, were two great big military policemen, who were called up to carry my kit ashore. They treated me as an invalid. I was an invalid until the MO said. They took me to a dockside room – in the customs hall, and there was an area screened off. There was breakfast. I had just had kippers on the ship. I ate it!

We got to the Endsleigh Hotel in London and a warrant officer came up to me. He asked me if I wanted a meal. Well, it was about two hours since I had eaten – or three hours. I ordered double egg and chips. Coming up! I didn't think I'd get it. I thought the country was starving. But I got it – with mushrooms and onions . . .

With 11 shillings I went to the cinema. I came out and was passing a pub. I hadn't had a pint since when. It was crowded – and I didn't know how much to pay for a pint of beer! There was a tall man next to me who

▲ **Housing is scarce for ex-servicemen and their families, so disused army huts are better than nothing.**

▼ **An optimistic toast by a family reunited – for now, with the war over, who cares about the future?**

was looking at my medal ribbons. I had this Atlantic, Pacific, and he looked at the Pacific one. He asked if I was in the Far East. He said, 'My lad was there too, he was a POW.' 'So was I. What was he in?' 'He was in ASR, in a high speed launch No 105.' 'Phillips!' Yes. He was this guy's father. Needless to say, he and I were there, quaffing pints of beer until they chucked us out.

At Cosford they examined me and gave me a warrant to go home. I wondered how I was going to feel. I was very weepy. I hoped there was nobody at the station. I wanted to walk down on my own.

Well, it was raining when I got home and I'd had a few beers on the way up, needless to say. I looked along the platform at Bangor and could see two girls and my mother. I couldn't see the old man, though. I jumped out of the train and these two girls came running to get on the train, I thought. They were my two sisters and I hadn't recognized them. They were looking for an invalid – they expected to see me staggering on crutches. Instead, here was a portly little 13-stone corporal walking along with all his kit on his back, as fit as a flea. My father had been there, but had got the flu so had gone home to keep warm. We walked back to the Railway Hotel. I was really sozzled leaving the first pub. I got down to the White Lion where my father was supposed to be, but he wasn't well and had gone home. It wasn't just the flu, it was the fact that I was coming home. I just broke down when I met him – especially knowing that my brother wasn't with me. ❞

RELUCTANT EMPIRES

As the winds of change blow through the Far East in the wake of Japanese occupation, former colonies see an opportunity to claim independence.

The war against the Japanese released powerful new forces in Asia. Many of the native populations had seen their colonial masters defeated with relative ease in the early stages of the conflict and, although Japanese rule proved oppressive, the desire for an end to colonialism gathered pace.

Thus, when the British, French and Dutch tried to reassert their power in 1945-6, they were fiercely opposed. To the Americans, a restoration of the old empires was counter-productive, and they did little to help the Europeans. But such non-involvement did not last long, particularly when it became apparent that insurgents in Indochina, Malaya and the Philippines were using Chinese communist methods of revolutionary warfare. By late 1946, in US eyes, a spread of communism was more dangerous than Western involvement in the Far East. This belief would culminate in Vietnam 20 years later.

Lieutenant-Colonel Hugh Astor was with a section of the SOE (Special Operations Executive) attached to Mountbatten's military mission to Indochina in 1945/46. He provides a unique insight into post-war planning in south-east Asia, and into the causes of the region's persistent turmoil.

" I was with an organisation called Force 136, which operated behind enemy lines, so we had people behind the lines in Burma and Thailand during the war – but Indochina was a different situation as it was not part of our (British) theatre of operations and this was a big problem for us. Initially, Roosevelt was violently opposed to colonialism, especially French colonialism, and he had told us on one occasion that he would approve of anything that would help defeat the Japanese, provided it didn't help restore the French to power in Indochina. He felt very deeply on it. Indochina formed part of the Chinese theatre of operations under Chiang Kai-shek, with whom the Americans had two military advisors – Wedemeyer and Stilwell – who naturally shared the anti-colonial views. And at one point it looked as though the colonial French Army, before they were disarmed in 1945, would stage a coup against the Japanese. We were trying to make contact to give them advice, supplies and encouragement when Wedemeyer got news of this and said it was a misuse of Lease-Lend equipment – aircraft and so on – and if we didn't cease the operation it would be withdrawn. For one ally to say that to another is not very helpful, but it does indicate how strong the feelings were among the Allies.

I was on Mountbatten's staff at the time and the main thrust we were planning was Operation Zipper, which was against Malaya. The plan was to invade Malaya but the Japanese HQ was in Saigon and our lines of communication went through Indochina to Malaya. So Mountbatten was anxious to secure control over Indochina. He had raised this on a number of occasions but it wasn't until the Potsdam meeting that we were given operational control over Indochina south of the

16th Parallel. North of that would remain in the Chinese theatre. This was the thinking behind the planning in 1945. But then the bomb was dropped and it all changed.

Indochina had been rather like Vichy France; it had retained a degree of autonomy and a titular head of state and they had not been very helpful to the Allies, but when the French saw that it would only be a matter of time before the Japanese were overcome, then the French started to identify themselves increasingly with our war effort and wanted to be part of the victory campaign. Until this time they had been sitting very much on the fence, although they were to say that they had been planning a coup against the Japanese and it was only because security was so bad that it failed. The Japanese had pre-empted them by confining all the troops to barracks and disarming them. And that is where we found them when we went in.

At first we re-equipped them, which wasn't wholly satisfactory as they became rather carried away and took some very vindictive action. It was very unpleasant. We first went in

◀Vietnam, November 1950: French tanks, manned by loyal Vietnamese troops, await the order to advance.

at the end of September 1945. I went in with the British Mission. We were sent because our government had assumed that the old colonial powers would take control of their colonies when the fighting was over, but as there were no French troops we had to do it for them and the Americans were anxious to keep them out as long as possible. It was always understood by our planners that we would only be there working with the Japanese who had unconditionally surrendered to us until the French came. But we were under constant criticism that we were fighting a colonial war to restore the country to the French. I didn't see it like this. Our job was not to restore anything to anybody – it was to release the prisoners who had been held by the Japanese for a very long time. It wasn't until we got there that we realised that the country was in a state of civil war, and now everybody asks why didn't we realise that the Viet Minh were the popular party with the backing of the majority, but the answer to this is that that certainly wasn't the impression I had or was given. In the north the situation was very different but in the south we were constantly told not to hand over power to the Viet Minh as they had very little popular support. When I travelled around the country

and entered the villages, I found that nearly all the headmen had been murdered, many had been impaled on stakes outside the villages and left to die. This was the way the Viet Minh exerted their authority – it was not true popularity.

When the Emperor made his declaration of surrender it was on the basis of being total and absolute. This was taken literally by the Japanese and in Indochina, as well as Burma and Thailand, the Japanese came under the authority of the Allies. When I arrived in Indochina the reception committee were Japanese. I drove around with a Japanese driver and I have no doubt that they fought on our behalf when ordered to. In the villages I saw the dread on the faces of the people if the communists were to take over but neither did they want the French back.

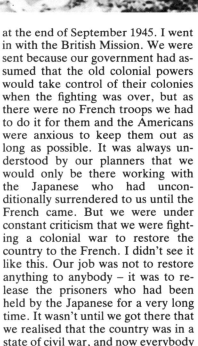

▲▲ A Viet Minh guerrilla captured by French troops, November 1950. Led by Ho Chi Minh, the Viet Minh were heavily backed by the Soviet Union and China.

▲ Malaya, November 1952: a police patrol wades through a mangrove swamp in search of elements of the communist Malayan Races' Liberation Army.

They wanted an independent government.

The Americans had a small OSS (Office of Strategic Services) mission there and we enjoyed very good relations with them, although they were busy arming the communists because they saw this as a way of impeding the return of the French. The US were strongly involved with the Chinese in the north and the Viet Minh received a certain amount of support from the US. The OSS had earlier parachuted into the north to train the communists to fight against the Japanese which, to a small extent, they did, but the main purpose was to stop the French returning. But the French eventually arrived and assumed control in the north after landing at Hanoi and were pretty much in control for a time. **"**

Major Derek Headly had spent the last five months of the war in occupied Malaya, leading a mission to promote Malay resistance to the Japanese. After the sudden surrender, he experienced considerable difficulty in persuading the Chinese communist guerrillas on the east coast to accept British control.

" By early August 1945, I and my party of seven Malays and two Britons had passed through the district of Raub, where Major Richardson and Yeop Mahadin, the District Officer in the Japanese Administration, had secretly recruited, trained and armed a 250-man Malay resistance unit.

The 6th Regiment of Chinese communist guerrillas was also based in this district. We knew that neither this regiment nor the 7th, with headquarters at Kuantan on the east coast, had heard of the agreement between South East Asia Command (SEAC) and the Malayan communist leaders, by which they agreed to accept liaison officers and to co-operate with SEAC during the war and the period of the British Military Administration. British Liaison Officers had already been posted to the five regiments in the west-coast states.

Major Leonard, who had dropped blind, had recently found 6th Regiment's headquarters. He reported that they were 'hostile'. We suspected that they thought they could seize power after the war. The

Malays hated communism on religious and political grounds and would certainly have fought any such move.

At this juncture, on 14 August, the Japanese suddenly surrendered. Richardson was ordered to take administrative control of central, and I of eastern, Pahang.

Allied troops could not arrive for weeks – it was important to persuade 6th and 7th Regiments to cooperate.

Lieutenant-Colonel Spencer Chapman, recently exfiltrated to India, had spent the war with the Chinese guerrillas in the jungle. He had considerable influence with them, and hoped to persuade 6th and 7th Regiments to obey SEAC orders. After lengthy argument, he persuaded the 'hostile' leader of the 6th Regiment to comply with Richardson's orders.

Chapman then came with me and my party to Kuantan. The Sickle and Hammer flag flew over the police station, which was manned by insolent armed Chinese, who refused to talk to us. Eventually we found the Commander of this, the 7th Regiment. The Japanese troops had handed the town over to him and he now refused to co-operate in any way. We still had no troops and my party was too small to overawe anyone. Chapman eventually reached a compromise – the Commander agreed to go to Kuala Lumpur with

Chapman to meet the Malayan Communist Party leaders, but would not hand over control to me unless ordered by them to do so.

I endured five days, hearing stories of death sentences by kangaroo courts and of government rice stocks being hidden in the jungle, until the Commander returned a chastened and obedient man.

I was then transferred to Trengganu. Two districts in that state were controlled by 7th Regiment detachments. It took me three hours to persuade the first to hand over – the second did so immediately.

Neither of the Malayan resistance movements was called on to make a fighting contribution to victory, but the British involvement with both yielded one very important consequence.

If there had been no agreement between SEAC and the leaders of the Malayan Chinese Communist Party, it is very likely that they, and the five regiments with whom they were in touch, would have refused to co-operate with our incoming troops, as 6th and 7th Regiments had done with me. This could so easily have resulted in armed conflict.

But the agreement resulted in the peaceful disbandment of the guerrilla forces and the surrender of most of their weapons. The Chinese communists remained within the law until June 1948. During that period the Civil Administration was rebuilt in

▲ Wary of ambush, a Dutch patrol fords a jungle stream in eastern Java, March 1949. Nationalist guerrilla forces achieved independence for Indonesia later this year.

▶ The French Minister for Indochina, Jean Letourneau, and (behind him) General Alphonse Juin, inspect the remains of a Moroccan unit decimated by a Viet Minh attack, October 1950.

▶▶ March 1974: Lt Hiroo Onada, who hid for 30 years in the jungles of Lubang Island, the Philippines, in the belief that his country was still at war, is reunited with his parents at Tokyo International Airport.

sufficient strength to withstand the strains of the 'Emergency', when the communists tried unsuccessfully to force communism on the people of Malaya. "

Battery Sergeant Major Douglas Greensmith was with 232 Battery, 114 Field Regiment, RA (Sussex) (TA) which was part of the 20th Indian Division. The battery arrived in Indochina after leaving Burma at the end of the war and, to their astonishment, found that Japanese troops were now under their command.

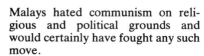

"One hundred troops were flown immediately to Saigon to try to hold the place. Then 100 Brigade followed. We were told to hold the communists, who got the blame for everything. Although the war was over I didn't mind going in, but I would say that more than 50 per cent of the regiment were of the mind that this wasn't our war. We had fought ours and if the country belonged to the French let **them** go and have a go because they haven't been doing much for the last five years.

However, we set sail for Saigon and coming up the Mèkong the landscape was beautiful. We were in a converted hospital ship and we sailed past lush vegetation and huge trees – we had seen nothing like it in Burma. The river was very wide and bendy – just like the Thames. When the noise from the ship's engines dropped we were just rounding a

▶ Sergeant-Major Douglas Greensmith (right), with an American friend in Vietnam. His account is a vivid evocation of the chaos ruling the country in the immediate post-war period of turbulence.

bend and into view on the left bank of the river was Saigon, a city only about 20 years old. The first thing we noticed was the tarmac roads which we hadn't seen since we left India, except in Rangoon. It fascinated us and this was new too – Japanese soldiers walking around the docks!

The Gurkhas with us were astonished because they had only seen ragged, filthy troops, riddled with malnutrition and disease and left behind by their own soldiers. These Japs were very clean and smart. There were cars with officers in the back and chauffeurs – big French and American cars. It was astonishing. Then when we started to unload, we walked past the Japs and they all bowed. We couldn't get over this, some Gurkhas just kept walking up and down laughing while the Japanese were continually bowing. This was great fun.

The Japs had run the country but once the bomb had gone off, the Emperor told them to surrender and co-operate. I couldn't believe this. The Japs would never, never surrender but they did – 95 per cent of them. The other five per cent went off to fight with the communists out there. It was a hell of a mix up. The Japs had gone out to free the natives from the white man's yoke, then they had collaborated with the

French; now they had turned around and joined us to fight the natives again. Fighting us were the people known as the Viet Minh and later still, the Viet Cong.

One of the more unpleasant moments on patrol came when we were driving through a village and three shots rang out from one of the bamboo huts. They didn't hit the vehicle but the Japanese were immediately out of their truck and went over to the hut, kicked the door down and then just sprayed it with automatic fire. Everything stopped. It really was brutal but we had been taking so much that it at least kept them quiet for a while.

Sometimes we came across rebels, mixed groups of the Viet Minh and Japanese. One group got very close to Saigon. They held a position about four miles from the airfield and about the same distance from the city. They were on the main road. The rebels had taken over a bungalow which had been occupied by a French plantation manager – he had been there right through the war. He and his family, including children, had had their throats cut. Then the rebels had dug themselves in, under the house which was built on stilts, raised up a couple of feet from the ground. They were holding up a whole French battalion, about

LAST OF THE SAMURAI

Not all members of the Japanese armed forces obeyed the order to surrender in August 1945. Many refused to abandon their code of behaviour which equated surrender with dishonour; others thought that the Emperor's radio broadcast ordering them to lay down their arms was an Allied trick; a few remained hidden on small Pacific islands and tried to carry on the war single-handed. Some, of course, never heard the broadcast and had no reason to believe that the fighting had finished.

The Americans slowly became aware of such 'diehards'. In 1951, for example, the island of Anaten in the Marianas was bombarded with leaflets, after which 19 Japanese soldiers emerged. Thereafter, rumours persisted that others were still at large: as late as 1975 Private Teruo Nakamura, then aged 57, finally gave himself up, having defied the Allies for 30 years.

SEPTEMBER

9 Soviet-occupied North Korea declares itself Democratic People's Republic; the US-occupied south becomes the Republic of Korea

17 Jewish terrorists kill UN mediator Count Bernadotte

DECEMBER

16 Cambodia becomes independent within the French Union

22 Tojo hanged for war crimes

1949

JANUARY

23 Mao's communists take Peking

29 Britain recognises the state of Israel

FEBRUARY

24 Israel and Egypt sign UN armistice

APRIL

3 Israel and Jordan sign ceasefire

4 NATO formed

27 Southern Ireland becomes a republic, Eire

MAY

1 Britain nationalises the gas industry

11 Israel joins the UN

12 Berlin blockade ends

23 US, British and French zones join to become a federal republic, West Germany

four or five hundred men. The French were badly trained, no discipline – awful colonial troops.

Only seven people were dug in under the house – two Japs with machine guns and five riflemen. They were holding up the complete French advance. They called us up with our guns. We positioned the guns about 400 yards away and engaged the house over open sights – like aiming a rifle. We were that close! We fired two rounds of solid shot, the type we used against tanks, and the shells went straight through the house. It just punched a hole through the walls, so we changed to high-explosive shells and fired ten of

those. It brought the house down – it was just rubble. By this time the French had decided that they would go in, so a whistle was blown and everyone was shouting and bawling and firing. We stood looking at them in amazement. We'd been used to the Gurkhas who went in like snakes through the grass. You never heard anything with them. What an army this lot were, bugles going and everyone shouting. In the melee the rebels had escaped through the back of the house into the jungle, this was their tactic. They had left behind an old man who had survived our shelling. He was about 60 and obviously a bearer. The rebels would go into a

▲Vietnam, November 1951: French paratroopers advance in the Hoa Binh sector, an important Viet Minh stronghold 60 km south-west of Hanoi.

▼In the early stages of the Tokyo trials, Japanese war leaders listen to the evidence amassed against them by Allied prosecutors.

village at night and take the bearers. If they refused to go, they cut their throat, so there wasn't a choice and no-one refused. They would keep them for about four days for interrogation.

The old man was terrified. The French had brought him back to the crossroads which were the headquarters. His hands were tied behind his back, he wore old pants and wooden sandals. The French were kicking and beating him, I'd never seen anything like it. It was terrible. They were interrogating him – well that's what they called it. We could see that he didn't know anything. In the end, our battery commander who spoke French, ran over and started to tell them what he thought of this. He was pushed aside and told to fight his war and let them fight theirs. He came back fuming. Meanwhile the French had put a length of telephone cable over a branch and placed a loop around his neck. We thought they were going to frighten him – 'If you don't tell us we'll hang you' sort of thing – he had nothing to tell them. Our officer went over to them again, he was mad with anger and frustration. He came back and told me to limber up, we were getting out. 'I will not stay and witness a cold-blooded murder,' he said to me. We pulled out and left them. Later that day he said, 'For two pins I would have turned the guns on them.'

If he had done so, he would have been fully backed up by the troops. That was French Indochina and we were glad to leave later that year and return home. It was the beginning of a mess the French were never going to get out of and, although I hated the Japanese, at least they were professional soldiers, however odd it felt to have them with you. **"**

JUDGEMENT IN TOKYO

On 4 June 1946, an International Military Tribunal met in Tokyo to try Japanese political and military leaders for alleged war crimes. Comprising representatives of 11 Allied nations, the Tribunal decided, by a majority vote, to grant immunity to Emperor Hirohito, but went ahead with the trial of other men. Altogether, 25 were found guilty: seven were sentenced to death and the rest to terms of imprisonment. They included General Hideki Tojo, Prime Minister and Minister of War, until July 1944, found guilty of permitting the 'barbarous treatment of prisoners and internees' and of bearing major responsibility for Japan's criminal attacks on her neighbours'. He was hanged in 1948.

Lesser war crimes trials were held in Hong Kong, Singapore and the Philippines, where over 900 Japanese soldiers and administrators were found guilty and many executed.

WAR IN PEACE

Territorial disputes mar the post-war period – troops are once more called upon to police the new troublespots.

A lthough World War II ended on 2 September 1945, universal peace did not follow. In a variety of countries, intense local enmities flared into war – a pattern that would soon characterise 'peace-time'.

In 1945-6 in Europe, a civil war raged in Greece between communists and monarchists, while at sea the Royal Navy suffered losses from mines laid by Albanians in the Corfu Straits. Throughout Eastern Europe, Soviet forces put down local opposition to communist rule, helping to produce the fear and mistrust that would lead to the Cold War, fraught with the danger of nuclear confrontation.

On a more active basis, Western powers faced the full force of nationalism in areas under their control. In Palestine, British soldiers came under guerrilla attack from Jews intent on creating a 'homeland', while the French and Dutch faced similar campaigns of insurgency in the Far East. It was violent and unstable world.

Sergeant Charles Elsey, of the 6th Airborne Armoured Recce Regiment, arrived in Palestine as part of the security force whose thankless task it was to keep the peace between the indigenous Arabs and the immigrant Jews who were homeless after the war – a problem which has never been adequately solved.

◀Haifa, July 1947: British naval and military personnel inspect the *Exodus 1947*, a Mediterranean fruit-ship crammed with 4,500 Jewish immigrants, after she had been intercepted and brought into harbour by the Royal Navy.

"" When we arrived in Palestine with a mixture of Tetrarchs and Locust tanks, we were put into camps in the desert. They set up an open-air cinema for us. It was bloody hilarious – the Arabs were running it, and you had to pay a couple of piastres to get in. An Arab had set himself up with a little counter with a few boxes in front of him, with sweets and drinks. So when the film came on, if you felt like a packet of fags or chocolate or something, you would go down to him. But he hadn't quite reckoned with the 6th Airborne Division who were a load of villains. When the lights went out and we were watching the film, there were people creeping down and helping themselves, so by the interval he hadn't got anything left! He was calling to Allah!

Some time after our unit had been taken over by the 3rd Hussars, our camp was raided by extremists. We had proper buildings of sorts – sergeants' mess and officers' mess – and opposite those, two whacking great marquees full of assorted ammunition.

Parked near the marquees we had all our tanks. I was a sergeant by then, and I remember sitting in the Mess and somebody shouting out, 'The Jews are raiding the ammo tents!' I was near the front door of the Mess, so I rushed out and ran

▲Illegal Jewish immigrants, part of a batch of 600 who landed on a beach near Haifa during the night, are escorted into temporary captivity by a British soldier. Their destination is a holding camp in Cyprus.

▶A British armoured car patrols an area of Jerusalem under martial law as part of Operation Hippo – the hunt for Jewish insurgents. During the operation all shops were closed, and postal and telephone facilities withdrawn.

over towards the ammo tents, thinking the whole Mess was behind me – but nobody had bloody well followed me!

I ran over and dived down between two of the tanks. There was shooting going on all over the place, and I looked up, and just between the two tanks in front was a lance corporal with a pistol. I didn't recognise him, but I said, 'Get down!' The bastard – it wasn't one of us, it was one of them – dressed up as a British soldier!

He fired! He just missed me – and he ran. There was shooting going on all around, and later on we found they were all dressed as British troops – there was a sergeant-major, several sergeants, a couple of corporals and about ten in dungarees. They had driven two trucks in and they were quietly loading ammunition on to them.

Just as that happened, an officer ran from the mess and dropped down beside me. The two trucks with the ammunition now drove off the square and came past us. The officer had brought down two pistols, one of which he gave me, and as they passed we fired into the back. We got a couple of them – one fell dead. We found a wounded one later on, and we heard that a second one had died.

For the soldier, Palestine was a difficult time. It was one big game of playing policeman. It was the sheer frustration of not being able to be soldiers as we'd been throughout the war.

Seaman Radar Mechanic Sidney Blurton left Portsmouth in January 1946, aboard HMS Voltage, to join 3 Destroyer Flotilla in Malta. From here the ship patrolled off Palestine to control the illegal immigration. After this, the ship was sent towards Argostoli, and Blurton, now a Petty Officer, experienced the Corfu Incident.

" I had very mixed feelings indeed about our job because of the conditions the emigrants were travelling under and what had happened to many of them during the war. They came typically from Trieste and other ports in northern Italy and we knew about the way they had suffered in eastern Europe and Russia. They travelled to Palestine in extremely crowded conditions – literally put into shelves or layers; babies were born *en route*. These ships and the conditions aboard them were really pretty horrific. The vessels had usually been purchased by a group of Jews and were abandoned when they got to Palestine and naturally their intention was to avoid being intercepted, so they would stay outside territorial waters until darkness and then make a run for it. Some would even swim ashore when they got close enough – many eventually did. We were only doing our duty. We just had to accept that it was unpleasant but it was a job that had to be done.

The RAF used to spot the ships about 100 miles out and then we would pick them up at about 23 to 30 miles out – but we were not allowed to board them until we were in territorial waters – three miles out. So we would escort them to well within territorial waters and then put a boarding party on board, but there was always a risk that they would try to run for it. Sometimes they did but we were always much faster, so we got them – the last resort was to open fire which we did once – and it made us notorious.

The boarding parties would often come under physical attack – it was the worst duty. It was unpleasant because of the way in which they had travelled. They had often spent everything to get a place on a ship and some had been on board for several weeks, literally living on board with absolutely no sanitary conditions whatsoever.

Then they came up against us, trying to stop them completing their journey to the Promised Land. It was unpleasant. The time we fired a gun sealed our fate. We had to fire one or two shots and from then on things became very different.

One old ship had refused to stop as it approached Palestine, it was decorated with banners as they always did when arriving, so we put a shot over it and eventually got aboard. Then, we found that it had failed to stop because this battered old ship had no reverse on it, so it couldn't go into reverse to take the way of it – it was very unfortunate

1949

JULY

14 Soviets test-explode an atomic device

19 Laos given independence within French Union

AUGUST

27 Soviet tanks gather on Yugoslavian borders

OCTOBER

1 China proclaimed a Communist republic

12 Stalin declares East Germany a democratic republic

16 Civil war in Greece ends

NOVEMBER

2 Dutch relinquish power in East Indies which become a federal state dominated by the Republic of Indonesia

1950

JANUARY

25 India declared a republic

APRIL

1 UN adopts plan to divide Jerusalem

JUNE

25 Communist North Korea crosses the 38th Parallel into South Korea

26 UN authorises 'such assistance as necessary to meet the armed attack'

28 South Korean capital Seoul falls to communists

AUGUST

29 British troops land in Korea

that we had fired on it. But we went alongside and put the boarding party on board and towed it in to Haifa from where the refugees were transferred directly on to a transport ship and taken to Cyprus, where the emigrants were put into holding camps. From here they would slowly dribble into Palestine, as only a quota of Jews were allowed to go over a given period – I think it was a case of only so many a month.

We were not popular on *Volage* now, and had a difficult time in Haifa, the Stern Gang and other Israeli organisations were determined to sink us. Frogmen were sent out to sink us.

For the whole time we were in port, we had to explode depthcharges over the side, day and night to prevent the frogmen attaching limpet mines to the side of the ship. Frogmen were not only seen but they succeeded in blowing up a tanker called the *Southern Cross*, which was berthed in the harbour. It burnt for several days while we were there. The threat of attack was pretty much for real and I was pretty glad when we got back into the Med.

When we had first arrived we could go ashore, but then only armed, to provide a guard for duty at the dockyard gates but that was all. It was at the time when the King David Hotel (the British headquarters) was blown up – a very lively period for so-called 'peace time.' In later years I felt rather sad at the role the Navy had played – it was an unhappy period.

On the morning of the 22nd October the captain told the ship's company what the mission was about. We would be going through the Corfu channel and we would be sailing at action stations. This was something that was new to me as I had not

been in action during the war.

We were given specific instructions to put on totally clean underwear in case anyone was wounded and to wear anti-flash gear. The instructions were entirely consistent with the chance that there might be a problem and that we would be prepared for it.

My action station was in the transmitting station which, on the destroyer, is the fire-control centre, from where the gunfire is controlled. We were totally enclosed and entirely reliant on conversation over the intercom to know what was going on on the outside.

We had been going for a while when we were fired on from the Albanian coast by a machine gun. Nothing was done, but if we were fired on again we were to return fire. Well, we were fired on again and so

▲ British soldiers on a beach near Haifa 'guard' the belongings of Jewish immigrants intercepted the previous night.

◄ The Corfu Straits, October 1946: HMS *Volage* lists following the mine explosion which tore off the bow and killed eight sailors.

I, in the transmitting station, heard the order go out 'All guns to take a bearing on the shore batteries on the Albanian coast and prepare for rapid broadsides.'

Fortunately for us, we had just got to the stage where the order was to

be given 'Rapid broadsides commence.' In fact, the order had been given, but immediately, and this was fortunate, 'Check, check, check,' was given too. (This is the control to stand down a particular order). *Saumarez*, the destroyer sailing in front

THE CORFU INCIDENT

On 22 October 1946 a British force of two cruisers and two destroyers entered the channel between Corfu and the Albanian coast. Albania had laid claim to the Corfu Straits – an international waterway – and, in May 1946, had fired on British ships. The aim on 22 October was to force a passage of the Straits, establishing international usage.

It was a disaster. Just before 3 pm, the destroyer HMS *Saumarez* hit a mine, laid (it was later alleged) by the Albanians. The ship lost power and steering and, with 36 crewmen dead, drifted towards shallow water. Her sister ship, HMS *Volage*, attached a towline, but then she too struck a mine, which killed eight more sailors, Eventually, *Volage*, managed to tow *Saumarez* out of danger, but with 44 men dead, it was an expensive way to set a precedent.

▶ Her bows ripped away by an Albanian mine, HMS *Volage*, as seen from her sister ship, *Saumarez*.

of us, had been hit.

The minutes ticked on and eventually the order came that the two cruisers were to move out of the immediate area to somewhere where they could keep us covered with their guns, some 5 or 6 miles away. *Volage* was to give assistance to *Saumarez*.

By then we were stood down from action stations as it was now a rescue operation. I was on the upper deck and saw *Saumarez* smoking very

board and a sick berth attendant. All we had was an attendant, so he was sent by boat to *Saumarez*. My immediate thoughts were that she had probably been fired on from the Albanian shore, but we soon learned that she had been mined.

We went to her help. It was a difficult task as the sea certainly wasn't calm and unfortunately, in trying to get alongside, we hit her and gashed an eight-foot hole, above our waterline, in the bow. This became very significant later, but we eventually got a line across and started to tow her to Corfu.

We were now feeling pretty pleased with ourselves because we had managed to get the *Saumarez* in tow in difficult circumstances and we were making very slow but steady progress. Then there was an almighty bang. I was on the upper deck and saw a 40-foot section of the bow just go straight up into the air – and it was coming down fast. I dived under the torpedo tubes for protection. There was a lot of metal coming down on the ship.

There had been a party of eight or nine men in the bow at that time, trying to plug the hole we had made earlier to make the ship as watertight as possible for the tow. Unfortunately the shoring-up party were still in the bows of the ship when the mine struck us. And that was where we sustained our main losses. So the incident of gashing earlier caused most of our casualties. We had lost the bow to the *Saumarez*, but although we had lost 40 feet of our bow, the watertight doors were closed so the ship was watertight and

▶ A launch from HMS *Saumarez* heads for the apparently stricken *Volage*, which had been towing her. Amazingly, the *Volage* was still seaworthy.

▶ After the Incident: the bowless HMS *Volage* awaits repairs in Corfu harbour.

badly. She had clearly been damaged very seriously – she was listing badly and drifting towards the Albanian coast which was less than a mile away. She asked us for assistance with fire-fighting but there was not much we could do. More particularly, she asked for medical aid. *Saumarez* was in fact, the flotilla leader, so she had the doctor on

still very seaworthy – perhaps surprisingly, bearing in mind the extent of the damage.

The difference between the mine that hit us and the *Saumarez* is explained by the fact that the *Saumarez* was travelling at speed and mines are designed to go out on the bow-wave and then come in, striking the ship amidships. We were going so slow that in fact this didn't happen. The mine was not pushed out by the bow-wave so it took the bows off. Now we were listing badly as the bow section had not come cleanly away but a skilful bit of manoeuvring got it off in the end and we went back, stern-first, to get another tow on to the *Saumarez*. This we did.

By now we also knew that we were towing in a minefield on our way back to Corfu town and we were by ourselves. I was assisting with the navigation by interpreting where we were on one of the radar plan indicators and while I was doing this, had the very sad sight of seeing Stoker Petty Officer Cyril Keaton, who had been on the bow of the ship when she was blown up, die alongside me. He died at about two or three in the morning. It was clear from his injuries that there was very little we could do for him except inject him with morphia to kill the pain.

The *Saumarez* was on fire throughout the night, they had no electricity and many dead, while *Volage* came out relatively intact; we still had our engines and electricity and life was tolerable. The trip back took roughly 12 hours. The next morning I remember we were all looking forward to a fairly relaxed time after the incident but no, it was not to be and I am sure it was the right thing for all of us.

Our first lieutenant, Lieutenant David Scott, instructed that we had to get the ship cleaned up and in a good state again. For all our health it was the best thing that could have happened to us.

We buried the dead in Corfu, left the *Saumarez* in Corfu where she stayed and we were towed to Malta to have the bow replaced. The end result of that day was that the Royal Navy had two destroyers mined, some 44 people killed, and the whole thing not a glorious episode in naval history.

It seems to me to this day that the Admiralty have totally played down these events. Neither the Government nor the Admiralty have ever paid a permanent tribute to those that were killed and have no known grave – just lost at sea. **"**

Rear Admiral Sir David Scott was First Lieutenant on HMS **Volage** *during the Corfu Incident, which took place off the coast of Albania in 1946. It was an act of war that went unrecognised by the British Government and was quietly and conveniently forgotten by the Admiralty. It led to the tragic deaths of many sailors.*

" The lunch break came and went before the ship's company was piped to anchor at 1300. The ships weighed together, and then slowly moved out of Corfu Bay, taking up formation line ahead in the order *Mauritius, Saumarez, Leander* and *Volage*. We had no cause to complain about being 'tail-end-Charlie'. We had cleared the bay, speed was increased to 12 knots. This was not to be a swift dash through the strait, but a deliberate demonstration of our right to be there. All was quiet on the radio

telephone channel connecting the ships. Suddenly, shortly after 1430, a machine gun opened fire on the *Volage* from the Albanian coast. The fire was wide and ceased after one burst. Once again silence reigned. We were now close to the Albanian coast. I was studying the shoreline in detail through my binoculars. At 1447 the silence was broken by *Mauritius* ordering a routine turn to port to go northwestwards on the final leg of the passage through the strait. I was still watching the khaki-clad figures manning the Albanian gun batteries on the shore, which seemed incredibly close. Now I swung my binoculars on to *Mauritius* to watch her begin her turn. I could hardly believe my eyes when *Saumarez* was suddenly engulfed by a great sheet of flame and black smoke. Because of her distance from us, there was no immediate sound of an explosion – there was no gunfire. The flame enveloped the bridge. Then came the rumble of the explosion followed by silence. The *Saumarez* and the flagship had been stunned. The voice of the signalman on the radio telephone came through. It was *Mauritius* calling *Volage* and the message was terse and simple. '*Volage* proceed to the assistance of *Saumarez*.'

We increased speed to 20 knots and key ratings who would be involved in a towing operation were told to fall out from action stations

▲◄ **The Corfu Incident, September 1946: following a mine explosion, the crippled HMS** *Volage* **(foreground) is made fast to a buoy with** *Leander* **and** *Saumarez* **in attendance.**

▲ **December 1947: a British armoured car on patrol in the City of Bethlehem.**

and muster amidships. As we approached the *Saumarez* I had no idea of the carnage and casualties which she had sustained. Her bow lay deep in the water and fires were burning near her fo'csle, in the bridge superstructure and amidships. We were manoeuvred into a position where the sterns of the two ships were only a few feet away from each other. I saw my opposite number, Teddy Gueritz, standing on *Saumarez's* quarterdeck. I shouted at him through a megaphone, asking whether he could pass us his tow-line, or did he want to take ours? He replied that he had very few hands and many fires on board and would rather take ours. We threw heaving lines across, and passed over a Ma-

nilla rope to which we were going to attach our main towing line. We manoeuvred to get the quarterdecks close together, but this time the manoeuvre went wrong. The bow of the *Volage* hit the *Saumarez* and a ten-foot hole was torn in the *Volage's* bow. At that moment we saw a boat coming towards us from the shore. It flew a white flag and the Albanian flag. In it were men armed with sub-machine guns. It came alongside and an older man, who seemed to be in charge, starting hectoring us in Italian as one of his wild-looking Albanians kept his gun trained on me. He shouted at me in an offensive way, demanding to know what we were doing. I replied

a difficult situation of reaching Corfu.

Then, at 1615 there was a gigantic explosion followed by the violent whipping up and down of the quarterdeck: *Volage* had hit a mine. I was thrown backwards to the deck and saw huge lumps of metal and debris falling about me. We had no casualties on the quarterdeck, but one officer and seven ratings in the forward part of the ship had been killed. The boiler-rooms were undamaged and we still had steam on both main engines. Shortly after the explosion there was a sound of grinding metal and the ship whipped up and down again. *Volage* then settled and I noticed there was no longer a

► Operation Hippo: a terrorist suspect waits in a British truck to be taken for interrogation. With the British departure from Palestine in May 1948, Jewish militia were faced with the Arab League and full-scale war.

in a tone no less offensive, telling him to use his eyes and common sense. He shouted a command to his crew and headed the boat back towards the shore, leaving us to our fate. By now the *Saumarez* had drifted far too close to the Albanian shore for comfort. The tow was taken and, at an even strain we made about 4 knots headway. The two cruisers had disappeared around the north corner of Corfu and I remember thinking we had a good chance in

list to port and the bow-down angle had been replaced by a bow-up angle. A 40-foot-long bow section had come away and sunk into the deep. Miraculously, there was no flooding. The tow to the *Saumarez* had slipped and so now we passed wires across to her quarterdeck from what remained of our bow. We set out for Corfu Bay with *Volage* proceeding astern at about two knots, towing *Saumarez* stern-first. By 2015 we were in safe waters. **"**

JEWISH INSURGENTS

◄ December 1947: men of the *Haganah* move into Jerusalem after Arab riots.

Between November 1945 and May 1948, the British faced an insurgency in Palestine by Jewish groups dedicated to the creation of an independent state. It was a guerrilla conflict which resulted in a British withdrawal and the emergence of Israel.

The insurgents were drawn from three groups. The largest, fielding up to 45,000 members, was the *Haganah* (Defence), formed in 19020 to protect settlements against Arab attack. Most of the *Haganah* were static 'village guards', but a more mobile unit and 'shock companies' were available for attacks on the British. More extreme was *Irgun Zvai Leumi* (National Military Organisation), whose 1,500 members were organised into hit-squads, while *Lohamei Heruth Israel* (Fighters for the Freedom of Israel, more commonly called the 'Stern Gang') fielded 300 dedicated fighters. Their most spectacular attack occurred on 22 July 1946, when bombs exploded in the King David Hotel in Jerusalem, killing 92 people.

1950

SEPTEMBER

15 Inchon landings: MacArthur's armada arrives to relieve Seoul and South Korea

25 Seoul recaptured

OCTOBER

5 MacArthur crosses the 38th Parallel into North Korea

6 China invades Tibet

27 UN forces advance towards China

NOVEMBER

27 Chinese troops force back UN troops at Manchurian border

DECEMBER

5 UN troops routed from North Korean capital by Chinese

12 Malays revolt in Singapore

1951

JANUARY

11 Viet Minh attack French at Tonkin

18 French push back Viet Minh from Hanoi

APRIL

11 MacArthur sacked by Truman over Korean war policy

JUNE

13 UN troops retake Pyongyang

OCTOBER

7 Shah endorses nationalisation of oil in Iran

18 British troops take over Suez Canal Zone

BECAUSE PEOPLE HAVE SHORT MEMORIES...

War is a paradox. Although it inevitably involves death, destruction and horror, bringing out some of the worst aspects of the human character, it is at the same time a period of great comradeship, selflessness and bravery. In the end, war is not about politics, technology or arrows on a map, but about people.

After 50 years, memories fade, exorcising the horror and stressing the more positive side – yet, to many who survived battles such as Stalingrad, Alamein, Kohima or Okinawa, who braved the dangers of Atlantic convoys, who flew through anti-aircraft fire over enemy positions, who suffered the effects of a firestorm or – perhaps worst of all – felt the impact of the Holocaust, the nightmares remain. Their stories – locked away for so long – are difficult to tell, but if both the horror and the laughter can be described, those who did not share the experience can start to understand the nature of war and try to avoid its recurrence.

The warring world paid a staggering price in lives – now it is for those who fought to evaluate the most momentous six years of the century.

Derek Glaister's post-war life was irreversibly changed by wounds he received when, as a para, he was dropped off target on the Rhine crossing operation.

▲ The sun goes down over the German cemetery at Cassino, Italy – a place where work for remembrance and reconciliation has done much to heal past wounds.

“ To be frank, I'd do exactly the same again, if it was the same officers and men. I think every expara would do the same – wartime ones, anyway.

I don't feel bitter about it – it's just something you've got to accept, you see. I was a professional soldier and joined the army when I was 14. They said that the life of a para in the war was three operations, and I got mine on the third. The thing I resented was being shot in the back after I was already wounded. I'll never forget the SS man who did it – six foot four and covered in boils! The Germans themselves are alright – it was just the system at the time. There were good Germans and bad, and it was the SS who were the evil ones.

At the time we thought it was important to fight the war as we did – but I sometimes wonder now if it really was, to be quite frank. A lot of us feel the same. Let's face it, Germany won the war – financially, anyhow. But then what would have happened if we hadn't fought? I think, if the situation came again in Europe, it would still have to be done. You can't let people like Hitler loose. When you were in the paras, this was part of you.

When my armoured division was broken up, we had people come round asking for volunteers for the paras. None of us knew much about them then, but I jumped in straight away. Within 24 hours, I was gone. The first thing you did was arrive at Chesterfield station, and you had all the different hats, cap badges and all the kit.

Certainly at the start, there were the men at the front and the generals running it were sitting at desks – doing it with flags! It was a bit scrappy at first because most of them were still living in the 1914 war. It was only after Dunkirk that they started to get their act together.

When I joined the Airborne, it was different – you had brigadiers,

the lot, and they all jumped with you. The paras were the best – every bloke was a volunteer and you didn't get skivers. You got such a close-knit unit that you'd know what the other bloke was thinking. It was a feeling that you knew what everybody was doing and you could always rely on them. That's a great feeling in the time of battle. It definitely was a time of greater camaraderie. We made a lot of friends.

You were always very vulnerable when you were first dropped, and I was dropped astray on top of a German HQ. I was unlucky to be wounded twice on the drop in ten minutes, but all the chaps I knew were killed, really, just as the war was ending in April. Up to about four years ago, they thought I'd been killed on the drop. I was three years in hospital and everyone thought I was dead. It was only by chance that someone saw me walking in Broadstairs wearing a Para tie, and passed it on to someone else who got in touch with me afterwards. **"**

John Hall was a night-fighter pilot – and, having experienced the highs and the undeniable terrors of his wartime career, is reconciled to the inevitable moral dilemmas which accompany a war.

" I would not have missed my six years in the RAF for anything. In some ways I am still an RAF pilot at heart. We had a lot of fun – and the fun comes to mind more easily than the other bits, though I still occasionally have a worry-dream when I am required, with no possibility of a reprieve, to climb into the cockpit of a Mozzie and take of into a dark and murky night.

England was a lovely place to be in those days, with villages and country

towns almost bare of traffic, and with friendly people whose beliefs and outlook were the same as yours. It's no good pitching it too high as far as I'm concerned – I wasn't full of noble thoughts all the time, but I did appreciate what a good place England was to fight for.

I still often think of four good friends in particular, who were killed on ops, and I still miss them. What's more, it never, ever crossed my mind that England would lose the war. I simply express as truthfully as I can the things that come to my mind.

I have a great belief that people recognise something which is true, even if trite or not particularly high-flown, and like it – but find high-flown thoughts rather boring. We did have a chap on our second squadron whose attitude was terribly solemn and serious, and he used to brood about killing Germans. It never crossed my mind to brood on those lines. After all, although it wasn't as dramatic as 'kill or be killed', it was something of that sort. I wouldn't have expected a German pilot to have been sorry about killing me. **"**

Jock Cairns, night-fighter navigator with 85 Squadron, saw action over Britain during and after the Blitz, then moved to fly night sorties over France after the D-Day landings.

" I personally had no difficulty with the morality of what we were doing. I was a fairly typical product of my generation – I lived by

▲ **Derek Glaister with a shield made for and presented to him by comrades from the paras, who only recently learned that he had survived his injuries from the Rhine crossing.**

◄ **John Hall, left, and 'Jock' Cairns – still inseparable friends 50 years after their night-flying partnership began, a testimony to the camaraderie of conflict.**

the values of my middle-class background. My poor old pop fought in the trenches of World War I, and was quite badly wounded, so my generation, we were pretty close to that war – much closer than the generation is now. I suppose I was imbued with patriotism and the justice of the cause. I don't think I was ever consumed with a hatred of Germans. I didn't think really in terms of killing men – combat was against an impersonal object of destructive machinery. I did carry out some operations which could have resulted in civilian casualties, but this is inevitable in modern total war, I think. I'm not proud at adding to the sum of human misery, but neither am I ashamed of my contribution to the overthrowing of an evil regime, if you want to put it as pompously as that. The regrets I do have are for the loss of many old chums.

The great quality engendered in war is an uplifting spirit of comradeship. It's binding and undying. I still meet old squadron companions regularly and my pilot, John Hall, as you know, has been my closest friend for nearly 50 years.

Did it change my life? Yes it did. It set me off in a completely different direction to my pre-war existence – but for the better, I think. Events and experience certainly caused me to examine my spiritual beliefs and to challenge many comfortable religious tenets which I had accepted without giving too much thought. My experiences have brought me to a rather atheistic viewpoint, in that I find it difficult to reconcile theological institutionalism with the scale of global suffering experienced during the war – any war – or life, for that matter. This is where I part company from 'organised religion' if you like. I believe in a Christian ethic, or perhaps you could say a set of Christian principles by which to live, but reject the fairy stories and all the piety in the light of my experiences during the course of the war.

What it brought me to is a tremendous faith in human nature. I believe in people and I think that anything that's good in life has come through human endeavour. There's a lot of evil too, but in my book, the good that comes out of it far outweighs the evil. **"**

Douglas Lyne, having witnessed the destruction of Monte Cassino monastery, is now consumed with a need to understand the human traits which seem to make war inevitable and to pour this understanding into a movement for reconciliation and for peace.

▲ **Douglas Lyne, centre, with MEP Madron Seligman at a service of remembrance at the British Cemetery, Cassino, with the rebuilt abbey in the background. Inset, the Commonwealth window from the new Benedictine chapel of remembrance.**

" I have come to believe in something like original sin – that there is some flagrant and absolute fault in the human condition which makes it virtually impossible to learn totally, absolutely complete lessons – which could not have been more complete than the time that people started hitting each other over the heads with clubs.

Spike Milligan made an odd, but I think quite illuminating remark when he said that the only way to stop having wars is to continue to have them. There is an appetite for war in the human condition and it

does seem, in some ways, to be the only means of solving certain insoluble difficulties. The bombing of Monte Cassino is an example — I cannot see, having been a soldier there, how the pressure of the opinion of the soldiery could have been allowed to go unnoticed, and how they could not have destroyed it. I can't see how there was the slightest chance that the Americans should not have dropped the atom bomb on Hiroshima at that time. I can't really see any alternative to the appalling things that have happened, except by a total and absolute change of informed opinion.

Perhaps populism of the century in which we have been involved has produced a mass emotional response to a mass emotional appeal by which the lowest common denominators of one's emotions are mobilised to do the most barbaric things. To do things that are worthwhile or to refrain from doing things which are abominable takes effort and training, and for both of those things you have to go to institutions where you can learn how to behave – how to do what is correct and refrain from doing what is incorrect. This is nowhere more clear than in the business of peace and war, which has become exceptionally technical at every level. It is extremely technical in the processes by which it is run – the equipment used.

As the generations pass, what I have found important is that younger people should be interested and that a new generation should believe that there is something to be learned from the past, and not have an entirely dismissive attitude that old soldiers are old idiots who like to meet together to clank their medals and cry into their beer and bore each other rigid with chats of their old days – which by and large is a totally justified opinion of most soldiers. But if one starts a movement with rules and regulations, people have to obey them. Emotion has to be cut down and to do that, the various strands which go to make up battles, and therefore reflect peace, have to be kept together, in my view, in order to maintain peace. It's exceedingly difficult to conceive of maintaining peace, because if you maintain peace, war would then become an ancient disease – like tuberculosis. I have the feeling that war is precisely the same. We hate to give it up because it is so complete in our mentality. **"**

Philip Murton, wartime Typhoon pilot with the RAF. He flew with the first Vampire jet squadron in 1946, and is still flying today.

" Was it worth it? Well presumably it was, because we stopped the jackboot from coming into England. And did I enjoy it? Well you remember the good things – the girlfriends, the travelling, the camaraderie. Then you tend not to recall the dreadful things – once we went across to Normandy we had to put up with the awful Normandy dust and we ate bully beef and biscuits – there were awful stomach upsets and of course there was the strain of doing what the Tornado pilots are doing today – going and sticking your neck out, flying low-level and

risking your life.

There were certain things where the memory is completely blank, presumably because there was nothing exciting, but there are other things that stuck in the mind vividly and have been there ever since. There were moments of high tension and real fear – being absolutely terrified at times. But then, on the other hand, when you got back, there were all your chums to talk to – the ones who got back – and there was all the excitement of discussing it. I think we all grew up very quickly. I know the Battle of Britain lads felt that they aged about five years in that one summer.

I didn't make any particular friends on the squadron that I've kept up with since the war, but there were two people I met during my training who are still friends. We have reunions – there was a 183 Squadron reunion at Apeldoorn the year before last, and five people turned up from the squadron who I hadn't seen since 1944. Because of the war I was able to go to America once, which was where I trained, and Canada twice, and then through France, Belgium, Holland and Germany. I had experiences in that wartime period which I would never have had otherwise.

We could cope at the time with the pressure because we were young and we all wanted to fly. It was great fun, and because we were young we didn't actually think, when we were attacking a convoy, that we were killing a lot of people.

Up until two or three years ago, I was having the most frightful nightmares about the war. My doctor said it was a natural thing and that it may last for a year or so, and then die away – and it did. I used to wake up screaming and in a cold sweat. Then I'd find it hadn't happened – it was just a dream. **"**

Sidney Lawrence emerged from three and a half years in Japanese POW camps and from under the Nagasaki bomb a changed and – he feels – a better man.

" I was asked by a young reporter, some five years ago, if I really believed in the war. I said yes. I believed I was doing my bit to fight for this country and for freedom.

I wouldn't have missed the whole experience of the war. I've learned so much. I've no room left for hate in my heart – hatred is a futile waste of emotion. All war is evil, but perhaps I am one of a very small number left in this world who knows what an evil, horrible thing **nuclear** war is. They say that nuclear weapons have kept the peace for 40 years, but in that time there have been 142 – no, 143 – different wars.

The experience I had changed my whole life from the word go. Speaking from the point of view of physics, its the principle where you drop a stone in the water and the ripples go out. By being a volunteer reservist

and being in the RAF, and having this experience, the whole of my life since has been affected.

I did learn that hatred is futile – it is human, but it's wrong. The only thing is love – and I still stick to that.

People today haven't a clue what it is like to endure this kind of suffering. I say it will do one of two things to you. It will either make you bitter and full of hate – what I call a mental wreck – or it will be the making of you. I consider for myself – and my wife will bear it out – that it has not

◄ Sidney Lawrence, survivor of the Nagasaki bomb. The experience would change the rest of his life – for the better!

◄ Philip Murton looks through an old log book – but still has his current flying records to keep up to date.

FEBRUARY

6 7 George VI dies; his daughter becomes Queen Elizabeth II

OCTOBER

20 British troops fly into Kenya to stem Mau Mau terrorism

MARCH

5 Josef Stalin dies

JULY

27 Korean war ends as armistice is signed

made me bitter. It has not given me a sense of anything else but a deep appreciation of life – and the conviction that loving is the most important thing in the world.

The only thing I think, 'Why me?' about, is the fact that I survived. I don't wonder why my life was pulled into this but I often wonder why I lived through it. I don't know why I was spared. It leaves you with a sense of guilt. Why am I alive when so many have died? Things hurt so much, particularly now, especially when I think of what is going to be in the Middle East, seeing the lads who are the age I was then. We had very much the attitude, 'Watch out, Hitler. We're coming now – and you're going to cop it.' Those boys are saying the same now. That's how you are when you're young – and I'm glad it hasn't changed. The point is what you learn from it – how to live your life afterwards. I used to say to myself, 'If I do get out of this – if I do get home – I'm going to be a better man, a better father and a better husband than I ever would have been if I hadn't had this experience.' I can only leave it to my family to say if that's so.

I was inclined, as a young man, to be rather arrogant. It was the arrogance of youth, but I came back a very different person and have tried to live to be that different person. I wouldn't behave the way I do, or have the attitudes I do without that experience. Every time August comes around, I am aware of the strange malaise that affects all of us who survived the bomb. I try to ignore it, but I begin to feel very strange. **"**

Bob Leonard, a merchant seaman on convoys throughout the war, still has pause for thought when he remembers the lack of foresight in British maritime planning.

" The thing that comes to mind that I have felt very strongly about really, was the huge unpreparedness of our maritime services – that is merchant ships and their escorts, or lack of them. Bearing in mind the shipping industry had been in such horrendous doldrums all through the Thirties, it would have been a precaution, from '36 on, to have designed a range of ships that could be built quickly and more efficiently. But more importantly, some research should have been done into building them 20 per cent bigger and 20 per cent faster, which would have meant that less ships would have been required, with less men to man them, less escorts to escort them – and the load-line would not have had to be lifted.

Looking at the memorial, 40 years on, I wonder why, with any kind of foresight at all, some of these wasting resources weren't applied to looking at what was bound to be a crucial weakness in the British armour – the need for a strong, well-trained and well-equipped merchant navy and escorts.

Had the Germans had more confidence in building up a powerful submarine arm instead of squandering their resources on the *Tirpitz* and the *Bismarck* and the like, the war could well have been lost, or Britain knocked out of it in 1941. We were saved by a combination of Hitler's shortsightedness (he probably mistrusted the submarine fleet because they weren't particularly ideological), and his failure to back the submarine arm and their associated back-up in aircraft, let us, if only just, get away with it. Also, there was the fact that the Americans designed and built the Liberty ship so effectively and so quickly. They were the things that saved us.

For myself, I think it was a hugely rewarding experience. My business career has been very strongly influenced by my service in the Merchant Navy – and particularly war service – being able to do with few resources, untrained people, and being able to become almost stress-proof.

I've been in the business-rescue-business for 27 years, and I think my Merchant Navy experience equipped me better than almost anything else that I could possibly have done for the fact that Sod's Law operates with unerring accuracy. It also gave me the capacity to direct people of modest ability and get them to do jobs outside or beyond their ordinary capability. The thing about a ship was that you had what you had – it was an isolated thing. You'd only got the people you'd got. Again, that kind of service, in wartime, gave you the capacity to make the best of what facilities you had. **"**

Gus Britton lived through the war as a submariner – oddly removed from events of the land war – and is still a submariner at heart.

" I wouldn't say that I wouldn't have missed it – but since I was there, I enjoyed it, although I didn't enjoy people shooting at me or dropping bombs or depth-charges on me.

No, it wasn't worth it. No war is worth it. What war in history has ever done anything for the good? I lost a lot of friends, but I was always sure it wouldn't happen to me – and it never did. I'm sure all my friends thought the same thing . . .

In submarines, it's very strange and paradoxical, I suppose, but you're cocooned away and you rarely if ever see the war. You come up on the surface at night for the submarine to charge its batteries, but most submariners never knew where they were. If you were a stoker, you never saw daylight, sometimes for three weeks.

I had joined the naval school at eleven and I wanted to be a submariner like my dear old dad. But the little people in the war, like me, we fought because we'd get a kick up the arse if we didn't.

Once we attacked a surface ship off Bari. There was a terrific explosion and I said to a mate, 'I hope we haven't killed anyone.' He said, 'What a stupid bastard you are.'

Now, I go back to see the submariners, and I'm a member of the German, French and Italian submariners' associations. As far as I was concerned, they were just like us, and the ordinary hairy matelot didn't know what was going on in concentration camps, and they hated the *Gestapo* too. **"**

▲ **Gus Britton, a navy man from the age of 15, is now Assistant Director of the RN Submarine Museum at Gosport, Hants.**

◄ **Bob Leonard – as for many enterprising young men, the war was a chance to cultivate the qualities of leadership.**

George Rhodes, hardened to the sight of death during the war, became a morbid anatomist. Since retiring, however, he has made a point of touring his old battlegrounds – a salutary reminder of the war.

" If only people would study history, they would find that man, being what he is, has fought wars on religious grounds and out of greed for power, throughout history. They should realise that appeasement and sanctions never work – for instance, South Africa has withstood 25 years of sanctions and still carries on . . .

Those people who preach pacificism are not only traitors, but cowards as well. Such people, in the period before 1939, were really responsible for the deaths of over 50 million people. A dictator must, at all times, be kept in his place, and not be allowed to bully smaller nations.

There is a very old saying which goes like this: 'The hand that rocks the cradle rules the world.' In a recent book there is a storyline of women gradually coming out of their shells and taking on more of men's jobs – which in time would mean that in future there should be no wars.

It won't happen in my lifetime, of that I'm sure, but it would shake the world if, after man has ruled the world for thousands of years, there were to be a reversal of roles – that would be a very interesting thing to observe!

As well as the deaths in World War II, thousands of illegitimate children were born – 70,000 to the Yanks alone – and the fashion today is not to get married. In the end, in my opinion, this has been the downfall of Britain. One can quote examples from Rome, Greece, France and so on, that when morals are thrown out the door, so the countries sink.

I am pleased to say that the forces today are being paid a decent wage. In World War II you started at a shilling a day – a gunner I was paid 4/6 a day.

In the pre-war days, in the Territorial Army, I was paid £12 bounty when I attended the annual fortnight's camp. Now the TA is paid £3,000 a year. "

Mirro Mansfeld, a Czech pilot, fought with the RAF from 1940. From that moment to the present day, having lost everything under the communist regime in his homeland, he is very emphatic as to where his loyalties lie!

" I may be Czechoslovakian – I may be British, but above all that is the RAF. If I have any order from the RAF, even today, I don't question it – I just carry it out, because I know it's good.

If I get any communication from Czechoslovakia, I say, 'Wait a minute – I'll have to look at it, because they are communists now.' If I get any sort of order from Britain, I still

▲ **George Rhodes – one for whom the war served to consolidate views which would last a lifetime.**

▼ **Mirro Mansfeld, second row from back, fourth from right, with RAF comrades from the Battle of Britain. After losing his homeland of Czechoslovakia, the RAF became his family – one to which he remains totally devoted.**

say, 'Wait a minute,' they may think I am an alien – they may not know that I'm ex-RAF.

In 1945, 6 and 7 there were 68 Squadron reunions here, and Czech boys came over. Two or three years later Czech boys from 68 Squadron came over. One of them contacted me and said he wanted to tell me something. He said, 'You have been sentenced to death in your absence for high treason. But because you were fighting with the RAF, it has been commuted to life imprisonment. You have been deprived of all rank and nationality. Don't tell anyone that I told you!'

I told him, 'I'm very proud that this has been done to me – by communists!' "

Hans Teske, born in Stolp in Pomerania in 1924, served as a German Paratrooper in North Africa. He was interned in America and England, and settled here, marrying a French woman.

" I was fortunate to serve in an élite regiment of the German parachute forces. Our experiences in war forged a comradeship, which has lasted until today. We are like a family, and included in our activities are many British, French and others.

The war was the key experience in my life. As we saw it, we were fighting for our country, which for me meant keeping Pomerania German. When the war ended, my part of Germany was given, temporarily as it was said, to Poland, subject to a peace treaty. This meant that the whole population of the Eastern territories, some 13.5 million people were expelled and 2.5 million of them died, either through murder, starvation or other acts. I can't return to my home, I can't ever meet my family or schoolfriends in my hometown. The ones who are still

alive are dispersed everywhere. They were all expelled without compensation. It is as if I died in 1945.

I accept that major war crimes were committed in the name of Germany, and I share that collective guilt, but my family and friends and millions of others were the victims of major atrocities by the other side. We are now 50 years on, but we still hear little of the crimes committed by the Russians, Americans and the British. But, on a human level, the wound is healed. I have major honours from many European countries for my services to peace and charity. I do, however, still bear a political grievance, and if a politician stands up to glorify what happened, I will put him in his place. "

Heinz Landau, as a Transylvanian Saxon, had supported the German cause whole-heartedly against the communist threat – but now he has lived in England for over 40 years as a British citizen.

" In a way I went to war with mixed feelings, because on the one hand, I was fanatically pro-German – and on the other hand, I disagreed very strongly indeed with the National Socialist Party. But, since the National Socialist Party and Germany became inseparable, I would still rather have fought for them, than for the people who were our enemies in the First World War. There were people in Germany who were very fanatically pro-German, but they would have very happily got rid of the Nazi Party.

I don't think, in the end, that anyone gained from the war. Wars are really such a terrible waste of time, and so many people suffered and died. And, in my case, Romania still managed to keep hold of the territories it had grabbed before. Then, of course they fell into the hands of the communists, and everyone knows what Romania has been through un-

der Ceaucescu.

It's very strange, but the Germans seem to have been doing better after the war than anyone else. Personally, I think it is very difficult for someone who has been through a war fought so fanatically to change his views on things. But I have been treated very well in this country, and I worship my wife and my English family, so I suffer a sort of post-war schizophrenia. I have spent 45 years amongst the English, 41 of those as a British subject – so I am very pro-British. You must remember, 45 years means two-thirds of my life. But the moment people start to talk to me about the war, I immediately revert to being a fanatical German.

I now have a daughter, who is English through and through (but very pro-German!), but since I have no sons, the name will die out. But if I had had sons, I would have been very keen to see that they didn't inherit any of my bitterness about the wars of this century, because there is nothing worse than living in a country to which you belong, and yet feeling you are an enemy of that country – as with me in Romania.

In spite of my own losses, I am glad Hitler lost the war, because I don't know what sort of a world it would have been to live in, and that includes myself. I, as a lieutenant of the Waffen SS, would probably have finished up, tucked away in Russia as commander of some silly little village. "

Karl Wahnig was born in Cotbus in what was the GDR. A former U-boat man, he is now a British citizen, with strong connections among submariners' associations.

" When the war finished, it was the best thing that could have happened – and for me personally, the best thing was that I came to England. I had no desire to go back to East Germany.

There's not one bad thing I can say about England and the way I have been treated here since. My biggest achievement was to work as an engineer with British Telecom (the GPO, as it was then). I was proud to work for a big national company.

I got married in 1948 to an English lady I met when I was a POW in Regent's Park. As my wife put it – I was the best export that ever came out of Germany!

With the help of a British submariner, I managed to meet up with my old crew again – that was eight years ago. And I've been an honourary member of the London branch of the Submarine Ex-Comrades for two years now. I have always been fascinated by the technology of submarines, and I've intensified my studies since the war, though I have no illusions about the awful side of war.

I'm not one of these people who try to make excuses for what Germany did – but through the 20s, people had been starving – then along comes this tin-pot soldier and offers you a loaf of bread. What do you say? 'No, thank you?'

To be honest, I've been delighted to have come to England, where I could let my hair down, and shake off all that 'Prussian' regimentation. The great thing about Britain is the tolerance. In my heart of hearts, I feel more English than German. To put it in a nutshell, my trouble is – I was born at the wrong time, on the wrong side. "

▲ One of many German POWs who have chosen to spend their lives in Britain, Heinz Landau admits that he worships his English family.

◀ Hans Teske devotes much time to the European Movement, whose work, he hopes, will draw nations together to avoid further conflict and promote strong European bonds.

▼ Karl Wahnig still can't stay away from submarines, which remain a consuming interest to him as an active member of the International Submariners' Association.

ACKNOWLEDGEMENTS

The publishers extend their thanks to the following agencies, companies and individuals who have kindly provided illustrative material for this book. The alphabetical name of the supplier is followed by the page and position of the picture/s.
Abbreviations: b=bottom, c=centre, l=left, r=right, t=top.

Max Arthur 122b; Associated Press 110b, 155, 158/159background; Auschwitz Museum, Wiener Library 182t; Barnaby's Picture Library 37t; Bibliotek fur Zeitgeschichte 88t, 120/121c, 130b, 132, 135tr & bl, 136/137t, 138cr, 138tl, 162/163background, 162cr, 167t, 168t; Ullstein Bilderdienst 16/17t, 21br, 22/23main pic, 24/25, 27t, 28tr, 29tr, 33cr, 44, 46t, 60t, 64/65t; Bildarchiv Preussischer Kulterbesitz 32/33t, 34t, 36tl, 64bl, 67, 68tr, 70t, 72t; British Official Foto 146/147main pic; Gus Britton 200b, r(inset) & bl(inset), 201t & cr, 202tl & cr(inset), 264tr; Bob Bruckner 13t; Herbert Brunnegger 22t, 60bl; Bundesarchiv-Koblenz 62tr, 75, 91tr & bl, 93t, 94/95t & b, 94cr, 95cr, 96t, 130/131t, 131cr & b, 132/133c, 166, 168b, 197b, 210cl, 214tl, 215tl; Camera Press 125b(inset); Bill Chalk 193t(inset); Cyril Cope/Narvic Association 45b & c(inset), 46/47c, 47t; Crown Copyright 142, 142/143, 144, 162/163b; Harry Despaigne, MC 187tr; Jack Durey 232t; Wilf Dykes 71t; RL Ferguson/TAB books USA 114c; Roland Feven 165cr; F F Fish 190c; R A Fogwill 34; John Frost Collection 32t(inset), 33t(inset), 37c(inset); D Glaister 207b, 261t; John Green 182b; D Greensmith 251tr; Josephine Harcourt 42b; Magit Harmsworth 237b(inset); Alois Hedwig 137cl & cr; James Hepburn 83, 83t; Hulton Picture Company 13br, 14/15t, 17cr, 30, 32t, 35cl, 38/39main pic, 39b, 40b, 40/41t, 41b, 61, 66tr, 73tr, 86/87b, 88c, 88/89b, 89cr, 206/207c, 206b, 230/231b, 245, 246br; Robert Hunt Library 12, 15b, 26/27b, 28cl, 31b, 32b, 36/37b, 49b, 50/51b, 65br, 65cr, 78b, 78/79c, 81b, 83cr, 86bl, 87t(inset), 100bl, 113c, 124, 150/151main pic, 183b, 216cr & b, 217t, 218tl, 219, 238t, 239tr & cl(inset), 242/243b, 243tr, 244tl, 253; Imperial War Museum 11, 48/49t, 56bl, 57, 59tr, 72b, 73br, 76/77t, 77b, 80/81c, 81tr, 82cl, 84/85main pic, 85br, 90, 103tr & b, 104tl & b, 104/105t, 105b, 106t, 107, 110t, 116/117, 118t, 118/119main pic, 119c, 120t, 121t, 126/127t, 127cr, 129, 132/133t, 134, 136tl, 136b, 138bl, 139, 149, 154t, 154b, 156t & b, 156/157c, 157b, 158b(inset), 159b(inset), 160t & b, 161t & b, 163tr, 165t, 170, 173b, 174tl & b, 179, 180/181main pic, 181, 183t, 186/187cr, 188b, 190b, 192/193t, 193b, 194cr, 195t & b, 198/199t, 198l, 199b, 205, 212b, 224/225main pic, 224b, 225t & b, 228, 229b, 233t, 247; Island History Trust   73cl; Leo Keys 58t, 211t & b; Kyodo News Agency 109b, 226/227c; Heinz Landau 167cr, 180t, 266tr; Sydney Lawrence 226tr, 263cr; Bob Leonard 48tl, 264b; J Leopard 209t; Michael Leszkiewicz 17b; Cannon William Loveless 194cl(inset); Mail Newspapers/Solo 264/265b; Mansfield & Kucera 14b; Len Matthews 133b; Tom McCarthy 243cr(inset); MOD, Air Historical Branch (RAF) 68cr & br, 73b(inset), 190br; Kurt Muller 63tr; Philip Murton 263 Naval Institute Press 113t(inset), 144t; Novosti 230t; Jack O'Keefe 234t; Peter Osbourne 69br, bl & b; George Page 69tl; James Palmer 39t, 77tr, 78tl & tr; Arno Pommerenke 21t; Popperfoto 31t, 46b, 54bl, 54/55t, 56/57t, 58/59b, 62bl, 62/63b, 66br, 68bl, 70bl, 92b(inset), 111b, 128tl, 140/141, 148, 150tl & b, 153t, 158cl(inset), 164t, 169b, 188/189background, 189cr, 190/191t, 207t, 229tl, 236, 237tr, 238, 240bl, 240/241cl, 244cr(inset), 246t, 251b, 252b, 254l & r(inset), 255, 256/257t, 257r, 258/259t, 259cr, 259b; Portfolio Pictures 101tr; Bruce Quarrie 214/215b; RAF Museum, Hendon 43; George Rhodes 40t, 265tr; George Rodger/Magnum 74b Roger-Violet 36cr, 58cl, 82/83, 86/87t, 92/93main pic, 96bl, 126b, 128b, 169t, 185t, 186t, 187b; R Rubinstein 185b, 221b & b(inset); Mark Sawicki 66cl, 80tl, 212cr; Sir David Scott 256c & b, 257c, 258cl(inset); SIRPA/ECPA 167b; Suddeutscher Verlag 13cl & br, 18/19b & t, 20, 22/23t, 23br, 24tl & b, 25t, 26t, 27cr, 28/29b, 42tl, 51tr, 71b, 240t, 241br(inset), 242bl, 248/249t, 248bl, 249cr, 250t, 250/251c, 252t; Tank Museum, Bovington Camp, Dorset 121b; Tass 213; Hans Teske 123cl & br, 266cl; Vicky Thomas 261b Topham 18, 34/35b, 35tr, 52/53t, 125t, 151t, 153b, 164b, 172/173t, 175, 184, 208t, 218cr; TRH 176t; US Air Force 152tl, 152b; US Army 115b US Army Airforces 143t; US Library of Congress 97, 98/99main pic & t, 221/222t; US Marine Corp 144/145c; US National Archives 98bl, 99br, 100t, 100/101b, 102/103t, 106b, 108/109t, 111t, 112/113main pic, 112t, 114/115t, 114b, 122/123t, 141cr, 159tr(inset), 176/177c, 177t & b, 196/197c, 196b, 204, 208/209main pic, 210cr, 222t, 222/223c, 223t & b, 226bl, 227cr, 230b, 231tr(inset), 232/233main pic, 232cr, 234b; George Vanden Heuval 191br(inset); Paul Verity Smith 260/261t, 262; Karl Wahnig 202b & b(inset), 266b; E Wood 196t & t(inset); Peter Wood 74t; Sydney Woolcott 178t, c & b.

Index prepared by INDEXING SPECIALISTS, Hove.

Healthy Me

Mental Well-being and Mindfulness

Ryan Wheatcroft   Katie Woolley

WAYLAND

First published in Great Britain in 2018 by Wayland

Copyright © Wayland, 2018

Editor: Victoria Brooker
Designer: Anthony Hannant, Little Red Ant

ISBN: 978 1 5263 0563 3

10 9 8 7 6 5 4 3 2 1

Wayland, an imprint of
Hachette Children's Group
Part of Hodder and Stoughton
Carmelite House
50 Victoria Embankment
London EC4Y 0DZ

An Hachette UK Company
www.hachette.co.uk
www.hachettechildrens.co.uk

Printed and bound in China

FSC MIX Paper from responsible sources FSC® C104740 www.fsc.org

Contents

What Is Mental Well-being?

You can't see mental well-being but you can feel it. Your mental well-being is all about how you think and feel. Some people call it 'mental health' or 'emotional well-being'.

Having good mental health doesn't mean being happy all the time. We all experience feelings of anger, sadness, fear and frustration. These feelings are perfectly normal. Mental well-being comes from finding positive ways to manage these feelings.

Your Mind Matters

Your mental well-being is just as important as your physical health. Good mental health helps you feel happy about yourself. It helps you cope with the everyday pressures of life. Part of being healthy is about understanding your own mental well-being.

Good mental health allows you to think clearly, have good relationships with your family and friends and learn new skills every day. It helps develop your self-confidence and self-esteem, too.

What Are Mental Health Problems?

Mental health problems are thoughts and feelings that can change the way you feel, think and behave. It can be frightening to think you have a mental health problem but it shouldn't be ignored.

Stress, anxiety and depression are all examples of mental health problems. Poor mental health can make you feel as bad as any other illness. Finding ways to deal with a problem can stop it getting worse, so that you can continue to enjoy life.

Stress and Anxiety

Everybody will feel anxious and stressed at some stage in his or her life. You might have felt anxious when you started school or if you have ever moved house. This anxiety and stress usually goes away after a little while.

If these feelings don't disappear, it can affect your mental well-being, your confidence and your self-esteem. You may become sad or angry and you might have difficulty sleeping. It's time to get some help.

Dealing With Change

We all deal with different situations in our lives differently. Most changes in life don't lead to mental health problems. But sometimes an event can trigger thoughts and feelings that lead to poor mental health.

For example, some children may feel excited about the arrival of a new brother or sister. Others may feel anxious about the changes to their home environment and will need to find ways to cope.

It's Good To Talk

Talking about your thoughts and feelings is an important way of looking after your mental well-being. If you are anxious or worried about anything, reassurance from your family and friends can help you deal with your feelings.

If you still feel anxious, it's a good idea to get some professional help. The first place to start is to talk to your doctor. There are also helplines, such as Young Minds, that offer advice and support.

Love and Affection

Your family and friends play an important part in your mental well-being. Human beings need secure and safe relationships to grow, learn and have fun.

The people you meet at home and at school help you understand the world, its cultures and its rules. As you grow up, you build a sense of your place within this world. Your mental well-being helps your feel confident about how you fit in.

Give Your Self-Esteem a Boost!

Self-esteem is how you see yourself. Having low self-esteem can affect your mental health. What affects self-esteem is different for everyone. An experience such as bullying, a mental health problem like stress or a difficult relationship can affect someone's self-esteem.

Giving your self-esteem a boost will boost your mental well-being, too! Try and focus on positive things in your life, such as your friends and any hobbies you enjoy. You could then try writing down a list of your achievements or talking to a friend or loved one.

Nurturing Your Mental Well-being

There are things that you can do to keep mentally well. Here is a list of ways to look after your mental health:

Make time to play and do something you enjoy.

Look after your body by exercising each day.

Eat a balanced diet, including lots of fresh fruit and vegetables.

Spend time with close friends and family who help you feel good about yourself.

Get a good night's sleep to rest your body and your mind.

These things will help you have the strength and resilience to cope with life's stresses, as well as find ways to solve problems.

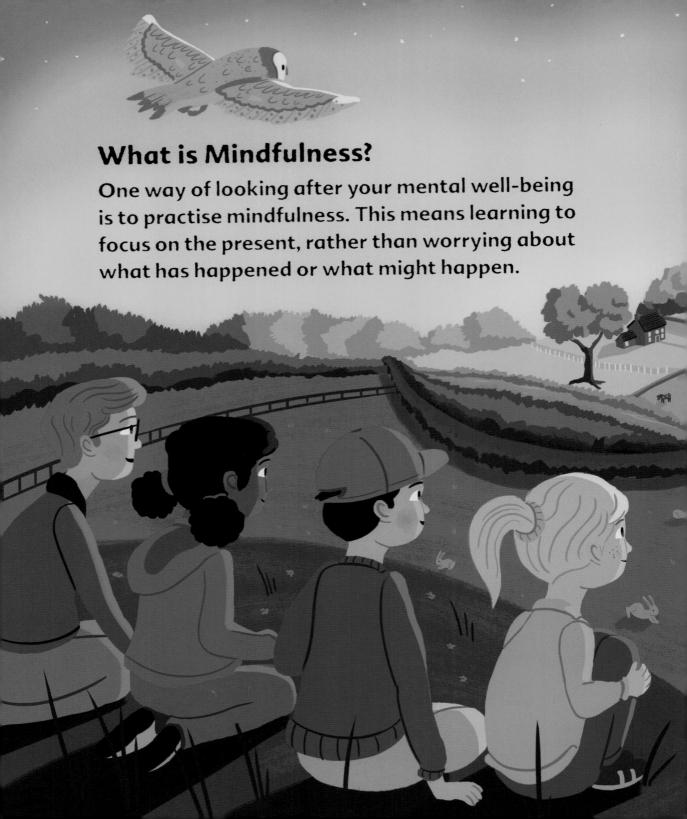

What is Mindfulness?

One way of looking after your mental well-being is to practise mindfulness. This means learning to focus on the present, rather than worrying about what has happened or what might happen.

Mindfulness exercises help you to focus on your breathing, the sensations in your body and your thoughts and feelings, as well as everyday activities, such as eating and walking.

Mindfulness Matters

At first, it can be difficult not to let your mind wander when you practise mindfulness. There is always something to think about! But, with time, you can learn to hold your attention for longer.

Thinking without being mindful

Stimulus

Reaction

Reaction

Thinking whilst being mindful

Stimulus

Reaction

Reaction

Mindfulness can help you concentrate and think more clearly, as well as feel less stressed and anxious. It can even help some people feel less depressed. This can all have a positive effect on your mental well-being.

Mindfulness Activities

Colouring calms the brain and helps the mind focus on one task. The best bit is that it can be done wherever you like. All you need is a colouring book and some pencils!

Mindful posing is another activity you can try at home. Doing funny poses, such as pretending to be a superhero can help you pay more attention to your body and its sensations as you strike a pose!

Go out for a walk and look for as many birds, insects and animals as you can. This uses all your senses and helps you focus on the present.

You could even look for the colours of the rainbow on your walk. Try and find objects that represent each colour. Some colours will be harder to find than others!

Top Tips!

Talking about your feelings isn't a sign of weakness. Having someone listen can give you the support you need.

Your mind needs vitamins and nutrients to keep well. A balanced diet will not only help your body but your mind, too.

Make time for yourself. Some 'me time' can reduce stress and make you feel happier.

Doing a little exercise every day will boost your self-esteem, help you sleep, help you concentrate and make you feel better.

Don't be afraid to ask for help.

Do something you are good at and that you enjoy. This will boost your self-esteem, help you forget your worries and lift your mood.

Parents' and Teachers' Notes

This book is designed for children to begin to learn about the importance of being healthy, and the ways in which we can look after our mental well-being. Read the book with children either individually or in groups. Don't forget to talk about the pictures as you go.

Mental health is just as important as physical health. It affects your thoughts and feelings, your relationships and even how you see yourself. Understanding about mental health is very important. Here are some discussion topics to encourage further thinking about mental well-being:

 Talk about the word 'healthy'. What do you think it means to be mentally healthy?

 Can you think of three ways you can look after your mental health?

 What advice would you give to someone suffering with low self-esteem?

 Mindfulness is one way to look after your mental well-being. Does it seem like something you might want to try?

Activities you can do:

 Grab a colouring book and some pencils and relax while you colour in a favourite picture.

 Have a go at the Mindfulness Jar activity. Fill a jar with water. Add some glitter glue and put the lid back on. Shake the jar. Imagine the glitter is your thoughts and feelings when you are worried or anxious. The pieces are hard to see clearly. When you feel anxious, it's hard to think clearly sometimes, too. Now, put down the jar and watch the glitter settle as the water clears. Your mind works in the same way. Once your thoughts start to settle, you can see things more clearly.

Further reading

Mindful Me: Breath by Breath: A Mindfulness Guide to Feeling Calm by Paul Christelis and Elisa Paganelli (Wayland, 2018)

Healthy for Life: Self-esteem and Mental Health by Anna Claybourne (Franklin Watts, 2016)

Glossary

culture the ideas, customs and way of life of a particular group of people. There are lots of different cultures around the world.

depression a feeling of great sadness and dejection. It is a medical illness so if you feel very depressed you should seek medical help.

environment the surroundings in which a person, animal or plant lives

mental health a person's emotional and mental well-being

professional someone who is an exert in a particular field, such as a doctor or counsellor

physical health the health and well-being of a person's body

resilience being able to recover quickly after a tough experience

self-confidence a feeling of trust in your abilities, qualities and opinions

self-esteem a feeling of confidence and happiness in your own worth as a person

trigger an event that causes a particular situation or feeling

Index

Titles in the series

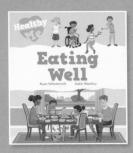

Eating Well
Ryan Wheatcroft · Katie Woolley

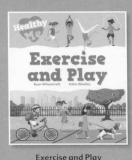

Exercise and Play
Ryan Wheatcroft · Katie Woolley

Keeping Clean
Ryan Wheatcroft · Katie Woolley

Keeping Safe
Ryan Wheatcroft · Katie Woolley

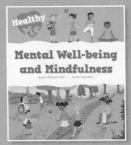

Mental Well-being and Mindfulness
Ryan Wheatcroft · Katie Woolley

Resting and Sleeping
Ryan Wheatcroft · Katie Woolley